VIETNAM'S STRATEGIC THINKING
DURING THE THIRD INDOCHINA WAR

New Perspectives in Southeast Asian Studies

KOSAL PATH

VIETNAM'S

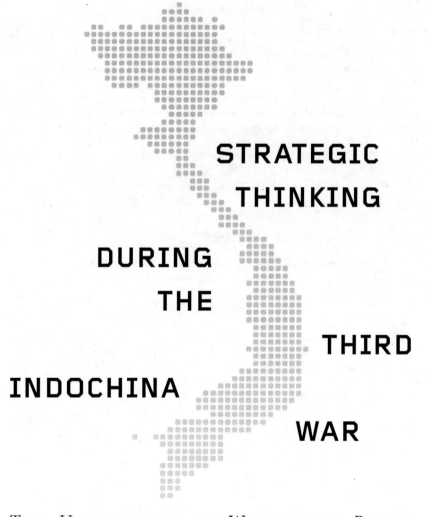

STRATEGIC
THINKING

DURING
THE

THIRD

INDOCHINA
WAR

THE UNIVERSITY OF WISCONSIN PRESS

The University of Wisconsin Press
728 State Street, Suite 443
Madison, Wisconsin 53706
uwpress.wisc.edu

Gray's Inn House, 127 Clerkenwell Road
London EC1R 5DB, United Kingdom
eurospanbookstore.com

Printed in the United States of America

This book may be available in a digital edition.

Library of Congress Cataloging-in-Publication Data
Names: Path, Kosal, author.
Title: Vietnam's strategic thinking during the Third Indochina War / Kosal Path.
Other titles: New perspectives in Southeast Asian studies.
Description: Madison, Wisconsin: The University of Wisconsin Press, [2020]
| Series: New perspectives in Southeast Asian studies
| Includes bibliographical references and index.
Identifiers: LCCN 2019017148 | ISBN 9780299322700 (cloth)
Subjects: LCSH: Vietnam—Politics and government—1975–
| Vietnam—History—1975– | Cambodia—History—1979–
| Indochina—History—1945–
Classification: LCC DS559.912 .P38 2020 | DDC 959.604/2—dc23
LC record available at https://lccn.loc.gov/2019017148

To my parents

who survived the Killing Field (1975–79) in Cambodia

CONTENTS

ACKNOWLEDGMENTS

I am grateful to Youk Chhang, who taught me early on the value of research and documentation during the second half of the 1990s when we documented the atrocities committed by the Khmer Rouge between 1975 and 1979. I am indebted to my early academic mentors Hayward Alker, Daniel Lynch, and John Wills at the University of Southern California for their advice and encouragement when I approached them in 2004 with my idea of writing on Sino-Vietnamese relations since 1950. I greatly appreciate Ben Kiernan at Yale University, Lien-Hang Nguyen at Columbia University, Sophie Quinn-Judge at Temple University, and Stephen Heder at SOAS University of London for their helpful comments on chapters of my book manuscript. Corey Robin, Mark Ungar, Jeanne Theoharis, and Janet Johnson, my colleagues at Brooklyn College, the City University of New York, offered me firm support to complete this project. I owe a great debt to the four anonymous reviewers who provided helpful comments and suggestions.

I am very grateful to Pham Quang Minh at the University of Social Sciences and Humanities, Vietnam National University (Hanoi), who strongly supported my archival research in Vietnam; he personally introduced me to the management and staff of the National Archives No. 3 in Hanoi in the fall of 2005, and I have kept going back to do archival research ever since. I also wish to thank the dedicated staff of the National Archives No. 3 in Hanoi during my research at their institution. The 2016 Whiting Fellowship at Brooklyn College enabled me to take spring semester off from teaching to complete a follow-up archival research in Vietnam. Last but not least I want to thank Gwen Walker, Adam Mehring, Janet Opdyke, Audree Chase-Mayoral, Margaret Copeley, and Nguyen Thi Tri for offering very useful editing advice. I dedicate this book to my family.

ABBREVIATIONS

ASEAN	Association of Southeast Asian Nations
BGD	Bo Giao Duc (Ministry of Education)
CCG	Cuc Chuyen Gia (Department of Experts)
CECC–Laos and Cambodia	Committee on Economic and Cultural Cooperation with Laos and Cambodia
CGDK	Coalition of Government of Democratic Kampuchea
CMC	Central Military Commission
CNRP	Cambodian National Rescue Party
COMECON	Council for Mutual Economic Assistance (Economic Community of the Communist bloc)
CPK	Communist Party of Kampuchea
CPP	Cambodian People's Party
CPV	Communist Party of Vietnam
DK	Democratic Kampuchea
DRV	Democratic Republic of Vietnam (North Vietnam)
FULRO	United Front for the Liberation of Oppressed Races
FUNK	National United Front of Kampuchea
FYP	five-year plan
GATT	General Agreement on Tariffs and Trade
IMF	International Monetary Fund
KR	Khmer Rouge
KUFNS	Kampuchean United Front for National Salvation
LPDR	Laos People's Democratic Republic
MoD	Ministry of Defense
MOFA	Ministry of Foreign Affairs
MOULINAKA	Movement for the National Liberation of Kampuchea
NAM	Non-Aligned Movement
NATO	North Atlantic Treaty Organization
NLF	National Liberation Front (Communists in South Vietnam)
PAVN	People's Army of Vietnam
PCC	Party Central Committee
PLA	People's Liberation Army

POW/MIA	prisoner of war/missing in action
PPA	Paris Peace Accords
PRC	People's Republic of China
PRG	Provisional Revolutionary Government
PRK	People's Republic of Kampuchea
PTT	Phu Thu Tuong (Prime Minister's Office)
QH	Van Phong Quoc Hoi (Office of the National Assembly)
RMB	renminbi (Chinese currency)
RVN	Republic of Vietnam (referring only to the regime in power in the southern part of Vietnam from 1954 to 1975)
SRV	Socialist Republic of Vietnam (official name of Vietnam since 1976)
UNCTAD	United Nations Conference on Trade and Development
UNICEF	United Nations Children's Fund
VND	dong (Vietnamese currency)
VVA	Vietnamese Volunteer Army

Vietnam's Strategic Thinking during the Third Indochina War

Introduction

In late 1978 Vietnam invaded Cambodia, toppling a pro-China regime, Democratic Kampuchea (DK), and installing a new pro-Vietnam regime, the People's Republic of Kampuchea (PRK). The decision to invade was a consequential one. Even as it ended the Cambodian genocide, it also triggered a wider Third Indochina War between Vietnam, backed by the Soviet Union, and Cambodia's DK, with its great power ally China.

Why did Vietnam decide to engage in a costly program of regime change and nation building and why did these efforts ultimately fail to establish a loyal client state in Cambodia in the 1980s? And what factors contributed to Vietnam's later decision to withdraw its forces from Cambodia and shift from military confrontation to reconciliation with China in the late 1980s? Within the debate over Vietnam's foreign policy decision making during the Third Indochina War, there is an unresolved question about whether the invasion of Cambodia was rational or irrational. To some western scholars, Hanoi's decision to invade Cambodia can only be explained by irrational factors, including Marxist-Leninist ideology or Vietnam's imperial ambition for the domination of Indochina engrained in Vietnamese elites' political culture. Yet a careful analysis of previously inaccessible archival materials produced by the Vietnamese government during that time challenges this line of argument and reveals how domestic imperatives and competing views between factions within the Vietnamese leadership influenced the country's domestic and foreign policy.

Internal reports and publications circulated within the top leadership of the Vietnamese party and government at that time, together with memoirs and other Vietnamese-language materials, show that Hanoi's decision to invade

Cambodia was driven by a rational need to address several pressing issues: an economic crisis at home, continuing military attacks on Vietnamese soil by Pol Pot's Khmer Rouge forces, and the Chinese threat to the north. The Vietnamese leaders' decision was a strategic one motivated by their belief that it would ensure full military and political support from Vietnam's great power ally, the Soviet Union; increase the flow of material aid and technology from the Soviet-led Council of Mutual Economic Assistance; and raise Vietnam's international standing in the Soviet-led socialist camp. By cementing its alliance with the Soviet Union, they reasoned, Vietnam would solve its domestic crisis at home and counter imminent threats posed by the Sino-Cambodian alliance. Vietnamese leaders thus came to view war as a cure-all that would resolve the country's economic crisis, reduce external threats to its territorial sovereignty, and solidify its alliances.

In addition to providing a crucial Vietnamese perspective on the decision to invade Cambodia, this book contributes to emerging scholarship on the shift in the Vietnamese political elites' thinking from the doctrinal Marxist-Leninist ideology during the last decade of the Cold War to the reform and opening of the post–Cold War era. During the decade-long war that had begun with DK escalating its attacks on Vietnam in early 1977, that shift in the Vietnamese leadership's strategic thinking was remarkable and transformative—that is, from a focus on socialist economic reconstruction and modernization at the Fourth Party Congress in December 1976 to a war decision in early 1978, fighting combined with offensive diplomacy to isolate China in 1984, and then to economic reform and opening, dubbed *Doi Moi* (renovation), at the Sixth Party Congress in 1986 in conjunction with the Vietnam-initiated process of reconciliation with China.

This book has three aims. First, it provides a political history of Vietnam's post-1975 economic crisis, and its invasion and occupation of Cambodia (1978–89), crafted based on a novel reinterpretation of Vietnam's motives for the war and regime change in Cambodia. In so doing, the book reveals historical details concerning hidden private information about internal deliberations within Vietnam's foreign-policy-making circle.

Second, this book offers an explanation for major shifts in the Vietnamese leadership's strategic thinking from the onset to the conclusion of the Third Indochina War, with emphasis on the influence of collective ideas on foreign policy. Unlike most existing scholarship, this book reveals hidden internal struggles between power groups within the Vietnamese government's collective policy-making structure rather than a monolithic and consensual decision-making body. At the heart of this fierce competition to dominate Vietnam's foreign policy are members of the conservative camp (conservatives and military-firsters)[1] who drew their power from militarism and Marxist-Leninist orthodoxy. On the other side were those in the reformist camp (economically minded leaders and economy-firsters) who advocated a gradual shift from a state-planned to a market-based economy and a broad-based foreign economic policy.[2]

Third, this book illustrates a crucial case of why a small state like Vietnam pursued war against a much more powerful alliance in an asymmetric conflict, as well as how a small country mobilized state resources.[3] Vietnam's decision to invade Cambodia qualifies as a crucial case of asymmetric war in which a weaker state, Vietnam, pursued a two-front war against a more powerful enemy, the anti-Vietnam Sino-Cambodian alliance. Vietnam was undoubtedly a pivotal actor in the war, and yet the Vietnamese leadership's strategic thinking behind its war decision remains elusive. Prior to Vietnam's massive military intervention in Cambodia in December 1978 and the subsequent invasion of Vietnam by China in February 1979, Vietnam feared a continuation or deterioration of the status quo of reciprocal military conflict along the Cambodian-Vietnamese border into a Sino-Cambodian-coordinated two-front war against Vietnam. Domestically, meanwhile, the economic crisis in Vietnam itself threatened to undermine the legitimacy of the Communist Party of Vietnam (CPV), which in turn emboldened the militant conservative faction of the country's leadership to churn Vietnam's war machine and turn to the open arms of the Soviet Union to gain economic and military support for its new war.

More broadly, an understanding of Vietnam's war and foreign policy decision making sheds light on the impact of revolutions and wars on Vietnam's national strategic culture. Vietnam's current foreign policy executive continues to build on traditional strategic thinking and a two-millennia-old national tradition of defending its sovereignty against foreign invaders, as its predecessors did during the military conflict with China in the 1980s following three decades of national resistance against French colonialism and American imperialism. Hence, this book both addresses a critical need for insight into the closely guarded "black box" of Vietnam's foreign policy decision making and contributes to the existing scholarship on the influence of ideas on foreign policy.

Previous Scholarship

Several excellent scholarly works have addressed these topics, notably Tuong Vu's *Vietnam's Communist Revolution* (2016) and David W. P. Elliott's *Changing Worlds* (2012). Vu argues that Marxist-Leninist ideology, in spite of periodic moderation, was the most important driver of Vietnam's foreign policy in the

1970s and 1980s. Elliott argues, however, that there was an internal disagreement between the conservatives, who favored security and military capabilities, and the reformists, who advocated performance-based legitimacy based on economic development. He contends that the transformative ideological shifts among Vietnamese political elites in the 1980s led to the CPV's rejection of the Marxist central-panning model and the decision to replace military confrontation with economic integration and engagement with the changing world.

Vu's book largely relied on publicly available party documents including the fifty-four volumes of *Van Kien Dang Toan Tap* (Collected party documents) as the most important sources. Although these public sources provide useful information in their own right, especially for the study of the CPV leaders' thoughts, they do not reveal internal debates as completely as internally circulated meeting minutes and reports do. Elliott primarily relied on publicly available sources written in Vietnamese supplemented with the memoirs of Vietnamese leaders and interviews with various former officials of the government. This study, however, largely relies on primary sources (archival documents produced by the Vietnamese government at the times when events were unfolding and actors' decisions were being made).[4] Elliott's *Changing Worlds* differs from my book in terms of temporality—that is, his book focuses on Vietnam's post–Cold War transformation from 1989 to 2005, not the critical period of 1975 to 1989 that this book covers. Simply put, this book fills the gap that precedes Elliott's work.

The main debate in the existing scholarship on Vietnam's foreign policy decision making has been between social constructivists, who emphasize ideological and historical-cultural factors (Marxist-Leninist ideology and political culture), and realists, who stress material forces (domestic and external opportunities and constraints), as the main drivers. Political scientist Tuong Vu argues that ideology is the overriding explanation for Vietnam's foreign policy from the decision of the Democratic Republic of Vietnam (DRV) to join the Soviet bloc in 1948 to Vietnam's normalization of relations with China in 1991.[5] For Vu, from mid-1976 to the late 1980s, in spite of some pragmatism in foreign policy and changes in the leadership, "The Vietnamese revolution by no means veered from doctrinal orthodoxy directed from Moscow."[6] Back then, Vietnam, in Vu's view, could not imagine a future outside the Soviet bloc. Stephen Morris contended that Hanoi's decision to invade Cambodia in December 1978 was an irrational one and therefore can only be explained by irrational factors, including Marxist-Leninist ideology and Vietnam's imperial ambition for domination of Indochina engrained in Vietnamese elites' political culture.[7] However, as international relations scholar David W. P. Elliott observes, "Vietnam's rulers have traditionally viewed international relations in starkly realist terms. . . . Vietnam's strategic thinking until quite recently has been almost exclusively focused on how to defuse the threat from a larger power and how to manipulate power balances to best advantage in order to defend its own territory, sovereignty, and independence—the emotional slogan that galvanized Vietnam's political class in 1945 and continues to resonate in today's interdependent world."[8]

In contrast to arguments that privilege ideological and irrational factors in Vietnamese decision making, my findings illuminate the "starkly realist terms" noted by Elliott. Hanoi's leaders, I argue, proceeded in accordance with what T. V. Paul describes as "subjective rationality," wherein "The values, beliefs, and expectations of a decision-maker are important factors that determine his probabilistic assessment before he undertakes a course of action."[9] In such a conception, "a course of action is rational only relative to a possessed body of information (beliefs and desires) in terms of which the merits of the available courses of action can be rationally evaluated."[10] At each step in their decision-making process, Vietnamese leaders rationally evaluated their available courses of action as these were informed by their values, beliefs, expectations, and desires.

Analytical Framework

Drawing on the neoclassical realist theory of international relations as an analytical framework for Vietnam's foreign policy decision making,[11] this study challenges this line of argument, which privileges ideological and historical-cultural factors by showing how domestic and external imperatives not only spurred competing ideas of how to achieve national security and economic development between the two main factions within the Vietnamese leadership but also caused one set of ideas to prevail over the other in different periods.

This study posits that decisions to pursue war and peace were made by decision-making elites with external and internal motives. As Paul stated, "War decisions are conditional, perception-dependent, and time-dependent, i.e., wars are initiated when favorable conditions are perceived by decision-makers who may pursue the war path for attaining their domestic and international goals."[12] This approach to domestic politics and foreign policy decision making incorporated the worldviews, positions, and interests of decision-making elites (e.g., economic, diplomatic, and military leaders) within the constraints and opportunities of evolving domestic and international correlations of forces. Joe D. Hagan calls this "domestic political explanations of foreign policy"—that is,

what Robert D. Putnam calls "two-level games," in which leaders cope simultaneously with the pressures and constraints of their own domestic political
systems, as well as with those of the international environment.[13] With the
notable exception of Elliott's *Changing Worlds*, Lien-Hang T. Nguyen's *Hanoi's
War* (2012), and Pierre Asselin's *Hanoi's Road to the Vietnam War* (2013), previous studies centered on Marxist-Leninist ideology or political culture tend to
treat the Vietnamese leadership as a monolithic political organization and have
therefore neglected important contentious politics—that is, competition, and
coalition building for influence in domestic and foreign policy decision making
between the conservatives/military-firsters and the reformists/economy-firsters
within the decision-making structure of the Vietnamese party and government.[14]

Who are the decision-making elites in this study? This book focuses on
three organizational levels of decision making, namely, the Politburo (top policy
makers), the Central Military Commission (CMC), and the Prime Minister's
Office (executive body), and ministerial leadership (senior policy implementers,
evaluators, and advisers to the executive body) at the policy input level. The
most important decisions in the late 1970s and first half of the 1980s were made
collectively by the Politburo of the Party Central Committee, which was dominated by the five long-standing leaders of the party and government, namely,
Le Duan, Truong Chinh, Pham Van Dong, and Le Duc Tho. However, power
groups of political elites, from ministers and vice-ministers to general directors
of departments or directorates, members of interministerial committees, and
senior leaders of the Prime Minister's Office, provided important policy input,
through a variety of research and intelligence-gathering activities, to top decision makers of the Standing Committee of the Government Council headed by
the prime minister.

With respect to Vietnam's regime change in Cambodia, Hanoi relied most
on the vice-ministers of various ministries who, as advisers to their Cambodian
counterparts, played critical roles in shaping Cambodia's domestic and foreign
policy. They were the ones who conducted assessments, produced reports, and
made recommendations to the top leadership. To be more specific, in addition
to Unit 478 (the committee in charge of military advisers) under the supervision of B68 (the committee that represented the Party Central Committee on
Cambodia affairs) and A40 (committee in charge of economic, educational,
and cultural advisers), the vice-ministers of each ministry directly served in
Cambodia as close advisers to their Cambodian counterparts within the PRK
government. On January 24, 1979, the Ministry of Defense issued Decision No.
30 to detach Unit 478 from B68 and placed it under direct supervision of the

Ministry of Defense. However, Unit 478 continued to work closely with B68 of the Party Central Committee. The reports from these committees to Hanoi provided valuable information about Hanoi's policy toward Cambodia.

In 1979–80, when Vietnam was conducting a two-front war in Cambodia and China on top of the growing economic crisis at home, two contending factions emerged in the CPV. These factions coalesced around the vital question of national security. The military-first conservative faction continued to push for military confrontation at all costs to defeat "Chinese expansionism" while relying on the Soviet bloc for political and material support. On the contrary, the economy-first reformist faction advocated the balanced use of resources for economic development and national defense, with a focus on economic over military threats to Vietnam's national security.[15] In terms of foreign policy, this faction, especially Foreign Minister Nguyen Co Thach, argued for gradual withdrawal of Vietnamese troops from Cambodia, a necessary condition for de-escalation of the conflict with China and opening a dialogue with the Association of Southeast Asian Nations (ASEAN) to assure it that Vietnam was not a threat to Thailand.[16] He also argued for a broad-based economic foreign policy that would expand economic relations with the West.[17]

In 1979, the leaders of the military-first conservative faction were General Secretary Le Duan and party organizational chief Le Duc Tho, who had dominated the party since their successful push for national unification through war in 1959. Under the Fifth Party Congress in March 1982, the real power was held by the five oldest Politburo members mentioned above and all were more than seventy years old.[18] Within this inner circle, real power was in the hands of General Secretary Le Duan[19] and his powerful allies Le Duc Tho[20] and Pham Hung,[21] who were the leaders of the military-first conservative faction with personal ties going back to 1958–59 when they advocated unification through war in opposition to the moderate faction's preference for unification through political-economic transition—that is, the socialist development of North Vietnam's economy, which it was believed would ultimately defeat the South.[22] Back then the moderate North-first faction of the party included Prime Minister Pham Van Dong, Deputy Prime Minister Le Thanh Nghi, and General Vo Nguyen Giap, and they wielded power within the executive.[23] However, Duan and Tho controlled the key appointments to the most important ministries, departments, and other bodies, especially the Ministry of Interior, Ministry of National Defense, Ministry of Foreign Affairs (MOFA), Ministry of Transportation and Communications,[24] State Planning Committee, and General Directorate and General Logistics Department of the People's Army of Vietnam

(PAVN).[25] General Van Tien Dung,[26] General Chu Huy Man,[27] and General Le Duc Anh[28] were key members of this faction, and they dominated the CMC after Vietnam's invasion of Cambodia in December 1978.

The economy-minded leaders were Prime Minister Pham Van Dong, Deputy Prime Minister Le Thanh Nghi,[29] and Deputy Prime Minister Do Muoi,[30] but they were not pro-market-economy reformists for they were in favor of central state planning, with the notable exception of Le Thanh Nghi, who turned to advocating decentralization of economic planning in the aftermath of the severe economic crisis in 1978. As Hanoi's top economic planner after the Fourth Party Congress in December 1976, Le Thanh Nghi warned the Politburo about the dangers of the wasteful use of resources and economic inefficiency inherent in state central planning and advocated decentralization of economic planning to the district level in 1978. Although Nghi was not a champion of market economy reforms, in 1978 he fired the first shot warning the party about a worsening economic calamity if Vietnam failed to improve its economic efficiency and rapidly increase its exports in order to import modern industrial equipment and important raw materials.[31]

By mid-1980s, the increasingly heavy cost of the protracted two-front war in Cambodia and against China weakened the conservatives/military-firsters faction within the CPV and elevated early reformers/economy-firsters.[32] The latter received strong support from the chief ideologist of the party, Truong Chinh—who Elliott called one of the "unlikely reformers"—and were appointed to prominent positions in the Vietnamese party and government.[33] In the first half of the 1980s, Truong Chinh,[34] Nguyen Van Linh,[35] Vo Van Kiet,[36] Tran Phuong,[37] and Nguyen Co Thach[38] became the leaders of the reformists. Simultaneously, the "new thinking" under the Soviet Union's Mikhail Gorbachev, which rejected the Stalinist bipolar worldview of the "two camps"—socialist and imperialist—and replaced it with the idea of world interdependence, lent support to the reformists within the Vietnamese government, allowing them to thrust their own "new-thinking" version of "*doi moi tu duy* or renovation of thinking" into foreign policy decision making in 1986.

Sources and Method of Analysis

Adopting an inductive analysis approach to Vietnamese archival documents, I set out to accomplish two main tasks. First, my interpretive task was to determine the parameters of Vietnam's national interests and priorities as defined by the Vietnamese political elites. Second, I traced the ways in which a specific elite group's foreign policy ideas became dominant in internal debates within the Vietnamese leadership with a careful analysis of the influence of domestic and external forces in mediating the rise and fall of competing strategic ideas at different periods. I relied on a large volume of internal reports circulated within the top leadership of the Vietnamese party and government at that time and now housed at National Archive No. 3 in Hanoi. The quality of internally circulated records of the Vietnamese government used in this study is superior to official party documents and memoirs used in the existing scholarship mentioned above. In addition, I also used selected internally circulated (*luu hanh noi bo*) publications and unpublished sources, including memoirs and dissertations in Vietnamese, as they provide useful corroborating information on Vietnam's domestic and foreign policy considerations during the Third Indochina War.

Since 2006 I have made five trips to Vietnam, conducting research at the National Archives No. 3 in Hanoi. Most of the archival documents I used to write this book came from various state collections, including the Prime Minister's Office (the Phu Thu Tuong, or PTT, collection), the National Assembly Office (the Phong Quoc Hoi, or QH, collection), the State Planning Committee, the Ministry of Finance, the Ministry of Transport, and the Ministry of Materials Supply. Notably, the PTT collection is the most important one for this book. This executive office was the central point where reports were sent vertically between top party and government leaders and those at the policy input levels, as well horizontally between the concerned ministries, with copies sent to the prime minister. For instance, the PTT collection contains internal reports circulated through the Prime Minister's Office from MOFA, Ministry of Defense (MoD), National Border Commission, State Planning Committee, and special committees such as B68, chaired by Le Duc Tho in 1979–80, and A40, chaired by Nguyen Con. In addition, reports by the provincial people's committees and foreign affairs committees reveal details concerning espionage activities, border skirmishes, refugees, and local socioeconomic and political situations, adding a local perspective on major events and conditions that influenced domestic and foreign policy at the national level.

In addition, the QH collection belonging to the National Assembly contains revealing information about the party and government's major decisions and policies and reports on their implementation. Minutes of National Assembly sessions contain detailed information about internal debates on foreign affairs and national security policy ranging from Vietnam's assistance to the PRK regime in Cambodia to the effects of military confrontation with China and the state of Vietnam's economy. National Assembly oversight reports reveal new information about the contentious politics within the CPV's crisis decision-making processes, showing that Vietnam's National Assembly did not simply rubber stamp the government's actions.

Taken together these collections reveal valuable new information about internal debates via minutes of top-level party and government meetings, minutes of diplomatic exchanges, and reports on domestic and foreign policy meetings circulated throughout the chain of command to and from the party's Central Committee Politburo, the Prime Minister's Office, and ministerial and provincial authorities.

An example will show how internally circulated documents reveal the otherwise hidden contentious internal deliberations within the Vietnamese leadership at that time. After China's invasion of Vietnam in February 1979, the Vietnamese leadership experienced a major national security shock after witnessing the horrendous destruction in border provinces by the Chinese invading troops. On February 11, 1980, the Government Council issued Directive 44-CP, which determined two strategic directions for the national defense in 1980. First, in a scenario in which war does not break out between Vietnam and China, key economic sectors, including transportation, telecommunications, electricity, coal mining, oil refining, and logging, were to be off-limits to state extraction for national defense. In addition, workers who operated machinery in agriculture, irrigation, construction, and so on would be exempt from military duty. However, in a scenario in which the country was at war with China, the MoD would automatically have the power to utilize the human and material resources of the nation at will, with a few restrictions, for the purpose of defending the nation against China's military aggression.[39]

This text revealed a compromise at that time between the leadership, dominated by General Van Tien Dung of the MoD, who advocated a military-first policy, and the leadership of the State Planning Committee (Le Thanh Nghi and his deputy Tran Phuong). Historically and institutionally, the State Planning Committee was largely dominated by economically minded leaders, including Le Thanh Nghi, who tried to reduce waste and improve the efficiency of the economy. These economy-first planners were increasingly alarmed by the continued deterioration of the economy as large quantities of national resources were funneled into the war machine instead of economic development.

Although the power of the military-firsters was on the rise, the economy-firsters pushed back against their increasing demands for resources in the name of national security. Such debates can be found in the up-and-down internal reports between various ministries and provincial People's Committees (the provincial governors) and decision-making bodies within the purview of the Government Council (the executive body). In a top-secret report from the MoD to Prime Minister Pham Van Dong, Vice-Minister of Defense Vu Xuan Chiem lodged a thinly veiled warning: "If we do not mobilize resources as planned now, we will not have time when war [with China] breaks out. Officials of the MoD have made three trips to the Ministry of Foreign Trade but did not reach an agreement."[40]

It is not obvious why the Ministry of Foreign Trade and the leadership of Hanoi city resisted the demands made in this report. However, after tracing connections to such infighting in other reports, I find from logistical logs attached to summary reports from other agencies that the State Planning Committee and those senior officials in charge of economic affairs at the Prime Minister's Office (economy-firsters) were increasingly concerned about the MoD extracting far too many resources from the economy in the name of national defense. By delving into records at ministerial levels, or what could be called the "policy input level," I was able to detect tension between the military-firsters and economy-firsters that was widespread below the surface of party unity on national security matters during this period. One of the economy-firsters, Tran Phuong, vice-chairman of the State Planning Committee, in May urged the prime minister to consider reducing quotas for allocating human and material resources for national defense and requesting urgent aid from the Soviet Union and other socialist countries to meet the basic needs of economic productivity and alleviate the Vietnamese people's economic hardship.[41]

Shifting Thinking

As a political history of Vietnam's domestic and foreign policy from 1975 to 1989, this book traces the evolution of Hanoi's strategic shift from military confrontation to economic reform and opening, known as *Doi Moi*, at the Sixth Party Congress in 1986 and the conclusion of the Third Indochina War. The first chapters (covering the period 1975–78) examine the failure of Vietnam's socialist economic development; the middle chapters (1979–85) interrogate the shift from an economic-political focus to the military-political priorities of national security; and the final chapters (1986–89) explore the rise of Hanoi's new strategic thinking, dubbed *Doi Moi* (renovation), and the importance of reconciliation with China to create a peaceful regional environment for Vietnam's economic reform and integration in the global economy.

The most plausible explanation as to why the Vietnamese leadership's view shifted from a focus on economic development and a broad-based foreign policy in 1975–77 to military strength and confrontation and a tacit alliance with the Soviet Union in 1978 is the disastrous failure of Vietnam's post-1975 economic development. Because of the economic crisis, Politburo member and Deputy Prime Minister Le Thanh Nghi, who was the top economic planner and a close ally of Prime Minister Pham Van Dong, was largely discredited. As the bloody conflict with Cambodia and the deterioration of Sino-Vietnamese relations escalated in 1977, the militant faction led by General Secretary Le Duan, Politburo member Le Duc Tho, and their military allies in the CMC, the most powerful body in charge of Vietnam's military policy, pushed for a decisive military action to end the military threat posed by the Sino-Cambodian alliance and for regime change in Cambodia. As early as January 1978, the CMC was planning an invasion of Cambodia,[42] following the major counteroffensives against the Khmer Rouge forces in the second half of 1977.[43] Its grand strategy required that Vietnam decisively shift from a balance-of-influence foreign policy to a tacit alliance with the Soviet Union to counter China's military threat and ensure alliance support for economic and military aid before the invasion in December 1978.

The continuing military attacks on Vietnamese soil by Pol Pot's Khmer Rouge forces and the even greater external threat that the Sino-Cambodian alliance posed to Vietnam's national security made it necessary for the conservative faction to push for war, but this military threat alone is not sufficient to explain Vietnam's decision to invade Cambodia in December 1978 and occupy it thereafter. I argue that what tipped the scale of the collective leadership in favor of an invasion and occupation of Cambodia is found in Vietnam's domestic and international imperatives—that is, the socioeconomic and political crisis in 1977–78, which threatened to destabilize a newly united country and delegitimize the CPV itself, as well as Hanoi's need to extract greater support from the Soviet Union and the Soviet-led Council of Mutual Economic Assistance to address both economic development priorities and national security threats. Vietnam's desire to dominate Indochina provided an additional incentive for promoting regime change in Cambodia. The invasion plan was put into action in late 1978 with the approval of the economy-minded moderate leaders, including Prime Minister Pham Van Dong.

Faced with criticism from their Politburo comrades, the country's top economic planners, headed by Le Thanh Nghi, conducted an internal investigation into why the economic crisis had worsened. They came to the conclusion in December 1977 that the root cause of economic stagnation lay in wartime "old thinking"—that is, party cadres' mind-set of dependence on material resources supplied by means of massive nonrefundable aid from China, the Soviet Union, and other socialist countries. This mind-set had derailed state central planning because it generated no incentive to produce quality goods that could be exported and incentivized self-preservation behavior (e.g., an exaggerated need for resources from the central government to meet state quotas and claims of success). Under new circumstances in which significant nonrefundable aid from the Soviet Union and China had ended and trade based on mutual interests had become the new norm, such wartime practices created a vicious cycle of shortages of raw materials and industrial equipment for the manufacture of quality products to increase exports. Without export growth and the resultant hard currency, by 1978 Vietnam had already accumulated an enormous debt, with the first payment plus interest due to the Soviet Union, Eastern European countries, and western creditors in 1979.

To resolve the financial crisis, the top economic chief, Le Thanh Nghi, called for "new thinking," that is, replacing top-down central planning with "local planning" at the district or city level.[44] With guidance from concerned authorities of the central government in Hanoi, local party leaders formulated their own economic plans, utilizing local resources and labor as the main resource and importing technology and equipment from other countries when necessary. This was a precursor to the *Doi Moi* policy of 1986. The idea behind decentralizing economic planning was to minimize waste, maximize the use of local resources, increase the quality and efficiency of production, and subsequently reduce foreign debt. Nonetheless, the economic crisis had crippled the economy-first faction's voices within the decision-making circle. The military-first faction was emboldened as the threat to national security that China and its Cambodian ally posed grew imminent after the DK's major attacks against Vietnam intensified during the second half of 1977. In his report to the Party Central Committee in December 1977, Le Thanh Nghi took personal responsibility for the economic crisis.[45] Eventually he was even stripped of his membership in the Party Central Committee in 1982.

Internal records show that Hanoi had three strategic objectives in Cambodia.[46] First, the overthrow of the DK regime in Cambodia was designed to deal a crushing blow to China's influence in Indochina once and for all. Second, the change of regime in Cambodia was also intended to ensure that a pro-Vietnam regime in the aftermath of genocide, similar to the one in Laos, would be long indebted to Vietnam's assistance and thereby would accept Vietnam's leadership role in Indochina. Third, Vietnam was to again proclaim itself the de facto leader of the socialist countries in Indochina and dominate the newly established Indochinese economic region,[47] including economic planning and oversight of international assistance for nation building in Cambodia in the aftermath of the Pol Pot genocidal regime.

Following the invasion, the Hanoi-installed PRK proved to be a rather difficult client state of Vietnam, having little resemblance to a conventional patron-client relationship . Behind the public display of camaraderie, Vietnamese archival evidence reveals contentious differences between the two countries over issues such as sharing the burden of support for Vietnam's occupying forces in Cambodia, territorial boundaries, transshipment of foreign aid to Cambodia via Vietnam, exploitation of Cambodia's natural resources, and the increasingly hostile relationship between Vietnamese troops and some segments of the Cambodian populace. However, documentary evidence in Vietnamese archives, as I discuss in detail below, shows that Hanoi exerted overwhelming influence over domestic and foreign policy in Cambodia in the 1980s. In addition, Vietnam gained nearly exclusive trade access to the rich natural resources, including forests, fisheries, fertile rice paddies, and rubber, of its two smaller neighbors, Cambodia and Laos. Documentary evidence strongly suggests that Hanoi's primary motive was to exploit the Indochinese economic subregion in order to bolster Vietnam's long-term objective of economic modernization.[48] By the same token, the Soviet Union deputized Vietnam as the de facto sheriff of Indochina during the Third Indochina War. Vietnam became the main interlocutor for Cambodia and Laos in the Soviet-led Council for Mutual Economic Assistance (COMECON), assuming far-reaching responsibilities, including economic planning and negotiations for foreign aid from the Soviet Union and other COMECON members on Cambodia's behalf. In Cambodia, as in Laos, the Vietnamese were advisers in chief in major fields ranging from foreign affairs and the economy to internal security at the district level.

In 1979–80, Vietnamese leadership's strategic thinking shifted from quick military victory to long-term militarization of the Vietnamese nation in a two-front war in Cambodia and against China. In 1980–85, Hanoi militarized the entire nation, subordinating economic development to the primacy of military confrontation with China and building a pro-Vietnam PRK in Cambodia in the aftermath of the genocide and national destruction conducted by the DK. The Council of Government's Decision 58-CP gave the MoD extraordinary power to extract material resources, manpower, and technological and professional assets from the national economy in support of Vietnam's two-front war. During this period, Vietnam achieved its aim of drawing economic and military aid worth US$4.5 billion from the Soviet Union, a reward for Vietnam's ironclad alliance with the latter.[49] Nonetheless, the economic pain of the entire nation resulting from the military confrontation with China, combined with the heavy cost of nation building and protracted military intervention in Cambodia, stifled Vietnam's economic growth in spite of massive aid from the Soviet Union and other COMECON countries.

By the end of 1980, one year into Vietnam's military intervention in Cambodia, it had become clear to Hanoi that China's strategy in Cambodia was to bleed the Vietnamese occupying force there and harass Vietnam from the north. In 1983 MOFA, under Foreign Minister Nguyen Co Thach, pushed for a political solution, beginning with a diplomatic offensive intended to isolate China, the China-backed Khmer Rouge, and other resistance factions in Cambodia. The strategy was to demonstrate to ASEAN Indochina's preference for dialogue over confrontation.[50] In the same year, a top-secret report by MOFA revealed that "[Cambodian] Foreign Minister Hun Sen has trusted us [Vietnamese] more in our grand strategy of partial troop withdrawal from Cambodia to pressure Thailand and China to cut their aid to the Cambodian resistance forces."[51] The report noted, "Hun Sen previously expressed strong concern" about Vietnam's first phase of withdrawal of its troops in July 1982.

The Vietnamese occupying forces' major summer offensives in 1984–85 intended to break the backbone of the Cambodian resistance forces was designed to turn victory on the battlefield into political and diplomatic leverage in the international arena, a classic military-diplomatic offensive strategy of the Vietnamese revolutionaries when they were contemplating a political compromise with their formidable enemy. On August 10, 1985, the two Politburos of the Kampuchean People's Revolutionary Party and the CPV held a joint meeting in Hanoi. They agreed on Vietnam's plan to withdraw all its troops from Cambodia by 1990.[52] The old guard, namely, Le Duan, Truong Chinh, Pham Van Dong, and Le Duc Tho, had already agreed on a major shift from military confrontation during the preceding six years to a political solution before the consequential Eleventh Conference of Foreign Ministers held in Phnom Penh on August 15–16, 1985.[53] Yet they also warned against so-called peaceful evolution, referring to the threat of western political and economic ideas to the socialist system.[54] The Vietnamese conservatives and their military-first allies must have been alarmed and shocked when observing Gorbachev's rejection of the long-standing Stalinist worldview of the "two-camps" and the doctrine of "military strength" around this time. On the other hand, reformists like Nguyen Co Thach saw the rise of Gorbachev and his "new thinking" worldview of global interdependence and cooperation with the West as an affirmation of their own new thinking. Combined with such a reckoning and the transformation in the Soviet Union in 1985–86, the threat of a prolonged and costly two-front military confrontation provided the political space for early reformists like Nguyen Co Thach to resurrect their post–Paris Peace Accords new thinking of 1973—a less ideological and more broad-based foreign policy, which also required reconciliation with China and the West.[55]

In 1987 Phan Doan Nam, a theoretician and senior adviser to Foreign Minister Nguyen Co Thach, attributed the shift in Vietnam's foreign policy from socialist internationalism, closely aligned with the Soviet Union, to a broader engagement with the world capitalist system after the 1986 Sixth Party Congress to one key element of Ho Chi Minh's thought on foreign policy and international relations: "Align the strength of the nation with the power of the age."[56] This philosophical belief came to influence the political report of the Sixth National Congress in 1986, which in turn guided Vietnam's multidirectional foreign policy. The "power of the age," as Foreign Minister Nguyen Co Thach elaborated in 1986, refers to the *quy luat phat trien* (law of development) at a critical juncture in human history. He argued, "This law determines the survival trajectory of a nation regardless of its political system and its future development. Great and small powers alike would lag behind if their leaders failed to align their national strength with the global trend."[57] Such structural changes required that Vietnam revise its concepts of national security, shifting the focus from *political-military* to *political-economic* strength.[58]

Consequential military and economic threats to Vietnam's national security, rather than Marxist-Leninist ideology or a political culture of hegemony, drove Hanoi's decision to invade Cambodia and occupy it from 1979 to 1988. The shift of collective ideas within the Vietnamese Politburo from a focus on socialist economic development in 1976–78 to massive military confrontation with China and China-backed Cambodian resistance forces in 1979 was caused by the duality of an economic crisis at home and military threats posed by the Sino–Khmer Rouge alliance. Simply put, material factors, rather than ideological or cultural ones, caused the shift in collective ideas and consequently a corresponding change in Vietnam's national security policy. Vietnam's costly two-front war in Cambodia and against China along its northern border during the first half of the 1980s, combined with entrenched economic hardship at home and the emergent collective belief by 1985 that the Soviet bloc's economic and technological development was lagging behind that of the West, made it possible for the newly empowered reformists' ideas to gain wide acceptance among members of the old guard. These reformist ideas were translated into the *Doi Moi* policy in 1986.

1

Impact of the Economic Crisis

1975-1978

In a short span of just a few years, the post-1975 euphoria of victory, unification, and the prospect of an industrialized socialist Vietnam embedded in the Soviet-style five-year plan (FYP) 1976–80 evaporated, and the leaders of the CPV found themselves confronting a severe economic crisis compounded by growing conflicts with Cambodia and China. Both domestic and external crises seriously threatened the legitimacy and survival of the party-state itself. In retrospect, although Vietnam's economic reform (*Doi Moi*) was officially launched only in 1986, its origins can be traced back to the economic crisis of what Adam Fforde and Stephan de Vylder referred to as the DRV model of the late 1970s—that is, Soviet-style central planning aimed at rapid industrialization, collectivization of agriculture, and strong central control of the economy.[1] Central to the focus of this chapter is the shift in Hanoi's strategic thinking from the celebratory years following national unification, 1975–77, to the dual threat of economic crisis and war with Cambodia and China in 1978–79. The existing scholarship has left a few important questions inadequately answered. How did Hanoi's leaders interpret the causes of the failure of their 1976–80 FYP and its relationship with the national security threat posed by the Sino-Cambodian alliance? How did their interpretation of these crises influence their strategic thinking and consequently domestic and foreign policy changes intended to address the economic and national security threats to the Communist regime?

This chapter, while building on previous studies, focuses on how the interactions between domestic and foreign policy, especially the economic crisis and escalated military conflict with the Khmer Rouge and China in 1977–78, influenced Hanoi's rethinking of national priorities and strategies. Vietnam found itself in territorial dispute with China as early as 1974 and at war with the Khmer Rouge soon after its unification in 1975. By 1978, Vietnam had plunged into economic crisis at home, while the border conflict turned into a two-front war with China and in Cambodia. I argue that how Hanoi's leaders interpreted the impact of the economic crisis on the socialist system in 1977–78 and the threat it posed to the party-state influenced the change in their strategic thinking about their country's national security orientation. As the economic crisis worsened in 1978, and the military threat the Sino-Cambodian alliance posed to Vietnam's territorial sovereignty grew, the conservative and military-first leaders within the CPV moved to bolster the country's military strength and mobilize the Vietnamese people for war against the Khmer Rouge and China. The economics-minded leaders, especially the chairman of the State Planning Committee and Deputy Prime Minister Le Thanh Nghi, were blamed for the economic crisis, although the sources of the crisis were impersonal and beyond their control. In early 1978, Le Thanh Nghi began to relax state central planning and focus on building local districts into an economic and national defense fortress in preparation for war. Hanoi decisively shifted from an attempted balancing position between the Soviet Union and China to a formal alliance with the Soviet Union against China in November 1978.

This chapter, however, does not focus on the objective reality of the failure of the FYP, which is the subject of many excellent studies,[2] but rather on the shift or lack thereof in Hanoi's collective strategic thinking in the face of a mounting economic crisis and national security threat in the late 1970s. In *Changing Worlds: Vietnam's Transition from Cold War to Globalization*, David W. P. Elliott revealed the change in Hanoi's collective ideas after 1975, but briefly touched on these crucial years, 1977–78.[3] Elliott observed—and I strongly agree—that "Although Vietnam's reforms were officially (if tentatively) launched in 1986, their origins were back in the late 1970s."[4] In Elliott's account, General Secretary Le Duan's mind-set of orthodox Soviet-style central planning conformed to the old thinking, that is, top-down economic management, at the Fourth Party Congress in December 1976, and Duan and his closest ideological ally, Le Duc Tho, were unyielding and dogmatic in clinging to orthodoxy.[5] The leading reformist, Vo Van Kiet, who served with the city-level leadership in Ho Chi Minh City, recalled that Le Duan's governing philosophy of Soviet-style central planning impeded the development of new thinking about economic policy.[6] Elliott discussed early reformists in the South, especially Vo Van Kiet and Nguyen Van Linh after 1975, but left out early reformists such as Deputy Prime Minister Le Thanh Nghi, who oversaw the national economy in the late 1970s. It was Le Thanh Nghi who advocated change and demanded "new thinking" (*tu duy moi*) to deal with the economic crisis in 1977–78. Leaving personalities aside, this chapter reveals, in greater detail than Elliott did in his book, the impact of the economic crisis in 1977–78 on the internal debate between the economics-minded leaders and the conservative and military-first faction over Vietnam's national security strategies. Elliott's work takes as its starting point an analysis of the shift in collective ideas about the economy in the early 1980s, not the late 1970s as in this chapter, and does not address Hanoi's internal debate about Vietnam's domestic and foreign policy in late 1977 and early 1978, which I argue led to a significant shift in domestic and foreign policy strategies.[7]

Newly available sources provide new insight into an internal debate within the Politburo in late 1977 and early 1978 about the problem of old thinking, which led to the decentralization of economic planning, that is, bottom-up planning, in response to the economic and national defense crises that Vietnam was facing at the time. The idea of decentralizing economic planning and delegating it to local authorities, especially at the district level, was accepted by the Politburo leadership and presented to the Third Plenum of the Party Central Committee in December 1977 as it was debating how to address inefficient economic management and national security threats from the Sino-Cambodian alliance in 1978 and toward the end of the FYP in 1980.[8] Compared to the *Doi Moi* reform policy at the Sixth Party Congress in December 1986, this was certainly an incremental and improvised change, as Vo Van Kiet later noted,[9] but it was also both a strategic and an ideological response to the domestic and international crises that Vietnam was confronting at the time.

While Elliott emphasized the coexistence of Marxist and nationalist components in the Vietnamese revolutionary mind-set,[10] with the former giving way to the latter—the view to which I subscribe—political scientist Tuong Vu contends that the Marxist-Leninist ideology of state leaders was the overriding worldview that shaped Vietnam's socialist revolution and external relations from the 1920s to the late 1980s.[11] Stressing that Vietnam's internationalism trumped its nationalism, Vu writes, "Although the Chinese invasion [of February 1979] aroused Vietnamese traditional patriotism in many Vietnamese, the conflict did not destroy the Vietnamese belief in internationalism precisely because of the way Chinese moves were interpreted—as an expression of feudalism and bourgeois chauvinism, and an act of 'betrayal' to the 'ideals' of internationalism."[12]

Portraying Vietnamese communist leaders like Le Duan as orthodox Marxists who could not imagine the future Vietnam outside the socialist bloc led by the Soviet Union, Tuong Vu's (2016) *Vietnam's Communist Revolution:*

The Power and Limit of Ideology asserted that Vietnam's vanguard socialist internationalism—that is, a two-camp worldview of Vietnam as the forefront of the socialist camp against the capitalist and imperialist camp—explained Vietnam's foreign policy behaviors with regard to the missed opportunity to normalize relations with the United States after 1975 and the failure to foresee Sino-Vietnamese hostility and the Chinese attacks in 1979.[13] While the ideological worldview of the Vietnamese Communist leadership played a role in Vietnam's foreign policy in the second half of the 1970s, newly available archival sources show that Vu's argument errs by privileging the explanatory power of Vietnam's Marxist-Leninist ideology. A social constructivist's lenses of Marxist-Leninist ideology, as Vu contends, are too confining; his ideational approach neither allows a nuanced analysis of Hanoi's strategic thinking about the linkage between domestic and foreign policy nor liberates analysts from the ideological-material dichotomy or, simply put, the either-or question that sets a constructivist theoretical and methodological framework apart from that of realism in international relations. Vu claimed that ideological affinity with the Soviet Union trumped pragmatism, writing, "There is simply no evidence that Vietnamese leaders ever considered leaving the Soviet camp. . . . Hanoi's quick fall back into Moscow's open arms indicated the more powerful pull of ideology compared to the push of the international structure."[14] As I show, such an argument overlooks a significant but much less visible shift in Hanoi's strategic thinking about the nexus between economic development and national security that began well before Hanoi's plan to invade Cambodia in December 1978.

On closer examination of Hanoi's strategic thinking, as revealed in the leadership's privately circulated documents, a more complete explanation would have to take into account the interaction between ideological (worldviews) and material factors (domestic and external pressures). Ho Chi Minh's diplomatic thought emphasized the single force of "combining the strengths of the nation with those of the era,"[15] a notion originating in the Marxist concept of class contradiction. This belief system is itself based on the decisive role of internal factors, as well as the influence of external factors, both the character of the Vietnamese revolution and the prevailing global trends in the paradox "who will prevail over whom" (*ai thang ai*).[16] This philosophical belief provides insight into Hanoi's interpretation and assessment of its position and the external environment at that critical juncture. In parallel with socialist orthodoxy, the Vietnamese art of diplomacy, as perfected by Ho Chi Minh himself, is also characterized by opportunistic maneuvering, that is, forecasting, creating, seizing opportunities, and analyzing the balance of power trajectory in order to predict opportunities, timing, and appropriate strategies and tactics.[17] Hanoi's top leadership in the late 1970s consisted of members of both camps—General Secretary Le Duan and his ally Le Duc Tho, the pro-Soviet conservatives, and more moderate and economics-minded pragmatists led by Prime Minister Pham Van Dong and Deputy Prime Minister Le Thanh Nghi. Nonetheless, they were all deeply influenced by Ho Chi Minh's diplomatic thought.

1975 to Mid-1977:
Domestic Determinants of Vietnam's Foreign Policy

During a short period of near-total peace (1975 to mid-1977), Hanoi's leaders attempted to translate their national glory and new geopolitical importance as the victor in the war of resistance against the United States into an action plan to build a socialist industrialized Vietnam that the developing world would envy. After its historic victory in April 1975, the CPV made national unification and socialist transformation of the South a top priority, focusing on dismantling the remnants of the Nguyen Van Thieu administration. The increasing conflict between China and the Soviet Union put major structural pressure on Vietnam's international relations immediately following the 1975 victory. A 1975 internal report by the MOFA declared that maintaining Vietnam's policy of a balanced position between the Soviet Union and China while adhering to unity in the international socialist camp remained the best course for Vietnam's postwar foreign policy.[18] Vietnam's victory, in Hanoi's view, proved to the socialist camp that the Soviet Union's and China's policies of peaceful coexistence with the United States were misguided and the great victory belonged solely to the Vietnamese revolution. Yet both China and the Soviet Union were quick to claim an important role in Vietnam's victory. In return, Hanoi expected both nations to continue to provide substantial aid for Vietnam's postwar reconstruction. However, after 1975 Beijing and Moscow were no longer enthusiastic about providing a huge amount of nonrefundable aid to Vietnam. They began to view economic cooperation with Vietnam as a matter of reciprocity and mutual interests.[19]

As senior Vietnamese diplomat Luu Van Loi put it succinctly, "We could obtain the assistance [in the form of loans to be repaid] only when our friends found the economic cooperation with us practically advantageous and when we could maintain their confidence in trade and cooperation."[20] Soon after Vietnam was unified in 1975, Moscow demanded that the Soviet Union be the first country to establish an embassy in Ho Chi Minh City and be granted exclusive access to captured American weapons so as to study their technology while gaining access to the strategic naval base in Cam Ranh Bay. Initially

Vietnam refused Moscow's navy access to Cam Ranh Bay, but it was finally granted at the end of 1978 when Vietnam was prepared to invade Cambodia. The Soviet Union also hoped to use Vietnam as a springboard to exert its influence in Indochina and Southeast Asia and roll back China's influence in the region. Moreover, it desired to integrate Vietnam into the Soviet-led COMECON, but again, to Moscow's disappointment, Vietnam was uninterested in establishing broad ties with the council at that time. Hanoi cited "the need to study the question of participating in the organization," which was perceived by the Soviets as a lack of interest in establishing broad ties with the COMECON.[21] Moscow also expected reciprocal economic cooperation from Vietnam (*hop tac kinh te co di co lai*), a key principle of economic relations between Vietnam and the Soviet Union after 1975.

Hanoi viewed China's significant reduction in its aid to Vietnam as Beijing's attempt to weaken Vietnam and limit its role in the region. In reality China wanted to use aid diplomacy to lure Vietnam into its orbit and limit the Soviet Union's influence, but Vietnam's request for Chinese aid for postwar reconstruction was enormous.[22] The Chinese historian Shu Guang Zhang observed, "Zhou Enlai, among other top PRC leaders, had shown serious concern over the ever-growing requests for aid from Hanoi and indeed tried to dissuade the Vietnamese from relying on China's aid in its postwar economic reconstruction, which gave rise to mixed feelings among the DRV leaders."[23] Hanoi asked Beijing to provide material aid worth 1 billion renminbi (RMB), including 100,000 tons of steel, 750,000 tons of fuel, 150,000 tons of fertilizer, 250,000 tons of coal, 100,000 tons of cement, 22,000 tons of thread, 2,200 vehicles, 300 train cars, 5 fishing boats, 350,000 tons of staple foods, and a few other consumption goods. To Hanoi's awful disappointment, Beijing only agreed to a loan of 100 million RMB (approximately US$50 million) to be used to import Chinese goods in addition to expanding the capacity of three China-aided projects (the Dap Cau power plant, Bac Giang fertilizer factory, and But-son cement factory).[24] This was an interest-free loan to be repaid with Vietnamese goods between 1986 and 1995. Premier Zhou Enlai and Vice-Premier Li Xiannian made it clear to Hanoi on several occasions that Chairman Mao Zedong and the Chinese Party Central Committee had made this decision after thorough deliberations. Zhang wrote, "On his deathbed in late 1975, Zhou Enlai met with the Le Duan delegation to try to convince them that China would continue to supply Hanoi with economic aid despite the almost unbearable burden of assisting the DRV's anti-American war, as long as the two countries remained friendly.[25]

More than a year before the Fourth Party Congress in December 1976, General Secretary Le Duan led a state delegation on an official two-month trip

(September 22 to November 22, 1975) to eight socialist countries, including the Soviet Union and China, to negotiate for economic assistance in support of the unified Vietnam's first FYP (1976–80). The delegation first visited China, on September 22–28, with the goal of improving Sino-Vietnamese relations, but the Chinese leaders warned that if Vietnam continued its pro-Soviet foreign policy it would not find support from them.[26] Le Duan ignored Beijing's warning, and in fact detested China's "big brother" attitude toward Vietnam.

Le Duan's successful trip to the Soviet Union and Eastern Europe resulted in pledges for 1.730 billion rubles in long-term loans from the eight socialist countries, including 946 million rubles for industrial projects and 695 million rubles to cover the import-export trade imbalance. The Soviet Union's pledge accounted for 844 million rubles (350 million rubles for heavy industrial equipment and machinery and 494 million rubles for raw materials), or about 50 percent of the total financial assistance from the eight countries. The Soviet Union and Eastern European countries agreed to charge Vietnam much lower than the market price for industrial equipment, estimated at between 80 and 180 percent below the international market prices. Hanoi's leaders viewed this as very advantageous to Vietnam, but far from replacing China's generous nonrefundable aid during the war.[27]

By comparison, China pledged Vietnam loans worth 200 million rubles to be used to import raw materials in 1976, only a quarter of the Soviet aid pledge, and Beijing used international market prices for these transactions.[28] During the war China had delivered nonrefundable aid worth 1.2 billion rubles (5.235 billion RMBs) in 1971–75.[29] Thus the combined aid and loans from the Soviet Union and other Eastern European countries for Vietnam's first FYP only amounted to around 50 percent (860 million rubles) of the wartime aid it received from China. In Hanoi's thinking, after 1975 the Soviet Union and the Eastern European bloc fell far short of replacing China's generous aid.[30] While the Soviet leaders urged Vietnam to substantially increase its exports in order to reach a balance in exports and imports, they made it known to the Vietnamese leaders that the COMECON would be willing to provide a long-term loan of more than a billion rubles for the next FYP (1981–86) on the condition that Vietnam become an official member of the organization.[31]

Although Beijing rapidly reduced its aid to Vietnam to an insignificant level after 1975, the aid pledged by China before 1975 was so significant that Hanoi strove to persuade Beijing to resume it in the ensuing years. Out of the 800 million rubles for industrial equipment that socialist countries had pledged before 1975, which Hanoi hoped to use to support its 1976–80 FYP, China was expected to deliver 475 million(never delivered due to the deterioration of

Sino-Vietnamese relations in 1977–78) and the Soviet Union 200 million.[32] Thus, in Hanoi's view, China's aid still played an important role in Vietnam's postwar economic reconstruction, which began in December 1976, although the Soviet Union clearly was the most important source of investment capital and technological know-how for the industrialization and modernization of Vietnam's socialist economy.

In 1975 Hanoi's leaders were highly confident, almost to the point of self-delusion, that Vietnam's important geopolitical position in the South China Sea and Southeast Asia and the vast economic potential of a unified country—including a young population and rich natural resources—would persuade many countries to establish economic relations with it. This belief was reinforced by the impressions of the Le Duan delegation during its first major trip to negotiate economic relations with socialist countries after unification in 1975.[33] However, the socialist camp, which served as the main prop for Vietnam's resistance against the United States during the Vietnam War and its national reconstruction in the first two years (1975–76) after the liberation of the South, was still deeply divided as the differences between the Soviet Union and China were still acute, especially in international relations.

After 1975 Hanoi strategically ranked countries in three ideological categories in order of their significance and the scope of their relationship with Vietnam: (1) socialist, (2) nationalist, and (3) capitalist.[34] The economics-minded leadership led by Prime Minister Pham Van Dong and Deputy Prime Minister Le Thanh Nghi desired to expand Vietnam's economic relations beyond the socialist camp in order to achieve the paramount objective of socialist economic development outlined in its first FYP without causing collateral damage to its main support from the socialist camp. General Secretary Le Duan, the leader of the conservative camp, stressed the importance of "combining economy with national defense" in his political report to the Fourth Party Congress in December 1976 and placed the tasks of building the technical and material basis of socialism to strengthen national defense at the center of the FYP.[35] In his political report, Duan stated that to prevail in the struggle between socialism and capitalism, "We must carry out the three revolutions in the relations of production, science, and technology and ideology and culture," emphasizing that "the technical-scientific revolution is key to demonstrating the superiority of socialism to capitalism.[36] Clearly Le Duan viewed economic relations through the "two-camp" lenses.

However, the pragmatic economics-minded leaders within the inner circle of the executive (Prime Minister Pham Van Dong's cabinet) believed that the international socialist camp was no longer the only source of support—though it was still the main prop—for Vietnam's FYP. They advocated expanding Vietnam's economic relations with nonsocialist countries while firmly adhering to the socialist camp politically and ideologically. With the urgency of economic reconstruction in the North, socialist transformation in the South, and no major war to fight, the conservatives yielded to the pragmatic leaders on exploring economic relations with the West, beginning with negotiations to normalize relations with the United States. For the first six months of 1975, the MOFA evaluated the US attitude toward Vietnam with an optimistic view toward establishing diplomatic and economic relations. While Washington declared its intention to impose economic sanctions on Vietnam, Hanoi took it as a positive sign when Washington passed along a diplomatic note via the Vietnamese embassy in Paris on June 12, 1975, expressing the possibility of establishing relations with Vietnam coupled with the fact that a number of American companies were already exploring the potential for doing business in Vietnam.[37] Hanoi certainly envisioned a broad-based foreign economic policy when in May of that year sixteen capitalist countries, including France, Sweden, Japan, and Norway, publicly criticized the US sanctions against Vietnam and explored economic cooperation with it. Such signaling by the West confirmed Hanoi's conviction that a unified Vietnam had great political and economic potential to establish economic relations with capitalist countries.[38] In addition, Vietnam began to explore building economic relations with Thailand, Indonesia, and other members of ASEAN and prepared its entry into the Non-Aligned Movement (NAM). Finally, the MOFA was instructed to prioritize Vietnam's membership in international organizations like the International Monetary Fund (IMF) and World Bank and organizations affiliated with the United Nations, such as the United Nations Conference on Trade and Development (UNCTAD), which it believed would help secure tangible national interests beyond the international community's recognition of a unified Vietnam.[39] Such deliberate efforts were further indicative of the pragmatist leaders' vision of Vietnam's future beyond the socialist camp.

Strategically, the resolution of the Twenty-Fourth Plenum of the Party Central Committee in August 1975 decided that the overarching objective of Vietnam's foreign policy would be to "secure favorable international conditions for the rapid construction of the material and technical bases of socialism and for the consolidation of national defense and security."[40] In an effort to translate this resolution into policy actions, the MOFA convened the Twelfth Foreign Service Conference and issued three foreign policy tasks for 1976: (1) to conduct research on general and economic foreign policy for important countries in each region; (2) to search for sources of fuel, capital, science, and technology and develop economic relations; and (3) to participate in border negotiations with Cambodia, Laos, and China.[41]

In the first six months of 1976, the MOFA observed a trend in global politics favorable to the socialist camp (led by the Soviet Union) as the position of the United States continued to weaken. Vietnam's relations with the Soviet Union and Eastern Europe were increasingly cooperative and economically beneficial, but Hanoi continued to engage in bilateral relations rather than officially joining the COMECON as Moscow desired. On the other hand, from the perspective of the MOFA leadership, Sino-Vietnamese relations continued to deteriorate as politically China was cold toward Vietnam and economically it intended to keep it suppressed. China sold goods to Vietnam at prices that were higher than those prevailing in the international market, bought only high-quality of goods from Vietnam, and slowed delivery of the goods that Vietnam needed most, including food and fuel. At the same time, China increased its aggression toward Vietnam along the Sino-Vietnamese border, especially in a number of strategic and economically important areas in Cao Bang and Lao Cai provinces.[42]

Vietnam's border disputes with Cambodia, Laos, and China resurfaced after 1975 but were not yet a serious threat to its national sovereignty in 1976. Hanoi was confident that it could resolve these disputes through negotiations with its neighbors and comrades in arms. The primary focus was on consolidating socialism in the North and socialist transformation of the newly liberated South with a view toward building a socialist industrialized economy. On July 2, 1976, the name of the country was changed from the Democratic Republic of Vietnam to the Socialist Republic of Vietnam (SRV).[43]

In the second half of 1977 the domestic and international situation changed rapidly, resulting in the onset of an economic crisis and escalating border conflicts with the Khmer Rouge and China, leaving Vietnam in a uniquely uncertain situation in which peace coexisted with the potential outbreak of armed conflict with its neighbors Cambodia and China, prompting the leadership to set two strategic tasks: successfully build socialism and be prepared to defend the socialist fatherland.[44]

To rapidly increase Vietnam's industrial production and extract technological know-how to speed up its socialist industrialization, one of the main objectives of the FYP, from 1975 to 1977, Hanoi increasingly relied on foreign specialists, especially from the Soviet Union and Eastern European countries, and sought to emulate their most advanced technology, while relying far less on Chinese specialists and China's less sophisticated technology. In Vietnam foreign specialists from socialist countries accounted for 90 percent of the total number of foreign specialists from twenty countries in 1976 and 85 percent in

1977.[45] The number of Soviet specialists increased from 19 percent (4,395) in 1975 to 23 percent (3,147) in 1976 and 27 percent (3,234) in 1977 while the number of Chinese specialists dropped sharply from 39 percent (1,719) in 1975 to 5 percent in 1976 and 3 percent in 1977.[46] As a result of China's unilateral takeover of some islands in the South China Sea in 1974, anti-Chinese sentiment in Vietnam had become widespread by 1977, accelerating the flight of Chinese specialists. The deterioration of Sino-Vietnamese relations in general prompted Beijing to reduce the number of foreign specialists it sent to Vietnam.[47] But it was Beijing's decision to cut off nonrefundable aid to Vietnam, not the return of Chinese specialists, that undermined Vietnam's economic reconstruction efforts. Hanoi attached greater value to Soviet technological know-how than to that of China, a policy directly lifted from the technical-scientific revolution (one of the three resolutions) that Le Duan stressed as "key" for the socialist victory over capitalism in his political report to the Fourth Party Congress in December 1976. Here socialist ideology was clearly intertwined with material interests, emulating the most advanced technology from the most advanced socialist great power, the Soviet Union, and then engineering a shortcut to apply it to socialist industrialization.

Hanoi's economic diplomacy was also deployed to fully absorb Soviet technology. In 1977 it increased its efforts to provide good living conditions for Soviet specialists who undertook industrial projects and trained Vietnamese technicians and engineers. Vietnamese officials were instructed to build close working relationships with Soviet specialists. In early 1977 the MOFA organized the first national conference on foreign service tasks at the city and provincial levels with the goal of improving working relationships with foreign specialists at the local level, especially in the newly liberated regions in the South.[48] In 1978 Hanoi increased its spending on foreign specialists by 44 percent to focus on eighteen agricultural and irrigation projects and fifty important industrial bases. It planned to substantially increase the number of Soviet specialists in 1978,[49] in part because the regime's oppressive policies had led to the exodus of a great number of experts and technicians, many of them ethnic Chinese.[50] In comparison, Vietnam spent on average 800 VND (US$88) for one Chinese specialist per month, compared to 2,200 (US$ 244.50) for every Soviet specialist and 2,400 to 3,200 (US$ 266.50–355.50) for every East European specialist.[51] Soviet and Eastern European engineers were allowed to bring their wives and families, although privately the Department of Foreign Specialists complained about the added cost.[52] In 1978 the Department of Foreign Specialists mobilized 2,500 Vietnamese cadres to provide direct services to foreign specialists working in Vietnam.[53] Clearly Hanoi's objective was to effectively learn and use the skills and technology of these Soviet and Eastern European specialists for Vietnam's economic benefit and to improve its scientific and technological base.[54]

Mid-1977 to Early 1978:
The Impact of the Economic Shock

In the MOFA's internally circulated report on foreign policy for the first six months of 1977, top Vietnamese diplomats definitively attributed the Soviet-led COMECON's suspension of industrial projects for Vietnam's FYP and rejection of its emergency aid request to address the food and fuel crisis to Vietnam's political position, specifically its refusal to officially join the COMECON and side with the Soviet Union.[55] It was also clear from that report that Moscow applied measured pressure by keeping Hanoi's hopes for substantial economic cooperation with the COMECON alive. Unless Hanoi officially joined the organization, the Vietnamese would not receive any generous aid packages from the Soviet bloc. Moscow expressed its intention to expand economic cooperation with Vietnam, stressing specific projects, but it denied Hanoi's request for emergency aid of 200,000 tons of fuel and 200 million rubles for the importation of consumption goods.[56] Moscow applied this pressure at a time when Beijing had suddenly suspended all material aid pledged during the previous decade, 1965–75, partly in response to the failure of provincial-level negotiations to resolve Sino-Vietnamese border disputes.[57] Clearly, Beijing was imposing economic sanctions to force Vietnam to make concessions regarding the territorial dispute and to increase the cost of Vietnam's tilt toward the Soviet Union. Simultaneously, Khmer Rouge attacks in southwestern Vietnam in April caused significant destruction of property and loss of life in a number of southern provinces bordering Cambodia.

By late 1977, Vietnam's normalization talks with the United States were on the verge of collapse because Washington had rejected Hanoi's demand for war reparations worth nearly US$5 billion. The Vietnamese pragmatic leaders' attempt to draw capital and investment from the West was met with delay and disappointment. In an attempt to court economic investment and technological transfer from the West, in late April 1977 Prime Minister Pham Van Dong made his country's first official visit to France with the aim of initiating economic (not political) relations with the West. Hanoi hailed Dong's visit as a diplomatic and political success, but it failed to yield any concrete economic deals. Hanoi also hoped to normalize relations with the United States in 1977 when the new administration under President Jimmy Carter expressed a serious interest in moving forward with the normalization process. As to why normalization failed in 1977, Tuong Vu points to the Vietnamese communist leaders' anti-imperialist ideology, placing the blame for the failure on the doorstep of the Vietnamese Communist leaders.[58] However, such an explanation is incomplete because it ignores the material factors at play. From a negotiation standpoint, Hanoi viewed the normalization process as the politics of reciprocity on top of a moral argument. Certainly Hanoi's anti-imperialist ideology and identity are a given, but their geostrategic and economic importance in 1977—which in retrospect can be seen as exaggerated and self-delusional—was also real in the Vietnamese leaders' minds, and their underlying objective was primarily economic and secondarily political when the negotiations took place. In fact Hanoi was badly in need of economic assistance in 1977. Given Vietnam's perceived geostrategic importance, its economic potential for American companies, and the assistance it was providing Washington with prisoner of war and missing in action (POW/MIA) issues, Hanoi's leaders believed they had the leverage to demand a large monetary reparations package. In the bilateral meeting in Paris on May 3–4, 1977, Assistant Secretary for East Asia Richard Holbrooke informed Vietnamese Vice-Minister Phan Hien that in addition to US$5 million in private humanitarian aid to Vietnam, despite the embargo, indirect aid after normalization might be possible. However, Phan Hien insisted that the United States carry through on President Nixon's commitment of $3.25 billion in grant aid and $1.5 billion in commodity aid.[59] In a top secret memo to the Party Central Committee in December 1977, Politburo member and deputy prime minister Le Thanh Nghi, who was also chairman of the State Planning Committee, lamented that Vietnam was annually losing US aid to the Republic of Vietnam worth $1 billion, unemployment was estimated at over three million people, and myriad social problems had arisen since 1975.[60]

One of the major factors that blocked US-Vietnam normalization was the issue of war reparations to which the Vietnamese believed they were entitled. Foreign Minister Nguyen Co Thach insisted on reparations worth US$4.7 billion as a precondition for the normalization of US-Vietnam relations in 1977. This demand created a problem for the Carter administration because the US Congress would not approve such a deal, and a major geopolitical shift (the China factor) in great power politics derailed the US-Vietnam normalization process.

The twists and turns of the subsequent negotiations from December 1977 to September 1978 revealed two indisputable facts. First, Hanoi showed greater flexibility than Washington, relaxed its demands, and finally agreed to unconditional normalization. Second, it was Washington's priority of strengthening the Sino-US alliance, in alignment with Deng Xiaoping's priority of normalizing

China's relations with the United States (as opposed to the Soviet Union),[61] that prompted the Carter administration to shelve the normalization of US relations with Vietnam. After meeting US secretary of state Cyrus Vance on August 24, 1977, Deng Xiaoping viewed the Sino-American alliance not just as a counterbalance to the Soviet threat but as an opportunity to access the capital and technology needed to modernize China's economy.[62] As senior diplomat Tran Quang Co, in charge of North America at the MOFA at that time, recalled, in early 1978 Washington had already decided to embrace the Sino-American alliance to oppose to the Soviet Union,[63] and it shelved normalization with Vietnam.[64] Citing Tran Quang Co's memoir as further evidence that Hanoi's anti-imperialist ideology was the main cause of the missed opportunity to normalize relations with the United States in 1977, Tuong Vu contends that the thinking of the Vietnamese Communist leaders simply did not prepare them for that,[65] suggesting diplomatic rigidity or "too little too late" flexibility in the context of rapidly evolving great power politics. Hanoi's ideology of anti-imperialism, though influential after 1975, hardly reduced the material (Hanoi's demand for massive war reparations from the United States) and structural (the convergence of Sino-American strategic interests) pressures on Vietnam that ultimately derailed the US-Vietnam normalization talks in 1977–78.

It was Hanoi's demand for $3.25 billion of US aid for postwar economic reconstruction in exchange for its cooperation with POW/MIA issues and American companies' access to economic opportunities in Vietnam that initially blocked normalization, and the United States' strategic alliance with China against the Soviet Union dealt the final blow to the normalization process in early 1978. According to Desaix Anderson, who was an American diplomat involved in the normalization process, it was Nguyen Co Thach who pushed a demand for the US$3.25 billion that President Nixon had offered to provide as part of the Paris Peace Accords (PPA). However, no American administration was obligated to pay this amount after North Vietnam violated its commitments under the accords.[66] Hanoi's release of Nixon's secret letter to Prime Minister Pham Van Dong, containing his promise of US$3.25 billion in grand aid and $1.5 billion in commodity aid, led to the passage of legislation by the US Congress prohibiting the Carter administration from negotiating reparations with Vietnam.[67]

In the third round of negotiations between Richard Holbrook and Phan Hien in December 1977, Hien proposed that normalization should occur first, leaving the issue of reparations to a later discussion. In the summer of 1978, as a gesture of flexibility, Hanoi turned over the remains of fifteen more American soldiers to a visiting US congressional delegation led by Congressman Sonny Montgomery. On September 22, 1978, after Richard Holbrook threatened to end talks twice during a meeting, Vice-Minister Nguyen Co Thach agreed to normalization without conditions. While awaiting the official signing scheduled for early October, national security adviser Zbigniew Brzezinski convinced President Carter to postpone normalization with Vietnam to avoid offending the Chinese.[68] Evidently the material factors played a major role in derailing the US-Vietnam normalization negotiations. In addition to the barrier to the US-Vietnam normalization process, Hanoi's lead negotiator (Nguyen Co Thach), by imposing a war reparations condition unacceptable to the Americans, affected broader strategic calculations (i.e., the Sino-American alliance) in Washington, and Beijing derailed Vietnam's efforts to normalize its relations with the United States.

Between mid-1977 and March 1978, the rapid deterioration of Sino-Vietnamese relations on the security front coincided with Beijing's drastic cuts in aid to Vietnam. The border negotiations between the two governments from October 1977 to March 1978 not only failed but the MOFA leaders who conducted the negotiations concluded that the Chinese were threatening the Vietnamese side with the use of force over the territorial disputes. The MOFA reported to the Politburo that Beijing's real motive was to expand its territorial claims along the border at Vietnam's expense while proposing negotiations to demonstrate its goodwill.[69] China's economic sanctions against Vietnam for building closer relations with the Soviet Union were intensified, worsening Vietnam's economic crisis.[70] Although Vietnam's economic crisis manifested itself in late 1977, its origins can be traced back to Vietnam's "DRV" model of central planning and its wartime reliance on foreign aid for over two decades.

The first FYP (1976–80) for the unified country was the most significant national policy in the postwar era, a product born out of monumental research by Vietnam's best and brightest economists and experts selected from all fields, along with three rounds of deliberations by the Politburo of the Party Central Committee before it was presented to the Party Central Committee in October 1976. On December 14, the Fourth Party Congress set forth the strategic tasks and objectives of the plan, which had two fundamental goals: (1) to build the material and technical bases of socialism and put in place a new economic structure to boost industrial-agricultural productivity; and (2) to improve the material and cultural life of the proletarian class, that is, peasants and workers.[71] The plan required resource balancing among (1) industrialization and agriculture, (2) central and local economies, (3) the economy and national defense, and (4) domestic and foreign economic relations.[72]

The Twenty-Fifth Conference of the Party Central Committee in October 1976 set agricultural production as a top priority of the FYP, stressing the goal of producing twenty-one million tons of food grains by 1980, more than one million hectares of industrial crops, and more than one million tons of meat, clearing an additional one million hectares of rice paddies, transferring a few million laborers from the delta and cities to New Economic Zones (remote virgin land to be cleared for agricultural production), and speeding up the process of mechanization in major rice-producing regions to yield an annual average crop increase of 8 to 10 percent. The strategic objective was to end food shortages in three years, by 1979.[73] Hanoi's economic planners expected to provide employment to seven million people by 1980.[74]

Besides the economic potential of 22 million young laborers, Hanoi's top economic planner—Deputy Prime Minister Le Thanh Nghi, who was also a Politburo member and chairman of the State Planning Committee—stressed the untapped potential of the technological revolution to increase productivity and called on his colleagues to pay special attention to technology in developing a long-term strategy for economic development and national defense.[75] This required importing technology from other countries, especially the Soviet Union and the nations in the West, because Vietnam did not have the ability to develop modern technology on its own. Emphasizing Vietnam's insufficient technological base for its economy, Le Thanh Nghi lamented to his colleagues during a debate over the FYP on November 30, 1976, that even if Vietnam could make the most efficient use of its existing resources in this area, this would only yield an annual average per-person allocation of 58 kilowatts of electricity, 140 kilograms of coal, 3.5 kilograms of steel, 16 kilograms of cement, 8 meters of fabric, 2 kilograms of paper, and 300 kilograms of staple foods. But actual productivity was even lower than that.[76] The national output could not keep up with an increase in population of 1.5 million people per year.[77] Vietnam lost a billion dollars' worth of nonrefundable foreign aid per year that had been provided mostly by China and the Soviet Union during the war of resistance against the United States from 1965 to 1973.[78]

However, Hanoi's leaders were highly optimistic at the end of 1976, believing that the traditional patriotism of the Vietnamese people, the combined strength of a unified Vietnam, and a people united in their belief in the party's farsightedness and Marxist-Leninist ideology after its victory over the United States would enable Vietnam to overcome the challenges the country faced.[79] Besides the heightened sprit of national unity, Hanoi's top economic planners looked to exploit Vietnam's national resources; a united Vietnam had diverse national resources, including oil deposits that could be used to develop the energy and various other industrial sectors, a total of five million hectares of rice paddies (which could be expanded to eleven million over time), fifteen million hectares of resource-rich forests, an annual extraction of several million tons of seafood from its seas, a labor force of nearly twenty-two million people, and a growing number of educated and skilled cadres and workers.[80] The political and economic potential of a united Vietnam, these economically minded leaders believed, would further create favorable conditions for expanding the country's economic relations and extracting technical know-how from sources beyond the socialist countries.[81]

The strategy of Hanoi's top economic planners at that time was to combine the country's internal strengths—that is, socialist ideology and traditional Vietnamese nationalism—with national resources at the center of the party-state's plan to mobilize national power and its projection of influence in international relations by leveraging its geopolitical significance in the region. In his address to the first meeting of the newly established Central Economic Zoning Commission (Uy ban Phan Vung Kinh Te Trung Uong) on October 1, 1977, the chairman of the State Planning Committee, Le Thanh Nghi, emphasized that the main duty of the commission was to "reorganize and redistribute production forces and material resources to enhance people's living conditions in localities and regions across the country; to advance the party's policy of building socialism, first and foremost the policy of socialist industrialization; to create a modern agricultural-industrial economic system, prioritizing heavy industry that appropriately relies on the bases of agricultural and light industry development; and to a develop central economy while simultaneously building the local economy."[82]

In December 1977, the Party Central Committee held its Third Plenum to assess the achievements of the previous two years (1976–77) of the FYP and to draw up a plan for 1978. On December 6, Politburo member and deputy prime minister Le Thanh Nghi, on behalf of the Politburo, delivered a three-part analysis of the state of the economy to the Central Committee for further debate. Nghi reported, "Although our economic foundation has developed, progress has not caught up with our country's demands. . . . Our economy is facing enormous difficulty and instability in 1977."[83] In 1977, although 22.1 million out of a total of 23.5 million laborers were employed, productivity was very low, yielding an annual income per person of 840 VND (approximately US$305 at that time). Le Thanh Nghi went on to describe the extent of economic hardship in terms of statistics. There was a severe shortage of staple foods and consumption goods. The state rice reserves were gone, and Vietnam had to import 1.1 million tons of rice. But even this was not enough to meet the national demand, greatly undercutting the plan to redistribute the labor force to designated production sectors, including irrigation, fishing, logging, and export-crop farming. Vietnam's transportation system was clogged, which significantly slowed production capacity, construction, and the movement of goods and people across the country. The transportation sector was extremely weak in 1977, operating at only 47 percent of its capacity in 1964 before the Vietnam War. A severe lack of building materials hampered the rising demand for construction. Vietnam continued to suffer from a huge trade deficit. With loans and financial aid from foreign countries, it could only meet 63 percent of its 1977 budget. Its gross national product had only increased by 2 percent in 1977, far too small a margin given the rate of population growth.[84]

Any progress had to be measured against 1974–75, when Vietnam's postwar economy was at its lowest point and experienced natural disasters beyond its leadership's control. As Le Thanh Nghi told his colleagues at the Third Plenum of the Party Central Committee in December 1977, "In 1974–75, our economy was in the situation of 'lam khong du an, thu khong du chi' or 'We don't make enough to eat and don't earn enough to spend.'"[85] According to Nghi, Vietnam's exports amounted to only one-sixth of its imports at that time. Besides the economic devastation of the prolonged war, Vietnam had to fill the void of a billion dollars that the United States had provided to the Thieu government of the Republic of Vietnam (the US ally) annually and the approximately 400 to 500 million rubles of nonrefundable aid from the eight socialist countries, including China and the Soviet Union, which punched an enormous hole in the country's economic foundation in the postwar era. In addition, more than three million people were unemployed and the country was beset with extremely serious social ills (te nan xa hoi in Vietnamese), including prostitution, crime, drug addiction, social and political instability, and the monumental tasks of national unification. In 1977 a prolonged drought created extraordinary difficulties for the economy because 50 percent of the country's national revenue came from the agricultural sector.

Under the socialist dictatorship of the party, mass mobilization became a solution to economic problems. One million hectares of rice paddies were cleared for cultivation in 1976–77 and 140,000 hectares in 1977 in spite of the drought.[86] This achievement would not have been possible without large-scale forced labor under the Vietnamese Communists' version of thought reform (cai tao tu tuong), programs lifted directly from the party's ideological and cultural revolution championed by the conservative leader Le Duan.[87] The industrial output for 1976–77 increased by 12 to 13 percent in spite of a severe lack of fuel, raw materials, and spare parts; basic construction increased by 30 to 40 percent, indicating a fast-growing sector of the economy. In 1977 Vietnam was able to produce enough basic consumption goods, and the export-import ratio increased from 20 percent in 1975 to 28 percent in 1976 and 31 percent in 1977. National revenue in 1976 covered 54 percent of the annual budget, which increased to 73 percent in 1977.[88] To the country's leaders, this achievement demonstrated the power of the Vietnamese Communists' revolution and mass mobilization of Vietnamese workers and combatants under the correct proletarian dictatorship of the party. Thus, in 1976–77, Hanoi's leaders, both the conservative and the economically minded, were steeped in their belief in socialist ideology and the power of authoritarian mobilization to solve economic problems.

The Deep Crisis of 1978 and New Thinking

Throughout 1977, the economic crisis was apparent at all levels and across many sectors of Vietnam's economy, with the most severe shortages occurring in food grains, staple foods, construction materials, energy, and hard currency. The main question at the heart of the debate at the Party Central Committee's Third Plenum in December 1977 was why the economy was stagnating. For top economic planners like Le Thanh Nghi, besides the proximate causes of the crisis—including the aftermath of the war, the reduced levels of foreign aid, and natural disasters—the wartime dependence mentality (old thinking") was also a major hindrance to progress. Nghi declared there were two main causes involving the party bureaucracy from the center to local authorities: (1) a lack creativity and motivation and heavy reliance on the outside, a reference to local production units' dependence on the central government and foreign aid; and (2) carelessness in the execution of one's duties, meaning a lack of attention to quality and the failure to take responsibility for one's work.[89]

In December 1976, as optimistic as his deputy Le Thanh Nghi, Politburo member and prime minister Pham Van Dong reminded party members to always remember Ho Chi Minh's teaching, which Pham Van Dong took as an instruction: "I do not fear scarcity, I only fear inequality; I do not fear poverty, I only fear the people having unquiet minds" (*khong so thieu, chi so khong cong bang; khong so ngheo, chi so long dan khong yen*). For 1978, the party set solving the food shortage as its top priority, attempting to produce 16.5 million tons of food grains, 3.5 million tons more than in 1977, to be used as reserves.[90]

To achieve this objective, the government increased the budget for the agricultural sector to 33.7 percent of the total national budget for 1978. This was a substantial increase compared to the 16 percent spent on agriculture in North Vietnam during 1955–75. As in the past, the funds were concentrated in two areas—large-scale irrigation schemes and state farms—both of which produced diminishing returns.[91] As economists Melanie Beresford and Dang Phong observed, "Expansion of irrigation schemes into less suitable areas tends to produce diminishing returns to investment, when higher returns might have been obtained from other sorts of investment such as high yielding varieties, fertilizer, [and so on].... Investment goods [tractors and other machinery] sent to the cooperative agricultural sector were often inappropriate to the needs of farmers, particularly given the shortages of necessary inputs such as fuel and fertilizer, lack of adequate repair facilities and so on."[92]

One-third of the total quantity of cement and steel were to be designated for basic agricultural construction and irrigation; approximately 30 percent of machinery and 20 percent of imported spare parts and equipment would be directly used to service agricultural production. For 1978 Vietnam required 4,325 heavy-duty tractors, 6,200 small tractors, 80 excavators, 70 pieces of machinery for irrigation, and many other types of equipment for agriculture.[93] But it could guarantee only 1.1 million tons of fertilizer and 740,000 tons of manure. Thus it needed to secure loans with which to import fertilizer to meet the goal of 2 million tons for the agricultural sector.[94] For example, 900 tons of rice per day were to be allocated to Ho Chi Minh City (the economic hub) and 500 tons to Hanoi (the capital). This quantity of rice would be sufficient for the large numbers people who would be moved to the New Economic Zones, as well as for housing, construction, forestry, industrial crop regions, logging export sectors, animal husbandry, and fishing.[95]

One of the consequences of Vietnam's economic stagnation in 1977 was that capital investment in its industrial sector in 1978–80 was greatly diminished, compelling it to consider officially joining the Soviet-led COMECON in mid-1978. Out of a total budget of 5.91 billion VND (US$2.15 billion), the Politburo allocated 2.8 billion (47.5 percent of the total budget) to agriculture, forestry, fishing, and the manufacture of consumption goods. Since 1.984 billion (33.7 percent) was used for agriculture and irrigation, this left only 1.839 billion (31.1 percent) for the industrial sector, which derailed Hanoi's FYP goal of modernizing and industrializing the economy. As Le Thanh Nghi told his colleagues at the Central Committee's Third Plenum in December 1977, "During this five-year plan, our industrial development has not made much progress. We have to make greater efforts to create favorable conditions to expand our industrial capacity in the next five-year plan (1981–85)."[96] According to Beresford and Phong, out of a total of 378 projects using imported equipment begun during the FYP, only 28 percent were completed in the end, and many of these were unable to function due to shortages of raw materials or lack of power.[97]

The weakening of the industrial sector provided an impetus for Vietnam to join the COMECON in mid-1978 in order to obtain modern industrial equipment and technology from the Soviet bloc.

By mid-1978, the economic crisis worsened dramatically, prompting Hanoi's top economic planners to search for emergency solutions. In the first quarter of 1978, in Hanoi's view, economic management, leadership, and organization for implementation of the economic plan still suffered from many serious problems, which were stifling progress. In April 1978, the Council of Ministers met to assess the causes of these problems.[98] They concluded, "Our economic situation now is very difficult—certain sectors have gotten worse than in previous years. Although natural disasters such as drought and foreign aid reduction were contributing factors, the main reason was our shortcomings in economic management and organization due to which we failed to execute our plan. And every field, level, and each one of us is partly responsible for this lack of progress."[99] During a three-day conference in May attended by representatives from the central government and provincial and city authorities,[100] the chairman of the State Planning Committee, Le Thanh Nghi, who was also deputy prime minister and a Politburo member, expressed serious concern in his opening remarks that "economic productivity during the first quarter of 1978 was in general low, and lower than that of the previous year, especially in the area of [the state] purchasing food grains and other agricultural products from [peasants], causing chaos in the market and enormous difficulties for people, especially government employees. We need to pay attention to the Mekong Delta [in southern Vietnam]; this is the region where food production per person is the highest in the country, but the government received the lowest amount of food grains from this region."[101] This was because a large quantity of rice was sold on the black market for a much higher price than the state offered and the black market itself had grown due to the increasingly corrupt practices of state bureaucrats throughout the country.

For 1979 Hanoi focused on agriculture, increasing exports, and importing of advanced industrial equipment and raw materials to improve the quality of export products. First, the most important mission was to meet the country's most basic needs, especially for food and consumption goods to support productivity and people's livelihoods.[102] Top economic planners set a target of increasing the production of staple foods from 16 million tons in 1978 to 18.5 million tons in 1979.[103] Hanoi's second priority was to concentrate on increasing exports in agriculture, forestry, fishing, and light industry, targeting a ballooning export market worth 600 to 650 million rubles, 50 percent more than in

1978.[104] Hanoi's third objective was to build up the material and technological base of the economy, especially electricity, machinery, metallurgy, construction materials, and transportation, in the coming years.[105]

However, achieving these three objectives would be no easy task without hard currency and additional financial aid from the Soviet Union and other COMECON countries. According to Beresford and Phong's estimate, between 1975 and 1978 Vietnam had already accumulated a $1.4 billion of debt owed to COMECON countries, almost equal to the total debt of the previous two decades. This was because, although after 1975 the socialist bloc agreed to continue aid on an expanded scale, the proposed nonrefundable aid dropped from an average of more than 60 percent in the decade prior to 1975 to around 43 percent in 1977–79.[106] Top Vietnamese planners knew that the economic imbalance had widened rather than narrowed on many fronts, including food supplies, electricity, construction materials, transportation, consumption goods, hard currency, the budget, and the export-import ratio. In the south, material goods left behind by the Thieu regime had been used up, and most of the industrial equipment had broken down or was badly in need of repair or replacement.[107] The population grew by 1.3 million in 1978, increasing the demand for food and consumption goods.

In addition to inefficient management, low labor productivity, and shortages of raw materials and spare parts due to sharp cutbacks from wartime levels of foreign assistance, escalation of the armed conflict with the Khmer Rouge in the southwest and China in the north resulted in a huge diversion of investment resources to a major military buildup in 1978. Vietnam's armed forces suddenly increased from 770,000 to 1.5 million soldiers and personnel in that year.[108] According to the MoD's official records, the total number of troops in 1978 increased by 18 percent compared to 1976. The 1978 defense budget suddenly increased by 44 percent, and expenses for equipping new recruits increased by 24 percent over the 1977 budget.[109] More than 200,000 military personnel who had been transferred to undertake economic projects beginning in mid-1976 were mobilized for war in early 1978, stalling Hanoi's plan to rely on the armed forces to make a major contribution to the economy.[110] The Fourth Plenum of the Party Central Committee issued a resolution in June 1978 to urgently mobilize a large number of Vietnamese civilians to build border defense belts in the southwest and north. The cost of the border conflict with the Khmer Rouge by mid-1978 was high: 45,000 injured soldiers treated at mobile military clinics at the border; 9,000 more seriously injured soldiers transported to Hanoi for treatment; and 9,000 tons of grain, 690 tons of food, and 25,000 tons of fuel used to fight the Khmer Rouge.[111]

Politburo member and deputy prime minister Le Thanh Nghi used the term *mat can doi lon* (enormous imbalance) to refer to Vietnam's transportation problems at the Third Plenum of the Party Central Committee on December 6, 1977. Vietnam's transportation capacity in 1977 was 47 percent of its 1964 capacity.[112] The Ministry of Transport came under additional pressure as Vietnam prepared for war with Cambodia and China in 1978. The country's transportation infrastructure was strained as resources were diverted from economic projects to the movement of troops, ammunition, food, medicine, and other military equipment as the border war with the Khmer Rouge and armed clashes with the Chinese rapidly increased in early 1978. From June to December 1978, 5,079 vehicles with the capacity to transport 15,569 tons per day were used for the war with the Khmer Rouge and the subsequent invasion of Cambodia.[113]

The economic and national security crises affected Hanoi's strategic thinking on its domestic and foreign policies. In the spring of 1978 the failure of the FYP left the CPV in a legitimacy crisis in the wake of a growing economic, social, and political crisis. At the same time, the economic policy of opening to the West had also failed and border disputes with Cambodia and China were unresolved. As the domestic crisis deepened, Vietnamese leaders were compelled to change their domestic and foreign policy strategies in preparation for war. At the national level they attempted to shake the party apparatus out of its wartime dependence mentality and instill self-reliance. Internationally, they shifted from broad-based foreign relations to membership in the COMECON in June 1978 and a strategic alliance with the Soviet Union in November. Thus Hanoi attempted an internal balancing act by making the best use of scarce resources and reorganizing economic life in the service of national defense and an external one by siding with the Soviet Union against China, reversing the course set by the Fourth Party Congress in December 1976.

At the May 12 conference with party leaders of the central government, provinces, and cities, Le Thanh Nghi vehemently declared the need to "attach special importance to economic efficiency. . . . [We] must eradicate the attitude of using production quantity and speed to project an image [of achievement] while we neglect product quality and value, which reduces economic efficiency."[114] Next Nghi pointed the finger at the provincial authorities.

Many local authorities still do not see the importance of managing the economy according to state planning; disobedience of the state's quotas is quite widespread. For instance, concerning expenses for the cost of producing agricultural products for 1978, many provincial authorities, especially in the south, set lower quotas for their subordinate production units than those determined by the central government. But they demanded greater investment in terms of funding and material resources from the central government. Regarding basic construction investments, many provincial authorities at their own discretion altered the central government's investment plan by exaggerating the resource need by 10 to 35 percent above the actual resource requirement to meet the target set by the central government in Hanoi.[115]

The shift to the new thinking occurred during the Politburo's internal debate about the 1978 economic plan prior to the presentation of its decision in a report by Le Thanh Nghi to the Third Plenum of the Party Central Committee in early December 1978.[116] At the Conference of the Central Committee of the CPV held on December 6, 1977, Nghi stressed the need to "renovate (*Doi Moi*) methods of [economic] planning" systematically in order to "give up the old and familiar ways of doing things for many years,"[117] referring to central planning, and to build effective economic planning from the bottom up. The central planners were to lead and coordinate economic planning and provide expertise, but the planning itself would be done by local officials to reflect the reality of local capacity. On May 12, 1978, in his meeting with leaders of the central, provincial, and city authorities, Le Thanh Nghi instructed, "We must do better in economic planning from the bottom up. We need to delegate control from the central to the local level. Planning the economy from the bottom up means that we will concentrate on democratizing the [economic] planning."[118] In a self-criticism, he frustratingly admitted, "Up to now, the work of bottom-up [economic] planning has not been good; that is an important cause of poor planning. We must work from the bottom up in the spirit of "*Doi Moi* or renovation" as set forth by the Decision of the Third Conference of the Central Committee of the CPV so that we can create real change in [economic] planning."[119] On the first day of the conference, Le Thanh Nghi talked at length about *doi moi tu tuong chi dao* (renovating the guiding ideology) in economic planning.[120]

What did the Politburo's reference to the *Doi Moi* of "planning as a guiding ideology" (*tu tuong chi dao*) from 1978 onward really mean? Certainly this was a precursor to the watershed transition from a centrally planned to a market economy, as the 1986 *Doi Moi* entailed, based on assessment from the top down and planning from the bottom up. It meant, rather, a shift from a top-down approach to economic planning (the old way) to a bottom-up approach (the new way). According to Le Thanh Nghi, in the process of debating what went wrong with the FYP and discussing the 1978 plan at the Politburo of the Central Committee of the CPV and the Council of Ministers, the leadership came to a deeper understanding and concluded that the real obstacle to the realization of the FYP lay in the guiding ideology—that is, that the party needed to instill the ideology of self-reliance (exploiting natural resources and labor to create economic value, cutting waste and unnecessary projects, and expecting less foreign aid) in addition to the three revolutions in the relations among production, science and technology, and ideology and culture).[121] Nghi described the guiding ideology of self-reliance as follows:

> First, we must rely on the most valuable and abundant source of investment, that is, the labor force, in conjunction with exploiting land, forest, sea, and other natural resources, and material-technological bases in our country to create economic value. Second, we must endeavor to procreate our capacity and unleash the hidden economic potential in our country and proactively take initiatives based on what we have to broaden our economic relations with foreign countries. Simply put, we must rely on our own energy, beginning with what we have, to develop economic plans; we should not rely on or expect assistance from the outside [foreign aid] to alleviate our economic difficulties and shortages. We must shelve or postpone certain industrial projects that we need but cannot afford or do not have the ability to build by ourselves at this time. We should not force ourselves to borrow too much from foreign countries. We need to know when to step back and wait for more favorable conditions.[122]

The question of how to maximize economic output based on the abundance of labor, land, and national resources, as well as how to reduce foreign debt resulting from a rapid rise in the demand for imported raw materials, spare parts, equipment, and investment capital, lay at the heart of the rethinking of the basic guiding ideology of economic planning and management at the top level of the Vietnamese leadership and the Politburo of the Party Central Committee in December 1977. Based on the country's economic performance in 1977, top economic planners came to view the top-down central planning approach as an inefficient mechanism for developing and optimizing the potential of Vietnam's enormous labor force of more than 22 million. Planners like Le Thanh Nghi believed this was because for many years the central planners, including himself, had followed the "old way" (duong mon cu). Since the 1960s the central planners had set production targets for local production units based on the available material resources, equipment, staple foods, consumption goods (in conjunction with Vietnam's ability to import these items), investment, and budget. This top-down planning did not factor in the effective use of labor, land, other natural resources and the existing material and technological resources at each locality. This wartime mentality led to a situation in which leaders of local production units inherently "expected and relied on outside assistance" to supplement a variety of economic shortages, and as a result Vietnam became increasingly dependent on foreign loans to meet a large portion of its need for spare parts and equipment.[123] The most important reason for the poor economic performance and ineffective management, the Politburo concluded, was that these local economic managers still followed the wartime habit of relying on nonrefundable aid for importing raw materials, spare parts, and equipment and lacked a "proactive, creative, and self-reliant mentality."[124] This conclusion was driven in large part by the debt accumulated in 1976–77 and the decision not to seek further credit from the West beginning in 1978.[125] According to the new guiding ideology of economic planning, the leaders of each production unit or sector were to create their own production, technological, and financial investment plan with guidance from the central government agencies, especially the State Planning Commission, and to use the locally available labor force and resources to ensure self-sufficiency. Any surplus was to be sent to the state. The local economy (*kinh te dia phuong*) and central economy (*kinh te trung uong*) were closely linked as one national economy, but local authorities were granted more control over their local economy in 1978; under the stewardship of the central government, they assumed primary responsibility for ensuring that the basic needs of the populations in their jurisdictions were met.

In a top-secret memo to the Party Central Committee's Third Plenum in December 1977, Le Thanh Nghi declared, "We must take the district as the compass (*lay huyen lam dia ban*) for balancing and managing the labor force in rural areas."[126] Although the importation of equipment still occupied an important place in the economy, any import plan had to match the ability to pay, and imported equipment would henceforth be treated as a "reserve" (*du bi*) for development and construction projects beyond the target.[127] Local managers and leaders of production units were to be instilled with the new thinking of stepping up their efforts and taking initiatives to ensure that they had sufficient materials for production. They were instructed to not depend on imports of raw materials by the cash-strapped central government. By way of example, Nghi stated:

> If local leaders do not have enough machinery, they must rely on manpower to produce raw materials locally, be economical with food grains or save them for more productive sectors of the economy, increase efficiency in the use of their equipment, and so forth. For instance, the Politburo raised the issue of tractor usage. Tractors, if properly taken care of and repaired in a timely manner, could be used for two to three shifts a day. Cumulatively, these economical efforts

would double their usage capacity and as a result reduce the need to import tractors while still meeting the target of mechanizing our agricultural sector. As another example, local leaders could lead a mass movement to raise animals, especially pigs and cows, to increase the production of phosphate fertilizer and offset the shortage of chemical fertilizer in 1978.[128]

Regarding food shortages, the Politburo instructed authorities at the provincial and district levels to cut down on waste and unneeded food so as to funnel these scarce commodities to the most economically productive sectors. For example, a larger quantity of food grains was to be set aside for the state plan to bring people in to clear farmland in the New Economic Zones, build irrigation systems, construct houses, plant and tend export crops, raise animals, and develop the fishing industry. As another example of increasing consumption goods domestically, bamboo, rattan, and other materials could be used to make furniture and other household tools because Vietnam suffered from a severe shortage of timber and nationwide production could only meet 30 percent of the national demand in 1977. Furthermore, Hanoi expected to increase exploitation of Vietnam's natural resources and export of Vietnamese workers to the Soviet Union and Eastern Europe to earn currency that could be used to import raw materials, spare parts, and modern machinery.[129] Clearly, the overall goal was to increase national self-sufficiency through the exploitation of national resources and therefore reduce the country's dependence on loans from foreign countries. Loans were to be used to import modern technology and machinery for economic development, not food and consumption goods. The evidence uncovered in internal documents of the Vietnamese government at that time lends support to Beresford and Phong's conclusion that "by the end of the 1970s, the combined effects of crisis in the planned sector, impending changes in the conditions of Soviet aid, increased market-oriented activity and political pressure for reform had created the conditions for a fundamental process of institutional change to begin."[130]

As Vietnam entered a new period of "peace coexisting with the potential outbreak of war" with Cambodia and China in 1978, the idea of delegating economic planning to local authorities to ensure local economic subsistence gained a stronger foothold. On January 24, 1978, the Politburo issued Directive 33-CT/TW to concentrate on "the district as the main agricultural-industrial unit, as well as the firm fortress of national defense."[131] From then on, the central government vigorously delegated more economic planning responsibility to provincial, city, and district authorities because, Hanoi believed, these local authorities would improve economic efficiency and self-reliance as they had direct knowledge of their labor force, land, natural resources, and production capacity. The central government was to provide guidance to provincial and district authorities as they developed their own plans, and it would set a realistic quota for each local authority's contribution to the central economy.[132]

In 1978 the CPV was in the midst of a deep economic crisis precipitated by domestic and external forces. Domestically, the crisis stemmed from both a deliberate attack on private ownership in southern Vietnam, especially Ho Chi Minh City, which was dominated by ethnic Chinese, and the failing centrally planned economy, which was suffering from severe shortages of everything from raw materials to food and consumption goods. In response to the worsening economic crisis, the campaign against private ownership in the south, inspired by Le Duan's concept of "the right to collective mastery (*quyen lam chu tap the*),"[133] was intensified in the spring of 1978, and the Chinese business class was deliberately targeted for economic repression. According to Tran Phuong, a close associate of reformist leader Nguyen Van Linh, Le Duan desired to "immediately solve the Chinese problem" in Ho Chi Minh city. He decided to replace Nguyen Van Linh with Do Muoi in early 1978 because he believed Muoi would be more amenable to banning participation in commercial activities by ethnic Chinese residents, at that time estimated to number more than half a million in Ho Chi Minh City.[134] The deterioration of Sino-Vietnamese relations hardened the party's policy—against the advice of southern reformist Vo Van Kiet—of uprooting the half million-Chinese residents of Ho Chi Minh City and dispersing them in provincial towns.[135] Le Duan even instructed the Ho Chi Minh leadership to immediately deport all Chinese residents from the city as Sino-Vietnamese relations further worsened that year.[136] In the south, of the 28,787 families designated as business compradors to be subjected to "reeducation," 2,500 had made contributions to the Vietnamese revolution.[137] Externally the intensified conflicts with the Khmer Rouge and China and the reduction of foreign aid from the Soviet Union and other COMECON countries, as well as natural disasters, especially floods,[138] deepened the economic and sociopolitical crises, creating a cycle of perpetual crisis and paralysis.[139] In September and October 1978, Vietnam suffered the most severe flooding in its recent history, during which it lost 3 million tons of rice, 500,000 houses, and 10 to 20 percent of its domestic animals, including cattle.[140]

1978:
The Party's Legitimacy Crisis

The crisis of 1978 and its sociopolitical impact on Vietnamese society undermined the legitimacy of the CPV. In 1978 top party leaders became aware that widespread corruption and self-interested behavior by party officials who deliberately exaggerated their resource needs to meet the output quotas set by the party were harming Vietnam's economy. For instance, local cadres at the district and city levels ballooned their budget and resource needs in their economic production proposals to the central government in order to easily meet the targets set by Hanoi. While meeting those targets earned local party leaders promotions and better living standards for their families, such practices further perpetuated economic inefficiency and wasted vital resources. Top economic planners like Le Thanh Nghi proposed a number of measures, mostly adding more layers of party and state control to the existing bureaucratic gridlock, hoping to increase labor productivity, cut down on waste, conserve resources, and eliminate corrosive phenomena such as corruption, bribery, embezzlement of state property, and abuse of power.[141] These were simply incremental changes, but the evidence shows that Hanoi failed to put a stop to the corrosive effects of the corruption, self-serving behavior, and wasteful practices of many local party leaders.

Throughout 1978 the economic crisis had serious political consequences for relations between the party and the people, causing popular resistance to the party's policies, self-preservation behaviors of many party members at the local level, and rampant corruption across the party apparatus. In *Vietnam under Communism, 1975–1982*, Van Canh Nguyen documented in detail the basic causes of graft and corruption in Communist Vietnam. He pointed out that these nonsocialist practices became widespread because wages and salaries were pegged so low that nobody could live on them. According to the official scale for 1978, in Ho Chi Minh City unskilled factory workers were paid 30 VND a month (a little over US$3), beginning high school teachers 40 dong, clerks employed by cooperatives 40 dong; engineers 60 dong, and doctors and pharmacists 70 dong. Even a government minister in Hanoi was paid only 215 dong."[142] The official price of a kilo of rice in 1978 was 0.45 dong, but it sold for 6 in a black market in Ho Chi Minh City.[143]

In 1978, the socioeconomic and political crises resulted in rising corruption, daily popular resistance to the party-state, and the mass exodus of an estimated 250,000 Vietnamese people from the country who played critical roles in the economy. These all converged in 1978, posing a grave threat to the party's legitimacy. From January to September, the Supreme People's Procuracy, also known as the People's Prosecutor,[144] was instructed to aggressively (1) promote workers' collective ownership (*quyen lam chu tap the*); (2) meet the goals of the 1978 economic plan; (3) strengthen national defense; (4) eradicate private ownership and markets; (5) strengthen sociopolitical order and security; (6) carry out the Politburo's Resolution 228 and the prime minister's Directive 159 regarding the crackdown on party and government officials' abuse of power and corruption, which tarnished the reputation of the party and government; and (7) crack down on transgressions against collective interests and peasants' livelihoods at various cooperatives across the country.[145] For the first nine months of 1978, to protect workers' collective ownership, the People's Prosecutor pursued corruption, abuses of power, and embezzlement of collective properties at 1,036 economic units at the local level, including 426 district-level administrative headquarters, 105 production units (agricultural, manufacturing, and logging), and 505 cooperatives. The People's Prosecutor arrested 1,735 "bad elements" and removed 717 others from the state apparatus.[146] In addition, to support the 1978 economic plan, the People's Prosecutor conducted investigations at 979 economic units and instructed 727 other units to conduct internal investigations in 282 districts of 25 provinces and cities, totaling 1,706 economic units. The result was that 1,129 units were instructed to correct a total of 2,227 violations of the central government's policies and regulations, 2,923 cases of infractions on socialist properties were prosecuted, and 2,035 out of 2,709 cadres involved were also prosecuted. In addition, reportedly provincial People's Prosecutors in 37 provinces and cities and 328 districts prosecuted 2,985 economic cases, including 558 cases of corruption and 1,365 cases of embezzlement of socialist property.[147] All this public corruption went on for several years while peasants and workers lived under harsh conditions in which food was scare and soldiers were sent to do farm work after the war. The CPV was internally corroded and on the verge of plunging into a political crisis.

By mid-1978, Hanoi's search for solutions to the economic crisis on its own terms reached an impasse. As Ngo Vinh Long has documented, per capita availability of rice declined precipitously each year from 15.4 kilograms per month in 1976 to 11.6 in 1978.[148] In 1978 Vietnam's food crisis was so dire that even households of the victorious Vietnamese army faced food shortages.[149] At the beginning of 1978, the growing economic crisis compelled the Hanoi leadership to search desperately for solutions, only to find that there was little it could do domestically, and escalation of the armed conflict with the Khmer Rouge and China in late 1977 and the spring of 1978 left Vietnam with no choice but to formally join the COMECON and sign an alliance agreement with the Soviet Union. On July 20, 1978, in his explanation of Vietnam's decision to join the COMECON to a joint conference attended by key members of the Council of Ministers and the Party Central Committee, Le Thanh Nghi spoke very highly of the leading role of the Soviet Union in the socialist economic bloc and the tremendous potential benefits to Vietnam from Soviet economic and technological power, as well as the Soviets' large reserves of fuel, raw materials, and industrial equipment, including oil, gas, iron and steel, electrical energy, fabric, aircraft, machinery and heavy transportation vehicles, and defense equipment.[150] Nghi cited two main reasons for the Politburo's decision to officially join the COMECON.

> First, all the Soviet pledges of material aid, including building the national north-south railroad, seven major industrial projects, and research on the mechanization of agriculture and so forth, have been delayed because Vietnam refused to officially join the COMECON from 1977 to mid-1978. Second, when China publicly adopted an anti-Vietnam policy in late 1977, the Politburo saw the need to join the COMECON and publicly disclose our political position and viewpoint, which was important to the organization if we were to obtain support and assistance from the Soviet Union and other members of the COMECON, as well as additional backing for Vietnam's resistance against China and the United States, which sought to weaken and do harm to Vietnam.[151]

According to Nghi, in the short term Vietnam requested that the COMECON increase its assistance for economic reconstruction and development and the building of the material and technological basis for socialism. In particular, Hanoi requested assistance from the COMECON for the following: (1) to begin work on the seven industrial projects it had pledged in principle to support during Le Duan's visit to Moscow in November 1975; (2) to speed up the mechanization of the agricultural sector in the northern delta; (3) to enlarge the railroad connecting Hanoi and Ho Chi Minh City; (4) to help build and provide materials and equipment to complete forty-nine industrial projects for which China had recently cut off aid; and (5) to provide raw materials and goods such as coal, fuel, and thread that Vietnam had once imported from China. The COMECON promised to study Hanoi's request immediately at the organization's thirty-second conference held on June 27–29, 1978, in Bucharest, Romania.[152] Nghi's explanation provides direct evidence of Hanoi's strategic thinking about the nexus between Vietnam's domestic priorities and foreign policies and the shift away from pursuing a balanced foreign policy toward the Soviet Union and China and a broad-based foreign economic policy and negotiating strategies for a peaceful resolution of border conflicts from 1975 to 1977 to a tacit alliance with Soviet Union in mid-1978 and an overt military confrontation with China. The nexus between domestic crises and national security threats was at the center of Hanoi's reconfiguration of its domestic and foreign policy strategies.

From 1975 to mid-1977 the CPV leadership's objective of building a prosperous, modern, and industrialized socialist state was paramount, even subordinating national defense to economic priorities during peacetime, and a rather broad-based and independent foreign policy and diplomacy were articulated and pursued to support the party's economic development agenda as set out at the Fourth Party Congress in December 1976. A significant amount of resources and energy was committed to economic statecraft and negotiations to solve border disputes with China, Cambodia, and Laos during this period. However, from late 1977 to mid-1978, the combined political pressure of the economic crisis at home and failure in foreign policy and diplomacy abroad compelled Hanoi to reverse its strategy by now subordinating economic development to national defense in a new period of "peace coexisting with the potential outbreak of war with Cambodia and China." The idea of "combining the economy and national defense" (*ket hop kinh te va quoc phong*) was translated into a national campaign to turn every district into a firm economic and national defense fortress in preparation for war. Toward that end, central economic planning (old thinking) gave way to local planning (new thinking). In preparing for war with Cambodia and China, Hanoi's decision at the Third Plenum of the Central Committee in December 1977 to decentralize economic planning—though only incrementally at this point—by allowing local authorities to draw up their own, more realistic plan was to serve as the beginning of an economic reform process. During this period, Vietnam failed to normalize relations with the United States, to solve border conflicts with Cambodia and China, and, more important, to maintain a balanced position between China and the Soviet Union due to the pressure of the Sino-American alliance against the Soviets. This failure profoundly affected Vietnam's economic and national security. It was in this context that Hanoi decided to shift from pursuing a broad-based foreign policy and steering clear of entanglement in the Sino-Soviet conflict to joining the Soviet-led economic bloc and concluding a tacit military alliance with the Soviet Union in late 1978. Domestically both the economically minded leaders and the conservative leaders in Hanoi came close to a common view in 1978 that Vietnam's alliance with the Soviets would help address both the worsening economic crisis and the threat the Sino-Cambodian alliance posed to the country's territorial sovereignty.

To Hanoi's leaders, in the first half of 1978 they were confronted with three major threats to the legitimacy of the CPV: (1) an economic decline worsened by inefficient economic management, public corruption, and other self-interested behavior by both provincial authorities and district officials; (2) the soaring cost of the border war with the Khmer Rouge in Cambodia and the general mobilization of troops in preparation for a two-front war with Cambodia and China; and (3) the withdrawal of aid from China followed by economic sanctions against Vietnam and the Soviet Union's significant reduction in nonrefundable aid after 1975. It was abundantly clear to Hanoi by mid-1978 that the three entwined problems had created a major national security crisis that could undermine the CPV's legitimacy if it were not resolved quickly. To address the first problem, Hanoi's leaders, driven by what they had learned from the ineffective top-down economic management of previous years, relaxed the Soviet-style central planning by allowing a bottom-up economic planning approach as a cornerstone of what they referred to as "renovation of economic management" (*doi moi quan ly kinh te*) whereby local economic units at the provincial and district levels made the plans and the central government provided investment resources. Simultaneously the government embarked on a nationwide crackdown on public corruption across the party-state apparatus, which had severely eroded people's trust in the party and caused rising popular resistance to the socialist system. Hanoi's goal was to ensure that each district would become a self-reliant economic unit and give any surplus to the central government. As 1978 marked the beginning of a new period of "peace coexisting with the potential outbreak of war" Hanoi's leaders embarked on a strategy of turning every district into a firm economic and national defense fortress. Documentary evidence from the Vietnamese archives, as presented in this chapter, illustrates the domestic-external determinants of Hanoi's foreign policy behaviors, the utility of the party-state's socialist ideology and identity in making use of national resources, and the shift in Vietnam's foreign policy orientation in service of its domestic economic and national security priorities.

2

The Decision to Invade Cambodia

DECEMBER 1978

This chapter focuses on the gradual change in Hanoi's strategic thinking and the corresponding policy shift from the peacetime focus on the twin goals of economic recovery and modernization and defense of national sovereignty—as spelled out in the first FYP after unification, which the Fourth Party Congress approved in December 1976—to its decision to invade Cambodia in December 1978. I argue that the wider strategic calculation—that is, the alliance between DK and the People's Republic of China (PRC), backed by the United States, which posed a serious threat to the SRV—played a more significant role in Hanoi's decision making vis-à-vis Cambodia than either local factors (border raids by DK forces or the territorial dispute between DK and the SRV) or geopolitical concerns steeped in long-term historical conflicts. Hanoi's decision to invade Cambodia in 1978 was a bold but calculated move intended to cement the Vietnamese-Soviet alliance and position Vietnam as the frontline state opposing Chinese expansionism in Indochina. Hanoi expected to use Vietnam's geopolitical position to draw massive economic and military aid from the Soviet bloc to address Vietnam's domestic economic crisis, bolster its national defense, and build pro-Vietnam socialist regimes in Cambodia and Laos.

Relying on new evidence from Vietnamese archives, this chapter revisits an old but still unresolved question: why did Vietnam invade Cambodia in late December 1978? The causes of the Third Indochina War have been the subject of a number of excellent studies.[1] However, fewer studies have focused specifically on the question of why Vietnam decided to invade Cambodia in December 1978 even though Hanoi's decisions and actions were arguably the most consequential triggers of the war as they led to China's invasion of Vietnam in February

1979 and the subsequent confrontation that turned into the Third Indochina War.[2] We know now that Moscow had little influence over Hanoi's decision to invade Cambodia.[3] Three contending accounts have emerged to explain the Vietnamese invasion. The first explanation attributes the invasion to Vietnamese leaders' irrationality and ideology. The main proponent of this theory is Stephen J. Morris (1999) in his book *Why Vietnam Invaded Cambodia*. His main explanation emphasizes "the imperial ambition of Vietnam's communist leadership" to dominate the formerly French Indochina (background cause) and the "ideological and paranoia-induced misperception" of all the three players (immediate or trigger cause).[4] Morris concluded, "Vietnam invaded Cambodia because it saw the action as a means of simultaneously achieving the two purposes of ending the military attacks begun by the Democratic Kampuchea (DK) and satisfying a long-standing ambition to dominate its weaker neighbor."[5]

However, the theory that Vietnam had a long-standing ambition to dominate Indochina explains its invasion of Cambodia is based on an implicitly faulty assumption that Hanoi's immediate concerns in the late 1970s had little effect on the course of its decision making.[6] As Gareth Porter succinctly argued, "Vietnam's invasion and occupation of Cambodia were not part of a plan which Hanoi had waited for nearly five decades to put into action, nor were they the inevitable outcome of the Vietnamese conception of Indochina."[7] In fact, as the Cold War historian Odd Arne Westad points out—and I agree—the invasion was not based on ancient resentments or predicaments but resulted from political decisions made by leaders who were bound by what they saw as the changing realities of their own time."[8] Historical and cultural lenses colored the Khmer Rouge's perception of Vietnamese intentions, but this cannot explain Vietnam's own perceptions and intentions in the late 1970s that led to its decision to invade Cambodia in 1978 and to occupy it for the next decade.[9] The Khmer Rouge (KR) anti-Vietnamese ideology and its provocative attacks were certainly contributing causes, but they are not sufficient to explain Vietnam's decision to invade. A fuller account needs to factor in Hanoi's tangible domestic and foreign policy objectives at that time, as this chapter will undertake.

In *China and Vietnam: The Politics of Asymmetry*, Brantly Womack (2006), to some extent, supports Morris's "irrationality" argument; for him the key cause of the Vietnamese invasion of Cambodia is located in the "systematic misperception" in Sino-Vietnamese asymmetric relations in a novel situation after 1975.[10] He writes, "Vietnam thought that it could present the region and the world with the *fait accompli* of its control of Indochina, and China and Southeast Asia would quickly adjust, as they had to Vietnam's victory in 1975."[11]

The second explanation contends that Marxist-Leninist ideology was the main cause of the Third Indochina War. Notably, political scientist Tuong Vu attributed the key cause of the Sino-Vietnamese conflict to Vietnam's Marxist-Leninist ideological belief in vanguard internationalism, which he defines as "a mixture of fervent national pride and fiery revolutionary ambitions."[12] Through such ideological lenses, Vietnam saw China's collusion with the imperialist United States as a threat to its identity and international socialism. Vu rejected Vietnamese nationalism and geopolitical factors such as the Sino-Soviet rivalry as the main cause.[13] He writes, "Hanoi's quick fall back into Moscow's open arms [in 1978] indicated the more powerful pull of ideology compared to the push of the international structure."[14] The problem with Vu's ideology-centered argument is that it cast the Vietnamese leadership as one monolithic group of pure ideologues rather than strategic thinkers who were factional at times.[15] This by no means rules out the role of ideology in this conflict, but a more convincing argument has to take into account a nuanced appreciation of Hanoi's tangible objectives in the context of the domestic and foreign policy crisis in 1977–78.

Unlike the studies mentioned above, which privilege leaders' irrationality, including their paranoia, misperceptions, and ideology, I argue that Hanoi's invasion decision in December 1978 was *rational* given the domestic and international imperatives at that time. By rationality, I mean "subjective rationality." As T. V. Paul stated, this concept posits, "The values, beliefs, and expectations of a decision-maker are important factors that determine his probabilistic assessment before he undertakes a course of action."[16] In such a conception, "A course of action is rational only relative to a possessed body of information—that is, beliefs, and desires, and priorities—in terms of which the merits of the available courses of action can be rationally evaluated."[17] The third explanation emphasizes key causes in 1977–78. Just two years after the war, Gareth Porter provided a penetrating analysis, with foresight, of Hanoi's decision making despite his lack of access to high-quality information at the time. Porter argued, "While the Vietnamese leadership approached their relations with Beijing and Phnom Penh with certain ideological, geopolitical and historical-emotional predispositions, it was a particular configuration of the external developments in 1978 that triggered the dramatic Vietnamese invasion of that year."[18] Specifically, he argued that the interplay between the two sides of Vietnam's foreign policy crisis—that is, an irreversible two-front conflict with China and its ally, the DK regime—led to its decision to invade Cambodia.[19] Similarly, the journalist Nayan Chanda argued that Vietnam reluctantly decided to invade Cambodia only after all prospects for effecting either a change in Pol Pot's hostile policy toward Vietnam or a coup against the DK leadership had failed.[20] Chanda's pathbreaking work provides an insightful and detailed account of the origins of the Third Indochina War, but his work does not provide adequate insight into the "black box" of Hanoi's decision making during the crucial years 1977–78. The focus on the overt threat posed by the Sino-DK alliance in 1977–78, however, overlooked a key connection between the economic and national security crises that converged during a rather brief period from late 1977 to mid-1978, which compelled Vietnam to recalibrate its prioritization of its national interests and make a radical shift in foreign policy.

As this chapter shows, Hanoi's decision to invade Cambodia was made as early as January 1978, and war preparations were under way well before Vietnam signed its alliance with the Soviet Union in November of that year. Building on these early works, I develop a rational explanation for Hanoi's decision to invade Cambodia by examining the link between the economic and foreign policy crises of 1977–78. Relying primarily on interviews, Hoang Minh Vu presents the qualified argument that after failed negotiations from April 1977 to February 1978 the invasion was ultimately a case of "preemptive self-defense" whereby the Vietnamese government responded with overwhelming force to what it misperceived to be a threat to its survival from a two-front war against an alliance between China and DK.[21] I agree with Vu's and Porter's conclusion that the immediate causes were located in 1977–78, not Vietnam's long-standing hegemonic tendencies. However, Vu's assertion that Hanoi's misperception of this two-front threat was the cause of its decision to invade is a post hoc or postinvasion argument. To my point, Vu asserts, "The story of the Vietnamese decision to invade Cambodia in 1977–78 should be best told as a tragedy in which Vietnam responded inappropriately to a conflict instigated by Khmer Rouge radicalism due to a series of misperceptions."[22] Was it misperception, ideology, or strategic interests?

I contend that Hanoi's decision to invade was a rational one based on its strategic interests in that by late 1977 and early 1978 all negotiations over border disputes with China and Cambodia had failed, military confrontations had escalated on both the southwestern and northern frontiers, and Vietnam was engulfed in economic and sociopolitical crises that threatened the survival of the party-state. Vietnam's invasion of Cambodia was driven by its leadership's rational political decision to cement its alliance with the Soviet Union with the objective of obtaining economic and military aid to address the national security threat and the economic crisis at home. This is a case in which post-1975 Vietnam plunged into domestic and foreign policy crises and then came to view the invasion of Cambodia and the alliance with the Soviet Union—a communist superpower with which it had forged an ideological affinity since 1970—as the most optimal solution. Unlike existing works that privilege the structural determinant, that is, the Sino-Soviet rivalry, of Vietnam's foreign policy,[23] I argue that the actual choice Vietnam made under such structural pressure had more to do with the strategic thinking and worldviews of Vietnamese leaders and Vietnam's domestic political constraints.

The Threat of the Sino-Khmer Rouge Alliance, 1975–77

Harboring irredentist nationalism and racial hatred toward the Vietnamese, DK identified Vietnam as its number-one enemy as early as 1973. Referring to the essence of DK nationalism, historian Ben Kiernan writes, "The DK defines as 'traitors' or 'Khmer bodies with Vietnamese minds' broad categories of the Cambodian population who do not accept the DK leadership in an anti-Vietnamese crusade."[24] From the DK perspective, the Vietnamese–Khmer Rouge alliance in 1970–73 was a necessity not a choice. From the very beginning, the Khmer Rouge chose to accept the more distant, more radical Chinese Communists as patrons because they had ideological differences with the Vietnamese, as well as complicated historical legacies.[25] In his announcement, on March 23, 1970, of the establishment of the National United Front of Kampuchea (FUNK), the deposed Cambodian head of state Norodom Sihanouk made no mention of the Vietnamese army's role in the war against the Lon Nol regime. However, from the Vietnamese perspective, the Cambodian revolution owed its existence and victory to the support of the Vietnamese Communists.[26] In the Vietnamese Communists' account, when the FUNK army was created on May 4, 1970,[27] they dispatched military advisers to help build and train Cambodian troops, and by the end of 1970 they had helped the Cambodian Communists create twenty-seven platoons, fifty-three companies, and nine battalions with a total of ten thousand soldiers. By the end of 1972, before moving their headquarters out of Cambodia, the Vietnamese Communists had assisted the Khmer Rouge in liberating thirteen of Cambodia's seventeen provinces.[28] Hence the Vietnamese believed that they had helped the Cambodian Communists grow from small units to a strong army that established a firm foothold in a large territory under its control and from there brought the armed struggle to a victorious conclusion in April 1975.

The stark contrast between the two communist parties' viewpoints of the consequences of the 1973 PPA was manifested in an unpleasant encounter between the two sides the following year. In September 1974, when the top leaders of Vietnam's Provisional Revolutionary Government (PRG) made a long, exhausting journey through the jungles of Cambodia to visit Cambodian Communist leaders in the liberated zone,[29] they received a cold reception.[30] The PRG delegation's mission was to make clear that the 1973 PPA, to which Cambodia was not a party, created favorable conditions for the Cambodian revolution rather than undercutting the struggle.[31]

Rather than dispelling Cambodian resentment, this reasoning by Vietnam was perceived by the Khmer Rouge leadership as adding insult to injury. In actuality, the PPA had two adverse consequences for the Cambodian revolution. First, the PPA led to the quick withdrawal of most Vietnamese Communist troops from the interior of Cambodia, and soon after, by accident or design, arms shipments from the Vietnamese designated for the Khmer Rouge were delayed or failed to arrive in Cambodia via the Ho Chi Minh Trail. Thus the Khmer Rouge fought alone on the Cambodian front. Second, Cambodia became the sole target of American bombing. To the Khmer Rouge, as Elizabeth Becker noted, "The accords were one more betrayal by their communist allies."[32] The Khmer Rouge response after the PPA was signed was "an undeclared war of revenge," to use Becker's words, against the Vietnamese Communists. Sales of Khmer produce and rice to the Vietnamese Communists were banned, and the Viet Cong was no longer allowed to travel through Cambodia freely.[33]

As soon as the Pol Pot regime came to power in April 1975, it wasted no time in eliminating any influence that its Vietnamese Communist ally had left in Cambodia. On April 21, 1975, five days after the liberation of Phnom Penh, the regime demanded that the Vietnamese terminate all broadcasts from Hanoi in support of the Cambodian revolution and began its own radio broadcasts from Phnom Penh. From August 1, 1970, to April 22, 1975, Hanoi had guaranteed uninterrupted radio broadcasts, even when the capital was under heavy US bombardment,[34] to support the Cambodian Communists' propaganda war against the Lon Nol regime. Two weeks after Phnom Penh was liberated and on the same day that the Vietnamese Communist forces entered Saigon, DK used military force to take over Vietnam's islands, which they believed had once belonged to the Khmer nation. On April 30, Khmer Rouge military units attacked Koh Tral (Phu Quoc in Vietnamese) to revive an old claim to the island. On May 3, they took over Koh Krachak Ses (To Chu in Vietnamese) and "evacuated" some five hundred Vietnamese inhabitants of the island, who were never heard from again. Two weeks later the Vietnamese launched a counterattack, killing many Khmer soldiers and taking about three hundred prisoners.[35] During a visit to Vietnam on June 11–14, 1975, Pol Pot expressed his gratitude to the Vietnamese for their assistance during the war against the Lon Nol regime in a deceitful attempt, however temporary, to dispel Hanoi's concerns about the DK border incursions. The Vietnamese leadership did not suspect that Khmer Rouge resentment over the 1973 PPA and cold relations thereafter would lead to attacks on Vietnam after 1975.

For its part, Hanoi privately acknowledged Vietnam's violation of Cambodia's territory in some cases. In a late 1977 report furnished to the Politburo, the Border Commission (Uy Ban Bien Gioi) of the Party Central Committee raised the issue of "local Vietnamese armed forces and authorities along the border unknowingly violating Cambodia's territory due to their poor knowledge of the border between the two countries."[36] The report further noted, "In some cases, local Vietnamese authorities did not know that Vietnamese land was being occupied by the Cambodians, and in some other cases, they mistakenly control Cambodia's territory."[37] This report shows that the status of the border was unclear when negotiations failed. Nonetheless, the Border Commission concluded, "It is overwhelmingly clear that Cambodia's intention is to take over Vietnam's territory as much as it possibly can and invent more cases of territorial dispute so that it can increase its leverage in subsequent negotiations with us."[38] This report evinces Hanoi's perception that its preference for the resolution of boundary disputes rather than bilateral negotiations was giving way to long-term concerns about the DK leadership using the pretext of wanting to negotiate to buy time to increase DK's territory. To understand how Hanoi reached such a conclusion, one only has to review the attempts of the DK regime to deceive Hanoi after 1975. From mid-1975 to late 1976, it was the Sino-Soviet conflict, not Khmer Rouge incursions into Vietnam, that seriously concerned the Vietnamese leadership due to its impact on the country's domestic and foreign policies. As mentioned earlier, the Border Commission viewed the early wave of Khmer Rouge territorial aggression as a ploy to gain leverage in tough negotiations.

On the domestic front, Hanoi's leaders were profoundly preoccupied with preparing for their first FYP (1976–80) after unification, and aid from both the Soviet Union and China was deemed critical to its success. In due course, Hanoi made concerted efforts to steer its foreign policy clear of entanglement in the rivalry between its two great power patrons in 1976–77. Maintaining its independent foreign policy orientation, or at least the appearance of it, in the new stage of its socialist revolution was of paramount importance because it allowed Hanoi to more flexibly address its most pressing concerns, that is, economic recovery and modernization, and a socialist transformation of newly liberated southern Vietnam. For a strategic reason, Hanoi preferred to negotiate rather than escalate border conflicts with the Khmer Rouge leadership, which had already received significant support from China right after it toppled the US-backed Lon Nol regime in April 1975. In July 1975, the Vietnamese MOFA circulated among the top leaders a report on foreign affairs, revealing Vietnamese diplomats' frustration and confusion about how best to respond to the contradiction between the DK regime's desire to strengthen relations between the two countries and its increasing military aggression along the border.[39]

After a series of failed negotiations over border disputes in late 1976 between the Communist Party of Kampuchea (CPK) and the CPV leadership, the land and maritime dispute escalated into armed conflict, often provoked by DK. The failure of the negotiations was as much due to the clash between the anti-Vietnamese irredentist nationalism of the Pol Pot regime and the Vietnamese assertion of territorial sovereignty as it was to the legacy of French colonialism, which left the boundary between Cambodia and Vietnam highly contested, with Vietnam gaining large areas of territory at the expense of Cambodia under French rule in the late nineteenth century. In November 1976, the Vietnamese Politburo proposed to use the French preindependence map (drawn prior to 1954) as the basis for delimiting the land and maritime boundaries between Cambodia and Vietnam. The CPK agreed to use it "*only* as a discussion document."[40] There were three major problems with the French map. First, certain portions of the border were not clearly drawn or demarcated. Second, there were a number of major discrepancies between the French map and French documentary records. Third, in the border regions along rivers, there were large discrepancies among the map, documentary records, and the reality of each side's territorial control. These three problems left ample room for different interpretations supporting each side's position. This Vietnamese internal record underscores the centrality of Khmer Rouge nationalism—that is, the loss of Mekong Delta (Kampuchea Krom) territory to Vietnam at the hands of the French colonialists and royal and feudal Khmer authorities.[41]

After 1975 Vietnam desired border security with Laos and Cambodia in order to develop its New Economic Zones, and Khmer Rouge attacks and Vietnamese refugees were disruptive to its socialist economic development plan.[42] This does not diminish the fact that the border dispute between Cambodia and Vietnam was a serious and complicated issue to which Vietnam partly contributed.

To the Vietnamese, the DK regime's preference for the use of force over bilateral negotiations was puzzling given their military superiority, and the only logical explanation for the Khmer Rouge's aggressive behavior pointed to Chinese ambitions. To the Khmer Rouge, this was a preventive war waged to reclaim large regions occupied by its historic enemy, Vietnam, while Vietnam was preoccupied with postwar unification and reconstruction. To the Vietnamese, Cambodian hostility with backing from China was part of Beijing's strategy to weaken Vietnam and expand its control over Indochina.

On April 14, 1976, the second anniversary of the DK victory, Chinese foreign minister Huang Hua left no doubt about China's commitment to Pol Pot.[43] In contrast, Beijing's desire to cut aid to Vietnam after 1976 was in stark contrast to its enthusiasm for aiding the Khmer Rouge.[44] On February 6, 1976, the deputy chief of the General Staff of the People's Liberation Army, Wang Shangrong, met with the DK minister of defense Son Sen and promised to supply the "necessary weapons and equipment for and training core officers on the spot."[45] A top-secret report in mid-1976 reveals that Vietnamese diplomats at the MOFA suspected that "China is attempting to incite conflict between Vietnam and Cambodia, as it did between Vietnam and Thailand, in order to limit Vietnam's role and influence in the region."[46] In Hanoi's view, the border dispute between Cambodia and Vietnam was complicated by China's divide-and-conquer strategy, which aimed to serve its broader objective of controlling Indochina. On the other hand, the MOFA was of the view that "China intends to find ways to pull Vietnam into its orbit to limit Soviet influence in Southeast Asia."[47]

A turning point in Khmer Rouge–Vietnamese relations came in 1977 as armed conflict between DK and Vietnam escalated rapidly toward all-out war. Armed clashes along the border—the majority of them initiated by the Khmer Rouge—increased rapidly from 174 in 1975 to 254 in 1976, 1,150 in 1977, and 4,820 in 1978.[48] All border negotiations with China throughout 1977 were futile, and armed clashes along the northern frontier also increased exponentially in the second half of the year.[49] Since the beginning of the year, relations between Vietnam and its neighbors China and Cambodia had deteriorated on all fronts, but, most notably, the open conflict between Vietnam and Cambodia in mid-1977 turned into war by the end of the year. Why did Vietnam decide not to invade Cambodia in late 1977? Internal records of the Vietnamese government at that time reveal that a cluster of issues, including Vietnam's fear of invasion by China, its declining military strength, and the growing economic crisis, along with dwindling Soviet economic and military aid, dissuaded Hanoi from launching a full-scale invasion at that time.

Throughout 1976, Hanoi informed Moscow with great confidence of its ability to make positive changes in its relations with DK, as it had done with Laos, bringing the latter out of China's orbit.[50] In July, in a conversation with Soviet ambassador B. Chaplin, the Vietnamese deputy minister of foreign affairs Hoang Van Loi declared that the Vietnamese leadership "deemed it necessary to have patience and work towards gradually strengthening its influence in Cambodia."[51] In the meantime, Hanoi attempted to demonstrate its good will toward DK through its emissary in Phnom Penh, Ambassador Pham Van Ba. In November 1976, at Ambassador Ba's insistence, the Ministry of Health was authorized to send help to the DK regime to combat widespread malaria among the Cambodian populace. On November 13, the DK Ministry of Foreign Affairs received antimalaria drugs at the Vietnamese embassy but refused to allow Dr. Nguyen Tien Buu, deputy director of the Anti-Malaria Institute at the Vietnamese Ministry of Health, and his associates to leave the embassy compound to train DK doctors.[52] Considering the DK regime's vigilance regarding Vietnamese spies, preventing Vietnamese officials from venturing into DK society was hardly surprising. Although Ambassador Ba hailed the delivery of the drugs as a step toward improving relations with DK and thanked the Vietnamese leaders for acting on his recommendation, Hanoi's leaders were far less impressed with the result of the mission.

Hanoi's strategic patience and hope of bringing DK into a joint effort to solve the border issue ended after Hoang Van Loi's confidential visit to Phnom Penh in February 1977. Pol Pot declined his proposal of a summit of top Vietnamese and Cambodian leaders.[53] Instead, the major Khmer Rouge attack on Vietnam on April 30 shook Hanoi's leaders out of their complacency as the Khmer Rouge overran Vietnamese border defense forces and penetrated deep into Vietnamese territory. Hanoi also knew that the Chinese were training and arming Khmer Rouge troops and building roads and military bases, including an air force base in Kampong Chhnang Province, from which planes could reach Ho Chi Minh City in half an hour.[54] The reason why the Vietnamese were ill prepared to mobilize an effective military response to the Khmer Rouge attacks goes beyond Vietnam's complacency toward the Khmer Rouge. The most plausible explanation can be found in Vietnam's economic crisis of 1977–78.

The Impact of the Economic Crisis on the Military, 1977–78

Since 1975 Hanoi had relied on diplomacy and bilateral negotiations at the party level to solve its territorial disputes with Cambodia and China as it strove to forge peaceful border relations with its neighbors so that it could focus on its top priority: economic recovery and the socialist transformation of southern Vietnam. Throughout 1976 Hanoi's confidence in the possibility of resolving the border dispute with the DK leadership through negotiations and goodwill remained very strong. General Secretary Le Duan ignored local authorities' reports that the Khmer Rouge was escalating its attacks on Vietnam with division-level forces.[55] In its internal report, the MOFA still referred to DK leaders as "comrades" whom Vietnam had to patiently pull back into alignment with its position, as it did with Laos.[56] In 1976 Vietnam did not position regular troops along the Cambodian-Vietnamese border, and the majority of Vietnamese troops were ordered to carry out economic duties outside their headquarters.[57]

The first large-scale Khmer Rouge offensive in Vietnam, launched on April 30, 1977, forced the Vietnamese to acknowledge the bitter reality of the Khmer Rouge military threat and the fact that Vietnam's superior military strength would not deter it. When the DK forces launched major attacks that day, the commander of Military Region 9, General Le Duc Anh, hastily reassembled Division 330 and prepared for combat.[58] Given its superior force, Hanoi was astonished that the Khmer Rouge had the audacity to attack Vietnam. The only logical explanation it saw for the continued provocation against Vietnam was China's military support of the Khmer Rouge.

While Hanoi's leaders had proudly shared their anti-US resistance lessons with other countries around the world after 1975, the Vietnamese military was in disarray just a few short years after unification and lacked the strength and discipline for an all-out invasion of Cambodia, especially given China's backing of the Khmer Rouge. As Hanoi prepared its military to crush the Khmer Rouge in the first half of 1977, it discovered many serious issues that had weakened its military strength since the unification of northern and southern Vietnam. In January 1977, the Politburo ordered the CMC to conduct a six-month assessment of military preparedness. On August 28, General Chu Huy Man, deputy secretary of the CMC and a Politburo member, submitted a report on a fact-finding mission to the Politburo and the secretariat of the Party Central Committee. Based on a meticulous study during the first half of 1977, the report delivered an alarming conclusion to the Vietnamese leadership: "Progress with our war preparedness on all fronts for the past six months fell significantly short of the actual capacity of our armed forces, and some other problems have become very serious. For example, our deployment of troops remains slow and ineffective, and our military strength has been eroded by our troops' weak discipline and sluggish performance."[59] So, as Vietnam was facing the threat of the Sino–Khmer Rouge alliance, a series of early military clashes with Khmer Rouge forces in the spring of 1977 raised long-term concerns about Vietnam's lack of military preparedness for war.

When the Khmer Rouge launched its offensive on April 30, a vice-minister of national defense, who served on the CMC, was dispatched to assess the military situation on the frontlines and provide guidance on border defense to the commands of Military Regions 5, 7, and 9 in the south. The lack of war preparedness among local armed forces and their poor combat performance were appalling to military leaders in Hanoi. In a series of counteroffensives against Khmer Rouge forces, regular Vietnamese troops also performed poorly, ranging from slow mobilization, erroneous assessment of the enemy's strength, and ill-conceived strategies to poor management of weaponry equipment and ammunition storage.[60] In May, the CMC issued an order to immediately correct these shortcomings as it ordered a general mobilization of troops in the south, and by July all troops were put on full alert for counteroffensives. Military Regions 7, 9, and 5 and the Third and Fourth Army Corps of the PAVN were already engaging the Khmer Rouge along the border.[61] The army quickly turned to increased political training and strict military discipline to raise morale. In 1977, now without substantial economic and military aid from the Soviet Union, the economic situation within the Vietnamese military went from bad to worse.

Certainly war weariness among the troops played a role in Vietnam's postwar lack of combat readiness, but it was economic hardship, worsened by the lack of foreign aid after 1975, that compelled Hanoi to direct the army to engage in economic work, which in turn undermined its military strength and combat readiness, especially in the south, where the economic crisis took a major toll on the military. In October 1976, the Politburo issued a resolution on the role of the military in building the economy to advance Vietnam's new revolutionary mission of socialist reconstruction throughout the country. The wartime slogan "Everything for the front" (*Tat ca cho tien tuyen*) was replaced with the peacetime slogan "Everything for production, everything for building socialism" (*Tat ca cho san xuat, tat ca de xay dung chu nghia xa hoi*).[62] In other words, the army was instructed to combat economic hardship, the new enemy after the war, by doing work such as clearing farmland, planting crops, and raising livestock and fish.

As laid out by the Fourth Party Congress in December 1976, Hanoi set two postwar national priorities: (1) economic recovery, modernization, and the socialist transformation of southern Vietnam; and (2) defense of territorial sovereignty. Certainly the first priority was the most important national goal. No Vietnamese leader emerging from this congress could have anticipated a major war with Cambodia and China in late 1978 and early 1979, let alone a war that would last a decade. The Politburo attached paramount importance to economic reconstruction and modernization in the first FYP (1976–80) and socialist transformation in newly liberated southern Vietnam. It began deliberating in earnest and drawing up its FYP in mid-1975, shortly after the Republic of Vietnam fell on April 30, enlisting hundreds of able and highly experienced economists and scientists to participate in the process and establishing twelve economic and scientific research committees to study the most critical areas of the economy. A draft FYP was circulated for in-depth discussion at the Council of Government. It was then reviewed and commented on by the Politburo on three separate occasions. In October 1976, the final version was presented to the Twenty-Fifth Conference of the Party Central Committee.[63] At the end of November, the Politburo assigned deputy prime minister and Politburo member Le Thanh Nghi the task of preparing a concise presentation to relay key points of the FYP to party members at the Fourth Party Congress to ensure that all of them would have a good grasp of party policy in the new revolutionary age.[64]

In December the Politburo set four main national goals: (1) stabilize and improve the standard of living, (2) build the economic and technical foundations of socialism, (3) train and improve the quality of government officials and workers, and (4) strengthen national defense. As a top strategic priority, the party was determined to solve the food crisis by 1978, or at the latest by 1980 (the end of the FYP), and it called on all party members, from the central government to local jurisdictions, as well as the masses, to help achieve this mission.[65] In the spring of 1977, the party launched a national campaign encouraging people to compete in building socialism and working to boost productivity while saving whatever they could and contributing any production surplus to the government.[66]

While the government focused on solving the economic crisis, Vietnam's military strength rapidly eroded. The Politburo tasked the army with both building the economy and defending national sovereignty after the Fourth Party Congress. In 1977 the MoD planned to release twenty thousand soldiers from the army (and at least an additional eighty thousand by 1980) while it reassigned a large portion of the armed forces to do economic work.[67] In 1977 the armed forces at all levels were ordered to engage in the economic mission. By mid-1977, the army reportedly had cleared new farmland and planted 20,000 hectares of food crops (60 percent of the plan) and raised 50,000 pigs, 20,000 cows and buffaloes, and nearly 140,000 chickens. It had farm-raised at least 6 million fish and created its own fishing units.[68] Its logistical department itself became a semiministry as the army's economic role was markedly expanded in the postwar era. But the CMC assessment report made a bleak observation: "Although the logistical department of the army made monumental efforts and all levels of the army leadership paid close attention to economic tasks, the living conditions of our troops in many places continue to be poor and will worsen due to the economic difficulties our country is facing today."[69] On top of its economic hardship, the Vietnamese army had to help the Laos People's Democratic Republic (LPDR) in Laos to strengthen its national defenses by dispatching Vietnamese advisers, as requested by Laos; building defense projects; accepting Laotian soldiers for military training in the Vietnamese military academy; and providing military aid as pledged in a bilateral agreement signed in May 1976.[70]

Nothing is more demoralizing to rank-and-file soldiers, perhaps, than a government's inability to provide proper burials for soldiers who die defending the nation. In the south, when a solider died the government offered a one-time state gift of 120 VND, as mandated by government Directive 10/ND, dated June 18, 1976, to the soldier's family to pay for burial. This amount fell far short of the actual cost of a proper burial, as the cost of new clothes for the deceased alone ranged from 280 to 700 VND. Facing growing criticism from veterans' families, in May 1977 the Ministry of Veteran and Social Affairs sent an urgent request to Prime Minister Pham Van Dong urging the government to increase the subsidy to families of deceased soldiers and government employees.[71] Deputy Prime Minister Pham Hung instructed people's committees at the provincial and city levels to urgently address the issue, but the subsidy remained unchanged. Thus the impact of Vietnam's severe poverty further contributed to the decline in soldiers' morale and discipline. For the second half of 1977, the CMC proposed to concentrate on elevating the war readiness of army units along the border and on islands, speeding up the implementation of economic tasks assigned by the Politburo; improving logistics, especially securing enough food for the troops; and enhancing military discipline and political indoctrination in the army.[72]

Hanoi was also concerned about the depletion of mid-level leaders within the army. While the number of high-ranking military officers increased significantly, accounting for 25 percent of the armed forces, infantry company commanders accounted for only 4 to 5 percent in 1977. There were too many generals and not enough well-trained mid-level officers to lead combat operations.[73] Vietnam also had to fulfill its international socialist duty of providing military aid and training to Laos,[74] which further drained the army's human and material resources. From the perspective of the CMC, the shortage of mid-level military leaders also contributed to the poor quality of political education and military training for new recruits from remote regions in newly liberated southern Vietnam.[75] As a result, the report concluded:

> Our soldiers [in the south] are not yet well equipped with correct ideological weapons to fight the new kinds of enemies and [perform] the twin tasks of building the economy while defending our nation. The majority of our troops lack political awareness, the will to fight, and the determination to overcome

difficulties; many try to avoid tedious work and evade their duty of building the economy and contributing their labor to boost production. A great amount of manpower has been wasted. The widespread violations of military discipline and the phenomenon of abandoning military duties at the local level need our attention.[76]

It is clear that Hanoi's military leaders were less than impressed by the combat readiness and performance of their troops, especially local forces in the south, and they only came to the realization in mid-1977 that much work remained to be done to prepare the army for war, especially in the event of a full-scale invasion of Cambodia and a possible military confrontation with China on the northern front. In the second half of 1977, the CMC, as reported by General Chu Huy Man to the Politburo on August 31, 1977, issued a resolution focusing on (1) enhancing the war readiness of Vietnamese soldiers, especially those who were defending border regions and islands [in the South China Sea], (2) quickly performing the economic tasks entrusted to troops by the Politburo, and (3) rapidly drawing up a military plan for 1978 and a long-term plan for building up the military and strengthening national defense.[77] As the military leaders were preparing their troops for war, Hanoi chose to launch major counteroffensives to send a clear message to the Khmer Rouge that military confrontation with Vietnam would not be in its best interest, hoping to force it into more fruitful negotiations on the border issue. But the Khmer Rouge was undeterred by the Vietnamese counteroffensives, which penetrated thirty kilometers into southwestern Cambodia in May and June, and it continued to attack Vietnam, killing Vietnamese citizens and plundering their property. Hanoi's leaders saw this as a defiant response by a radical anti-Vietnam Khmer Rouge regime, which remained characteristically antagonistic and merciless toward Vietnamese people along the border in spite of Vietnam's goodwill.

The Economic and Security Nexus and the Soviet Factor

In 1977 Hanoi made a last-ditch effort to maintain amiable relations with Beijing in the faint hope that it would renew the aid programs that Vietnam desperately needed to support its FYP and to enlist China's support in putting pressure on the Khmer Rouge regime to cease its attacks along the border. Although Hanoi tilted closer to the Soviet Union, it refrained from officially joining the Soviet-dominated COMECON simply because an open alliance with

Moscow would certainly antagonize Beijing.[78] In a demonstrative display of national independence and a play for capital and technology from the West to support its economic agenda, Hanoi sought to speed up normalization of relations with the United States and to diversify its economic relations with a number of capitalist states.[79] The head of the US Division of the MOFA, Tran Quang Co, who participated in the first round of negotiations for normalization of US-Vietnamese relations on May 3, 1977, recalled in his memoir that Hanoi's demand that Washington pay war reparations of US$3.2 billion as an important precondition for normalization was problematic for the Carter administration because the US Congress would oppose such a demand. Because of that demand, in Co's view, Vietnam missed an important opportunity to normalize relations with the United States in 1977.[80] Hanoi did not abandon this demand until September 1978, preventing Washington from moving toward normalization of relations until it was too late because Hanoi's intentions vis-à-vis Cambodia and the Soviet Union were clear by that time. The Carter administration saw American national interests as lying with China as a way to contain Soviet ambitions in Southeast Asia.[81] Thus, by mid-1978 Hanoi had no choice other than joining the Soviet-led COMECON, and it signed a military pact with Moscow to ensure the flow of economic and military aid from the Soviet Union and the rest of the Soviet-led socialist bloc to address both its economic and political crises at home and the security threats posed by the anti-Vietnam alliance between China and DK in Cambodia.

Evidently, the Vietnamese leaders decided to join COMECON only after Beijing's intention to oppose Vietnam was clear to them. On July 20, 1978, Politburo member, deputy prime minister, and chairman of the State Planning Committee Le Thanh Nghi told the Council of Government, "As China has openly opposed us, the Politburo saw the need to officially join the Council for Mutual Economic Assistance to demonstrate our stance and seek support and assistance from the Soviet Union. This has become necessary."[82] Nghi further reasoned, "Our membership in COMECON has increased the political influence of the Soviet-led socialist camp . . . [as well as] the Soviet Union's trust [of Vietnam] and our closeness with the Soviets and other members. With this our country will win other socialist countries' accord, support, and assistance to us in all fields."[83] The Soviet Union and other COMECON members quickly pledged to replace China's aid programs. Hanoi wasted no time in making a request to COMECON for assistance in a number of important areas of critical need in order to (1) expedite the design and construction of seven industrial projects pledged by COMECON, (2) speed up mechanization of Vietnam's agricultural sector, (3) build a railroad connecting Hanoi and Ho Chi Minh City, and (4) continue to provide industrial equipment and parts to complete forty projects for which China had terminated aid.[84]

By early 1978 Vietnam was in a deep economic crisis that poisoned the political atmosphere and aroused popular resistance, alarming the CPV. Without US$3.2 billion in reparations from the United States and 1.9 billion RMB in aid and loans from China, Vietnam's first FYP was stalled. The worsening economic crisis precipitated a corresponding sociopolitical crisis across the country. In the south, Vietnam lost the $1 billion per year aid package the United States had provided to the Republic of Vietnam, leaving a great financial burden for the victorious Communist government.[85] Le Thanh Nghi, on several occasions, lamented that the DRV (and by extension the later SRV) had lost US aid to the government of the Republic of Vietnam. Since the burden of postwar reconstruction in southern Vietnam after 1975 was enormous, Hanoi's leaders believed that they were entitled to US aid for war reparations as a condition of normalization of US-Vietnam relations in 1977–78.

On December 6, 1977, Le Thanh Nghi lamented, "While the imbalance of our economy since the war ended has not yet been resolved, we have to rely on our own strength to meet a great domestic demand for food, raw materials, spare parts, industrial equipment, and hard currency to cover our large trade deficit.[86] On an optimistic note, Nghi emphasized the potential of Vietnam's national resources, including five million hectares of farmland (potentially to be increased to eleven million by 1980), a large amount of rich forestland, and undertapped maritime resources and freshwater fishing. In addition, Vietnam had a large labor pool of 22 million people, a modest number of educated people (3,000 cadres with higher education degrees, 160,000 with university degrees, and 350,000 with high school diplomas), a million technicians, and tens of millions of farmers and experienced leaders of cooperatives.[87]

The economic situation continued to spiral downward in the spring of 1978. In his address to the Third Conference of the Central Committee of the CPV, Le Thanh Nghi presented an extraordinarily bleak assessment of Vietnam's economic crisis: "Our national economy is in a situation in which we cannot produce enough food to eat (*lam khong du an*), earn enough income to cover our expenses (*thu khong du chi*), and export enough to cover our imports (*xuat khong bu nhap*)."[88] As the FYP was on the verge of collapse, Nghi attributed the worsening crisis to the loss of foreign aid in the amount of US$1.5 billion per year ($1 billion in the south and 400 to 500 million rubles in the north), leaving a large gap in the foundation of the national economy.[89] In addition, Vietnam suffered a severe drought in 1977, increasing the severity of the food shortage as the country lost half of the agricultural harvest that year except in the Mekong Delta.[90]

In 1978 the economic crisis had serious political consequences for the party-state, threatening to escalate into a breakdown of the sociopolitical order with a damaging impact on the government's legitimacy. During the crucial years 1977–78, the Central Committee of the CPV appeared to lose control over local affairs and was blindsided by many self-serving local party officials. Rampant corruption and abuses of power at the local level profoundly worried Hanoi's leaders. From January to September 1978, the General Prosecutor arrested 1,735 so-called "bad elements and reactionaries" at the district authority level and "eliminated"—a euphemism for "executed"—717 individuals from the state apparatus. In addition, from September to December, the General Prosecutor was authorized by the Politburo's Resolution 228, reinforced by the prime minister's Directive 159, to investigate more than 6,000 government officials who were suspected of having committed economic crimes. A total of 51,892 complaints against government officials were filed with the General Prosecutor, indicative of rising popular resistance to the party-state. Civil disobedience in the form of refusing to relocate to the New Economic Zones, avoiding military duty, or simply disregarding state rules and regulations was reportedly widespread.[91] In 1978 alone, the bureau investigated a total of 28,342 cases of violations of state laws, a sharp increase of 46 percent compared to 1977. Three million people were unemployed in the south alone.[92] The political crisis, intensified by the socioeconomic crisis, Hanoi recognized, had the potential to explode into social upheaval, particularly in the south, giving more ammunition to enemies inside the country (e.g., resisters from the Thieu regime and the United Front for the Liberation of Oppressed Races, better known as FULRO, a guerrilla group fighting for autonomy for the Montagnard tribes) and outside it (Khmer Rouge and Chinese reactionaries) to exploit and expand internal instability and undermine the party-state. It was overwhelmingly clear to the Hanoi leadership by 1978 that many party officials at the local level were undermining party policies in the pursuit of personal gain, generating increasingly tense relations between the populace and the party-state. But Hanoi's worst fears of dire political consequences would be realized if it failed to find a solution to the intensified crisis soon. While Hanoi faced domestic crises in 1977, the external threat to Vietnam's national security was gathering strength as 1978 approached.

If in 1976 Le Duan could afford to ignore Khmer Rouge attacks along the southwestern border out of confidence in the superiority of Vietnamese military strength as a deterrent and in diplomacy as a gesture of goodwill and patience, he came to full realization in 1977 that the major attacks by Khmer Rouge forces had been ordered and planned by the DK leadership. Hanoi's leaders concluded that the Khmer Rouge regime's tenacious defiance indicated that it would continue its attacks on Vietnam unless the regime was toppled. After personally touring the battlefield along the border after the April 30 Khmer Rouge attacks, Le Duan came to the conclusion that Pol Pot's explanation that previous attacks were launched by insubordinate or undisciplined local commanders was in fact a CPK strategy intended to deceive the Vietnamese leaders into believing that the conflict could be resolved at the party level.[93] When Vietnamese ambassador Pham Van Ba raised the issue of border conflicts with Pol Pot on September 2, 1977, the latter shifted the blame to "enemies within the Party ranks."[94] Hanoi had had enough of Pol Pot's excuses by this time. But as it contemplated a decisive military response to eliminate the DK threat, it feared military retaliation by Beijing from the north. At the end of 1977, during his visit to the southern region, in response to a group of confused local officials who frankly criticized Hanoi's feeble response to the Khmer Rouge attacks and brutal killings of Vietnamese people along the border, Le Duan remarked, "Comrades have correctly pointed out the situation that has puzzled the whole country. We [leaders] have had a lot of headaches and lost a lot of sleep over this issue. The issue is not DK and Pol Pot but those who are behind them [referring to China]. We have a powerful army; they cannot resist us, but if we attack them, China will attack us. If we do not take over Cambodia, China will not attack our country."[95]

Le Duan's view was grounded in Vietnam's territorial dispute with China. By mid-1977, the dispute had turned into open armed conflict and all negotiations at the provincial level had failed. The tension gave way to a sense of relief, however temporary, as Beijing suggested that top-level negotiations should take place at the end of the year, offering Hanoi hope for a peaceful resolution of the conflict.[96] It was not unreasonable for Hanoi to believe that a resolution of the border conflict with China would lead to a renewal of Chinese aid to Vietnam. In November Vietnamese Deputy Prime Minister Le Thanh Nghi sent a letter to Chinese Vice-Premier Li Xiannian requesting that China provide material aid and consumption goods worth 1.1 billion RMB on credit and a loan of 900 million RMB without interest over the period of three years from 1978 to 1980.[97] According to Le Duan's assistant, Tran Phuong, in late 1977 when the Vietnamese army launched a major offensive that penetrated thirty kilometers into Cambodian territory in the southwest,[98] it captured military documents that confirmed Hanoi's suspicion that China was behind the Pol Pot regime's aggressive behavior toward Vietnam.[99]

At the end of 1977, the Vietnamese Party Central Committee declared war on the Pol Pot regime and began to view China as enemy.[100] Only then did Hanoi begin to place an emphasis on enhancing the country's strategic relations with extraregional powers, especially the Soviet Union and the United States. Hanoi repeatedly sent high-ranking officials to Phnom Penh to try to bring DK in line with its ideology and away from China's, but this failed utterly. After a chain of increasingly hostile actions by Beijing, combined with its cold reception of Vietnamese leaders, Hanoi concluded that China was intent on weakening Vietnam.

Through a series of economic negotiations and exchanges of letters between top leaders of the two countries in the second half of 1975, Beijing made it clear to Hanoi that from 1976 onward China would no longer provide nonrefundable aid to Vietnam. To Vietnam's further disappointment, China only agreed to provide an interest-free loan of 100 million RMB (roughly US$50 million) to import consumption goods from China in 1976 and refused to negotiate a long-term trade agreement as Hanoi repeatedly requested.[101] Beijing also postponed the delivery of materials and equipment for a total of eighty economic projects, which would significantly undercut Vietnam's FYP.[102] In late 1975, Beijing also cut off military aid to Vietnam, including a large amount of military supplies.[103] On December 2, 1976, Vietnamese deputy prime minister Do Muoi stopped over in Beijing on his way to Moscow, and the Politburo instructed him to stay two additional days to persuade Beijing to provide additional aid to Vietnam. Chinese Vice-Premier Gu Mu, a top leader in economic circles in the Chinese government, again pointed out China's own economic difficulties and its obligation to provide aid to sixty other countries.[104]

The mood in Hanoi had taken on an increasingly apprehensive edge as Beijing entered into an extraordinarily public feud with Hanoi in defense of the Khmer Rouge after late 1977, and its condemnation of the Vietnamese military response as incursions into Cambodia had intensified. On June 2, 1977, General Vo Nguyen Giap stopped in Beijing on his way back from Eastern Europe, but his counterpart, the Chinese minister of defense, did not show up to receive him at the airport. Giap, a great general and the face of the Vietnamese army, was reportedly furious during his entire stay in China. As the Vietnamese ambassador to China, Nguyen Trong Vinh, recalled, "China treated General Giap's delegation with disrespect. . . . On the train back to Vietnam, the Chinese used rice bowls with chipped edges to serve the Vietnamese delegation."[105] On June 10, in front of other high-ranking officials on both sides, Chinese Vice-Premier Li Xiannian and Vietnamese Prime Minister Pham Van Dong had a heated exchange over who had caused the deterioration of Sino-Vietnamese relations. Vice-Premier Li chastised Pham Van Dong for not honoring his own 1958 letter, which purportedly recognized China's sovereignty over the Spratly and Paracel Islands in the South China Sea.[106] During Le Duan's visit to Beijing on November 20–23, he also received a cold reception from the Chinese leadership. Duan soon felt Deng Xiaoping's hostility,[107] as Deng did not come to welcome him at the airport.[108] Deng's indifference to Le Duan at that time was taken as a sign that Sino-Vietnamese relations had gone from bad to worse, and Hanoi's leaders were bracing for some kind of confrontation and certainly more Chinese pressure as Deng consolidated his power at the helm.

The Decision to Invade Cambodia and the Soviet Factor

Rather than demonstrating its generosity and willingness to replace China in supplying aid to Vietnam, Moscow saw these events as an opportunity to put more pressure on Vietnam to join COMECON and eventually draw Vietnam into the Soviet orbit. On October 27, 1977, Soviet ambassador Chaplin came to the office of the Foreign Affairs Committee of the Party Central Committee to inform Xuan Thuy, a top Vietnamese diplomat, of the Soviet government's reply to Pham Van Dong's request for Soviet military aid to Vietnam for the period 1976–80.[109] Moscow pledged far less than the amount of military aid Hanoi had requested. For example, it agreed to provide only two patrol boats and six fishing boats converted for use as patrol boats, three land-based radar systems, and other, less valuable items. Notably, Moscow did not honor Hanoi's request for major state-of-the-art weaponry for its air force, navy, and infantry, including twelve Mig-21MF fighter jets and two Mig-21US training jets, two missile ships (183R type) equipped with three missile systems, two submarine hunter ships (Gorisna type) with three torpedo systems, two fully equipped survey ships, twenty attack boats, and three bridging tanks.[110] After Xuan Thuy briefed the Politburo on the results of his meeting with Soviet Ambassador Chaplin, there was a strong sense of apprehension and anxiety among senior Politburo members about what they saw as the Soviets' opportunistic behavior. But Moscow's intended message was clear: until Vietnam joined COMECON and sided with the Soviet Union, Hanoi would have to make do with whatever aid it decided to deliver. In the spring of 1978, Hanoi's leaders felt isolated as they strove to implement their first FYP after the 1975 unification while the two-front military threat to Vietnam's territorial sovereignty from the Sino-Cambodian alliance was omnipresent on both the northern and southwestern frontiers.

Nonetheless, in January 1978 Hanoi adopted a political-military solution to the Cambodia problem. According to Chanda, it was a Soviet general who suggested in January that Vietnam "do a Czechoslovakia" in Cambodia.[111] But Vietnamese internal reports corroborate Morris's assertion that Moscow had little influence on Hanoi's marked shift from counteroffensives in 1977 to a full-scale invasion and occupation of Cambodia in early 1978.[112] Although the Vietnamese welcomed Soviet support for the invasion, its leaders knew that the Soviet Union would not commit ground troops other than military advisers.

The Conservative and Military Leaders at the Helm

As early as January 1978, the CMC proposed decisive military action to overthrow the Pol Pot regime and put an end to DK attacks on Vietnam. To rally the population around a new regime and justify the invasion, Hanoi saw the need to create a Khmer revolutionary front. On April 21, the Vietnamese Politburo issued Resolution 34 establishing Committee 10, headed by Vice-Minister of Defense Tran Van Quang. The committee was given two specific tasks: (1) recruit revolutionary armed forces among Khmer refugees and defectors and (2) research and advise the CMC on the plan to assist the Khmer revolutionary army.[113] On May 12, at Camp 977 in the Thu Duc district of Ho Chi Minh City, Hanoi established its revolutionary army, the Kampuchean United Front for National Salvation (KUFNS), and appointed former Khmer Rouge military officer Hun Sen commander of its first unit. This unit consisted of only 125 officers and soldiers.[114] In January, as the Vietnamese army pounded the DK forces, the Chinese ambassador in Hanoi condemned "Vietnam's invasion of Cambodia and accused Vietnam of killing Cambodians and plundering Cambodians' properties" and personally asked the Vietnamese government to withdraw all troops from Cambodian territory.[115] But by this time Hanoi was oblivious to Beijing's condemnation.

In January the Border Commission of the Party Central Committee informed the Politburo that during a series of border negotiations in 1976–77 "Beijing's main intention was to weaken Vietnam. . . . China wants to take over our territory where there are rich natural resources and islands of strategic importance to its military, undermine our ability to develop our economy, obstruct our cooperation with the Soviet Union and our neighbors, and prevent us from opening and developing the border region."[116] On March 23, 1978, Vice-Minister of Foreign Affairs Phan Hien, who headed the Vietnamese border negotiation team, concluded that "future negotiations would be in vain" because China was continuing to pressure Vietnam to accept its positions and recently had brought up the border conflict between Vietnam and Cambodia during negotiations over territorial disputes between China and Vietnam.[117] Moscow was kept informed all along about the results of these negotiations. In February the Ministry of the Interior reported a sharp increase in Cambodian and Chinese incursions into Vietnamese territory along the southwestern and northern borders,[118] generating the perception in Hanoi that Vietnam was under siege.

At a major conference on January 26, 1978, as the CMC pushed for an invasion of Cambodia, the MOFA leadership proposed to launch a diplomatic offensive to justify any military interventions in Cambodia. It put forth three scenarios: (1) Cambodia continues attacks in Vietnam, anti-Vietnamese nationalism and public denunciation of Vietnam rise, and Cambodia refuses to negotiate; (2) Cambodia continues all these activities while negotiating with Vietnam, but negotiations fail; and (3) Cambodia ceases all military attacks along the border, negotiates with Vietnam, and takes steps to resolve the border problem.[119] In the MOFA's assessment, the situation was evolving in the direction of the first scenario because the DK leadership was not intimidated by Vietnamese counteroffensives into cooperation and compromise at the negotiation table. The MOFA further reasoned that if Cambodia were to be soundly defeated by military force an internal split within the DK leadership would occur, for it would realize that its policy of relying on China to militarily oppose Vietnam was doomed to fail. Cambodian leaders would be condemned by their own populace—possibly by means of an internal uprising—as well as by world opinion.[120] They would be forced to negotiate to buy time to restore domestic order, and the situation would evolve according to the second scenario: futile negotiations. However, if DK suffered a devastating military and political defeat it would be forced to give up its belligerent policy toward Vietnam, and if China faced more internal struggles among competing factions in its domestic politics, became isolated internationally, especially within the socialist bloc, because of its support of anti-Vietnamese Cambodia, and failed in its attempt to drive a wedge between Vietnam and Laos, then the third scenario would develop.[121] Although the MOFA agreed with the CMC that the third scenario was the best option, it cast doubt on Vietnam's economic and military ability to successfully carry out an invasion of Cambodia and engage in nation building there without the military, economic, and political backing of the Soviet bloc.[122]

Based on MOFA's rationalization, it could be argued that Hanoi's "two camps" worldview—that is, the ideological conflict between communism and capitalism—in which victory was shifting in favor of the Soviet bloc, remained influential,[123] but such an ideology does not necessarily conflict with Hanoi's rational decision making. In fact, this ideological underpinning eased Hanoi's decision to join COMECON and ally itself with the Soviet Union by silencing potential resisters and doubters, especially the pro-China faction, within Vietnam's domestic politics, and those economically minded leaders who were concerned about the adverse impact of the war on Vietnam's economy. But if this ideology was a cause of Hanoi's decision to ally itself with the Soviet Union against China, why did Hanoi hesitate until mid-1978 and why did it make a sudden move at that point?

In planning its invasion of Cambodia, Hanoi closely observed the internal struggles in both Cambodia and China, looking for an opportune time to invade. On January 1, 1978, the Vietnamese leadership received an important piece of intelligence reporting that the internal struggle for power between Chinese leaders Deng Xiaoping and Hua Guafeng had intensified.[124] In May 1978, Hanoi received news that DK had pulled some of its troops from the border region to quell an internal uprising in the Eastern Zone.[125] These were all encouraging signs as Hanoi was preparing for military intervention in Cambodia.

Against this backdrop, the MOFA proposed to launch a diplomatic offensive, far greater than it had done before, to prop up its "self-defense" justification when the military intervention in Cambodia was under way because it recognized that Vietnam was losing in the court of world opinion as it intensified its counteroffensives in Cambodia in the spring of 1978. To the MOFA, the pendulum of world public opinion appeared to be swinging in favor of Phnom Penh's anti-Vietnam propaganda, amplified by Beijing, claiming that "Vietnam has an ambition to establish an 'Indochinese Federation,' orchestrating regime change in Cambodia with the intention of propping up its client state there."[126] To disrupt this public perception, the MOFA instructed its diplomatic corps to redouble its efforts to elicit favorable public opinion around the world that would cast Vietnam's military actions as much as possible in the light of self-defense. The rationale, in the words of MOFA officials, was "If Cambodia refuses to negotiate or prolongs negotiations, we will win politically because we will shift world opinion to support our self-defense actions and Cambodia will be more politically isolated."[127] It is overwhelmingly clear that by late January 1978 a collective decision had been reached to deal the Khmer Rouge a decisive military blow and follow it with regime change in Cambodia. The MOFA sought to launch another round of diplomatic offensives to justify these military interventions.[128]

By mid-1978, the economic crisis worsened and there was enough blame to go around all branches of the government. From May 12 to 15, Chairman of the State Planning Committee Le Thanh Nghi, who was deputy prime minister and

Politburo member, presided over a conference on the state of economy with district and provincial leaders. He opened his address to high-ranking party and government officials with a self-critically candid view of the state of the economy: "Now we are facing [economic] difficulty, and it's going to get worse. It's partly due to the economic reality, but our shortcomings with regard to economic management and organization are the main cause. All levels of the party and government are responsible for this, and therefore we must face our own shortcomings head on and accept our responsibility. We must not put blame on other people."[129] This rare admission of failure by the economic chief of the Vietnamese party and government reflected the severity of the economic crisis in the run-up to Vietnam's decision to join COMECON in June of that year. This provides another important immediate background to Hanoi's decision to join COMECON in June and sign a military alliance with the Soviet Union in November of 1978.

On the battlefront, from December 1977 to June 1978, 6,902 Vietnamese soldiers died and 23,742 were injured during border clashes with DK forces, and 4,100 Vietnamese citizens were killed or injured in brutal attacks.[130] It was not difficult for the Vietnamese government to channel the population's rage into emotional support for a decisive military action against the Khmer Rouge. On November 3, Hanoi officially signed the Soviet-Vietnamese Treaty of Friendship and Cooperation, but the alliance agreement was agreed on in June during which time the Soviet deputy foreign minister, Nikolai Firuybin, made an unannounced trip to Hanoi to smooth out the remaining differences in the draft.[131] Hanoi was to decide on the timing of the public announcement of the treaty to deter Beijing from contemplating military action against Vietnam.[132] Nonetheless, in August Moscow demonstrated its commitment in material terms. At Hanoi's request, the Soviet Union began an unprecedented airlift and sea transport of arms, including long-range artillery pieces, missiles, and Mig-21 fighter planes to bolster the country's defenses against China.[133] On December 23, Prime Minister Pham Van Dong made the case for all-out war against the Khmer Rouge regime and an invasion of Cambodia to the fourth session of the Sixth Plenum of the National Assembly.[134] His entire speech was aimed at convincing his comrades that with the full backing of Soviet political, economic, and military might Vietnam was assured of victory and that China, which he described as a "paper tiger," would not dare attack Vietnam.[135] On the same day, a combined Vietnamese force of three army corps and troops from Military Regions 5, 7, and 9 under the command of General Le Trong Tan launched an invasion of Cambodia. But the Khmer Rouge regime was not taken by surprise as it had already withdrawn its major forces westward toward the Thai border.[136]

The bulk of the documentary evidence reveals that the wider strategic calculations of Vietnam's national security (i.e., its alliance with the Soviet Union to counter the alliance between DK and the PRC and to draw the Soviet bloc's greater assistance to address its domestic economic crisis) in 1977–78 played a more significant role in Hanoi's decision making vis-à-vis Cambodia than either local factors (such as KR border raids) or geopolitical concerns steeped in long-term historical conflict. Vietnam's decision to invade Cambodia was made in the context of domestic and external imperatives in 1977–78, not as a result of its long-standing hegemonism. Certainly, the threat to Vietnam's national sovereignty of the Sino–Khmer Rouge alliance was growing before Vietnam's invasion of Cambodia in December 1978; Hanoi's ideological affinity with the Soviet Union had grown after 1975; and the Vietnamese had a strong desire for revenge for the atrocities the Khmer Rouge troops committed against thousands of innocent Vietnamese civilians along the Cambodia-Vietnam border. These factors facilitated Hanoi's decision to invade Cambodia in December 1978, but they were not necessary and are insufficient to explain Hanoi's external and internal motives, that is, to enlist Moscow in an alliance that would preempt China's attacks and attract economic and military aid from the Soviet Union to relieve Vietnam's economic crisis and boost its military strength. The convergence of strategic interests between Vietnam and the Soviet Union explained the formalization of an alliance between them.

In January 1978, the Vietnamese CMC recommended a decisive military intervention and a regime change in Cambodia. Vietnamese leaders made this consequential decision in early 1978 when they were under siege domestically (from the socioeconomic and political crisis) and externally (from the two-front threat of the Sino-Cambodian alliance). Almost all doors were closed around them; they had missed the opportunity to normalize relations with the United States in 1977, and they blamed China for undermining it.

Hanoi's rational calculation of benefits from the Vietnamese-Soviet alliance for Vietnam's national survival against the Chinese threat and alleviation of an economic and sociopolitical crisis alarmingly detrimental to the legitimacy of the CPV were the main drivers of Hanoi's decision to invade Cambodia and form an alliance with the Soviet Union. As a continued revolution by other means, war provided the CPV leadership with the power to extract resources and sacrifices to defend the Vietnamese nation and a rationale for subordinating economic development to the priority of national defense. Also revealing is the rising influence of the military-first faction spearheaded by the CMC in the decision-making process as the economy-first faction, including the chairman of the State Planning Committee, Le Thanh Nghi, was largely discredited due to the worsening economic crisis. This shift was manifested in Hanoi's return to military-security priorities and the Marxist-Leninist "two-camp" worldview in late 1977 and early 1978, ending its earlier attempt to employ a broad-based foreign policy of economic engagement with the West. As I discuss in chapter 3, the military-first priority heightened after China's invasion of Vietnam on February 17, 1979, which suddenly pushed Vietnam to mobilize the entire nation for a two-front military confrontation in Cambodia and against China along its northern border.

3

Mobilization for a Two-Front War

1979-1981

Following the Chinese invasion on February 17, 1979, the Vietnamese leadership declared that Vietnam had entered a new era of a "two-front war" with Cambodian resistance forces in Cambodia and with China along the northern border.[1] This chapter examines the impact of China's invasion of northern Vietnam. It specifically addresses two questions: (1) why did the Vietnamese leadership fail to anticipate the invasion in spite of a highly militarized border conflict months before and (2) what impact did Vietnam's military confrontation with China after 1979 have on Hanoi's strategic objective of balancing economic and military priorities and domestic politics within the Vietnamese leadership? In answering these questions, this chapter traces the Vietnamese leaders' strategic thinking about how to deal with the Chinese threat as they planned a massive military intervention in Cambodia in December 1978, as well as the rise of the military-first policy and its consequences for economic development in the aftermath of the Chinese invasion in 1979–80.

The shock of China's invasion prompted the Vietnamese leadership to militarize nearly all aspects of national life, subordinating socialist economic development to expanding military and security capabilities during the last two years of the first FYP after unification. In 1979–81 the SRV turned itself into a powerful resource-extractive state in preparation for a two-front war in Cambodia and against China. This chapter reveals two major consequences of the Chinese invasion. First, the main explanation for Vietnam's military underpreparedness when massive numbers of Chinese troops crossed the Sino-Vietnamese border has to be found in Vietnam's overconfidence in its military strength vis-à-vis China's PLA, amplified by its leaders' underestimation of China's military resolve and overestimation of great power support from the Soviet Union. As a result, the shock of China's blitzkrieg invasion of northern Vietnam in February and March 1979 caused a sudden shift from a strategic balance between economic development and national defense to total mobilization for national defense against another anticipated invasion by China. Second, China's military pressure on Vietnam's northern border in 1980 and in Cambodia enabled the military-first faction to continue to dominate policy making in Hanoi. The economy-first and moderate factions were either demoted or co-opted into supporting the massive mobilization of national resources for military confrontation with China. Anti-Chinese nationalism and socialist ideology combined with the power of a police state enabled the CPV and the government to extract enormous amounts of resources for the two-front war. Although Vietnam relied heavily on Soviet economic and military aid to support its military intervention in Cambodia and boost its military capacity to confront China, the human and material costs of the military conflict stifled its economic development. Previous scholarship has privileged ideology as the major explanation for Hanoi's failure to anticipate the Chinese invasion,[2] but new evidence pointed to the combination of the Vietnamese leaders' overconfidence in Vietnam's military strength, underestimation of China's military resolve, and strong belief in the deterrence effect of Vietnam's alliance with the Soviet Union as a major cause of Hanoi's failure to anticipate the Chinese invasion.

The Stalinist "two-camp" worldview of Vietnamese leaders swelled their confidence that they were on the winning side in the ideological conflict with China because China under Deng Xiaoping had betrayed the international socialist movement by aligning itself with the imperialist United States. Ideology was certainly a facilitating factor, but it is insufficient in itself to explain Hanoi's failure to foresee the Chinese invasion. Hanoi's overconfidence in its military power vis-à-vis China's military resolve, combined with much anticipated support from the Soviet Union, was decisive in the Vietnamese leadership's strategic thinking that China would not dare invade Vietnam. That turned out to be wrong, but it does not mean that Hanoi's decision making was not rational.

In retrospect the fact that Deng Xiaoping used the invasion of the Soviet Union's smaller ally, Vietnam, to forge a new anti-Soviet strategic relationship with western countries in order to draw capital and technology for his economic reform agenda was beyond Hanoi's prevailing thinking at that time.[3] Military historian Xiaoming Zhang writes, "Despite several months of saber rattling by Beijing, China's invasion still caught Hanoi off guard."[4] In addition to various battle reports of the PLA, Zhang points to the absence of anticipation and strategic military preparedness on the part of the Vietnamese political and military leadership.

General Secretary Le Duan's son, Le Kien Thanh, had planned his wedding for the day of the Chinese invasion, and it lasted for only an hour.[5] Le Kien Thanh publicly rejected the argument that the Chinese invasion of Vietnam on February 17, 1979, came as a big surprise to his father. Documentary evidence of internal debates within the Vietnamese government before and after the Chinese invasion suggests otherwise, that the Vietnamese military leadership failed to anticipate the Chinese invasion in spite of the deterioration of Sino-Vietnamese relations in 1977–78. First, blindsided by its great victory over the United States, after 1975 the Vietnamese leadership was overconfident, lacked vigilance against, or even found unthinkable the prospect of China's invasion of Vietnam. The perception of "China as a paper tiger" was prevalent within the Vietnamese military leadership at that time. Vietnam kept its one million troops on active duty and had acquired sophisticated weaponry left behind by the United States and its Republic of Vietnam ally, as well as from the Soviet Union. Chinese troops were not well equipped and had little war experience; its last war had been with India in 1962.

Today, forty years after the war, most Vietnamese nationalists and historians continue to repeat the party narrative of "the great victory of the war to defend the motherland against the Chinese invaders" in February 1979. However, a few Vietnamese scholars have begun to openly question Vietnamese military preparedness before the Chinese invasion. Among these few but well-known historians, Vu Duong Ninh told *VNExpress* (a popular online news source), "Vietnam did not correctly evaluate the adversary and itself."[6] He suggested that Hanoi's leaders failed to see the strategic importance of normalizing relations with the United States in 1977–78. Former vice-minister of foreign affairs Tran Quang Co called it "a missed opportunity" when Vietnam rejected Washington's demand for "unconditional normalization of relations" in 1977 and insisted on reparations of US$3.2 billion from the United States.[7] This allowed Deng Xiaoping to push for the normalization of Sino-American relations, which compelled the Carter administration to shelve its normalization talks with Vietnam. In retrospect, Co blamed the rigidity of Vietnam's foreign policy thinking at that time, and its disconnect with changing world politics.[8]

Second, and more important, having secured a military alliance with the Soviet Union against China in November 1978, the Vietnamese leadership failed to anticipate China's large-scale invasion from the north. Based on an important eyewitness account from the Soviet side, Soviet military advisers did not anticipate China's invasion of Vietnam either. In December 1978, the Soviets were busy building a naval base in Vietnam's Cam Ranh Bay in anticipation of the arrival of their Pacific Fleet; in January and February 1979, a number of Soviet warships were dispatched to the South China Sea to send a strong message to

Beijing of Soviet support for Vietnam. As General A. G. Gaponenko, head of Soviet military advisers in Laos recalled, in mid-January, just after Vietnam's invasion of Cambodia and several weeks before China's invasion of Vietnam, tensions between the twenty thousand Chinese army engineers, who were building roads in Laos, and the two Vietnamese divisions stationed in Laos escalated.[9] On the day China invaded Vietnam, there were fifty Soviet military advisers under the command of General Vladen Mikhailovich Mikhailov, but Mikhailov was in Moscow receiving medical treatment. General Gaponenko, as the second-highest-ranking officer in Southeast Asia, was ordered by the Soviet Union's Central Military Commission to rush to Hanoi's aid. According to General Gaponenko, Moscow decided to put six Soviet army divisions on war readiness; two infantry divisions were sent to the East, of which one division went to Mongolia. By the end of February 1979, two weeks after the Chinese invasion, the first Soviet infantry troops, Division 106, commanded by General E. Podkolzin, arrived at the Gobi Desert on the Mongolian-Chinese border.[10] By the end of February, thirteen Soviet warships had arrived on Vietnam's seacoast, and the number increased to thirty in March 1979.[11] The presence of Soviet warships there prevented some three hundred Chinese warships at Hai Nan Island (China) from participating the Chinese invasion of Vietnam.[12] These developments just before and after the Chinese invasion further suggest that the Vietnamese military leaders, and their Soviet military advisers, did not anticipate a large-scale military invasion by the PLA and so the Chinese military achieved an element of surprise. The war damage and reactions on the Vietnamese side, as I discuss in details below, provide further evidence of Vietnam's lack of military preparedness.

On February 17, 1979, when massive waves of PLA troops crossed the Sino-Vietnamese border and stormed Vietnamese defense positions in the province of Cao Bang, Prime Minister Pham Van Dong and chief of the General Staff of the PAVN Van Tien Dung were in Phnom Penh to sign a friendship treaty between the SRV and the new pro-Vietnam regime, the PRK.[13] On February 27, the entire PAVN Second Corps (thirty thousand soldiers plus armory) in Cambodia received orders to immediately return to defend the northern border of Vietnam.[14] In terms of scale, speed, and distance, the colossal transfer of an entire army corps from Cambodia to battle positions in northern Vietnam, nearly two thousand kilometers away, was unprecedented in Vietnam's military history. Soviet military units provided almost all the means of transport to move troops and the armory, which included airplanes, ships, trains, and vehicles.[15] It took two weeks. On March 6, the Second Corps command arrived at Noi Bai International Airport in Hanoi and immediately began planning the military response to the Chinese invading army. Infantry Division 304, Artillery Brigade 164, Air Force Brigade 673, and all regiments arrived in Hanoi on March 11 and took up battle positions the following day.[16] Their arrival was a little too late, for the Chinese troops had already inflicted heavy damage.

Details of the destruction caused by the Chinese invading forces are further evidence of the Vietnamese government's lack of anticipation of the Chinese attack. On March 18, the Chinese withdrew their troops, declaring that the military attacks into Vietnam had satisfied Beijing's main objective of "teaching the Vietnamese a lesson" for their anti-China behaviors. On the same day, Prime Minister Pham Van Dong dispatched three groups of cabinet officials to assess the damage. The report of the fact-finding mission reveals that the losses could have been minimized had the Vietnamese not been caught off guard. In a March 1979 summary report by a senior government delegation appointed by Pham Van Dong, the preliminary assessment based on local reports stressed four notable areas of destruction. First, almost all the houses in villages in the provinces of Lao Cai, Lang Son, Cao Bang, and Mong Cai had been destroyed by the invading Chinese troops. Second, the Chinese had laid waste to nearly all the industrial factories, equipment, and infrastructure of the central and local governments in the war zone. Third, almost all bridges, roads, and railroads were blown up by the Chinese army's mines before it withdrew. Fourth, nearly 7,000 tons of food were taken by the Chinese as trophies. Fifth, material goods worth tens of millions VND were lost. Sixth, an estimated 560,000 Vietnamese people out of 800,000 in Lang Son, Cao Bang, and Hoang Lien Son alone were homeless refugees. And, seventh, the Chinese had confiscated large quantities of weapons from military storage facilities.[17]

Just two days before the invasion, on February 15, Office 8 (Van Phong 8, or VP8) of the Prime Minister's Office—one of its major tasks was to assist the prime minister in national security matters—carried out its business as usual, mostly focusing on strengthening the six northern border provinces against China's aggression and addressing economic difficulties and emergency assistance to the newly installed PRK regime in Cambodia. The only reference to military affairs in its February activity report to the top leadership was "military and police recruitment in 1979, and the duty and power of the unified military command."[18] From the end of 1978 to the day before the Chinese invasion, Office 8 was assigned two major tasks: (1) to lead provincial authorities along the northern border to strengthen border defense and (2) to relocate all Vietnamese citizens of Chinese ethnicity from the border regions to areas inside the country,[19] as Hanoi viewed them as potential collaborators or sympathizers with China. It was not until after the Chinese invasion that Office 8 expanded its national security tasks to include recruitment of soldiers and reservists and mobilization of resources and manpower in preparation for an all-out war with China. It took the shock of the invasion to push the government to issue orders to militarize the entire nation as stipulated in Council of Government Directive 83 of March 5, 1979, which was sent to the Ministry of Defense.[20] Had Vietnamese leaders anticipated China's invasion of Vietnam in response to Vietnam's invasion of Cambodia in December 1978, they could have significantly mitigated the war damage.

To understand why Hanoi failed to anticipate the Chinese invasion, we need to return to late 1978, when Hanoi was planning a military intervention in Cambodia. Members of Hanoi's Politburo attached the highest value to Soviet aid, as they were planning the invasion while contemplating Chinese military responses. The memory of massive economic and military aid from the socialist bloc led by the Soviet Union was very strong, and Hanoi's leadership anticipated an outpouring of support from the Soviet-led socialist bloc as a reaction to China's alliance with the imperialist United States. During the resistance war against the United States for national salvation, as the Vietnamese veteran diplomat Luu Van Loi noted, military and economic aid to North Vietnam from 1955 to 1975 was valued at 6.067 billion rubles, which came mainly from the Soviet Union, China, and other socialist countries.[21] In response to China's increased aid to the Khmer Rouge and strategic cooperation with the United States, Vietnam moved closer to the Soviet Union. On June 25, 1978, Vietnam officially joined the Soviet-led COMECON, and on November 3 it signed with the Soviet Union the Treaty of Friendship and Cooperation, which would be valid for twenty-five years. In a tit-for-tat escalation of the conflict, Beijing took three major actions: mobilize members of ASEAN into a regional front of opposition to Vietnam, normalize relations with the United States, and intensify the alliance with the Khmer Rouge.[22] In mid-December 1978, China mobilized troops from five military zones to concentrate them at the Sino-Vietnamese border,[23] but Hanoi was not deterred by China's looming military threat.

On December 23, 1978, Prime Minister Pham Van Dong made the case for an invasion to topple the DK regime during the fourth session of the Sixth Plenum of the National Assembly. The Treaty of Friendship and Cooperation between the Soviet Union and Vietnam was front and center in Dong's attempt to convince his colleagues that the full backing of Soviet political, economic, and military power would preempt a Chinese retaliatory attack on Vietnam for its invasion of Cambodia. Dong hailed the Soviet Union as Vietnam's "strongest supporter" during its resistance against the French and the Americans and now in a war of "national defense" against its neighboring enemies. He told his comrades, "Provision 6 of the mutual defense treaty is the most important one. In any case where one of the two nations is attacked or threatened with attack, the two allies immediately will join force to eliminate the threat and take appropriate measures to guarantee each other's security. Comrades, do you want me to read it to you again? Let me read it again because this is a matter of utmost importance!"[24]

Dong further assured his comrades that the Treaty of Friendship and Cooperation was different from the Sino-Soviet Treaty of Friendship, Alliance, and Mutual Assistance of 1950 or the Security Treaty between the United States and Japan in 1951. He emphasized, "This treaty is not just for mutual military defense. It is a more comprehensive treaty, which will assist Vietnam with our socialist economic development and defense of our territorial sovereignty and peace and security in Southeast Asia by providing us the means to mount a resistance to Beijing's expansionism and its reactionary forces."[25] He stressed at least three times the importance of Soviet aid to Vietnam's economic development in his speech.[26]

Pham Van Dong, a moderate and economically minded leader, was attempting to persuade the economy-first faction within the party and the government that the invasion of Cambodia would not result in the deterioration of Vietnam's economy. In fact Dong made the case that the war would allow Vietnam to draw more economic aid and advanced technology from the Soviet Union and other Eastern European members of the COMECON. From 1975 to 1979, Moscow had provided financial aid of more than 4 billion rubles to Hanoi. In 1979 Moscow pledged—in addition to material aid in the form of food, fertilizer, oil, and consumption goods—to double its financial aid to approximately 8.7 billion rubles for the next five years (1980–85).[27]

In this unpublicized speech to the National Assembly on December 23, Prime Minister Pham Van Dong called for mobilizing forces and taking necessary measures to defeat Beijing's "four treacherous plots" against Vietnam, meaning the border war between Cambodia and Vietnam, Chinese residents in Vietnam, the Sino-Vietnamese border skirmishes, and Chinese propaganda against Vietnam on the world stage.[28] It is quite clear from this speech that Dong did not anticipate China's large-scale invasion of Vietnam as it later unfolded but attempted to dispel his economically minded colleagues' fear of further exacerbating the economic crisis. Ideologically aligned with the socialist superpower, the Soviet Union, even a moderate leader like Dong believed that China was "further isolated on the world stage" on the diplomatic front, drawing condemnation from the NAM. India, an important NAM leader and a South Asian great power that lost a 1962 border war with China, expressed its support of

Vietnam in the Sino-Vietnamese confrontation in material terms, reaching an important trade deal with Vietnam. Viewing world politics through the lens of the "two-camp" struggle between the socialist and capitalist blocs, Hanoi's leaders believed that their socialist bloc was on the winning side in juxtaposition with the weakening capitalist bloc in 1978. "The victory of the Cambodian revolution will also be ours," Dong remarked, referring to Vietnam's international duty to build a socialist country in Cambodia.[29] China also lost support in Africa for opposing Marxism-Leninism, dividing international socialism, and undermining national liberation movements.[30] The West, in Dong's view, would not side with China against Vietnam because it wanted to maintain trade relations with both countries. He therefore concluded, "China would not dare attack Vietnam."[31] On the border clashes with China, Dong called for vigilance and readiness to respond quickly to any emerging threat, but nowhere did he mention even the possibility of China's full-scale invasion of Vietnam. From Hanoi's vantage point, Beijing would not risk a major war with Vietnam and its ally the Soviet Union to save the DK regime in Cambodia.

Dong also emphasized the economic and political benefits of the military alliance with the Soviet Union. Hanoi's expectation was consistent with what international relations scholars call "external security," whereby the alliance would bring about closer economic and political cooperation between Vietnam and the Soviet Union. He stated, "In the treaty we have just signed with the Soviet Union, economic cooperation, as Comrade [Le Thanh] Nghi mentioned this morning, is the most important part. If we can forge effective economic cooperation with the Soviet Union and other members of the Council of Mutual Economic Assistance, then we will be able to accelerate our economic development much faster than we can now."[32] Dong stressed, "We must know how to trade and do it well. When I talk about economic cooperation, I mean we must make efforts to import modern industrial equipment and advanced technology to industrialize our socialist economy."[33] Thus Prime Minister Pham Van Dong's speech revealed Hanoi's strategic thinking that the treaty of November 3, 1978, committed the Soviet Union to providing comprehensive economic and security assistance to Vietnam. In effect, Dong made a very strong case for the invasion of Cambodia by preempting domestic concerns about China's retaliation against Vietnam and the deterioration of Vietnam's economy. With this convincing speech, he silenced any remaining dissent.

This proved to be a costly mistake when massive numbers of Chinese troops crossed the border on February 17, 1979, and the military leadership drew fierce criticism from a number of National Assembly members for its lack of preparation. Rather than having been ideologically blinded by its socialist internationalism, the Vietnamese leadership erred with overconfidence in its military power and expectations of great power support from the Soviet Union. The Vietnamese scholar Ngo Thi Thanh Tuyen observes regarding Vietnam's overconfidence, "As Vietnam won victory after victory against France and then the United States, the Vietnamese from the top leadership to cadres became delusional about their military victory, and their excessive self-confidence fed their prevailing thinking that no country would dare to invade Vietnam, at least over the next few decades."[34] Until mid-1977, it never occurred to Hanoi that the Khmer Rouge would have the audacity to launch a major military attack on Vietnam. Just days before the invasion, Pham Van Dong boasted in front of his National Assembly colleagues, "Our country is a powerful one in the region now. We defeated the French, the Japanese, and the Americans because our country has two strengths. First, we are a brave nation and possess abundant natural resources. Second, since we defeated the United States and united our country, we are stronger than ever, and no country will dare invade us again."[35]

Throughout 1978 the Vietnamese government cleared the Sino-Vietnamese border of Chinese residents suspected of siding with the Chinese government. Chinese residents along the border had been evacuated and moved deeper into the interior before the invasion. Dong told his National Assembly colleagues in regard to these relocations, "It is our sovereign right and authority to deal with our own domestic affairs, not negotiate them with China. If we do our job [of assimilation and reeducation of Vietnamese citizens of Chinese ethnicity] well, other countries with Chinese residents will learn from our experience."[36] This statement is indicative of Hanoi taking pride in imposing a policy of forced assimilation of Chinese residents, which further widened the rupture in Sino-Vietnamese relations. In material terms, as Christopher Goscha reports, Chinese in the south lost an estimated $2 billion in the late 1970s due to the nationalization of their property, businesses, and industries.[37] In all more than two hundred thousand Chinese, the majority of them people from the commercial class, fled to China, while more than six hundred thousand repatriated to non-communist countries in Asia and elsewhere.[38]

In actuality, at the national and local levels, the security threats the Vietnamese perceived regarding the Hoa Kieu (Chinese residents) of Vietnam in the late 1970s became a justification for extraordinary measures taken by the authorities. In March 1978, refugees from Vietnam started to cross the Sino-Vietnamese border; in the months of May and June of that year, the Chinese recorded 118,253 Chinese refugees crossing into southern China (mainly Guangxi, Guangdong, and Yunnan provinces), which compelled the Chinese government to allocate hundreds of millions of US dollars to address the refugee crisis.[39] Beneath the conflict between China and Vietnam, the lived experiences of Chinese residents fleeing to southern China demonstrated the Vietnamese government's systematic persecution of them, including purges of Vietnamese cadres with Chinese spouses, arrests of cadres for spying for China, and expulsion of a wide range of teachers and professionals of Chinese descent.[40] A Chinese researcher wrote in 1980, "Most bitter are the stories of old revolutionaries who fought hard for Ho Chi Minh and Vietnam. No matter what wonderful work was done, wounds, privations, rank, decorations, all of those with Chinese blood in their veins were thrown out of office and either managed to get to China, or else were sent to the waste lands [the so-called New Economic Zones].[41]

Well before the Chinese invasion, Office 8 of the Prime Minister's Office was put in charge of recruitment to beef up the armed forces (military and police) and reported to the standing committee of the Council of Government on this issue.[42] Office 8's main task from the end of 1978 to early 1979 (before the Chinese invasion) was to assist the Council of Government in strengthening national defense and war preparedness to prevent China from invading Vietnam.[43] Office 8 played a more important role in shaping the military-first policy after 1979 by actively recruiting young men and women with talent in various fields into the army and introducing various pro-military policies, including increasing payments to families of disabled veterans and deceased soldiers.[44] In his internal assessment, Phuong Minh Nam, vice-chairman of Office 8, wrote, "When the Chinese invaded, we were able to recruit and build local defense forces and mobilize local resources swiftly."[45]

The second task of Office 8 was to provide policy input to strengthen social and political order (domestic security). Office 8 was to report on efforts to combat corruption and bribery, abuses of power, oppression of the population, and violations of state law, as mandated by Directive 228. In its report to the Council of Government, Office 8 stated, "Law enforcement remains weak and has failed to address people's complaints." However, it took great pride in its ability to "prepare northern border provinces well and strengthen border defense" well before the Chinese invasion in February 1979. That included "relocation of ethnic Chinese people from the border region to areas deep inside the country" and neutralizing ethnic Chinese residents' ability to collaborate with and offer intelligence to the invading Chinese troops.[46] Ethnic Chinese residents (Hoa Kieu) in Vietnam had a changing relationship with the CPV, evolving from being seen as favorable in the 1950s and 1960s to threatening in the second half of the 1970s in parallel with the deterioration of Sino-Vietnamese relations.[47]

Immediately Hanoi claimed a military victory over the Chinese invaders with an official figure of Chinese casualties. According to a report by the SRV

Council of Ministers dated May 29, 1979, "Our army and people had heroically fought back the Chinese invading troops in six border provinces, causing them heavy losses: Over 60,000 Chinese troops were put out of action [dead or injured]. 550 military vehicles, including 280 tanks and armored vehicles, were damaged or destroyed. Hundreds of artillery guns and large caliber mortars were destroyed. A great number of weapons and invading troops were captured.[48]

Internal Vietnamese documents suggested that the Chinese succeeded in adding an element of surprise to its invasion of Vietnam by sounding false alarms of a pending Chinese invasion as early February 1978, one year before the actual invasion in February 1979. But besides small border skirmishes, there was no Chinese invasion. A series of secret reports by the Police Command of the Ministry of the Interior revealed that Chinese villagers in Lung Hiu (China) had spread the rumor that China would launch a major attack on Vietnam during the New Year (Tet) in late February 1978. Vietnamese villagers were scared, and many left their homes near the border. In Quang Ninh Province, villagers also spread rumors that on New Year's Day, February 29, Chinese troops would attack Hoang Mo and that, as Chinese troops mobilized, Chinese villagers had left the border area, suggesting a pending invasion. The Police Command of the Ministry of the Interior instructed local forces and authorities to stay alert but also be vigilant about the Chinese use of psychological warfare to scare Vietnamese people along the border.[49]

Internal Criticism of the Lack of Military Preparedness

Although Vietnamese propaganda lauded the party and government's farsightedness and accurate assessment of China's treacherous intention behind the Khmer Rouge attacks on Vietnam, internal debates were contentious.[50] Many party members criticized the party and government for a "lack of vigilance and overconfidence," which had resulted in a significant loss of life and property during the Chinese invasion.

Evidence from internal reports and debates immediately after China's invasion of Vietnam in the five-month period from the fourth session to the fifth session of the Sixth Plenum of the National Assembly clearly reveals that Vietnam did not anticipate and was therefore not well prepared for a large-scale invasion by China. Before the Chinese withdrew their troops from Vietnam on March 5, 1979, Vietnam's own records revealed additional war losses: "Many villages and towns were razed to the ground and communications lines, production equipment, medical stations, and schools were destroyed completely.

The towns of Lang Son, Cao Bang, Lao Cai, and Cam Duong were reduced to ruins. About 330 villages, 735 schools, 428 hospitals and medical stations, 41 farms, 48 forestry enterprises, 81 enterprises and mines, and 80,000 hectares of food crops were destroyed. About half of the 3.5 million people in the six border provinces lost their residences; thousands of Vietnamese, including the elderly, women, and children, were killed or wounded, not counting the cultural and historical monuments that were reduced to rubble."[51]

Shocked by the scope of the devastation, Prime Minister Pham Van Dong's fact-finding delegation proposed that the government take urgent action to address three pressing issues: (1) stabilization of people's livelihoods, restoration of social order and security, resumption of agricultural production, and provision of food and shelter in the border provinces; (2) emergency assistance for the military buildup and war preparedness along the border; and (3), most important, instilling new thinking within the government and party apparatus, a shift from a peace to a war mentality.[52]

While the prime minister's delegation was assessing the situation, the Vietnamese government's delivery of emergency aid to the Sino-Vietnamese border regions was under way. The management of the aid further revealed Hanoi's unpreparedness for the attack. In the first week of March, as China was about to withdraw its troops, the Vietnamese Ministry of Internal Trade was able to transport its first major shipment of food to forces at the front, a total of 750 tons of food (320 tons of fish sauce, 300 tons of dried meat, and 130 tons of fresh meat and canned fish) along with 300,000 salted eggs. The MoD made an urgent request for a further 800 tons of meat by the end of March.[53] The Organization Committee of the Party Central Committee under Le Duc Tho made a request to the Ministry of Internal Trade that party officials from the district level up in the six provinces along the Sino-Vietnamese border be offered an extra food ration of 1 kilogram of sugar, 4 cans of condensed milk, and 1 kilogram of canned meat per month on top of their base salaries.[54]

With respect to emergency transportation, Hanoi was ill prepared for war against China and the state bureaucracy was so fractured that transportation to the frontlines along the Sino-Vietnamese border was slow and often interrupted by poor road conditions and ruined bridges. For three weeks, from the day of the invasion to the day China withdrew its troops from Vietnam, the ministry was able to transport only half the planned 2,700 tons of food to eight provinces affected by the war and internal displacement. Worse, due to transportation problems, mountainous border provinces such as Cao Bang, which was devastated by the invasion, received less than 10 percent of the planned food shipment.[55] Food shortages became a national security issue as the Vietnamese attempted to beef up its border defenses against future Chinese attacks. The Ministry of Internal Trade shifted the blame to the Ministry of Transport for the failure to meet the critical need for sufficient food for the Vietnamese population and troops along the Sino-Vietnamese border. In its report to Prime Minister Pham Van Dong, the Ministry of Internal Trade pointed to the poor infrastructure, including jammed rail systems, shortages of transportation vehicles and fuel, and poor coordination and organization. It also highlighted the fact that "some [government] agencies, particularly in the area of transportation, have not yet transformed their old thinking and practices from peace to wartime,"[56] referring to the country's dependence on foreign aid during the anti-American resistance period of 1965–75. For instance, the Lai Chau Provincial Committee's urgent request for rice was approved on March 3, 1979, but by March 12 no rice trucks had arrived in the province.

To guarantee timely transportation from Son La to Lai Chau, a mountainous province bordering the province of Yunnan in China, the government approved a plan to reinforce the Ministry of Transport with three hundred new trucks, but by mid-March it had received only thirty. At a number of train stations, the General Railway Directorate was not able to mobilize enough workers to unload cargo, which significantly slowed rail transport. An average of thirty-three train cars were left unloaded for days at the Luu Xa train station and seventeen others at the Quang Trieu station (Thai Nguyen Province) connecting Hanoi and the Cao Bang Plateau bordering the Chinese province of Guangxi. Despite a desperate need for material aid, some local authorities failed to organize enough manpower to unload, transport, and store goods, further impeding delivery of aid to the border provinces.[57]

Following the Chinese withdrawal, Hanoi mobilized over 200,000 people to work on border defense projects. Each worker was allotted 21 kilograms of food per month, including 18 kilograms of rice and corn, half a kilogram of meat, one kilogram of fish, one kilogram of tofu, half a liter of fish sauce, and three salted eggs in addition to a salary of 24 Vietnamese dong (VND) per month.[58]

In actuality, as it was about to launch its full-scale invasion of Cambodia in late 1978, the Hanoi leadership called for preparation to defend its northern flank against a Chinese invasion plot, but it clearly did not contemplate a large-scale invasion with massive numbers of Chinese soldiers. From late 1978 to early 1979, Office 8 of the Prime Minister's Office played a crucial role in assisting the Council of Government with war preparations along the northern border. On the day China invaded Vietnam, the government quickly disseminated the party's and government's directives to local authorities and mobilized local armed forces to defend the country. They moved swiftly to secure the loyalty of ethnic minorities living along the Sino-Vietnamese border and convinced them to fight the Chinese. They pledged more state aid to take care of the minority population and the families of combatants.[59]

Xiaoming Zhang has repudiated the claim that "Vietnam had committed only militia and local forces, who executed constant attacks against Chinese invaders."[60] He writes, "Vietnam's 1979 war records remain unavailable. However, the publication of PAVN unit histories reveals that a significant number of Vietnamese regular forces fought against the Chinese invasion, including some that engaged in 'last-stand' actions before being overwhelmed by resolute PLA attacks."[61] Internally circulated documents corroborate Zhang's argument. On May 28, 1979, war hero General Vo Nguyen Giap, a ranking member of the Politburo, deputy prime minister, and minister of defense, reported to the National Assembly that three types of armed forces, including regular Military Region forces,[62] local armed forces, and citizen-soldiers of the six provinces along the Sino-Vietnamese border, were involved in the battle against the Chinese invaders.[63]

The state's official articulation of Vietnamese heroism and patriotism was rendered by none other than Vietnam's war hero, General Vo Nguyen Giap, at the fifth session of the Sixth Plenum of the National Assembly in May 1979. On behalf of the Council of Government, Giap presented a lengthy report entitled "The Great Victory of the Two Wars to Defend the Motherland and the Duties of Our People and Army in the New Situation" on May 28."[64] According to Giap, the fifth session was convened mainly to discuss "the meaning and causes of Vietnam's victory" in the two wars, "China's intentions," "Vietnam's international duty in Cambodia," and "the Vietnamese people's duty in the new situation."[65]

The handwritten minutes of the National Assembly representatives' discussions of General Giap's report, which was kept secret at the time, revealed some notable criticisms of the report and raised additional issues about the conduct of the wars.[66] Although all representatives agreed with General Giap's conclusion regarding the causes of Vietnam's victories—"the capable and farsighted leadership of the Party, the bravery of Vietnamese people and soldiers, and the strength of Vietnam's national unity"—many suggested that the report fell short of acknowledging local realities or shortcomings. Most important, the National Assembly debate arrived at this conclusion: "Our victory could have been greater if we had not been blindsided by overconfidence, which led to mistakes in the conduct of the war."[67] Chairman of the National Assembly Standing Committee Truong Chinh and eleven other high-ranking Assembly members from Hanoi, Ho Chi Minh City, and Hai Phong called for a thorough investigation of the causes of negligence and heavy punishment for officials who made the mistakes that caused serious loss of the state's and people's property in order to restore people's trust in the party and the government.[68]

Some members of the Assembly directly blamed the party's leadership for its "lack of vigilance" and "incorrect assessment of China's intentions" in direct opposition to General Giap's rosy report. Assembly member Nguyen Ky Uc from the province of Cuu Long (in southern Vietnam) stressed the colossal lack of vigilance of the top leadership.[69] He recalled that at a conference on counter-offensives in the southwest against the Khmer Rouge in late December 1978, a number of provincial authorities raised the issue of China's retaliatory attacks in the north, but the leadership appeared to ignore such concerns and did not anticipate China's invasion of Vietnam. Shortly before the war in the north broke out, even some high-ranking party officials from the Nguyen Ai Quoc School (political training school of the Central Committee of the CPV) stated with great confidence, "The Chinese do not dare face off with us yet."[70] Echoing his southern colleagues, Vo Van Pham, a representative from Ben-Tre, pointed out, "We underestimated the enemy. In previous reports, our Vietnamese military leaders called China a 'paper tiger.'"[71]

Regarding military strategy, Nguyen Ky Uc criticized the Vietnamese military leadership for its underperformance. In an internal debate, Uc said, "There was nothing new about the Chinese military strategy in their invasion of Vietnam [referring to China's dispatch of large expedition forces to invade Vietnam in the distant past], but why didn't we achieve a decisive military victory like the battles of Dong Da or Bach Dang?"[72] Uc's colleagues Vo Van Day, Le Thi Sau, and Tran Thi Minh Hoang, from the three southern provinces of An Giang, Kien Giang, and Dong Nai, joined the fray, arguing that "due to our lack of vigilance and incorrect assessment of the threat from China, all the Cambodian cadres we trained were killed by the Pol Pot–Ieng Sary clique and our economic foundation in the north was destroyed by the Chinese invaders."[73]

After China withdrew its troops from Vietnam on March 18, 1979, military confrontations continued along the border. From the Vietnamese perspective, China was still engaging in sustained sabotage against the Vietnamese government. Various local reports convinced Hanoi's leaders that China was trying to create ethnic conflict by stirring up animosity between ethnic Vietnamese (the Kinh people) and other ethnic minorities in Vietnamese provinces along the Chinese border and was using Chinese residents inside Vietnam as a Trojan horse for Beijing's plot to incite an internal uprising in Vietnam. In one internal debate, a National Assembly member warned, "China has attempted to connect with reactionaries in our society to start internal rebellions. China is appealing to Chinese residents, especially in the south, to side with them against our party and government. We need to pay attention to the problem of Chinese residents in the south, especially their political tendencies and economic power. We need to issue an appropriate policy regarding the Chinese residents."[74] Evidently Chinese residents in Vietnam faced more severe persecution by the Vietnamese government after the Chinese invasion in 1979.

Nguyen Tan Lap, a representative from the southern province of Hau Giang, suggested that the party should cleanse itself of the remaining Chinese influence in the leadership and the country's major economic sectors because Vietnam had tolerated excessive Chinese influence in the past.[75] However, Assembly members Luu Huu Phuoc and Duong Viet Trung from the province of Hau Giang (in the Mekong Delta in southern Vietnam) warned that, although the war further justified persecution of the remaining Chinese residents, who were already being treated as "suspected collaborators with Beijing" in the south, "In our propaganda, we must make sure that our people understand clearly that our enemy is the Chinese expansionists' clique in Beijing, and we must not call them our 'hereditary enemy'—the term used by *Nhan Dan* [the party newspaper]—because we need to seek harmony with Chinese people and persuade them to oppose Beijing's expansionist policy."[76]

In 1979, as Vietnam's economic crisis continued, the Vietnamese government demanded that people make more sacrifices for national defense. In internal debates, a representative from the province of Tien Giang (southern Vietnam) complained that the majority of the seven thousand teachers in his province had quit their jobs because they could not bear the hard life of their profession.[77] The representative from Dong Thap called for a "Vietnam-first" policy, suggesting that the Vietnamese government should curtail aid to Cambodia and instead help Cambodia help itself by "exploiting its rich national resources, including its fisheries and forests."[78] Clearly criticism of the Vietnamese government veered into Vietnam's heavy burden of nation building in Cambodia.

Many challenged General Vo Nguyen Giap's claim that the Soviet Union was doing its part under the 1978 Treaty of Friendship and Cooperation. To be sure, General Giap wrote, "The Soviet Union immediately condemned China's invasion of Vietnam and provided timely aid in many fields to meet our needs. On March 2, 1979, Comrade Brezhnev declared, "We are absolutely united with Vietnam, and no one should have any doubt about the Soviet Union's commitment to the Treaty of Friendship and Cooperation that binds our two countries."[79] However, National Assembly member Lam Thi Mai from the province of An Giang argued that the Soviet Union's condemnation of China's invasion of Vietnam was "rather weak."[80]

In summary, postinvasion debates within the party circle reveal an element of surprise and miscalculation in Vietnam's strategic thinking about the defense of the northern flank against China. Party officials privately criticized their party and government leaders for not sending PAVN regular forces to fight the invading Chinese troops sooner. As a result, the loss of property and lives was enormous. Nevertheless, the overriding narrative that emerged after the Chinese invasion, as General Giap emphasized, is filled with heroism and the victories of local citizen-soldiers and armed forces in districts along the Sino-Vietnamese border. The historical narrative is registered as another episode of Vietnamese people fearlessly standing up to northern Chinese invaders, as their ancestors did against Chinese dynasties for two thousand years in the distant past.

The Primacy of the Military-First Policy

Rising in power and influence behind this heroic narrative is the military wing of the party and government. General Giap took pride in his strategy of treating the entire district as a defense fortress (*Ca huyen la mot phao dai*).[81] From February 17 to March 18, 1979, Vietnam claimed to have removed (killed or injured) more than 60,000 Chinese soldiers from battle, destroying three Chinese regiments and sixteen battalions. In addition, Vietnam claimed to have destroyed 550 military vehicles, including 280 tanks and armored vehicles, 115 artillery pieces, and many heavy mortar cannons; captured a large quantity of weaponry and military equipment; and taken many Chinese prisoners.[82] Vietnam's estimate of Chinese casualties is close to that of western observers: 26,000 killed and 37,000 wounded.[83] This is three times higher than the 20,000 killed and wounded that Beijing acknowledged publicly. According to historian Xiaoming Zhang's calculation of casualties in two Chinese military regions, based on Chinese sources, PLA casualties totaled more than 31,000 soldiers (5,103 dead and 15,412 injured in Guangxi and 2,812 killed and 7,886 wounded in Yunnan).[84] We may never know the full truth due to the fog of war and each side's propensity to inflate the casualties of the other side to justify its own narrative of victory.

The Chinese claimed to have killed 57,000 Vietnamese soldiers, captured 2,200 prisoners of war; destroyed 340 pieces of artillery, 45 tanks, and 480 trucks; and captured 840 pieces of artillery and more than 11,000 small arms, along with many other types of military equipment.[85] In addition, the Guangzhou Military Region claimed that its forces captured 226 tanks, 457 artillery pieces, 8,298 small arms, 230,000 rounds of shells, 8 million rounds of small arms ammunition, and 2,635 tons of food.[86] General Giap's official report to the

National Assembly on May 28, 1979, did not give an accounting of the Vietnamese casualties in this war but focused solely on the "meaning and causes of Vietnam's victory in the two wars in defense of the motherland," as General Giap termed it.[87]

Focusing on the number of casualties may miss the point because what fueled the war machine on both sides in the 1980s was the *truths* manufactured by Hanoi and Beijing to perpetuate their respective narratives of great victory, transmit a collective memory of heroism, and instill patriotism in the minds of the citizenry.[88] For Hanoi's leaders, the purpose of the narrative of "the great victory in the two wars in defense of the motherland" was to situate contemporary Vietnamese heroism in the historical metanarrative of defeating foreign invaders, particularly China, in order to arouse the Vietnamese people's patriotism and ask them to make the ultimate sacrifice for the nation.[89] The CPV was determined to draw on Vietnamese nationalism to mobilize resources and manpower for its two-front military confrontations in Cambodia and against China.

On December 22, 1979, General Secretary Le Duan stated on the thirty-fifth anniversary of the establishment of the PAVN: "The People's Army must be a large and popular school for the younger generation, training our youth to become new [revolutionary] men, good soldiers, and good producers."[90] Military hero General Vo Nguyen Giap wrote, "Our people's tasks of building our country and defending our nation are closely linked. As Uncle Ho reminds us, 'Our ancestors, the Hung Vuong (King Hung), built our nation, and you and I together have a duty to protect our country.'"[91] Like other Vietnamese nationalists in the 1950s and 1960s, General Giap emphasized the fighting spirit of the Vietnamese in the tradition of resistance to foreign aggression dating back to King Hung.[92] While nationalism evoked patriotic emotion in the Vietnamese people, the government backed it up with strict law enforcement and the full power of the state, asserting its control over every aspect of national life. Following a short-lived peace after 1975, Vietnam turned into a heavily militarized state in 1979–80, on top of having been a police state before that.

Throughout 1978, in preparation for national defense, the People's Prosecutor—the highest and most powerful law enforcement organ of the state—launched a sweeping operation to cleanse the country of internal "bad elements," including those who engaged in abuses of power, corruption, bribery, extortion, avoidance of military duty, and refusal to move to the New Economic Zones.[93] The People's Prosecutor also played a crucial role in spreading propaganda, disseminated the law on military duty, punished those who evaded military duty, and reeducated them to return to military service. In addition, the People's Prosecutor hunted down enemies burrowing within the masses and the party apparatus who were suspected of sabotaging the state policy of military conscription, committing bribery, or issuing fake documents to those who evaded military duty and those who stole salaries, embezzled the state benefits of military families, or stole the belongings of dead soldiers.[94]

In June 1978 the People's Prosecutor called an urgent meeting and instructed officials at its branches in the seven provinces along the Sino-Vietnamese border to discuss urgent measures for dealing with China. In September it held a similar conference for representatives from Military Regions 5, 7, and 9, the PAVN regular army, and the CMC to purge hidden enemies in the local population along the southwestern border with Cambodia. Internal purging was intended to strengthen local armed forces, enhance military discipline, and tighten political and social order in the border regions.[95] The People's Prosecutor's report to the National Assembly read, "Internal social and political order is a high priority [for this office]. Especially when the reactionary leaders in Beijing have betrayed and opposed us, the reactionary elements [ethnic Chinese citizens in Vietnam] in our country may have the idea that the opportunity to sabotage us has arrived."[96] The People's Prosecutor stressed that in the battle against China in the north and the Khmer Rouge in Cambodia, it was important to raise the political understanding of local people and local authorities in the border regions and alert them to enemy elements hiding among them.[97]

The year 1979 was very difficult for Vietnam as it was engaged in both the military confrontation with China and the rebuilding of the PRK, under a pro-Vietnam regime, in postgenocide Cambodia in addition to contending with socioeconomic hardship at home. On the home front, Hanoi focused on three strategic tasks: (1) stabilizing people's livelihoods, (2) strengthening national defense and security, and (3) building a material and technical base to meet national defense needs. Vietnamese leaders also called on the nation to focus on two urgent economic duties: (1) concentrating on agricultural production, mainly grains and other foodstuffs, to stabilize farmers' livelihoods, and (2) increasing exports to guarantee imports of vital goods and pay down the national debt.[98] The Politburo's Resolution 228, augmented by the prime minister's Directive 159, granted more power to the People's Prosecutor to tighten social and political order and eradicate abuses of power, corruption, and waste of government property in order to increase people's trust in the party and government.[99] From the outset, the CPV and the government systematically fueled anti-China nationalism and Vietnamese anger over Chinese brutality during the four-week invasion of Vietnam in 1979. General Giap summed up the most important lesson of the war against the Chinese invaders in his report to the National Assembly on May 28, 1979, as follows:

The heroism of our local armed forces and citizen-soldiers in the six provinces along the Sino-Vietnamese border defeated the might of 600,000 Chinese regular troops. This victory marked a new military capability—that is, the combined power of our three types of armed forces, the police, and the people at the locality. One Vietnamese person killed 100 or even 150 Chinese invaders. On average the ratio of those killed and injured is 1 Vietnamese soldier to at least 30 Chinese soldiers. The enemy prepared to inflict this war on us for two decades, and even though our country faced much difficulty after thirty years of war, we still defeated the Chinese.[100]

General Giap's report spoke of the brutality and the policy of total destruction of the Chinese invaders, including the Chinese policy of "kill all, loot all, and destroy all"; indiscriminate killing of the women, children, and the elderly; and vicious killing methods such as beheading and burning people alive.[101]

Defining Vietnam's military confrontation with China as a life-and-death national security imperative, the conservative and military-first faction within the party and government demanded that the entire populace and military demonstrate their loyalty to the party and government and make further sacrifices for the cause of national defense. As mentioned earlier, the conservative leader Le Duc Tho, who controlled the powerful Organization Commission of the Party Central Committee, had already demanded that more resources be diverted to party cadres in the border provinces to boost national defense.[102] The state reiterated the importance of rebalancing the country's economic production and national defense, demanding that local people be economically self-sufficient and ready to fight the Chinese invaders under the slogan "Every district is a fortress."[103] General Giap wrote, "Every district is a comprehensive economic management unit, a strong agricultural-industrial economic foundation for building a new life in the countryside and a strong fortress ready for battle to defend its local territory and capable of meeting its logistical needs on site."[104] On March 5, 1979, the Standing Committee of the National Assembly approved the Council of Government's request for the "total mobilization of the nation's manpower and resources to defeat the invading [Chinese] troops and defend its independence and territorial integrity."[105]

As Vietnam was at war, economic corruption was singled out as a "social evil," which served to further discredit top economic planners, especially those who managed the economy and state resources. In particular, Deputy Prime Minister Le Thanh Nghi, chairman of the State Planning Committee, and Deputy Prime Minister Vo Chi Cong, minister of agriculture, soon took the blame. The call for harsher punishment of corruption within the party apparatus came from National Assembly members. As the country was at war, these law-makers pointed to the disease of chronic corruption and waste in the party and government, which eroded people's trust. Regarding food distribution, for instance, party members Ha Ke Tan and Hoang Minh Giam from Ha-Son-Binh called attention to the fact that there remained "many cases of corruption and waste of state assets in the economic field."[106] Party officials Nguyen Tho Chan and Pham Thi Ngam from Hai Phong leveled harsher criticisms against the party and government, stating, "The National Assembly met many times, and there has been a lot of criticism about social evils like corruption, waste, and abuse of power, but we have not yet seen any improvement on this front."[107] During a span of five months from December 1978 to May 1979, the Standing Committee of the National Assembly received fifteen hundred complaints about local party officials' corruption and abuse of power.[108] This was a serious issue that would further erode people's trust in the government. Discontent with the government was high even before the Chinese invasion, and people were now being asked to consume less and contribute more to support a prolonged military confrontation with China while corruption and abuse of power were rampant.

In 1979–80 Truong Chinh remained firmly in the conservative camp. The party's leading theoretician, Truong Chinh believed that the pendulum of history had once again swung in Vietnam's favor, with the Soviet Union and the international socialist bloc strongly supporting its stand against reactionary China, which was aligned with the imperialist United States. In his opening remarks to the fifth session of the 6th Plenum of the National Assembly in early March 1979,[109] Chinh also attributed Vietnam's victory to the long-standing Vietnamese nationalist tradition of "fighting the enemy and protecting the country" (*danh giac giu nuoc*), recalling the Vietnamese people's resistance to northern aggression by Chinese dynasties.[110] Thus Marxist-Leninist ideology and traditional Vietnamese nationalism colored Chinh's assessment of Vietnam's position in the world and its national strength.

In 1980, in a grand scheme of mass propaganda, one of Truong Chinh's books, *On Kampuchea*, was published in both Vietnamese and English. In this book, he began with a historical analogy to characterize China's strategy of using to the Khmer Rouge to weaken Vietnam from the south in December 1978 before Chinese invasion of Vietnam from the north in February 1979. Chinh wrote, "In implementing its anti-Vietnam policy, Beijing repeated the offensive strategy applied time and time again by feudal China in its history of invasions against Vietnam, namely, combining a direct offensive with rear attacks. In the eleventh century, when Vietnam was ruled by the Ly dynasty, the

Sung dynasty in China, in collusion with the king of Champa, used the Cham army in incursions on Vietnam's southern border to weaken Vietnamese resistance to the Sung army's attack from the north."[111] Hanoi's leaders did not take this historical lesson to heart in 1978–79.

On March 5, 1979, the National Assembly's Standing Committee, under Provision 53 of the 1959 constitution, issued an order for general mobilization for war. On the same day, the Council of Government issued Directive 83-CP, militarizing the entire population to defend the country, and instituted a new regulation mandating that every citizen work ten hours per day—eight hours for production and two hours for military training or national defense duty.[112]

There were also key changes to the membership of the Council of Government in the first half of 1979. On February 23, 1979, Deputy Prime Minister Vo Chi Cong was stripped of his portfolio as the minister of agriculture, and Nguyen Ngoc Triu was appointed in his place.[113] Ho Viet Thang replaced Ngo Minh Loan as minister of grains and foodstuffs, and Deputy Prime Minister Huynh Tan Phat was given another portfolio as chairman of state construction.[114] On May 24 Vice-Minister Nguyen Co Thach was appointed minister without portfolio to assist the prime minister with foreign affairs.[115]

Notable was the rising influence of military leaders, including Lieutenant General Hoang Van Thai and Major General Dang Kinh on the Standing Committee of the Council of Government, the highest executive committee. On January 24, 1979, Lieutenant General Hoang Van Thai, vice-chief of General Staff of the PAVN, on behalf of the Council of Government, delivered a fervent speech on the military victory in the two-front war against the Khmer Rouge in December 1978 and against China's invasion in February 1979.[116] On the same day, Vo Dong Giang, vice-minister of foreign affairs and a former army general, was appointed to replace Pham Van Ba as Vietnam's ambassador to the PRK.[117] On February 23, after Prime Minister Pham Van Dong's report to the Standing Committee of the National Assembly about the signing of the Treaty of Peace, Friendship, and Cooperation between the Socialist Republic of Vietnam and the People's Republic of Kampuchea, Major General Dang Kinh, second vice-chief of General Staff of the PAVN, delivered a nationalistic speech about China's invasion of Vietnam, glorifying the heroic fighting of local Vietnamese forces. On April 23, Major General Cao Van Khanh, third vice-chief of General Staff of the PAVN, reported to the Standing Committee on "the great victory of the Vietnamese people and army in their resistance to China's invasion."[118] On the same day, after Khanh's report, Vu Tuan, minister of the Prime Minister's Office, reported on the government's measures undertaken to overcome the effects of China's invasion in the six provinces bordered with China; Vice-Minister of

Foreign Affairs Phan Hien then reported on the Sino-Vietnamese diplomatic negotiations at the vice-ministerial level, which began on April 18 in Hanoi.

In contrast to the military leaders' glorious victory speeches, Vu Tuan, minister of the Prime Minister's Office, reported massive destruction in the northern border provinces caused by the invasion and underlined the monumental and urgent tasks of restoring normalcy to people's livelihoods and economic productivity. In April and May 1979, the Standing Committee of the National Assembly conducted its own on-site visit to the northern border provinces impacted by the invasion. It appointed Dao Van Tap, a member of the Standing Committee and vice-chairman of the Planning and Budget Committee of the National Assembly, as head of the National Assembly delegation to study the situation in war-affected regions in provinces bordered with China.[119] After on-site visits, the delegation also witnessed the heavy burden of rebuilding the war-ravaged regions in the northern border provinces.

In an attempt to glorify military service and restore morale, the Vietnamese government began to pay more attention to veterans and military personnel. On May 24, 1979, acting on a request from the Council of Government, the Standing Committee of the National Assembly awarded sixteen Ho Chi Minh medals to Vietnamese military leaders for their outstanding contributions to the anti-American resistance along with Military Achievement (Quan cong) and Combat Achievement (Chien cong) medals to 10,218 soldiers from 938 units for defending the border against the Khmer Rouge's and China's aggression in 1978–79. The committee awarded Resistance (Khang chien) medals to 263 families that had many family members serving in the army during the anti-American resistance period. Glorious Soldier (Chien si ve vang) medals were awarded to 91,011 cadres and soldiers in the police force and army.[120] The Vietnamese government's attempt to glorify military service after the Chinese invasion stood in stark contrast to the rather poor treatment of veterans and families of deceased soldiers when the war ended in 1975.

On February 11, 1980, the Council of Government issued Directive 44-CP calling for military mobilization in two different scenarios: one in which war had not yet broken out between Vietnam and China, and the other in which the two countries were at war.[121] In the first situation, workers in key economic sectors, including transportation, telecommunications, electricity, coal, oil refineries, and logging, and workers who operated machinery in agriculture, construction, and irrigation were exempt from military service. Also exempt were core leaders of villages, schools, and production units at the local level and heads of household or family breadwinners, the only remaining son of a military family, the only son of a family, cadres of agricultural cooperatives and forestry units in northern border provinces and the Western Highlands, high school teachers, lecturers at professional schools and universities, students in professional schools, and students who had passed their exams to enter university in 1980.[122] Military conscription was carried out in two rounds. The first round was to be completed in April, followed by a second round in September of that year. In the case of war with China, conscription would be widened to include grade twelve high school students and first- and second-year university students.

Directive 44 was the result of a debate between the military and economic factions of the government, namely, Minister of Defense General Vo Nguyen Giap and Chairman of the State Planning Committee Le Thanh Nghi.[123] This executive directive determined two strategic directions for national defense in 1980. First, if war did not break out between Vietnam and China, key economic sectors were to be off limits to the state's extractions for national defense. However, if the country was at war with China, the MoD would automatically have the power to extract the nation's human and material resources at will, with a few restrictions, for the purpose of defending the nation against China's military aggression.[124] The policy compromise reflected the tensions between two necessities: national defense and economic development.

On February 25, 1980, the Council of Government issued Directive 58-CP, granting the MoD far-reaching authority to mobilize human and material resources in all fields at all levels of the state apparatus—not even local authorities were spared military obligations—to support the war effort. Provision 3 of Directive 58-CP granted more authority to the minister of defense to coordinate with vice-ministers in all ministries, general directorates, government agencies of the Council of Government, and the general secretary of People's Committees (governors) in all provinces and cities under the leadership of the Central Committee of the CPV. The minister of defense was instructed to sign contracts for resource mobilization with other government agencies by March 15. If war broke out with China, Directive 58-CP would automatically become the general order for war. The State Planning Committee was responsible for issuing reports on this issue to the Standing Committee of the Council of Government.[125]

Shortly after the directive went into effect, various ministries and local authorities raised serious concerns about the adverse effects of the MoD's military conscription plan on agricultural production and the food supply. On February 29, Deputy Prime Minister To Huu, a conservative in the government, was instructed by Prime Minister Pham Van Dong to issue urgent instructions to all general secretaries of People's Committees in provinces and cities under the supervision of the party and all ministries under the leadership of the Council of Government to temporarily freeze military conscription.[126]

Balancing military capability and economic productivity was increasingly difficult as a result of the protracted war in Cambodia and military confrontation with China. In a top-secret letter to the prime minister dated March 19, 1980, Pham Nien, director of the General Directorate of Telecommunications and Post, complied with the MoD's demand that he conscript 103 university graduates or seniors in this field to serve in the army. He reserved only 25 out of 75 transport vehicles the MoD had requested.[127] In asking the prime minister to let him supply fewer vehicles, Nien reasoned that if the state took such a large quantity of vehicles from his department he would not be able to perform his political duty—that is, dissemination of the party's political works.[128] By October 1979 the Ministry of University and Professional Training Schools signed a contract with the Ministry of Defense to enlist into the army a total of 1,819 university graduates in various fields from construction to engineering.[129]

The Ministry of Transport met the MoD's demand for a total of 1,300 transport vehicles for military service but fell short on providing small vehicles, ships, ferries, and boats. It could provide only 69 out of 190 engineers and technicians and 400 out of 580 electricians and mechanics requested by the MoD.[130] Vice-Minister of Transport Binh Tam asked Prime Minister Pham Van Dong to exempt his ministry from military training because his officials were busy transporting material aid to Cambodia and Laos.[131] For 1980, 60,000 tons of rice, of which 11,000 tons were to be urgently dispatched to the six provinces along the Sino-Vietnamese border by April 1980, further constrained the Ministry of Transport's capacity.[132] The debate over logistical priorities further demonstrated Hanoi's sudden shift from a balance between economic development and national defense priorities to "everything is for the frontlines" against China. On April 15, in an agreement penned by Vice-Minister of Defense Major General Dinh Duc Thien, the Ministry of Health was to directed provide 90 medical doctors, 40 pharmacists, 300 medical school graduates, and 265 out of 533 assistants to medical doctors, which was the quota set by the MoD.[133] In addition, a large quantity of medicine and equipment, including 8,000 patient beds and 12 vehicles that served as mobile clinics, were funneled to the military.[134]

National defense trumped economic concerns. In a top-secret report sent by the MoD to the prime minister on September 4, 1980, Vice-Minister Vu Xuan Chiem expressed that he was pleased with the results of resource mobilization for 1980. The MoD signed agreements with 21 out of 28 ministries and 13 out of 19 provinces in Military Regions 2, 3, and 4 and the Special Zone of the province of Quang Ninh.[135] By September, the MoD had recruited 82,000 soldiers (73,900 male and 8,100 female) out of the quota of 100,000 in the north. The remaining 20,000 were to be recruited in the south. A total of 6,121 technicians and 3,108 university graduates and final-year students were conscripted into military service that year. Military conscription, however, was not yet carried out in the south by September 1980.[136]

In addition, 3,530 vehicles, the majority of which were transport vehicles, were transferred from various economic sectors to the military.[137] For 1980, the Ministry of Materials Supply allocated for national defense 5,425 tons of iron, 144 tons of corrugated sheets, 11,448 tons of steel, 34,900 tons of coal, 410 tons of aluminum, 7,000 sets of tires, and 2,000 tons of fuel.[138] The vice-minister of the Ministry of Materials Supply informed Prime Minister Pham Van Dong of the ministry's inability to provide all the materials requested by the MoD and asked that the number of engineers the MoD demanded for military service be reduced so that it would not adversely affect economic productivity, materials planning, and maintenance technicians within the ministry.[139]

On May 16, the Ministry of Materials Supply sent another letter to both the prime minister and the minister of defense indicating that it was preparing to deliver 13,765 tons of hardware, out of 17,198 tons requested by the MoD, but 4,282 tons were imported goods. Therefore, the Ministry of Foreign Trade and the Ministry of Transport were to be responsible for delivery and transport of those materials to a location determined by the MoD. A total of 7,281 tons of hardware were scattered in three storage facilities in Hai Phong (the main seaport in the north), Ha Bac, and Vinh Phu, and therefore the Ministry of Transport was to transport those to the MoD's preferred location.[140] Tens of thousands of workers in the provinces were diverted to food production, transport, and firearms repair for national defense in 1980 alone. Vietnam's militarization penetrated every aspect of the economy, pumping out enormous resources. With this national security emergency, the MoD was granted broad power to mobilize resources for war.

The Ministry of Foreign Trade and Ministry of Health were not able to meet their respective quotas due to shortages. The Ministry of Health could only provide fifteen out of seventeen types of medicine mandated by the MoD, and it could not produce enough medicine due to a shortage of materials and delays in the delivery of imported aid. Few who refused to cooperate with the MoD were forced to comply. The Ministry of Foreign Trade and the city of Hanoi were singled out for noncompliance with Directive 58-CP. Vice-Minister of Defense Vu Xuan Chiem complained, "If we do not mobilize resources now, we will not have time when war breaks out. Officials of the Ministry of Defense have made three trips to the Ministry of Foreign Trade, but they did not reach any agreement."[141] Clearly, those who observed the MoD milking resources from the economy in the name of national defense pushed back on the MoD's demands.

The State Planning Committee and senior officials in charge of economic affairs at the Prime Minister's Office (economy-firsters) were increasingly concerned about the siphoning of resources from of the economy into national defense. An urgent secret report from the Ministry of Materials Supply on May 26, 1980, noted that out of a total of 18,612 tons of raw materials the MoD requested, the Ministry of Foreign Trade had to import nearly 7,000 tons, including 3,173 tons of steel, from the Soviet Union and other socialist countries by the end of 1980.[142] Since the Ministry of Transport had to surrender 1,224 vehicles to the MoD, its transport capacity was further weakened by the urgent demand that it move military equipment and supplies to Cambodia and strategic military positions along the northern border with China. This produced a cascade of resource diversions from economic productivity into national defense, a trend that increasingly alarmed the economy-firsters.

Detailed records at ministerial levels reveal increased tension between the military-firsters and economy-firsters beneath the surface of party unity on national security. In May one of the economy-firsters, Tran Phuong, vice-chairman of the State Planning Committee, urged the prime minister to consider reducing quotas for human and material resources for national defense and to request urgent aid from the Soviet Union and other socialist countries.[143] On October 7, another economy-firster, Phuong Minh Nam, vice-minister of the Prime Minister's Office, in a report on the implementation of Directive 58-CP, privately informed the prime minister that "all the government agencies have tried very hard to allocate manpower and material resources, including tractors and construction equipment, for national defense, but resources fell short in many areas."[144] He pleaded with the prime minister, "While resource mobilization for war was necessary, the difficulty that local authorities are experiencing in balancing the need to prepare for war and the need for economic productivity is a major problem."[145] However, the worsening of the two-front war in Cambodia and against China silenced those who raised economic concerns.

In 1980 diplomacy reached an impasse. Vice-Minister Phan Hien reported on the failed border negotiations in a meeting at the vice-ministerial level between Vietnam and China in Hanoi on April 18, 1979, although both sides agreed on an exchange of prisoners of war.[146] China terminated all negotiations by the end of 1980.[147] At the same time, the military intervention in Cambodia shifted from offense in 1978–79 to a defensive posture in 1980. Cambodian resistance forces dominated by the Khmer Rouge quickly regrouped and turned to guerrilla and psychological warfare,[148] combined with sneak attacks, to destroy bridges and transportation convoys and kill Vietnamese soldiers.[149] On the northern front, China continued to put military pressure on Vietnam with "offensive Operations against the Enemy's Controlled Points" along the Yunnan-Vietnam border.[150]

In October 1980, Council of Government Directive 333-CP granted more power to the minister of defense, General Van Tien Dung,[151] than had Directive 58-CP to implement compulsory military service to a larger segment of the entire population. It states, "In accordance with the request of the minister of defense, approved by the chairman of the State Planning Committee, from the second phase of military conscription scheduled to begin in October 1980, all male citizens (from eighteen to twenty-five years of age) in all rural areas, towns, offices, state enterprises, and professional schools in whatever positions, as long as they meet the requirements of military conscription as set by the annual state plan, will serve in active military duty for the duration set by the Law on Military Duty."[152] In addition, the government decided to recruit single women from eighteen to twenty years old in rural areas to serve in the army for three years.[153]

Still exempt from military service were cadres, technicians, engineers, and leaders in important economic-defense sectors, including electricity, metallurgy (e.g., steel manufacturing), coal mining, the production of construction materials, light industry, and food production.[154] China continued its military harassment in northern Vietnam. Between 1979 and 1984, it launched about 7,500 armed attacks into Vietnam along the border and continued pounding residential areas. The Vietnamese reported 2,000 Chinese violations of Vietnamese air space.[155] Vietnam's protracted war with the Cambodian resistance forces, mainly backed by China and Thailand, from 1979 to 1984 also forced Vietnam to increase military spending, which took a major toll on its already weak economy.

In summary, after China's invasion of Vietnam in February 1979, the Vietnamese leadership experienced a major national security shock after witnessing the horrendous destruction in border provinces by the invading Chinese troops. The documentary evidence pertaining to the internal debate over how to confront the Chinese military threat reveals a compromise, kept private at that time, between the leaders of the military (General Chu Huy Man and General Van Tien Dung, who were promoted to Politburo members in the March 1982 Fifth Party Congress), who advocated a military-first policy, and the leaders of the State Planning Committee (Chairman Le Thanh Nghi and Vice-Chairman Tran Phuong). Historically and institutionally, the State Planning Committee was largely dominated by economy-firsters, including Le Thanh Nghi, who tried to cut waste and improve the efficiency of the economy. These economy-first planners were increasingly alarmed by the continuing deterioration of the economy as large quantities of national resources were funneled into the war machine instead of economic development.

The Worsening Economic Crisis in 1979–81

The economic crisis in 1979–81 had both domestic and foreign causes.[156] The failure of the state's central planning of the economy was caused by a number of internal and external factors, including disastrous flooding in 1978, widespread corruption among party officials, wasteful use of state resources as a residue of Vietnam's wartime reliance on foreign aid, low productivity, an increased trade deficit and debt, constant shortages of raw materials, and the detrimental effect of the two-front war on the economy. As David Wurfel summed it up, "By 1982, imports from capitalist countries had dropped to forty-eight percent of their 1979 value, while imports from socialist countries had risen from fifty-two percent to eighty-one percent of Vietnam's total. Overall imports dropped fourteen percent in 1980, thus cutting supplies to state enterprises."[157]

In response, the political leadership took the first steps in adjusting to the new economic conditions with "spontaneous bottom-up reforms" in both industry and agriculture,[158] the idea the chairman of the State Planning Committee, Le Thanh Nghi, proposed in 1978. The party endorsed "output contracts" (*khoan san pham*), an innovative approach to increasing agricultural productivity. Wurfel wrote, "The essential characteristic of this contract was that the cooperative, which had its own production quota, agreed with farm families on quotas for set pieces of land, to be delivered at the state price, with the family free to sell any excess over the quota on the open market."[159] On January 13, 1981, the Party Central Committee in Hanoi issued Instruction 100 C/TU, making the contract system national policy in an attempt to curb farmers' opposition to collectivization of the land. In December of that year, the contract system was extended to the south.[160] Bottom-up reforms in industry, which Le Thanh Nghi called for in December 1977, took the form of "fence breaking" (*pha rao*), which allowed individual factories to break through the constraints of the central planning system. The first key reform decree for state industry, in January 1981, allowed state factories to diversify their products outside the plan as long as they met state quotas. The reforms increased economic growth but also produced the new problem of inflation as demand grew more rapidly than supply. The inflation in 1979, registered at 43 percent, rose to 83 percent in

1982. Alongside this inflation were "negative phenomena," including specula-
tion, smuggling (mostly goods pouring into black markets in southern Vietnam from Thailand after passing through Cambodia), and various forms of
corruption.

The dominant conservative leaders were alarmed and sought to reassert
tight control over the economy. In September 1981, a Council of Ministers resolution moved to limit the free market activities of state enterprises, directed at
the south, especially Ho Chi Minh City.[161] The March 1982 Fifth Party Congress
put a brake on the urgency of reforms, marked by the removal of Nguyen Van
Linh, party secretary in Ho Chi Minh City, from the Politburo and the Central
Committee secretariat. Within the conservative camp, Deputy Prime Minister
To Huu voiced the need for the party to provide close guidance to the coopera-
tivization movement, and Hoang Tung, a Central Committee spokesperson,
emphasized the need to eradicate private ownership.[162] As the conservatives
and military-firsters won the ideological battle, the economy slowed and the
costs of escalated military confrontation and nation building in Cambodia and
against China rapidly increased in 1979–81, a trend that continued into the en-
suing years, 1982–85, in spite of increased aid from the Soviet bloc. As Vietnam's
economic crisis persisted and the costs of its two-front war rapidly increased,
by 1982 the conservative and military-first faction had begun to rely more
heavily on economic and military aid from the Soviet bloc.

Hanoi's overconfidence in its military capability, fed by its underestimation of
Beijing's military resolve and great power support from the Soviet Union as a
deterrence against China's retaliatory attacks prevented Hanoi's leaders from
anticipating China's invasion of Vietnam with such massive numbers of troops.
Information from internal documents also shows that behind Hanoi's public
claims of military victory, Vietnam suffered massive economic damage as a
result of the government's underpreparedness for such an invasion. In public
Hanoi claimed another historic victory over the Chinese invaders, another episode of the Vietnamese tradition of resistance against foreign aggression. In private, however, the Vietnamese leadership came under heavy criticism by many
National Assembly members who had warned that such an invasion by China
might occur in retaliation for Vietnam's military intervention in Cambodia.

Ideologically, the Vietnamese leadership, with its "two-camp" worldview,
believed that the pendulum of history had once again swung in the direction of
the socialist bloc and that Vietnam was on the winning side of international
socialism in its opposition to China's shift to the capitalist world. This belief
certainly influenced Hanoi's assessment that Beijing was in a weak position and

therefore unlikely to wage a major war against Vietnam. However, the ideological factor is neither necessary nor sufficient to explain Hanoi's failure to anticipate China's invasion of Vietnam in February 1979. As archival documents from that time show, in Hanoi's strategic thinking, however erroneous in retrospect, the deterrence effect of the Vietnamese-Soviet alliance and leaders' confidence in the superiority of Vietnam's military capability prevented Hanoi from anticipating a major invasion by China.

The most consequential impacts of the Chinese invasion were the rising influence of the military-first faction in Hanoi's decision making and the militarization of the entire nation at the expense of economic development. The revolutionary socialist state of Vietnam was by nature a resource-extractive state during wartime. However, what was new after the Chinese invasion was the excess of the military-first policy in reaction to constant fear of another Chinese invasion of Vietnam. The heavy militarization of the northern border defenses in anticipation of such an invasion inflicted a heavy toll on economic productivity as material and human resources were pumped out of the economic sectors and into national defense. To economy-firsters within the Vietnamese government, this military excess was detrimental to Vietnam's economy but the two-front war dictated a military-first policy. In retrospect, the shock of the Chinese invasion, amplified by the Vietnamese underpreparedness for such a large-scale invasion, prompted the dominant military-first faction to favor excessive militarization and mobilization of resources for national defense.

Wang Dongxing's delegation arrived in Democratic Kampuchea on November 5, 1978 (*left to right*): PRC ambassador to DK Sun Hao, PRC vice-minister of foreign affairs Han Nienlong, director of the party's Organization and Propaganda Department Hu Yaobang, PRC vice-premier Yu Quili, DK foreign minister Ieng Sary, vice-chairman of the Party Central Committee and member of the Politburo Standing Committee Wang Dongxing, director of the CPC Central Committee Investigation Department Luo Changqing, and deputy director of the CPC International Liaison Department Shen Jian. (Documentation Center of Cambodia Archives)

The Vietnamese and Cambodian army on the day of the liberation of Phnom Penh, January 10, 1979. (Documentation Center of Cambodia Archives, photo by Dinh Phong.)

Hun Sen with Cambodian refugees in Vietnam in 1977. (Documentation Center of Cambodia Archives)

Villagers in the 1980s watch a Khmer Rouge cadre arrested by PRK soldiers being prepared for punishment. (Documentation Center of Cambodia Archives)

Vietnamese advisers trained Cambodian soldiers before they pulled out of Cambodia in 1989. (Documentation Center of Cambodia Archives)

4

The Two-Faced Enemy in Cambodia

1979–1985

Against the backdrop of Vietnam's socioeconomic crisis precipitated by the failed planned socialist economy in the post-1975 unification and the embargo imposed by the United States after 1975, the Vietnamese invasion and occupation of Cambodia from December 1978 to 1989 contributed significantly to Vietnam's economic stagnation and caused military conflict with China and political confrontation with ASEAN, further isolating Vietnam in the region during this period. To political elites in Vietnam today, the invasion of Cambodia in December 1978 was a justified response to Khmer Rouge provocations but the occupation of Cambodia for the next decade was a costly mistake.[1] In addition to economic stagnation in Vietnam, the cost of the occupation was estimated at US$2 million a day throughout most of the 1980s, mostly covered by Soviet aid to Vietnam. Vietnamese casualties were estimated at 117,000 between 1977 and 1989.[2] Today in Vietnam's official history the Vietnamese army "gloriously fulfilled its duty to help the Cambodian people wholeheartedly and unselfishly."[3] If so, why is Vietnam's military presence in Cambodia during this period deeply contested in Cambodia? This chapter provides a narrative of seldom discussed events during Vietnam's military intervention in Cambodia in 1979–83.

Today in Vietnam, behind the official history of its noble mission in Cambodia, there is a debate over why Vietnam stayed on to occupy Cambodia for another decade after the invasion. The common explanation is that the PRK, the regime that Hanoi installed after 1979, would not have survived without the Vietnamese military opposing Cambodian resistance forces,[4] a joint anti-Vietnamese alliance represented by the Coalition of Government of Democratic

Kampuchea (CGDK), established in June 1982. The anti-Vietnamese and PRK alliance among the royalist faction (with Sihanouk as its leader), republicans (led by Son Sann), and communists (led by Khieu Samphan) was backed by China, the United States, and ASEAN, and, with the support of those nations, it retained the Cambodian United Nations seat after October 1979.[5] The PRK under its first president, Heng Samrin, along with Vietnam itself, was isolated and politically delegitimized by the West as Hanoi's puppet regime.

The historical representation of Vietnam's invasion and occupation—or liberation and nation building—of Cambodia during the decade from 1978 to 1988 is controversial and deeply contested in public political discourses in Cambodia.[6] This emotionally and politically charged issue divides the Cambodian people and rallies factions behind two radically different historical representations of the event by the two major political parties in Cambodia: the CPP, the ruling party; and the CNRP, the opposition. While branding itself as democratic, the CNRP has articulated and perpetuated an anti-Vietnamese nationalist discourse and exploited the CPP's political debt to its Vietnamese patrons in Hanoi in the late 1970s and 1980s.[7] On the other hand, the ruling CPP has always emphasized Vietnam's assistance in the liberation of the Cambodian people from the Pol Pot genocidal regime, a legacy that the CPP inherited and incorporated into its political identity of terminating the Khmer Rouge political and military movement and bringing total peace to Cambodia. The CPP has accused the CNRP leadership of stirring up anti-Vietnamese racism in Cambodia and fomenting Cambodian-Vietnamese antagonism for its own party's political gain.

This chapter provides insight into the murky period of Vietnam's occupation of Cambodia (1979–83) during which, we now know, the CPV attempted to export the Vietnamese revolution and socialist model to Cambodia after overthrowing the DK, better known as the Khmer Rouge, regime in January 1979. Documents, memoirs, and interviews reveal the human and material cost of Vietnam's bloody war in Cambodia and Vietnam's occupation. The bulk of the evidence presented below shows that the moral urgency with which the Hanoi leadership carried out its mission of nation building in Cambodia after overthrowing the Pol Pot regime in 1979 was soon challenged by the reality of Cambodia's growing insurgency and resistance against the Vietnamese occupying forces.

The Vietnamese Volunteer Army (VVA), dubbed "Buddha's army" by Cambodian prime minister Hun Sen,[8] was given a mission under the slogan "Helping our [Cambodian] friends is helping ourselves."[9] To be sure, the Vietnamese volunteers were regular soldiers. Cambodian popular perception of the Vietnamese troops changed from seeing them as "liberators" to seeing them as "occupiers" in just a few years. The CPV's self-proclaimed moral high ground in liberating Cambodia from the Pol Pot regime and making considerable sacrifices for the new Cambodian revolution it established gave leaders of the Vietnamese occupying forces the moral self-license to take extraordinary measures, including the arrest and torture of many Cambodian officials suspected of serving as a fifth column for Cambodian resistance forces against the Vietnamese. Moral self-license is a phenomenon whereby behaviors that initially establish people's morality can subsequently disinhibit them and allow them to behave in ways that are immoral or frivolous.[10] Moral self-license, a concept I borrow from social psychology,[11] best captures the behaviors and attitudes of some Vietnamese generals and political leaders who oversaw Cambodian affairs that occurred as part of Vietnam's "noble mission" in Cambodia. These actions rapidly eroded Vietnam's moral capital and inspired resistance, defection, and mistrust among the general populace and Cambodian authorities, causing major damage to Vietnam's nation-building mission.

Vietnam's determination to prevent a humanitarian crisis, including mass starvation, after the collapse of the Pol Pot regime in early 1979 was admired by the Cambodian people. But as Vietnam's nation-building mission shifted from an emphasis on restoring livelihoods and economic productivity while building a socialist system between 1979 and 1980 to achieving military victory on the battlefield from 1981 to 1983, the Vietnamese military saw the need to purge the "two-faced authorities" (*chinh quyen hai mat*) and "hidden enemies" (*dich ngam*) within Cambodian society. The impact of the Vietnamese purges gravely soured the relationship between the Vietnamese army and the Cambodian people, rapidly eroding Vietnam's goodwill and moral capital just a few years after it liberated of the Cambodian people from genocide in 1979.

Exporting the Vietnamese Revolution to Cambodia

In mid-1979, Military Region 7 of the PAVN was confronted with a tough guerrilla war against Cambodian resistance forces with between 22,000 and 25,000 combatants in the northeastern region of Cambodia.[12] This vast region includes the two northern provinces of Battambang and Siem Reap and the four central and northeastern provinces of Kampong Thom, Kampong Cham, Kratie, and Svay Rieng. But the majority of the Cambodian resistance forces, with nearly 20,000 combatants, operated in three important provinces: Battambang, Siem Reap, and Kampong Thom. In the first half of 1979, the forces of Military Region 7 concentrated on wiping out the enemy forces, protecting convoys, and retaining control over strategic territory along the main national roads, especially

National Roads 5 and 6 connecting Phnom Penh and the provinces of Battambang and Siem Reap.

From February 12 to March 20, 1979, the Third Army of the PAVN was ordered to take charge of the battle in Siem Reap and Battambang so that Military Region 7 could dispatch its three main divisions—5, 302, and 303—to wipe out regrouped Khmer Rouge forces in Kampong Thom Province. The Military Region 7 commander claimed a major victory; according to the Vietnamese Ministry of National Defense, Vietnamese troops killed 546 enemy combatants and took 1,221 prisoners while 11,124 enemy combatants defected. The Vietnamese also liberated some 20,000 villagers from enemy control, confiscated 3,515 tons of rice and 20 tons of salt, and provided food to save these villagers from starvation.[13] However, having won this military victory, the Vietnamese would find it much more difficult to retain control over the acquired territory. At the urgent request of the Military Region 7 command, in April 1979 the Vietnamese MoD dispatched the newly established Division 317, consisting of six regiments (five infantry regiments—775, 747, 115, 770, and 329—and one artillery regiment, 774) to keep control of this strategically important central province of Cambodia.[14]

With the approval of the Central Military Commission, Military Region 7 separated its main force of volunteer troops and military specialists into two fronts, Front 479 and Front 779. On April 14, 1979, the Front 479 command was established.[15] On May 11, the MoD issued Decision 553/QD-QP to place Front 479 under the direct command of Military Region 7, and it was put in charge of the northern region of Cambodia, including the provinces of Battambang, Siem Reap, and Uddar Meanchey. General Bui Thanh Van, a native of the Vietnamese province of Tay Ninh on the border with Cambodia, was appointed commander of Front 479, and Major Le Thanh was named political commissar.[16] Early on, the organizational structure of Front 479 included the central command, three departments (general staff, political, and logistics), four divisions (5, 302, 309, and 317), six infantry regiments (6, 7, 160, 205, 726, and 740), and five army regiments.[17] Mimicking the military regions in Vietnam, the central command of the VVA in Cambodia was established to directly command the newly created fronts. Front 479 assumed major responsibility, including raids to wipe out enemy forces, liberate people from the enemy's control, help build the Cambodian revolutionary armed forces, and consolidate the Cambodian revolutionary government under its jurisdiction.[18]

Before overthrowing the Pol Pot regime, Hanoi devised a two-stage plan to stabilize the Cambodian people's livelihoods and restore economic productivity. The first phase, from December 1978 to January 1979, entailed rapid distribution of supplies to meet basic needs, including food and medicine. In the second phase, Hanoi planned to continue its assistance until aid from the Soviet Union and other socialist states arrived.[19] By the end of January 1979, the Vietnamese government had transported a total of 3,771.7 tons of emergency supplies to Cambodia, including 250 tons of salt, 5.5 tons of sugar, 16.2 tons of fuel, 3,500 tons of grain, and medicine of all kinds to prevent mass starvation. This saved many Cambodian lives after the genocide. Vietnam also sent a number of other basic household goods, including cloth (530,000 meters), plates, bowls, knives, and spoons. Hanoi also ordered eight southern provinces of Vietnam to send similar temporary material aid to Cambodia. These deliveries accounted for less than 50 percent of the planned supplies; Hanoi planned to send the rest by June 1979.[20] The main reason for the delay was simply that Vietnam was also a poor country that had just survived its own twenty-year war.

To support the new regime in Cambodia, Hanoi looked to the Soviet Union to provide what it could not, especially grain, cloth, medicine, communications equipment, means of transportation, vehicles, fuels, steel, cement, construction materials, and other raw materials for manufacturing.[21] Nevertheless, Vietnam's emergency aid prevented mass starvation in the first few weeks after the end of the Pol Pot regime.

From October 18 to November 24, 1979, a powerful conservative leader, Le Duc Tho, chief of Vietnam's nation-building mission, and General Le Duc Anh, commander of the VVA in Cambodia, convened a general conference on the tasks to be undertaken by Vietnamese specialists in Cambodia. By October 1979, 1,284 Vietnamese specialists were already working in Cambodia, 300 specialists served the central government of Cambodia, and 1,300 more had been dispatched to assist the provinces. Committee B68 and the on-site military commands were in charge of Vietnamese specialists in the provinces and districts, while A40 was in charge of supervising economic and cultural specialists at the Party Central Committee in Phnom Penh.[22] All leaders of the military specialists (code named 478), economic-cultural specialists (group A40), and public security (state police) specialists (K79) were instructed to attend the 1979 conference.[23]

In a speech delivered at the conference, Le Duc Tho expressed his pleasure over Vietnam's historic achievement in building a revolutionary government and army in Cambodia during the previous twelve months. He reported that by the end of 1979 the Vietnamese had helped the PRK establish 46,000 production groups, known as "solidarity groups" (*krom samaki* in Khmer), in the liberated territory throughout Cambodia. Each group included a cluster of ten to fifteen families with twenty to thirty workers who were to cultivate some twenty hectares of land. Central to the establishment of these collective farming co-operatives was the idea that they would boost production efficiency, share any grain surplus with the state, and strengthen communal resistance against infil-tration by the enemy, thereby enhancing national defense. At the conference Tho remarked, "These production groups not only restore economic produc-tivity, but they also strengthen political stability and provide a security buffer at the local level."[24] This idea was lifted directly from the Vietnamese Commu-nists' socialist political economy manual, introduced in North Vietnam be-tween 1958 and 1961.[25]

Tho reminded the Vietnamese specialists to uphold three principles when working with their Cambodian counterparts. They were to (1) respect Cambo-dia's sovereignty, laws and regulations, and people; (2) refrain from big-country chauvinism; and (3) let the Cambodians make their own decisions. In other words, the Vietnamese were to assist their Cambodian comrades without pa-tronizing them and encourage their self-reliance. The Vietnamese were to simply offer recommendations and leave final decisions to their Cambodian comrades. Tho remarked, "In the beginning, our friends [the Cambodians] lack knowledge. We have knowledge, and our Cambodian comrades learn [from us]. Then our Cambodian comrades start to join us in doing some work together. Next they carry out these tasks, and we simply observe or help when necessary. And fi-nally, they can take over the work and do it independently, and we gradually withdraw."[26] Central to Tho's instructions to the Vietnamese specialists and ad-visors was the importance of always being sensitive to the "political issue" of Cambodia's independence and sovereignty.

On December 20, 1979, on Le Duc Tho's recommendation, the People's Revolutionary Council of Cambodia decided to collect agricultural taxes and force peasants to sell all their farm yields to the state (at well below the market price). In addition, the state supplied rice seeds, fertilizer, and other agricul-tural necessities to the peasants and ensured the availability of irrigation.[27] Tho and his associates were pleased that this policy speedily encouraged people to join "solidarity groups" and that Cambodian villagers were able to feed their families, which in turn reduced their dependence on aid from Vietnam and other socialist countries. However, these policies were not tenable over the en-suing years as the PRK needed many more resources to wage a protracted war against the Cambodian resistance forces mainly backed by China, the United States, and Thailand, feed the population, and contribute to the feeding of nearly 200,000 Vietnamese troops in Cambodia.

During the first two years (1979–80), the Vietnamese under the leadership of Le Duc Tho attempted to build an image of Vietnam as a selfless neighbor and friend in a time of need. But this image was short-lived. Tho was credited with saving the Cambodian people from starvation and laying the political and economic foundation of the PRK. But in February 1980 he was called back to Hanoi to assume more important party functions as a member of the Politburo. In a Politburo meeting in November 1980, he spoke highly of the power of Vietnam's state bureaucracy and system, which enabled the party to achieve victory in two wars of aggression (waged by the Khmer Rouge and its patron, China) and fulfill its international duty to help build the Laotian and Cambodian revolutions.[28] For the conservative leader Le Duc Tho, building the new socialist state in Cambodia not only eliminated the threat to Vietnam's national security in the southwest once and for all but also was part of the CPV's export of its socialist model to the new regime in Cambodia, dressed up in an "international socialism" suit.[29] This justified Vietnam's all-out assistance to the new socialist regime in Cambodia. According to the first Vietnamese ambassador to the PRK, Ngo Dien, Tho single-handedly selected and formed the first group of leaders of the PRK in 1979–81. During this period, all major decisions were made by the Vietnamese and handed over to Party Secretary Pen Sovann, who then presented them to the party as the ideas of the Standing Committee.[30] However, as I point out in the next chapter, the economically minded leaders were of the view that Vietnam as a poor country was not in a position to provide nonrefundable aid to Cambodia and Laos for long and had to form mutually beneficial economic relations with Cambodia and Laos under Vietnamese leadership.

General Le Duc Anh was also credited with the military victory in Cambodia in the first eighteen months after the invasion. Notably, from October 1979 to May 1980, Vietnamese troops achieved significant success in their dry-season offensives across the Cambodian frontline. They claimed to have driven 20,255 enemy combatants from the battlefield, confiscated 11,296 rifles of various kinds, destroyed the enemy's ability to regroup and reassemble its forces, and attempted to create two territories and two authorities in various battle zones. As a reward, the Politburo appointed Le Duc Anh commander in chief of all Vietnamese volunteers and specialists, both civilian and military.[31] Now it was General Anh's turn to deliver a success during his tenure in Cambodia.

Under General Anh's leadership, building Cambodia's military capability was paramount as protracted guerrilla warfare had developed. As General Anh replaced Le Duc Tho at the helm of nation-building in Cambodia in late 1980, the military assumed more responsibilities and, simultaneously, vast power in Cambodia. This constituted a major shift from Le Duc Tho's mission, which focused on restoring basic livelihoods and building a revolutionary government at the district level from 1979 to 1980.[32] Le Duc Anh continued Le Duc Tho's district fortification strategy, but this time it was the Vietnamese military leaders who called the shots. In 1981, General Anh ordered the withdrawal of economic and cultural specialists at the district level and ordered Vietnamese battalions stationed at each locality to defend the territory and strengthen Cambodian district authorities.[33]

In August 1985, General Anh planned to create three to five local battalions for each Cambodian province, and he instructed the Vietnamese military to play an important role in assisting the PRK in building civilian authority at the local level. Cambodian and Vietnamese military leaders were to work jointly to establish each battalion. At first the ratio was one Cambodian combatant for every two Vietnamese soldiers. Over time the Vietnamese were to be phased out, leaving all responsibilities to the Cambodians.[34] But initially the newly created battalions of revolutionary Cambodian armed forces were placed under the supervision of the general political department of the Vietnamese occupying force. For instance, in 1980 Division 302 of Military Region 7 swiftly helped build civilian authority in eight districts, seventy-one communes, and 1,360 villages; on the military side, it built nine companies consisting of 1,821 combatants and 2,840 commune militiamen and equipped them with 4,106 rifles. In addition, it helped local authorities build seven schools, forty-six headquarters for people's committees, and ten commune clinics. In the same fashion, every military division was deeply involved in this strategy as the Vietnamese drove Cambodian resistance forces toward the Thai border.[35] The Vietnamese believed that this strategy would allow the PRK to control newly liberated territory and strengthen local revolutionary governments to cut off popular support from the Cambodian resistance forces.

To assert military control over Cambodia, on June 6, 1980, the Vietnamese MoD issued Resolution 62/CT-TM, creating a military command structure that gave each provincial military division a code name to mimic the three military regions (5, 7, and 9).[36] In the second half of 1980, each military region was given total responsibility for civilian and military affairs in the region under its control. Each military region was tasked with helping its Cambodian counterparts to establish and strengthen PRK commune and district authority, build local armed forces, maintain political order and security, distribute food and medicine, and help the Cambodian people return to their livelihoods.

General Anh was pleased with the progress over a short span of eighteen months. By mid-1980, the three military regions claimed to have reintegrated nearly 400,000 Cambodians who had left with the Khmer Rouge and gone to the Thai-Cambodian border, provided them with shelter and food, and restored their means of food production and their livelihoods.[37]

On the military side, throughout the rainy season (May–October) of 1980, the Vietnamese army and the PRK armed forces together dealt a serious blow to the newly reinforced seven divisions of Cambodian resistance forces, forcing five divisions to flee across the Thai border. They then fortified a defensive belt stretching 740 kilometers along the border and strengthened their control over a number of strategic outposts, including Preah Vihear, Samroang, Nimit (Uddar Meanchey Province), Malai, Pailin, Samlot (Battambang Province), and Koh Kong Province (in the northwestern region of Cambodia bordering Thailand). Their main objective was to prevent the enemy from infiltrating from the Thai border. However, the success of these efforts would soon evaporate as the Cambodian resistance was able to rebuild its military power and strengthen its political standing with the help of China, the United States, Thailand, and their allies.

Growing Hostility between the Vietnamese Army and Local Cambodians

From 1981 to 1983, the Cambodian resistance employed a strategy of entrenched guerrilla warfare with the objective of controlling the jungle and mountainous regions, rural areas, and towns and cities surrounding river deltas. From 1980 onward, a number of refugee camps were created along the Thai-Cambodian border, including at Anlong Veng (Uddar Meanchey Province); Preah Vihear Province; and Dang Rek, O' Da, Kamrieng, Malai, and Ta Sanh (Battambang Province). In these camps, the Khmer Rouge and its resistance allies received foreign aid, conducted military training supported by foreign specialists, and developed their armed forces.[38] From these relatively safe bases, they launched raids against the Vietnamese and attacked convoys to cut off their food supply and break their will to fight in Cambodia. In early 1981, one-third of the Khmer Rouge forces penetrated undetected the interior of the country into the seven provinces along the Thai-Cambodian border. A large number of them surrendered and, according to the Vietnamese, became "two-faced enemies" hidden among the villagers, acting as spies for the Cambodian resistance or working against the Vietnamese at the local level. Some even infiltrated the local authorities.[39] By 1982 the Cambodian resistance forces had gained control of large areas of Battambang, Siem Reap, Preah Vihear, and Stung Treng provinces. They would use these bases to expand their military offensives in the interior of the country.

From 1982 onward, the image of Vietnam as a nation builder changed to one of an occupying force, and resentment crept into the Vietnamese-Cambodian fraternity. The Vietnamese commanders at the frontline began to harbor distrust toward the local Cambodian people and authorities. They became convinced that two-faced enemies with allegiance to the resistance forces were hiding among the general populace. The perception of being surrounded by enemy fighters and a hostile population at the local level created a siege mentality within the Vietnamese army in Cambodia.

By 1982 the Vietnamese military leadership in Cambodia, including General Le Duc Anh, had come to the conclusion that the resistance forces had already penetrated the Cambodian revolutionary authority and the general populace in order to conduct espionage, becoming a sort of Trojan horse to conduct military attacks, incite popular uprisings, plunder food supplies, and destroy the local economy.[40] In a new phase of psychological warfare, Front 479 decided to elevate its three-pronged strategy combining military, political, and diplomatic efforts. It stressed the necessity of eliminating the two-faced enemies among the population and local Cambodian authorities. It also emphasized the importance of intensifying propaganda campaigns and mobilizing popular support to counter the enemy's psychological warfare.[41]

Vietnamese convoys on National Road 5 passing through Siem Reap to the frontline were frequently ambushed by Cambodian resistance forces. According to one Vietnamese source, more than 30 percent of troops protecting convoys suffered casualties every year, forcing the high command to provide additional troops to protect the convoys, repair bridges and roads, and clear land mines.[42] In the rainy season of 1982–83, Cambodian resistance forces were able to launch raids into Vietnamese army camps, increasingly destroying economic foundations and exhausting the Vietnamese fighting capability throughout the frontline in the provinces of Battambang and Siem Reap, under the control of Front 479.[43] The fact that many of these ambushes took place near villages or in town centers, combined with the Vietnamese perception of the threat posed by the two-faced enemies hiding among local Cambodian people and authorities, undoubtedly had a profound psychological impact on the Vietnamese troops. The command of Front 479 was under tremendous pressure to achieve Hanoi's objectives.

For many rank-and-file soldiers, a prolonged war seemed to make no sense as they faced an increasingly hostile local population. Nguyen Thanh Nhan, a Vietnamese veteran of Front 479, reflects in his memoir *Away from Home Season: The Story of a Vietnamese Volunteer Veteran in Cambodia*, "We weren't like the soldiers of the years 1978–80. They fought to drive away Pol Pot's cruel army that was burning and killing innocent [Vietnamese] people along the Vietnam-Cambodia border. They all absolutely understood the meaning and purpose of their jobs. They deserved to be called 'volunteers.' For us soldiers after 1980, things weren't as clear and simple as that."[44] Thanh Nhan's account reveals that many Vietnamese soldiers at the frontline in Cambodia questioned the whole notion of Vietnam's "noble mission" as they increasingly encountered hostility from Cambodian villagers who saw them as "occupiers."

However, the conduct of the Vietnamese toward the Cambodians contributed directly to their deteriorating relationship. Le Duc Tho's admonition to the Vietnamese working in Cambodia to respect Cambodia's sovereignty and aspirations was not carried out well in practice, especially in battle zones like Siem Reap Province. For instance, in the district of Chi Kreng, the relationship between District Chief Kham Sokhom and his Vietnamese adviser, Major Nguyen Van Bao, was one of "student-teacher" or "subordinate-superior," to use Kham's words. This was the standard practice throughout the battle zones in northeastern Cambodia. The Cambodian district chief was required to submit to the Vietnamese adviser a daily report on three important issues: the enemy's activities, food production, and local party affairs. On important issues like this, the Vietnamese adviser made decisions and instructed the district chief to execute them as he saw fit.[45] In Major Bao's absence, Chief Kham was instructed to seek advice from his deputy, who was also a political commissar.[46] The overwhelming presence of the Vietnamese army and military advisers dominated Cambodian authority in this region.

By 1982, as Cambodian resistance forces launched frequent raids and the Vietnamese suffered a growing number of casualties and loss of food supplies and equipment, the relationship between the Vietnamese military adviser and the district chief became increasingly strained. The deteriorating relationship between the Vietnamese troops and local Cambodian people worsened the already bleak situation. Food was in short supply for Vietnamese troops as deliveries were delayed due to the Khmer Rouge raids. Throughout 1982, villagers lodged complaints with the Cambodian authority about Vietnamese soldiers' transgressions, from stealing chickens, dogs, pigs, cows, and vegetables to aggression against Cambodian women, including cases of rape. A cloud of fear hung over local villagers when Vietnamese troops moved in.[47]

Since 1979 when the Vietnamese first entered Cambodian territory, the issue of some soldiers' misbehavior had been brought to the attention of the Vietnamese government at that time. For instance, on May 29, 1979, a member of the Vietnamese National Assembly reported to the party and the government that "a small number of Vietnamese soldiers did bad things in Cambodia, and some Cambodian people have become suspicious of us. If this drags on much longer, it will erode the Cambodian people's trust in us."[48] These misdeeds increased from 1981 onward, partly because Vietnamese soldiers in Siem

Reap bore the brunt of the Cambodian civil war and, as Vietnamese army newspapers describe, they were exposed to daily hardships such as nutritional deficiencies and malaria.[49] They would stop villagers along the road or go to their homes to "ask for" things they lacked.

District chief Kham Sokhom recalled his fear of retaliation every time he reported villagers' complaints to his Vietnamese adviser. Feeling sympathy for the Vietnamese soldiers who endured so much hardship and risked their lives in Cambodia, he chose to ignore some trivial issues.[50] In Kham's recollection, such misconduct by Vietnamese soldiers caused the villagers to harbor resentment and fear of the Vietnamese and to become sympathetic to the Cambodian resistance, including the Khmer Rouge. Villagers who in 1979 saw the Vietnamese soldiers as their saviors from the genocide later became sympathizers of the Cambodian resistance.[51] Some sent their sons to join the resistance, while others provided food and shelter to the resistance fighters and spied on the Vietnamese to help their cause.[52] In effect, this fed the Vietnamese suspicion of the two-faced enemy hiding among the populace, resulting in a cycle of mistrust and misunderstanding between the Vietnamese military and the local population. Eventually, the Vietnamese occupying forces took steps to purge Cambodian officials suspected of supporting the resistance.[53]

In his memoir, Nguyen Thanh Nhan recounts the following conversation between a Vietnamese solider, Huy, and his superior, Quan,[54] at a Cambodian wedding ceremony in a village adjacent to their camp that captures the Vietnamese soldiers' mistrust mixed with frustration with Cambodian villagers.

"The villagers are so kind and simple, aren't they?" Huy asked Quan.

"Most of them are like that," Quan answered.

"But in our unit, there are some guys who don't like them. They say that the villagers are just pretending to like us, because they're all enemies. They ask how anyone who has children and relatives who followed Pol Pot could like us, Vietnamese soldiers. Our friend Thien treats the villagers as his enemy. He's always suspicious of them and looks down on them."

Quan answered, "Some Vietnamese soldiers actually like the Cambodians, but some befriend them only to take advantage of them, and consider them fools and inferior. The minds of such men are full of prejudice and discrimination against people of other colors and races." . . .

Huy said, "I think that for anybody of any nation or race, if other people treat him kindly, he certainly has to treat them the same. Isn't it better to be good and honest with everyone, brother Quan?"[55]

Quan replied, "It's easy to say that, but it's not easy to do, Huy. It's noble of you to think like that, but sometimes we do the right thing to help people, but all we get in return is misunderstanding and hostility."

According to Chief Kham, local villagers' distrust of and resentment toward the Vietnamese reached an all-time high after news of the arrest of Prime Minister Pen Sovann, who was in office for a little more than five months, in December 1981 reached the general populace. Pen Sovann was widely known as a staunch nationalist, especially among residents of Kampong Khleang, a fishing village located on Siem Reap's Tonle Sap Lake. Cambodian fishermen had been complaining about the influx of Vietnamese fishermen and saw the arrest as an attempt by the Vietnamese to assert their colonial control over Cambodia.[56] After Pen Sovann's arrest, fear and mistrust replaced gratitude toward the Vietnamese in the minds of many state cadres.[57]

The Campaign against the "Two-Faced Enemy" in Siem Reap

Beginning in the summer of 1982, there were reports of people who worked for the government of Cambodian leader Heng Samrin during the day and for Pol Pot at night. In April 1983, as fear of enemy infiltration into Cambodian local authorities ran high in Siem Reap Province, the Front 479 command received what it believed to be "concrete evidence" warranting a crackdown on the two-faced enemies among the people and the entire Siem Reap authority. The evidence came from a confession by a deputy head of a Khmer Rouge regiment who defected to the Vietnamese.[58] Such events likely confirmed Front 479's belief that it had to hasten the arrest of local officials before they had a chance to escape.

The perceived and real two-faced enemy compelled the Vietnamese leadership to take drastic measures, and the pressure to succeed became even greater for local Vietnamese commanders at the frontlines in Cambodia. On January 20, 1983, the Central Military Commission issued resolution 05/NQ-QU regarding military duty in Cambodia. It stressed the "urgent need" to strengthen the ability of the Cambodian armed forces to "undertake major responsibility for combat along with Vietnamese troops, independently manage their armed forces, and assume greater control over the liberated zones."[59] The resolution underscored the necessity of launching major military offensives against the enemy and eliminating the two-faced enemies among the population and local authorities.[60] Under these conditions, the Vietnamese military leadership began to sidestep the principle of equality and noninterference with the Cambodian government and engaged in what Huy Duc,[61] a Vietnamese veteran in Cambodia, called "big-country chauvinism" (*tu tuong dan toc nuoc lon*).[62]

What happened next was a terrifying campaign of arrest, interrogation, and torture of Cambodian officials in Siem Reap Province in 1983. In that year, the Vietnamese military in Siem Reap arrested several hundred suspected resistance sympathizers, including district and provincial officials and security officers.[63] In April at least forty Cambodian officials—most of whom had received lengthy political training in Vietnam and were installed in these positions by the Vietnamese themselves—were arrested, and the governor of Siem Reap Province committed suicide when Vietnamese military officials came to arrest him.[64] These events sent a shock wave through Cambodia. Some officials who feared arrest fled into the jungle. Many of those who were arrested were detained in Vietnamese military barracks to await interrogation, and some were tortured when they refused to confess to aiding the resistance.[65] The purge prompted thousands of Cambodians to head for the border, many of them arriving at the refugee camps accusing Vietnam of "colonialism."[66]

A First-Person Account of the Purge

Kham Sokhom, chief of the district of Chi Kreng in Siem Reap Province, became one of the victims of the purge by Front 479. Between 1980 and 1982 Kham received political training in Thu Duc (Ho Chi Minh City) on three occasions and was promoted from commune chief to district chief after he completed his first political studies in Thu Duc in 1980. He was one of many Cambodian officials in Siem Reap Province who were arrested for the alleged crime of working or spying for the Cambodian resistance forces. In other words, he was accused of being a two-faced enemy who had infiltrated the PRK regime. In 2016 Kham recounted the story of his arrest and torture by the Vietnamese, and I will summarize it as follows:

> One morning in May 1983, Kham Sokhom left home in Prasat village (Kampong Kdei subdistrict, Chikreng district, Siem Reap Province) for his office in a small town in Kampong Kdei subdistrict. At eight o'clock his Vietnamese adviser, Major Nguyen Van Bao, summoned him to an adjacent room for a routine meeting. Major Bao asked Kham, "Do you know about the arrest of Cambodian provincial officials in Siem Reap?" Kham replied, "Yes, I heard about it. Why?" Without replying, Bao told Kham to wait in the room and left. At the same time, six other district officials were being questioned in different rooms of the district

headquarters. Two Vietnamese soldiers came to stand guard at the door of the room where Kham was held. A Vietnamese military officer entered the room, instructed the guards to confiscate all of Kham's belongings, and gave Kham a pen and three sheets of paper with which to write his revolutionary autobiography. Accused of secretly colluding with the Khmer Rouge enemy, Kham was placed under arrest and detained in the district office. The next day he was told to write a self-criticism report about his antiparty and anti-Vietnamese activities. But he wrote nothing, instead telling the Vietnamese officer that he had done nothing wrong.

On the third day, the Vietnamese officer threatened to send Kham to the regional Vietnamese military headquarters for interrogation if he refused to confess his secret collusion with the Cambodian resistance. Again Kham declined to write a confession. The officer said to him, "A lot of our soldiers were killed in your district. How come you don't know anything?" That night two Vietnamese army trucks arrived at the district headquarters. Kham was blindfolded and thrown into one of the trucks. Locked in a military prison inside the Vietnamese army compound, he was about to face a harrowing ordeal that would last for three weeks.

Kham was shackled to the floor in an isolated makeshift hut and guarded at all times. For the first three days he was told, "If you write your confession, we might consider reducing your punishment, but if you refuse, you will certainly die." Every day two guards walked him blindfolded around the military camp, occasionally firing shots to frighten him before he was sent to an interrogation room. On the seventh day, at midnight, he was transferred to a smaller bamboo hut, which he called a "chicken cage" because of its small size. Day in and day out, he was harangued to confess his reactionary activities. On the tenth day he was threatened with transfer to a harsher prison in Phnom Penh. Yet he still refused to admit any wrongdoing.

On the twenty-first day of his captivity, at about nine o'clock in the morning, Kham was taken to a room that was somewhat nicer than his prison cell. He heard a helicopter arriving at the camp. Minutes later a man who appeared to be a ranking leader arrived with an entourage of twelve military officers.

"Just talk," he told Kham. "No need to write anything. Just talk about your antiparty activities and I will reduce your punishment."

Kham replied, "I was chosen by the Vietnamese army to lead my people. I was trained by the Vietnamese, and I speak Vietnamese. Why would I betray my Vietnamese comrades?"

The interrogator pointed out, "Pol Pot speaks Vietnamese fluently and even fought side by side with us, but he still betrayed us."

Kham answered, "I helped my people, and the record shows that I called on thousands of people to defect from enemy territory."

The interrogator smiled and said, "Then I'll send you to the Phnom Penh prison." He ordered Kham to put on a suit and tie to be photographed. As the Vietnamese photographer was about to take his picture, the interrogator said, "Don't forget to smile!" Kham replied, "I can't smile. I've had little sleep for three weeks."

After the photograph was taken, the interrogator banged his fist on the table and shouted, "We treated you well but you refuse to confess. You show no fear. Why aren't you afraid?"

Kham replied, "Because I've done nothing against the party."

The interrogator turned to the guard and said, "Ask him if he's right- or left-handed." When Kham answered that he was left-handed, the guard tied his left thumb behind his back with a rope slung over a wooden beam above him and began to pull him up by his thumb while the interrogator was forcing him to confess. The interrogator warned, "This is your last chance to confess." Kham replied, "I am innocent." Through a fog of pain he heard the interrogator remark, "He's honest." Kham soon lost consciousness from the pain. When he gained consciousness, the interrogator had already returned to the helicopter awaiting him in the military compound and left.

Two days later Kham was released and summoned to meet a visiting representative of the CPV in the city of Siem Reap. He did not know at the time that the head of the eight-member delegation was Politburo member Chu Huy Man, Hanoi's top party official. In addition to an apology for what happened, Kham was given gifts of a bottle of Russian vodka, a case of crackers, two tea bags, a box of instant noodles, and 500 riels (roughly US$250) in cash. He continued to serve as chief of Chi Kreng district for the next two years. He was offered a promotion to a judiciary position in the Siem Reap provincial administration. He accepted it but resigned two years later in 1985.[67]

The Vietnamese Response to the Purge

When news of the arrests and torture in Siem Reap reached Hanoi, the Politburo of the CPV became deeply concerned about the political and military ramifications of the event. Prime Minister Pham Van Dong was furious and called on the Politburo to punish the commanders of Front 479, which had direct oversight over the provinces of Siem Reap and Battambang, and Command 719, which was in charge of the entire VVA in Cambodia.[68] The Siem Reap incident involved forced confessions and torture of Cambodian officials under the command of Front 479.[69] Ngo Dien,[70] the first Vietnamese Ambassador to the PRK at that time, recalled, "The arrests, coercion, and torture caused the unjust death of many [Cambodians]. . . . It was so bitterly painful when I heard the Cambodian public and officials ask, 'Why did the Vietnamese officials do something like this?'"[71]

Huy Duc, the former Vietnamese military specialist who served in Cambodia in 1983, later interviewed a number of retired Vietnamese leaders. He asserts in *Ben Thang Cuoc* that before the "Siem Reap case" (*vu Xiem Riep* in Vietnamese), some top officials of the PAVN were well aware of what Front 479 was about to do.[72] Coincidentally or not, when the purge was carried out, General Le Duc Anh, commander in chief of all Vietnamese volunteers in Cambodia, was in the Soviet Union for eye treatment. Confronted with this politically sensitive matter, Le Duc Tho sent a telegram on behalf of the Politburo recalling General Anh to Vietnam to deal with the problem.[73] General Anh asked the Politburo for advice.[74] He recalled in his memoir, "I returned to Hanoi, and the Politburo called a meeting to discuss this incident. At the time, Brother To [Prime Minister Pham Van Dong] expressed strong criticism and proposed heavy punishment for all officials of Front 479 and Command 719 who were involved in this incident."[75] However, General Anh proposed to the Politburo that only those high-ranking officials of Front 479 and Command 719 who were directly involved in the incident be disciplined. According to General Anh, General Ho Quang Hoa, his deputy, came to Hanoi to ask for instructions from the upper echelon. There is no direct evidence to indicate that General Hoa received a tacit order from Hanoi's leaders. However, General Anh did not reveal which officials were briefed and who issued the order for the purge in Siem Reap. General Anh made no attempt to identify the senior leaders in question, preferring instead to put the blame on a few Vietnamese generals in Front 479, and therefore he left it to the Politburo to determine the responsibility of those upper-echelon leaders.[76]

No available evidence specifically names those leaders, but in all probability the purge in Siem Reap was carried out with the knowledge of the Department of Political Affairs of the MoD, if not the minister of defense (General Van Tien Dung) himself. General Anh, who was put in charge of the investigation, knew that it was beyond his power to pursue those military leaders. Nevertheless, the Politburo accepted General Anh's proposal to discipline a few local commanders and dispatched General Chu Huy Man, a Politburo member and chairman of the General Political Department of the PAVN, to Phnom Penh to offer an official apology to the PRK party and the government of Cambodia. General Anh ordered the leadership of Front 479 to immediately release all Cambodian detainees and cease all interrogations and physical abuse. He ordered all relevant departments of Front 479 and Command 719 to submit "situation reports" to him. General Anh recalled in his memoir, "At the beginning [of my investigation], some comrades did not understand and called me 'a traitor.' And some even shifted blame to the Hanoi leadership because they said 'they had already asked for instructions from Hanoi' before they took such extreme measures."[77]

After his investigation in Ho Chi Minh City and Cambodia, Anh came to this conclusion: "Our [Vietnamese] comrades did not have any ill intention or harbor revenge against the Cambodian officials [in Siem Reap], but premature evidence and excessive hastiness led to these mistakes. . . . It would not have been right if we did not discipline some officials, but it would not have been right to impose heavy discipline either."[78] According to General Anh, in May 1983, the Front 479 command depended on unverified sources for its analysis and concluded that in June 1983 there would be an uprising in Siem Reap Province, that the enemy controlled the Cambodian revolutionary authority in the province, and that 80 to 100 percent of the people, the number varying from place to place, supported the enemy.[79] Thus the official narrative, according to General Anh, attributed the Siem Reap purge to "an error in judgment and the unwarranted hastiness of local military commanders of Front 479," thereby protecting the upper echelon in Hanoi from accusations of wrongdoing.[80]

In the end, two military officials were disciplined. Ho Quang Hoa, deputy commander of Front 719, was demoted from general to colonel and removed from the Central Committee of the CVP, a position he was elected to in March 1982. General Le Thanh, commander of Front 479, was demoted to the rank of colonel. When General Le Duc Anh reported back to the Politburo, Prime Minister Pham Van Dong remarked, "Dealing with the issue this way is good. And such internal disciplinary action is correct!"[81] In addition to an official apology to the PRK Politburo, General Chu Huy Man led a party delegation from Hanoi to visit families of Cambodian officials who were wrongly arrested and present them with gifts. As General Le Duc Anh recalled, the PRK Politburo told Chu Huy Man, "The shortcomings are not worthy of mention because Vietnamese comrades sacrificed the flesh and blood of tens of thousands of Vietnamese soldiers and specialists to rescue the Cambodian people from the genocide and reconstruct our country."[82] This obsequious attitude reflects the PRK leadership's inferiority to and dependence on the Vietnamese leadership imposed by the powerful conservative leader Le Duc Tho from the heyday (January 1979) of the PRK regime.[83] As his memoir reflects, Vietnamese ambassador Ngo Dien, who was a close adviser to then foreign minister Hun Sen, must have been disheartened by the purge as he was trying to show the world that Vietnam respected Cambodia's national sovereignty. According to Ngo Dien, "The origins of the Vietnamese mistakes like the 'Siem Reap case' was rooted in *tu tuong dan toc nuoc lon* [the nationalist ideology of a big nation], and the obvious evidence of this ideology was the fact that we [the Vietnamese leaders at that time] assigned ourselves the role of rearranging the Cambodian revolution."[84]

The Aftermath of the Purge

The long-term effects of the purge perpetuated the Cambodian people's distrust of the Vietnamese beyond 1983. According to Ambassador Ngo Dien, the villagers' terror and anger toward Vietnam spread to the entire province of Siem Reap and then quickly to the entire country.[85]

Just two years after the Siem Reap arrests, in May 1985, another shocking incident took place in the village of Kandal in the Svay Check district of Battambang. This time, a Vietnamese soldier from a public relations battalion stationed in the area raped a young Cambodian girl in front of two other girls and elderly villagers on the outskirts of the village. He then shot his victim and those who tried to flee the scene, killing five innocent Cambodian women.[86] The village was outraged and called for revenge. This terrifying news spread like wildfire. To appease the villagers, the military court of Front 479 condemned the Vietnamese soldier to death after a public trial.[87] In a public statement, the court declared, "The Front Military Court sentences the accused to death for his savage murder of many innocent Khmers, which has driven a wedge between the soldiers and people of the two countries and destroyed the Vietnamese army's honor and prestige. . . . We would like to ask for your forgiveness. There were always short and long fingers on our hands."[88] The Vietnamese essentially explained to Cambodian people that these were just misdeeds committed by a few men in the Vietnamese army. To the Cambodian people, mindful of their long history of anti-Vietnamese resistance, such incidents happened too often and fueled their fear and distrust of the Vietnamese. Their gratitude for Vietnam's liberation of Cambodia evaporated quickly when these incidents continued unabated.

The extent of the purge shocked the Cambodian populace and played into the hands of the Coalition Government of Democratic Kampuchea, in short the Cambodian resistance. Its contagious effects significantly undermined Hanoi's twin objectives of "continuing to win the trust of the Cambodian people and bring about mass defection of the enemy forces,"[89] as the Vietnamese Ministry of Foreign Affairs expressed it.

The souring relationship between the Vietnamese troops and local people tipped the psychological warfare in favor of the Cambodian resistance forces, unleashing deadly consequences for Vietnamese soldiers who passed through rural villages and making it difficult for the public relations units of Front 479 to win the hearts and minds of the local people after 1985.[90] To further drive a wedge between the Vietnamese troops and Cambodian villagers, the resistance forces often launched surprise attacks on villages through which Vietnamese troops were passing or in which they were temporarily stationed. As a result, many villagers fled their homes when the Vietnamese arrived. The resistance forces rewarded villagers who concealed their agents or spied on the Vietnamese.[91]

To the Cambodian people, the Siem Reap purge of local officials in 1983 definitively marked the beginning of the end of Vietnam's moral high ground and claim to have respect for Cambodia's national sovereignty, which in turn tilted the psychological warfare in favor of the resistance forces. Even before the Vietnamese invasion of Cambodia in December 1978, the Vietnamese leaders, including Prime Minister Pham Van Dong, warned of the danger of Vietnamese chauvinism toward their Cambodian comrades, and yet military victory on the Cambodian battlefield was a priority, and other political and economic issues were considered secondary. Consequently the Vietnamese occupying force's mistreatment of Cambodian civilians and officials was not properly addressed by the top Vietnamese leadership. The VVA and the advisers themselves ended up being seen by the Cambodian populace and local cadres as occupiers instead of liberators.

The Vietnamese mission in Cambodia during the early years 1979–83 evolved from saving the Cambodian people from genocide and preventing mass starvation after toppling the Pol Pot regime to full-fledged nation building. This was achieved by exporting Vietnam's experiences with revolution and building socialism to Cambodia, oddly enough a country with a very different culture and a long history of anti-Vietnamese nationalist sentiment. As the Cambodian resistance grew with the increased support of China, the United States, and ASEAN—particularly Thailand—Hanoi's strategy emphasized military victory over the resistance forces more than political correctness, that is, respecting Cambodia's sovereignty and noninterference in its internal affairs. The arrest of the first PRK prime minister, Pen Sovann, in 1981 and subsequent purges in Siem Reap are symptomatic of Vietnam's "big-country chauvinism," which fed Cambodia's traditional fear of Vietnam's southern expansion at its expense.

As leadership of Vietnam's nation-building mission in Cambodia passed from Le Duc Tho to General Le Duc Anh after 1981, operational power also shifted from intellectual and civilian committees like B68 and A40, which were in charge of military affairs and economic and cultural affairs, respectively, to the supreme command of the Vietnamese occupying army in Cambodia. Reports from Cambodia were often glowing until the Siem Reap purge incited overt Cambodian anger toward the Vietnamese. The Vietnamese military's heavy-handed measures to get rid of perceived and real two-faced enemies in Cambodia caused the goodwill and moral capital earned during 1979–80 to evaporate quickly. In retrospect, from the vantage point of political and psychological warfare in Cambodia, General Le Duc Anh's emphasis on a big military victory on the battlefield to quickly strengthen PRK control was counterproductive, causing the blowback effect of growing anti-Vietnamese sentiment toward Vietnamese soldiers in Cambodia.

The purge is an example of large-scale "moral self-licensing," under which the commanders of the Vietnamese occupying forces in Cambodia justified and ignored immoral acts committed by their officers based on Vietnam's immense sacrifice for Cambodia. To this point, the first Vietnamese ambassador to the PRK, Ngo Dien, attributed the purge to ethnocentric superiority embedded in big-country chauvinism and manifested in Vietnam's self-proclaimed "role of forging the Cambodian revolution from start to finish."[92] Vietnamese military commanders, however, including General Le Duc Anh, rather than considering their officers' and soldiers' conduct as emblematic of a larger offense against the Cambodian people's trust, cast these problems as isolated incidents or random mistakes and concluded that disciplining a few officers would be sufficient. A few top Vietnamese leaders, such as Prime Minister Pham Van Dong, Le Duc Tho, and Ambassador Ngo Dien, recognized the costly political and diplomatic fallout. But the Vietnamese military leadership in Cambodia believed that it had a moral license to conduct the purge. As Vietnamese veteran Huy Duc keenly observed, "Over the period of ten years [1979–89], the Vietnamese soldiers did a great deal to prevent the return of the Pol Pot regime. Many made the ultimate sacrifice of flesh and blood in Cambodia. At the same time, however, the Vietnamese leaders also interfered significantly in the decisions of the Cambodian government."[93]

5

Economic Regionalism in Indochina

1982–1985

Why did Hanoi's leaders engage in costly nation building in Cambodia given the widespread economic hardship in Vietnam in the early 1980s? The conventional wisdom offers two different explanations, one emphasizing the role of ideology and the other pointing to the security imperative as a determining factor in Vietnam's occupation of Cambodia in the 1980s. First, the Vietnamese leadership was motivated by the Marxist-Leninist belief in two ideological camps. Through this lens, Hanoi's leaders viewed Vietnam's intervention in Cambodia as part of the global ideological conflict between the Soviet-led socialist camp and the imperialist camp spearheaded by the United States.[1] Thus, Hanoi viewed the military intervention in Cambodia and the construction of a new socialist regime after toppling the Pol Pot genocidal regime in January 1979 as Vietnam's international socialist duty. Opposing the return of the Pol Pot regime in Cambodia, which was backed by reactionary China aligned with the imperialist United States, is therefore consistent with Hanoi's ideological line. This was the publicly expressed view of conservative leaders like Le Duc Tho.

In contrast, other scholars have attributed Vietnam's occupation of Cambodia to the security imperative of countering the Chinese threat in Cambodia. Evan Gottesman, who studied the relationship between Vietnam and the PRK in the 1980s, concluded, "Vietnam's role in Cambodia was not exactly colonial. Its reason for occupying Cambodia was more strategic (to protect Vietnam from China) than economic. Its justification for the occupation (to protect Cambodians from the Khmer Rouge) also seems more valid to modern historians than the racist theories spun by colonial Europeans."[2] Yet he went on to

134

argue—which contradicts his preceding claim—that "Vietnam's economic relationship with the PRK, which included the exploitation of Cambodia's natural
resources and the manipulation of its currency, was similar to the Soviet Union's
domination of Eastern Europe. Like the Soviet Union and its satellites, Vietnam
and Cambodia couched their agreements in terms of 'friendship' and 'solidarity,' but in fact, benefits flowed mostly to the stronger party."[3] This chapter ad-
vances an eclectic argument that goes beyond the either/or dichotomy between
strategic interests and ideological Marxist-Leninist orthodoxy. New documentary evidence from the Vietnamese archives corroborates Gottesman's argument,
which stressed Vietnam's strategic interests, but also reveals that in pursuit of
such interests Hanoi's leaders utilized Marxist-Leninist ideology as an instru-
ment to ensure Vietnam's long-term strategic domination of Indochina.

I argue that Hanoi aligned Vietnam's strategic and ideological interests in
Cambodia with a grand strategy of a Vietnam-dominated regionalism within
the hierarchical order of the Soviet-led socialist bloc. To be clear, it is the export
of Vietnam's economic model or the integration of Cambodia and Laos into a
Vietnamese-led regional system. Rather, it was an asymmetrically interdependent economic community that would enable Vietnam to employ its large population of skilled labor and more sophisticated equipment to exploit the relatively
untapped natural resources (rice paddies, forests, fisheries, etc.) of Cambodia
and Laos. Over time Cambodia and Laos were to become economically dependent on the larger and more advanced economy of Vietnam. This economic
community was expected to create "security externality" for Vietnam and by extension for its two smaller socialist neighbors. Building a viable pro-Vietnamese
and anti-China regime in Cambodia contributed to the defense of Vietnam's
national sovereignty and the security on its southwestern flank. Moreover, by
bringing Cambodia into the Soviet-led socialist camp, Hanoi hoped to raise
Vietnam's stature and role as the vanguard of Indochinese socialism within the
international socialist hierarchy. As I discuss below, such a role would bring
with it material benefits, including massive aid from the Soviet Union and other
members of the COMECON and preferential trade agreements between Vietnam and the Soviet bloc and Vietnam and Laos and Cambodia in a system of
Vietnam-dominated economic integration. There is no evidence that Vietnam
planned to impose outright colonial rule over Cambodia or Laos. However, the
bulk of documentary evidence from the Vietnamese archives clearly demon-
strates that in 1982–83 Hanoi hatched a grand strategy, inspired by the French
colonial scheme,[4] of controlling Indochina via association rather than assimilation to ensure Vietnam's long-term domination of Indochina through economic
integration like the Soviet domination of Eastern Europe.

In explaining Vietnam's role in assisting the Cambodian revolution after 1979 to various government ministries and provincial authorities, the Vietnamese Prime Minister's Office wrote, "The Politburo has placed the issue of assisting the Cambodian revolution as Vietnam's national duty, which involves the party, army, and people. First and foremost, this duty serves the need to defend our motherland. At the same time, it is also our supreme international duty; given the immense difficulty the Cambodian revolution is facing, Vietnam's assistance is an important and decisive factor that would guarantee the victory of the Cambodian revolution."[5] The statement indicates that national security and ideological considerations were inseparable in Hanoi's thinking. As I discuss below, more concrete evidence reveals that under the cover of its international socialist duty, Hanoi had both short-term and long-term plans to establish Vietnam-led economic regionalism.

Beginning in 1983, Hanoi's strategic thinking shifted from outright military and political control of Cambodia and Laos, as the bulwark against economic encirclement by Thailand and China, to economic access to the markets and natural resources of Cambodia and Laos in order to boost Vietnam's economic growth and competitiveness within the Soviet bloc. By 1984 this was the prevailing view and action plan for economic regionalism put in place by the economically minded leaders and later reformers in Hanoi. This was the next logical objective since growing popular Cambodian resistance and international opposition to the occupation of Cambodia cast doubt on the conservative faction's plan for a lasting pro-Vietnam regime there.

It is important to recall that on the eve of Vietnam's invasion of Cambodia (December 23, 1978), Prime Minister Pham Van Dong emphasized, "It is the issue of Cambodia's national sovereignty, the aspirations of the Cambodian people, and their revolution that Cambodian people have to decide for themselves."[6] Dong stressed, "Vietnam's role was to provide all-out support for the Kampuchean United Front for National Salvation to overthrow the Pol Pot–Ieng Sary regime and establish an independent government in Cambodia."[7] Hanoi's main objective before the invasion was the neutralization of the Khmer Rouge threat by means of military intervention and regime change in Cambodia, leaving unstated its intention to install a pro-Vietnam socialist government that could stand up to the Cambodian resistance forces dominated by the Khmer Rouge. In the aftermath of overthrowing the DK regime in January 1979 and the Chinese invasion of Vietnam a month later, Hanoi's leaders believed that Beijing's intention was to engage China in a protracted military conflict with Vietnam along the northern border while the Chinese ally, the Cambodian resistance forces, adopted a long-term strategy of a guerrilla warfare to "bleed the Vietnamese" in Cambodia. Hanoi believed, however, that the strategy of the Cambodian resistance was bound to fail in Cambodia due to the critical lack of popular support in the aftermath of the Cambodian genocide (1975–79).[8] As was discussed in the preceding chapter, that turned out to be not completely true. It was the Vietnamese who had to face growing resistance in rural Cambodia.

As a propaganda tool, the Vietnamese helped the Cambodian government establish the People's Revolutionary Tribunal, which tried the Pol Pot–Ieng Sary clique for the crime of genocide on August 15–19, 1979. It saw the Vietnamese troops as liberators, revealed Khmer Rouge hideouts to them, and even identified enemies burrowing among the masses. The Cambodian people were concerned that Vietnam would withdraw its troops soon, fearing that the Khmer Rouge would return to terrorize them.[9] This sentiment was short-lived as the Vietnamese troops were soon seen as occupiers in the eyes of Cambodian populace. On the economic side, Vietnam shifted from nonrefundable aid to the PRK for most of 1979–81 to primarily economic cooperation based on the principle of reciprocity and technical assistance in 1982–85.

Given the complete destruction of the socioeconomic system in Cambodia by the DK regime, the Vietnamese leadership concentrated its assistance on helping their Cambodian comrades on three major fronts: (1) building a new revolutionary government in Vietnam's image (armed forces, political system, economy, and culture) from the central government to local authorities; (2) stabilizing people's livelihoods, restoring production capacity, and educating the masses about the importance of collective ownership; and (3) helping the new Cambodian armed forces to wipe out the remaining resistance forces of the enemy, that is, the retreating Khmer Rouge.[10] Towards that end, Hanoi expected to tap into Cambodia's rich natural resources and agricultural potential with the help of Vietnamese experts and equipment to build a viable socialist economy for the People's Republic of Kampuchea (PRK) regime.[11]

In the chaotic years 1979–80, Hanoi counseled the Cambodian revolutionary government to adopt a combination of state central planning and private exchange of the goods it could not provide. Markets quickly responded based on such private exchange. While rice was the medium of exchange for inexpensive goods, more expensive items from Thailand were paid for in gold.[12] As discussed below, by 1982 Hanoi was alarmed by the flow of gold from Cambodia, Laos, and Vietnam to Thailand due to unofficial cross-border trade. Hanoi's other idea was to create solidarity groups for agricultural production (*doi doan ket san xuat nong nghiep* in Vietnamese, *krom samaki* in Khmer).[13] According to Margaret Slocomb, the distribution of agricultural production within the *krom samaki* was to be transparent, equitable, and reasonable. An individual's share of the rice harvest was to be proportional to his or her labor input. However, the elderly, children, and those without the strength to do labor also received a portion of food to guarantee their livelihood.[14] By 1980, as the food crisis persisted, family economy was encouraged and promoted to increase food production to compliment the collective economy.[15]

After January 1979, with respect to the construction of the Cambodian revolutionary government, Vietnam played three specific roles. First, at the central level, the Vietnamese government assisted its Cambodian counterpart in building organizational structures of governance from the central to local levels regarding the two specific tasks of state administration and economic management. The Vietnamese trained Cambodian civil servants to fill the bureaucracy of newly established government ministries. Vietnam also assisted the Cambodian government in developing a professional bureaucracy and a budget for each Cambodian ministry. In addition, the Vietnamese government helped the Cambodian government develop a plan for economic and cultural recovery, including proposals for material aid from the Soviet Union and other socialist countries for the years 1979–80.[16] The Vietnamese continued to play a mentoring role for their Cambodian comrades well into the mid-1980s.

Second, at the provincial and city levels, Vietnamese authorities in the south were instructed to train and assist their Cambodian comrades in implementing various directives and resolutions of the Cambodian party and government. They also helped their Cambodian counterparts organize provincial and city administrations, especially with respect to economic and cultural affairs. That effort included on-site training of provincial-level Cambodian cadres by provincial Vietnamese experts. In cases in which Cambodian cities or provinces did not have enough cadres, technical officials, or professionals, Vietnamese provincial authorities dispatched Vietnamese experts to Cambodia on the condition that the two governments agreed to it. Finally, Vietnamese provinces were to assist Cambodian provinces with material supplies, including agricultural equipment and fertilizer, and consumption goods as determined by the Vietnamese government.

To have clear oversight of Vietnamese assistance to Cambodia, in February 1979 Hanoi established sector-specific advisory committees, including B68 (a party committee in charge of political organization and the state apparatus from the central government to the district level), A40 (a government committee in charge of economic, social, and cultural affairs), Group 478 (a military advisory group charged with building the Cambodian revolutionary armed forces), K79 (in charge of building the public security and police forces), and A50 (in charge of rebuilding the capital of Phnom Penh).[17] On June 16, 1978, Work

Committee Z (Ban cong tac Z) of the Party Central Committee with the code name Committee B68 was established by the Politburo to carry out four tasks. First, it followed and researched the Cambodian situation on all fronts and reported to the Politburo to determine Vietnam's policy direction and assist the Cambodian revolution. Second, it implemented resolutions and instructions of the Politburo and CMC (the highest political and military decision-making bodies) concerning the building of Cambodian armed forces and the planning of military operations. Third, it assisted Cambodian comrades with establishing the Cambodian revolutionary government and training Cambodian cadres step by step. Fourth, it provided material aid to Cambodian revolutionaries as instructed by the CMC.[18] On December 12, less than two weeks before the invasion of Cambodia, the CMC issued Decision 129/QD-QU, establishing a military advisory group with the code name Group 478 under the supervision of B68.[19] The establishment of this military advisory group shows that Hanoi's leaders had a clear strategic plan to stay in Cambodia long after the invasion to train the armed forces and build a new government there.

On February 26, 1979, the Council of Government issued Decision 72-CP to establish the economic, social, and cultural committee A40 to assist the People's Revolutionary Council of Cambodia. Notably, A40's main objective was to assist the Cambodian government in economic-cultural recovery and development and implement various economic projects that the Cambodians were not yet capable of doing. The A40 committee dispatched Vietnamese vice-ministers to build ministries of the Cambodian government in their respective field of expertise.[20] For instance, a Vietnamese vice-minister of agriculture was appointed to lead a group of Vietnamese agriculture experts to mentor their Cambodian counterparts in the areas of irrigation, fishing, and forestry. For the central planning, a Vietnamese vice-chairman of the State Planning Committee was to lead a group of Vietnamese economic experts to help the Cambodian government with policy planning from finance and pricing to salaries of government civil servants.[21]

On August 24, 1979, of the same year, the secretariat of the Party Central Committee issued Resolution 19/NQ-TW to establish a unified Work Committee K (Ban phu trach cong tac K) in charge of all of Cambodia's economic, military, and political affairs and its foreign relations. Committee K was scheduled to act on behalf of the Vietnamese Party Central Committee, the government, and the CMC in its relations with the Cambodian government and serve as the central office in Cambodia in charge of overseeing all Vietnamese experts. Le Duc Tho was appointed chairman of this powerful committee,[22] making him the most influential Vietnamese leader in charge of Cambodian affairs and directly accountable to the Politburo in Hanoi from 1979 to 1980. General Le Duc Anh was appointed the first vice-chairman of the committee and Nguyen Con and Hoang The Thien vice-chairmen.[23]

As the planner of the invasion in December 1978 and architect of the PRK in Cambodia after January 1979, Le Duc Tho was the most powerful Vietnamese leader acting on behalf of the Politburo in Hanoi. As a trusted confidant of General Secretary Le Duan, Le Duc Tho's civilian expertise as chief of the party organization and member of the Politburo, according to General Le Duc Anh, was the right leader to lead Vietnam's mission in Cambodia.[24] At the Prime Minister's Office in Hanoi, Deputy Prime Minister Do Muoi was in charge of Vietnam's economic assistance to Cambodia while Nguyen Con, the chairman of A40, worked directly with the top leadership of the new Cambodian government and came up with a plan to be presented to the Politburo via Le Duc Tho. The case in point was the urgent reconstruction of the capital of Phnom Penh as the nerve center of the new government.[25] In February 1980, the Politburo decided to establish a General Group of Experts (Tong doan chuyen gia) under the leadership of General Le Duc Anh, who additionally served as the commander in chief of the Vietnamese volunteer troops in Cambodia.[26] Under Tho's leadership, the slogan of Vietnam's assistance in the civil and political affairs was "*Nganh giup nganh, tinh giup tinh, huyen giup huyen*" (Branch helps branch, province helps province, district helps district),[27] meaning that a Vietnamese branch of government and party was to assist its counterpart in the Cambodian government and party from the center to the district levels. In short, it was Hanoi's export of the Vietnamese model of revolutionary socialist governance to Cambodia.

At the provincial or city level, deputy heads of a specialized department or deputy secretary generals of the People's Committee (provincial governors or city mayors) were appointed to lead a group of four experienced cadres, including one expert on agricultural production, one on distribution, one on transportation, and one on public health. In major cities in Cambodia, Hanoi added three more Vietnamese experts on industry, commerce, and public transportation systems to the expert groups.[28] The model of "sister provinces or cities" was applied to implement the government system in provinces and cities. For instance, Ho Chi Minh City assisted the Cambodian capital Phnom Penh.[29]

By February 1979, Hanoi established a viable system for constructing and molding a new socialist regime in its own image in Cambodia, consisting of the B68 committee in charge of building the political bureaucracy and administrative offices of the party and government and first-rate Vietnamese experts to help their Cambodian counterparts from the center to the district level. These included A40 (economic and cultural advisers), Group 478 (military advisers), K79 (the security expert group, which assisted the Cambodian authority in building a police force and ensuring political security and social order), and the Command 917 of the Vietnamese volunteer troops (Vietnam's occupying force). With the Vietnamese military advisers, these groups undertook three tasks: (1) conducting joint military operations with the PRK armed forces to eliminate the enemy (including the Khmer Rouge), (2) helping build and strengthen the PRK revolutionary government armed forces at the provincial and district levels, and (3) preventing mass starvation and restoring people's normal livelihoods so they could resume economic production.[30] By October 1979, 1,284 Vietnamese experts had been dispatched to Cambodia; in January 1980, the number reached 1,600 (300 experts sent by the Vietnamese central government and 1,300 by Vietnamese provincial authorities). This figure excluded the group of Vietnamese military experts (the exact number is still not known) with the code name Group 478. The two main special committees, B68 and A40, were in charge of overseeing civilian Vietnamese experts in Cambodia.[31] Provincial assistance was under the jurisdiction of B68,[32] while A40 oversaw all Vietnamese experts in the field of economy and culture dispatched to Cambodia by the Vietnamese government.[33]

For 1980 Hanoi planned to increase the number of Vietnamese experts in Cambodia from 1,600 to 6,000.[34] In March 1980, the Organization Committee of the Central Committee of the CPV headed by Politburo member Le Duc Tho issued Directive 384 TC/TW, instructing Office 6 of the Prime Minister's Office, in charge of Cambodian affairs, to dispatch more Vietnamese cadres who spoke Khmer or Laotian languages to Cambodia and Laos and to increase funding from 15 to 25 percent for Vietnamese cadres to learn Khmer and Laotian languages. Except for Vietnamese translators, the directive prohibited Vietnamese workers in the field of economic production and construction and Vietnamese drivers from regularly contacting Cambodian people or officials.[35] The move was meant to reduce the political sensitivity of the increased Vietnamese presence in Cambodia. From the very beginning, the Vietnamese leadership was aware of the political sensitivity of their ubiquitous presence there. Hanoi's leaders told Vietnamese soldiers and experts:

> Helping the Cambodian revolution is our noble international duty and defends our motherland. In helping our Cambodian friends, we have to respect Cambodia's sovereign independence and maintain solidarity and friendship between Vietnam and Cambodia. The Khmer Rouge reactionaries spent four years indoctrinating Cambodian people to hate the Vietnamese, and they will continue

to stir up such ethnic hatred to lure Cambodian people to their side and use them as the support base for guerrilla warfare against us. All our soldiers and cadres who perform their duty in Cambodia must treat our Cambodian comrades and their citizens with respect, obey their laws, avoid the attitude of big power chauvinism in any form, and refrain from transgressing on Cambodian people's lives, property, and cultural traditions.[36]

Vietnamese Aid to the PRK, 1978–80

On December 23, 1978, on the eve of Vietnam's invasion of Cambodia, the Vietnamese government decided to allocate the first economic assistance package, including 50,000 to 70,000 tons of food grains, 600 tons of salt, 10 tons of sugar, 20,000 cans of condensed milk, 2 million meters of cloth, and other household products to restore people's livelihoods in the liberated zone.[37] As Le Duc Tho represented the Politburo of the Central Committee of the CPV on Cambodian affairs after Vietnam's invasion in 1979, at the Office of the Prime Minister, Deputy Prime Minister Do Muoi assumed oversight over Vietnam's economic assistance to Cambodia.[38]

In March 1979, Prime Minister Pham Van Dong issued an emergency assistance plan. From March to October of that year, the Vietnamese Ministry of Transport, with security for transportation guaranteed by the Vietnamese MoD, transported a total of 142,000 tons of material aid to Cambodia, including 11,000 tons of economic aid and 131,000 tons of military aid—that is, an average of 16,000 per month. A total of 124,500 tons of material aid and equipment were to be shipped from Ho Chi Minh City to Phnom Penh, an average of 14,000 tons per month. The remaining 18,000 tons were to be transported by sea via Kampong Som (the main seaport of Cambodia), which amounted to an average load of 2,000 tons of cargo per month or approximately 70 tons per day. The Vietnamese MoD oversaw the receipt of material aid in Kampong Som and Phnom Penh and then transported it from these two port cities to designated areas deep inside Cambodia.[39] In addition, Vietnam helped the Cambodians with transshipment of the much larger quantity of material aid from the Soviet Union and other socialist countries that passed through Vietnamese ports. To that end, the Vietnamese Ministry of Transport was instructed to undertake the enormous task of assisting its Cambodian counterpart in restoring various national roads connecting southern Vietnam to Cambodian cities and provinces near the border. Inside Cambodia, Vietnam helped restore the railroad from the Kampong Som seaport to Phnom Penh.[40]

In March 1979, Hanoi's leaders counseled their Cambodian comrades to ask for material aid from the Soviet Union and other socialist countries, and the Vietnamese advisers were to provide the idea and draft the aid request.[41] By April 1979, starvation in postgenocide Cambodia had reached an alarming scale. According to a report of the Vietnamese government, starvation was occurring in various provinces, including Kampong Thom, Kampong Speu, and Pursat, and other newly liberated regions in the western part of Cambodia. For the rest of the year, Hanoi ordered the Vietnamese military in Cambodia to distribute food supplies they captured from the enemy and some of their own food supplies to local Cambodian authorities so that they could distribute them directly to Cambodian people who faced starvation.[42]

For economic recovery, Hanoi's top economic planners used Cambodia's economic potential in the last two years (1968–69) of the Sihanouk regime as a benchmark for economic recovery after 1979. First and foremost, Hanoi made it an urgent priority to restore Cambodia's agricultural sector, which was its strongest. Cambodia already possessed 2.4 million hectares of rice paddies out of maximum cultivatable land of 2.8 million hectares, which yielded 3 million tons of rice per year in 1968–69. However, in 1979 the rice yield was very low, only 1 ton of rice per hectare, and only half the available land was cultivated for one rice season per year due to the severe shortage of labor in the aftermath of the genocide. The entire Cambodian labor force, according the Vietnamese study, consisted of 1.5 million people in 1979. Each laborer could produce only 250 kilograms of rice per year.

To increase productivity, the Vietnamese planned to help mechanize Cambodia's agriculture on a large scale, undertake irrigation projects, and create other favorable conditions for rice cultivation. The second priority for economic recovery went to Cambodia's transportation sector, which was severely damaged.[43] Hanoi referred to transportation recovery as a decisive factor for Cambodia's national defense and economic development. Speedy recovery in the two critical foundations of the PRK economy, namely, agriculture and transportation, required importing large amounts of machinery, vehicles, and other agricultural equipment from the Soviet Union and other socialist countries.[44] As an aid-receiving country, Vietnam was not able to assist Cambodia in acquiring sophisticated equipment and technology.

However, Vietnamese planners felt that the country could play a crucial role in human resources, and it dispatched tens of thousands of Vietnamese technicians and skilled laborers to directly advise their Cambodian comrades from the central government down to the various district authorities. Such a large presence of Vietnamese cadres and workers, as Hanoi's leaders speculated in April 1979, would become a major political issue that could arouse suspicion among Cambodian people and lend support to the enemy's anti-Vietnamese propaganda.[45] Vietnamese leaders were sensitive to Cambodia's suspicion of Vietnam's intentions. Hanoi's rationale, however, was that Cambodia's economic recovery would be too slow to recover if the PRK regime was to depend only on Cambodia's small labor force.[46] To minimize the political fallout of the heavy Vietnamese presence in Cambodia, Hanoi limited the number of unskilled Vietnamese workers and used more Cambodian workers in the areas of road construction and other public works. In the beginning, Vietnamese economic professionals and managers were to directly help the Cambodian government and directly work within the Cambodian administration from the central down to the district level.[47] Thus, for Cambodia's economic recovery, Hanoi's formula was to combine Cambodia's rich natural resources, Soviet modern technology and machinery, and Vietnam's basic but long-term assistance in the areas of skilled labor, technical and economic experts, and training Cambodian officials in socialist economic management.

On January 24, 1979, Vice-Minister of Foreign Affairs Vo Dong Giang was appointed to replace Phan Ba as Vietnam's ambassador to the PRK.[48] In September 1979, B68 officially assigned eighteen Vietnamese education experts to build a socialist educational system in eighteen of the twenty provinces of Cambodia. By January 1980, every Cambodian province had a Vietnamese education expert, and Phnom Penh had two.[49] In April, A50, a Ho Chi Minh City group of experts in charge of rebuilding the capital city of Phnom Penh, recruited 360 teachers who had suffered under the Khmer Rouge regime and had diplomas from the Sihanouk and Lon Nol regimes to teach at 70 schools with a total of 90,000 students in Phnom Penh.[50] For a period of one year, from January 1979 to January 1980, Vietnamese experts trained more than 20,000 teachers and went on to train more than 10,000 more in 1980.[51] Vietnam's training focused on both political ideology and technical professions, with the latter serving the former. The training emphasized (1) the ideological orientation of the Cambodian revolution, (2) the crimes of the Pol Pot–Ieng Sary clique, and (3) Cambodian-Vietnamese-Laotian unity and international socialist solidarity.[52] To Vietnamese education experts, the *colonial and feudal* influence of the old educational systems remained strong, posing a major challenge to the building of a socialist education system in Cambodia.[53] Through their socialist lenses, the Vietnamese viewed the old education system of the Sihanouk era of the 1960s as "heavily influenced by French colonialism, reactionary, and backward."[54] The eradication of the colonial, feudal, and reactionary influence of the previous regimes and ideological indoctrination of a new socialist man became the paramount political and ideological objective of the new socialist education system.[55]

The Vietnamese experts claimed a historic achievement in their assistance to Cambodia in the field of education.[56] The educational task of the Vietnamese education experts in Cambodia was divided into two phases. The first five years (1979–84) were the most important phase, as they were to eradicate the influence of the old educational system and build a new socialist one to serve the PRK. In 1982–83, the Vietnamese experts helped Cambodia enroll 1.6 million middle school students, which was almost twice the number of students during the Sihanouk era.

In 1979 Vietnam provided Cambodia with nonrefundable aid of 130 million VND.[57] In a top-secret report dated April 12, 1980, to the top Vietnamese leadership in Hanoi, chief economic adviser to the PRK and chairman of Committee A40 Nguyen Con counseled, "Vietnam's 1980 assistance to Cambodia had to factor in the maximum use of the latter's existing material resources and foreign aid from other socialist countries and international organizations."[58] To reduce Vietnam's aid burden, Con only proposed to provide nonrefundable aid worth 150 million VND for 1980 to continue assisting Cambodia in the recovery of agriculture, food production, transportation, telecommunications, culture, health, and education. More than one-fourth of the fund (40.2 million VND) would be used to the strengthen the Cambodian revolutionary forces.[59]

In 1980, as Hanoi was planning to increase the number of Vietnamese experts from 1,600 in 1979 to 6,000 and train 3,000 Cambodian officials, the planners began to face the increased cost of building a regime in Cambodia.[60] In December 1979, B68 requested that each Vietnamese expert working in Cambodian provinces receive a monthly ration of 24 kilograms of food supplies, 3 kilograms of meat, 2.5 kilograms of fish and shrimp, and 1.2 kilograms of peanut, salt, and sugar per person. Citing a proposal by the Ministry of Foodgrains and Foodstuffs that food rations be reduced due to food shortages, deputy prime minister and vice-chairman of the Council of Ministers Do Muoi, who was in charge of economic affairs and assistance to Cambodia, decided that from April 1 of that year onward the monthly food ration would be reduced to 16 kilograms for each Vietnamese expert who worked in Cambodian provinces and 15 for those who worked in Phnom Penh.

In response to the increased expenses for Vietnamese specialists working in Cambodia in 1980, Deputy Prime Minister Do Muoi suggested a more pragmatic solution; that is, the Vietnamese experts utilize a portion of their rice ration to purchase meat at local markets in Cambodia. In 1978–79, expenses

for all Vietnamese experts in Cambodia were covered by the General Department of Logistics of the MoD, but in February 1980 three thousand Vietnamese
specialists were present in Cambodia and this figure excluded Vietnamese experts dispatched by the CPV and Vietnamese provinces for short-term assistance to the PRK. In 1980, the structure of managing assistance to the PRK
changed; material supply, including food for Vietnamese military experts, remained the responsibility of the General Department of Logistics of the MoD;
the Prime Minister's Office was in charge of all expenses for Vietnamese economic experts headed by Committee A40; and the secretariat of B68 was in
charge of meeting the needs of all Vietnamese specialists the CPV sent to Cambodia. In February 1980, Tran Xuan Bach, head of Committee B68, asked for
twenty vehicles for Vietnamese experts in Cambodian provinces (one vehicle
for each province), but Deputy Prime Minister Do Muoi approved only ten.[61]
Much less enthusiastic about Vietnam's international duty to assist the Cambodian revolutionaries than Le Duc Tho, economically minded Do Muoi was a
strong advocate of saving Vietnamese resources and using as many Cambodian
resources as possible for nation building in Cambodia.

In 1981, due to Vietnam's economic difficulties, Hanoi planned not to increase its aid significantly and desired to use Cambodian resources and foreign
aid from the Soviet Union and other socialist countries to cover the majority of
the postgenocide recovery. As a conservative (one of Hanoi's ideological hard-
liners), Con warned the Cambodian leadership against accepting aid from
western organizations for fear of political infiltration.[62]

Vietnam was Cambodia's patron but it was still a poor country. Hanoi's
leaders expected to build Cambodia's new revolutionary government in their
image using their human resources. Yet, with Vietnam's limited ability to provide Cambodia with sophisticated and high-value material aid, Hanoi's leaders
looked to the Soviet Union and other, more developed Eastern European countries of the COMECON to assist their nation-building efforts in Cambodia. In
just one year after liberating Cambodia from the Pol Pot genocidal regime in
1980, Hanoi looked for ways to reduce Vietnam's economic burden. Counseling
Cambodia to exploit its natural resources and ask for more aid from the Soviet
Union was the next logical step.

The Role of Soviet Aid to the PRK, 1979–81

In 1979 the Soviet Union provided the PRK with significant nonrefundable
material aid via Vietnam. The Soviet aid package included 20 diesel electricity
generators, 200 tractors, 360 transport vehicles,[63] 250 small vehicles,[64] 35 buses,

5 ambulances, 3 mobile clinics, 50,000 tons of fuel,[65] 8,300 tons of steel, 1,000 tons of iron, 2,000 bicycles, 5,000 tons of cement, 200 tons of aluminum, 50,000 tons of rice, and a long list of consumption goods including 3 million meters of cloth to 2 million dishes.[66] In September of 1979, the PRK regime, as the Vietnamese counseled, requested supplementary aid from the Soviet Union, including 20,000 tons of rice, 50,000 tons of corn, 30,000 tons of fuel, and other items.[67] Thus, Soviet material aid played the most significant role in building a material foundation for the PRK regime.

In enlisting Vietnamese help with the transshipment of its material aid to the PRK, the Soviets distrusted their Vietnamese comrades' handling of such aid and desired to have their own economic experts directly assess Cambodia's need for Soviet aid. On June 16, 1979, Moscow dispatched a seventeen-member delegation from the Committee for Foreign Economic Relations, headed by the committee vice-chairman, to Phnom Penh to assess the PRK's economic situation and determine what part of its aid request was urgently needed. Later it presented its findings to the Soviet government.[68] The Soviet delegation met with its Cambodian counterpart led by the Minister of Economy and Livelihood Ros Samay. To Soviet dismay, the Cambodian side allowed its two Vietnamese economic advisers from the Vietnamese Ministry of Foreign Trade to attend the bilateral meeting.[69]

The Soviet delegation concluded its visit to the PRK by offering a few recommendations and a specific suggestion that aid should be shipped directly from the Soviet Union to the PRK. First, the Soviets agreed to assist the PRK in technology, industrial equipment, and machinery to help restore factories and transportation. Second, they prioritized their material aid to many fields, including health (e.g., the Khmer-Soviet Friendship Hospital), transportation, telecommunications and television, fisheries, agriculture, and technical training.[70] For transportation especially, the Soviets planned to immediately restore the means to ship Soviet aid directly to Cambodia via the Kampong Som seaport and Phnom Penh River port. The Soviets also pledged to provide more transportation vehicles for the second phase of transportation infrastructure recovery.[71] In addition, the Soviet government desired to immediately establish an economic representative in Phnom Penh.

One of the reasons behind Soviet frustration with the transshipment of Soviet aid to Cambodia for 1979 via the Vietnamese port in Ho Chi Minh City was the lack of transparency on the part of the Vietnamese government regarding the handling of Soviet aid. A few factors contributed to this lack of transparency.

First, Vietnam's decentralized system of transshipment, under which each Vietnamese ministry was responsible for shipping its own Soviet aid, did not work smoothly and in fact led to confusion, which in turn created friction in Vietnam's relations with Cambodia and the Soviet Union. While the Ministry of Foodgrains and Foodstuffs received Soviet material aid on behalf of the Cambodian government, the Ministry of Transport was in charge of transporting all of it from Vietnamese ports to various destinations in Cambodia. For instance, in 1979 the Vietnamese Ministry of Foodgrains and Foodstuffs received 50,000 tons of food from the Soviet Union, and the Ministry of Transport was to ship it to Cambodia. In 1980, Vietnam was to ship 130,000 tons of Soviet food aid to Cambodia, and the Vietnamese Ministry of Materials Supply was responsible for receiving Soviet aid in the form of fuel, steel, iron, and agricultural machinery on behalf of the Cambodian government. As a result, two issues created disputes between the Soviets and the Vietnamese. At times the Soviets transferred "Soviet aid to Vietnam" to "Soviet aid to Cambodia" due to the emergency. According to the Vietnamese, Soviet ship captains sometimes failed to keep a clear record of this change. As a result, when the Vietnamese took a portion of "Soviet aid to Cambodia" to pay for that loan, a dispute between the two sides occurred. On the Vietnamese side, when Soviet aid to Cambodia had not yet arrived, the Vietnamese shipped its own food supplies, including rice and instant noodles, as emergency loans. However, the Vietnamese would then take some of Soviet aid to Cambodia in rice and corn to pay back these loans. When the Vietnamese side did not make this clear to their Soviet and Cambodian comrades beforehand, it created a misunderstanding between Vietnam and the Soviet Union on the one hand and between Vietnam and Cambodia on the other.[72] To make it more transparent, the Vietnamese Ministry of Finance proposed to Prime Minister Pham Van Dong that all transshipments of aid from other countries to Cambodia should be under the central control of the Vietnamese Ministry of Transport. In doing so, it would create unified control, including management and delivery of foreign aid to Cambodia via Vietnamese ports.[73]

On May 2, 1980, the Soviet Union signed an agreement to significantly increase nonrefundable economic and military aid to the PRK. The most notable items of Soviet aid for 1980 consisted of 130,000 tons of food supplies (50,000 tons of rice, 20,000 tons of flour, 30,000 tons of rice noodles, and 30,000 tons of corn), 350 vehicles (of the 500 Cambodia had requested), 130,000 tons of fuel (10,000 more than the quantity requested), and 45 more items of economic assistance from cloth and bicycles to agricultural machinery.[74] In addition, the Soviets provided substantial military aid, including 91 military transportation trucks (30 Zil-157-KD heavy-duty trucks and 61 GAZ-53 light trucks) for 1980, 102 GAZ-66 light trucks and 3 helicopters for 1981, and 33 other items of military necessities from 800 tons of fuel to medical supplies.[75] In addition, the PRK received supplementary aid in food and consumption goods from Bulgaria, Mongolia, Czechoslovakia, Poland, and the German Democratic Republic (East Germany).[76]

In a letter to Prime Minister Pen Sovann dated June 6, 1980,[77] Deputy Chairman of the Council of Ministers of the Soviet Union Ivan Arkhipov expressed his displeasure with the slow transshipment of Soviet material aid, including food supplies, from Cambodia's Kampong Som seaport to other parts of the country where such aid was needed. Arkhipov told Sovann:

> What is most important to us is that all Soviet aid, including food supplies, is effectively used and quickly transported to regions where such aid is needed. In the spirit of comradeship, I want to convey our concern about the situation of transporting Soviet material aid from Kampong Som port to other regions. Due to poor preservation and slow transportation, most of the goods were damaged due to the Cambodian side's neglect. For example, 6,000 tons of corn [from the Soviet Union] has been stored at the port since October of last year [1979]. Two thousand tons of cement arrived at the port in January of this year [1980], but due to poor storage the cement was largely spoiled. In addition, 20 of the 50 tractors we sent you are still parked at the port and have not been used.[78]

Arkhipov told Sovann to increase his shipments from six hundred to fifteen hundred tons of cargo per day, which was roughly equal to the daily quantity of imports arriving at the Kampong Som port.[79] The Soviets pledged to send two ships for sea and river transport, together with a group of fifty Soviet experts and equipment to upgrade the Cambodian port facility.[80] Arkhipov urged Sovann to mobilize transportation and the labor force to increase capacity as the rainy season was approaching, which meant that transport was going to be even more difficult.[81] The PRK's overreliance on the Vietnamese for transportation must have appalled the Soviets.

In 1981, two years after the collapse of the DK regime, Vietnam largely curtailed its nonrefundable aid to Cambodia and began a new era of bilateral trade based on mutual interests between the two countries.[82] The majority of Vietnam's exports to Cambodia consisted of high-value products, including machinery, equipment, spare parts, rice and fruit tree seeds, cloth, medicine and medical supplies, school supplies, construction materials, handicraft products, and processed food. On the other hand, Cambodia's exports to Vietnam comprised mostly low-value items, including agricultural products, forest products, fish, poultry, and domestic animals.[83] Vietnam's nonrefundable aid to

Cambodia was reduced to technical assistance, including research studies; design, repair, and recovery of thirty-five economic and cultural projects; the dispatch of Vietnamese experts to Cambodia; and scholarships for Cambodian students.[84]

In April 1981, Vietnam and the Soviet Union signed an agreement on "the coordination of economic assistance to the recovery and construction of the PRK concerning projects in the agreements between Cambodia and the Soviet Union."[85] This trilateral agreement stated, "Vietnam will assist in the implementation of the work under the responsibility of the Cambodian government as stated in the agreement with the Soviet government. Such assistance in the form of sending Vietnamese experts to the Soviet-aided projects in Cambodia will be carried out in agreements between the Vietnamese and Cambodian authorities. When necessary, the Cambodian authority will transfer to the Vietnamese government all important documents on structural design and technological equipment from the Soviet Union."[86] Thus, Vietnam's role as the coordinator and implementer of the Soviet aid projects in Cambodia further suggests the Soviets' delegation of responsibility for assisting Laos and Cambodia to Vietnam as the de facto leader of socialist Indochina.

Vietnam-Led Indochinese Economic Regionalism, 1983–85

The year 1983 saw a major shift in Hanoi's strategic thinking from an all-out military confrontation with China and ASEAN to the partial withdrawal of Vietnamese troops from Cambodia and a long-term strategic plan for Vietnam-led economic integration of the three Indochinese countries, a model inspired by the Soviet-led COMECON. Such a shift in strategic thinking was driven by both international pressure and domestic economic imperatives at home. In 1980–82, the decline of the Soviet economic power in the last few years of Brezhnev's rule, compounded by economic competitiveness between Vietnam and other Eastern European members of the COMECON, converged with Hanoi's growing fear of the economic and political threat emanating from China and Thailand, which were aligned with the United States.

By late 1982 and early 1983, Vietnam's two main strategic objectives— building socialism and defending national sovereignty— in Hanoi's view were more threatened by economic and political factors emanating from China and ASEAN than by Chinese military attacks.

At the center of this change was the rising influence of reformist leaders, including Foreign Minister Nguyen Co Thach. Against the growing military costs of the two front-war and the prospect of protracted warfare, their ideas about economic reform and opening gained more support from the old revolutionary guards, namely, Le Duan, Le Duc Tho, Truong Chinh, and Pham Van Dong within the Politburo of the Party Central Committee, after four years of costly military confrontation with China and military intervention in Cambodia. In 1983 this gradual change in Hanoi's strategic thinking was by no means a move away from the Soviet camp toward the West but rather a reorientation of strategies from a focus on military confrontation with China and Thailand toward deescalation of military conflicts and dialogue with China and Thailand in the hope of reaching an acceptable political solution to the Cambodian problem. Such regional stability would allow Hanoi to focus on economic integration within the socialist Indochinese bloc. The reformists used the language of "peaceful economic and political evolution" engineered by China and ASEAN to convince the military-first faction within the CPV and its smaller Communist allies Laos and Cambodia to support a shift from short-term military confrontation to long-term economic security as the Soviet bloc was becoming a less reliable base for Vietnam's economic development.

The ultimate motivation behind the economy-first faction's strategic idea of Vietnam-led economic regionalism was to provide a short- and long-term material foundation for its twin strategy of building socialism and defending its national sovereignty against the Chinese threat, as well as for expanding Vietnam's political sphere of influence within the Soviet-dominated hierarchical structure of international socialism.

The bulk of available documentary evidence reveals that, although Hanoi's leaders did not have the motive of physically colonizing all of Indochina per se, they sought to establish a Vietnam-dominated Indochinese regionalism to advance Vietnam's economic development and security environment and confront the economic and political threat emanating from China, Thailand, and other ASEAN members.

In March 1979, just two months after toppling the Pol Pot regime, Prime Minister Pham Van Dong instructed economic experts in Office 6 of his cabinet to conduct a thorough study of Cambodia's economic potential. On April 30, a report on "Cambodia's economic situation after liberation," was submitted to the prime minister. In this report, Vietnamese economic experts wrote, "Based on our early assessment, Cambodia's long-term economic potential is rich and diverse in many fields, from agriculture and forestry to fisheries and so on. Its rich natural resources will be a strong foundation for developing an independent socialist economy."[87]

In the summer of 1982, the Council of Ministers instructed the MOFA and the Committee of Economic and Cultural Cooperation with Laos and Cambodia to take charge of organizing an economic experts conference on economic cooperation between Vietnam, Laos, and Cambodia to be held for six days in Ho Chi Minh city in January 1983 in preparation for the first high-level party and government leadership summit of the three Indochinese countries.[88] In an internally circulated report dated August 24, 1982, the MOFA and the Economic Advisory Committee of the Prime Minister's Office wrote, "Today the process of the international division of labor and economic cooperation between socialist countries has created the need to build economic alliances with the three Indochinese countries to collectively confront the threat of the West-led economic globalization and the economic threat posed by China and Thailand respectively."[89]

To understand why Hanoi's strategic thinking was shifting in late 1982 away from military confrontation, which began in 1978, it is important to discuss how Hanoi viewed the decline of Soviet economic and political power in the early 1980s following the Soviet invasion of Afghanistan in 1979. In addition, one needs to take into account the trend of great power rivalry moving away from military confrontation toward peaceful coexistence and dialogue between the Soviet Union and the United States, on the one hand, and reconciliation between the Soviet Union and China in the context of troubled Sino-American relations on the other. Vice-Minister of Foreign Affairs Vo Dong Giang believed that the troubled relations between China and the United States would compel China to shift its strategy from military confrontation to reconciliation and dialogue with Vietnam and the Soviet Union.[90]

Hanoi's leaders must have been alarmed by the deterioration of the political and economic foundations of Soviet power in the last few years of Brezhnev's rule (1980–82), which was in part affected by the renewed Cold War tensions between the Soviet Union and the United States and heightened military confrontation between Warsaw Pact and North Atlantic Treaty Organization (NATO) forces following the Soviet invasion of Afghanistan in 1979. The US Carter administration's economic sanctions against the Soviet Union after the invasion of Afghanistan had already exacerbated economic tensions inside the Soviet bloc.[91]

The Polish political and economic crisis of 1980 revealed the precarious position of the Soviet Union. Moscow injected US$4 billion to prevent the collapse of Poland's economy that year, while food shortages in the Soviet Union worsened.[92] From 1980 onward, a number of Warsaw Pact countries, including East Germany, Czechoslovakia, Hungary, Romania, and Bulgaria, became increasingly dependent on NATO countries for loans.[93] The worsening economic and political crisis within the Soviet bloc had a direct negative impact on Vietnam, along with Cambodia and Laos, as they had shifted to far greater reliance on foreign aid from and trade with the Soviet-led COMECON; Vietnam's exports to the COMECON accounted for more than 70 percent of its imports coming from these countries in the early 1980s.[94] To the Vietnamese, the Polish crisis demonstrated the limits of Soviet economic power as a socialist bulwark against the invasion of western capitalism. The Vietnamese also learned that members of the Warsaw Pact were engaging in limited economic relations with NATO countries even though they were ideological rivals engaged in military confrontations.

In close proximity, Vietnam in the early 1980s not only faced ideological conflicts and military confrontations with China and Thailand, the latter a key member of anti-Vietnam ASEAN, but it also came under growing economic threats from its neighbors. As Vietnam continued to suffer economic stagnation and food shortages in the early 1980s, unofficial cross-border trade with Thailand was depleting Vietnam's and Cambodia's reserves of gold and foreign currency. As large numbers of commodities, including secondhand motorcycles, popular foreign cigarettes, Thai beer, and clothes were smuggled from Thailand through Cambodia to southern Vietnam, Vietnamese and Cambodian gold, diamonds, and foreign currency ended up in Thailand.[95] Imports of goods from Thailand had to be paid for in gold or foreign currency. As Beresford and Phong explain, "Although they could be purchased in Phnom Penh with Vietnamese dong [VND], they had first to be purchased in Thailand with Thai baht or US dollars. In this case the imports have been paid for. The deficit, which was certainly large, could be covered either by Cambodian exports to Thailand or by dollars available in the Vietnamese market and transferred to Cambodia."[96] According to Beresford and Phong's estimation, Vietnam's annual unofficial imports from Cambodia amounted to no less than US$200 million. With respect to the balance of unofficial imports and exports, Vietnam suffered a large trade deficit with Cambodia.[97] Unofficial cross-border trade with Thailand via Laos followed the same pattern; cheap Thai shoes and clothes were the two most popular goods in Vietnam.[98] As a result, the constant flow of foreign currency and gold from Vietnam to Thailand became a major concern to Hanoi's leaders.

Deng Xiaoping declared at the Twelfth Party Congress on September 1, 1982, that "economic construction" was the fundamental determinant of China's success in solving international and domestic problems.[99] Since 1980 China had actively engaged in a new mission in its economic diplomacy, that is, to promote its economic development. China had already developed a working relationship with the United States to obtain economic and technological assistance.[100] With the cooperation of the United States and Thailand, China sent economic and military aid to the Cambodian resistance forces, including the

Khmer Rouge, to increase the human and economic costs to the Vietnamese occupying forces.

Proponents of reforms and opening, especially Foreign Minister Nguyen Co Thach, argued that the greatest threat to the Socialist Republic of Vietnam and its smaller Communist allies in Cambodia and Laos was by 1982 *political* and *economic*; to them, the military threat posed by China and its ally, the resistance forces inside Cambodia, had become secondary to the growing threat of China's economic and political rise. In other words, from the perspective of the economy-first faction, the fear of Vietnam being left behind the global economic change and lagging behind its Communist great power neighbor China presented a long-term threat.

Hanoi's idea of a Vietnam-dominated Indochinese regionalism emerged in the context of (1) the deterioration of the economic and political foundations of the Soviet bloc and uncertainty about the Soviet commitment to aiding Vietnam, Laos, and Cambodia; (2) Hanoi's fear of a repeated economic crisis and domestic political instability and desire for more autonomy from the Soviet Union; and (3) the immediate threat China and Thailand posed to the political, economic, and security interests of Vietnam in Indochina. Internal discussions at the policy-input level, precisely in specialized committees and agencies such as the Committee of Economic Relations with Foreign Countries, the Committee of Economic and Cultural Cooperation with Laos and Cambodia, and the Prime Minister's Office, reveal Hanoi's strategic shift from a posture of military confrontation to one of economic integration and political solidarity in Indochina in late 1982 and 1983.

On February 22–23, 1983, on Vietnam's initiative, the three Indochinese socialist countries convened the first high-level party and government summit in Vientiane, the capital of the LPDR. Hanoi attached historic and political importance to the summit and dispatched a Vietnamese delegation to assist Laos in organizing it.[101] Internationally this summit was primed to boost Vietnam's public diplomacy, demonstrating the nonmilitary nature of the Indochinese socialist bloc to dispel the ASEAN security concerns often raised by Thailand, Singapore, and Malaysia about a Vietnam-dominated Indochinese military alliance. The Vietnamese hoped to drive a wedge within the ASEAN community and between ASEAN and China. The summit was timed to launch a diplomatic surprise to derail China's attempt to isolate the Indochinese countries at the seventh NAM summit in New Delhi, India, on March 7–11, 1982, during which the issue of Cambodia's country seat at NAM was expected to be a hotly contested issue. The Vietnamese top diplomat Nguyen Co Thach and Prime Minister Pham Van Dong declared a major success in isolating China at the NAM summit.[102] There was a split near the middle, with twenty-five countries supporting the Cambodian government in exile and nineteen supporting the Heng Samrin regime.[103] Only Singapore and Malaysia condemned Vietnam's occupation of Cambodia. Seventeen countries voted to leave the Cambodia seat vacant.

In Nguyen Co Thach's view, this was a notable success because China had hoped to enlist fifty countries to support the Cambodian government in exile.[104] Foreign Minister Nguyen Co Thach told the Council of State in a two-day meeting on March 29–30, 1983, "Many countries are still concerned about us and have not yet understood our intention. They raised concerns about 'The Indochinese Federation.' We explained to them that the declaration of the three [Indochinese] countries' summit did not use the language 'federation' or 'military alliance.' The three countries only talked about 'economic cooperation,' and this does not resemble the [Soviet-led] Council of Mutual Economic Assistance either."[105] Clearly the Vietnamese leadership publicly suggested that Vietnam did not seek to dominate Cambodia and Laos economically as the Soviets dominated Eastern European countries. However, evidence from internal records of the Vietnamese government in 1983–85 indicate otherwise, that Vietnam-dominated Indochinese economic regionalism was exactly what the economically minded leaders of the Council of Ministers in Hanoi had in mind.

One of the major successes of the Indochinese summit in March 1983, as Nguyen Co Thach told the Council of State, was that the three countries shared a common stance that "under present international circumstances, the three Indochinese countries' solidarity with the Soviet Union and other socialist countries is a very important factor and that the unity between the three countries is a decisive factor in achieving victory."[106] The first major achievement at the Indochinese summit, Nguyen Co Thach stressed, was that "Laos and Cambodia recalled Uncle Ho's teaching about 'unity and victory' of the Indochinese Communist Party and valued the important role of Vietnam in the Indochinese revolution today."[107] Thus, ideologically even the economy-first reformists, including Foreign Minister Nguyen Co Thach, still saw Vietnam playing a central role in building Indochinese economic regionalism within the Soviet-led international socialist hierarchy.

The second achievement at the summit was a trilateral agreement on (1) the relations between the three countries and their strategies and tactics vis-à-vis other countries and (2) the issue of Vietnam's troops in Cambodia. Vietnam intended to reemphasize the principle of independent and national sovereignty, voluntarism, and equality in the relations between the three countries to refute the accusation leveled by China and ASEAN that Vietnam's intention was to create the Indochinese Federation under its control.[108]

Yet Hanoi's more concrete success was achieved behind closed doors, that is Vietnam obtained the consent of Laos and Cambodia to its long-term plan for economic integration of the three countries. According to the Vietnamese MOFA report, "Laos and Cambodia with good faith want to enhance the co-operation of the three economic cooperation committees. Besides, Laos desired to quickly establish a system of economic cooperation between the three countries modeled after the Council of Mutual Economic Assistance."[109] Vietnam's top economic planners were very pleased that their Cambodian and Laotian comrades were enthusiastic about Hanoi's long-term plan for Vietnam-led economic integration in Indochina. But the Vietnamese explained to them that

> because we cannot afford to allow our enemy to accuse Vietnam of establishing a military alliance and to cause our ASEAN neighbors to fear us, we did not mention the trilateral military cooperation in the summit declaration. However, in our dialogue the Laotian comrades proposed that we help them by maintaining a long-term presence of [Vietnamese] volunteer troops in their country. As for the Cambodian comrades, they completely agreed with us regarding the strategy of gradual withdrawal of Vietnamese volunteer troops, and they praised and thanked our soldiers in Cambodia. Especially, the three countries completely agreed with each other regarding the assessment of regional and international politics, China's ambitions in Indochina and Southeast Asia, and the orientation of our foreign policy.[110]

In 1983, Laos and Cambodia were also in accord with Vietnam's strategy of the gradual withdrawal of Vietnamese troops from Cambodia to demonstrate the corresponding ability of the Cambodian revolution to stand on its own and to emphasize Vietnam's desire for peace consistent with the international trend of deescalation of confrontation in the world and Southeast Asia.[111] In a top-secret report on the March summit delivered to the Council of State, the MOFA wrote:

> After three years of bitter struggle and victory, the position (*the*) and strength (*luc*) of the three countries have never been as strong as they are today. We have circumvented the most difficult test in the years 1978–80, during which the Sino-American cooperation against our Indochinese revolution was at its peak. Our Indochinese unity and cooperation with the Soviet Union have also never been this strong. China's policy of putting pressure on ASEAN countries to oppose the Indochinese countries has failed. Dialogue and peaceful coexistence

in Southeast Asia is the emerging trend. The recent Sino-Soviet negotiations marked the failure of China's policy of using the Sino-American alliance against the Soviet Union.[112]

Foreign Minister Nguyen Co Thach warned, "We must educate our cadres well to defeat the enemy's attempt to divide our three [Indochinese] countries and to reject the ideology of big-country chauvinism and the ideology of narrow-minded ethnonationalism. Especially we need to be prepared to confront China's shift from the policy of using the military to a new policy of peaceful evolution, using political and economic tools to divide our three countries, foster regime change, and sabotage our revolution from the inside."[113] In essence, Indochinese economic regionalism was to replace each country's economic nationalism.

A series of conferences had been convened to find common ground on the substance of the joint communiqué of the three Indochinese countries well before the summit even took place. Nguyen Co Thach told the Council of State on March 29, 1983, that the two preparatory conferences at the foreign minister and economic expert levels were organized in such a way as to guarantee secrecy well before the high-level party and government summit in Vientiane.[114] On December 9–10, 1982, the vice-ministerial conference in Vientiane concluded with an agreement to hold a follow-up conference of economic, cultural, and technological experts from the three countries in January 1983.

Tran Xuan Bach, secretary of the party secretariat of the Party Central Committee, was appointed chairman of the preparatory committee (*ban tru bi*) for the high-level summit, and the vice-minister of foreign affairs, Vo Dong Giang, was appointed as one of the members of this committee. On December 27, 1982, Bach's preparatory committee authorized the Standing Committee of the Council of Ministers to organize a six-day conference of economic experts from the three countries in Ho Chi Minh City in January 1983. Each country was to send a six-member delegation to the conference. The Vietnamese delegation was headed by Tran Quoc Manh, who was vice-chairman of the Committee on Economic and Cultural Cooperation with Laos and Cambodia (CECC–Laos and Cambodia).[115] In an all-day meeting on December 30, the CECC–Laos and Cambodia circulated an economic cooperation policy draft prepared for the conference of economic experts from the three countries. Senior economic officials of the Council of Ministers, including Hoang Kim An, attended the meeting.[116] The draft of the policy proposal to be presented to the Laotian and Cambodian delegations only contained a summary of (1) "content of cooperation," (2) "procedure on the forms of cooperation," and (3) "methods of implementation."[117]

In a nutshell, Vietnam's proposal was that for 1983–85 the implementation of bilateral trade agreements would continue and focus on trilateral cooperation that benefited the three countries in the most important areas, especially food supply, consumption goods, processing of forest products for export, transportation and telecommunications, and technical cooperation.[118] Six forms of economic cooperation listed in the proposal included nonrefundable aid, loans, joint projects, trade, subcontracting, and plan coordination for the economic FYI for 1985–90.[119] The three countries agreed that the Soviet ruble would be used as the currency for trade.

Vietnam by design was going to be the dominant country in Indochinese economic regionalism, although the Vietnamese planners spoke of sovereign equality and socialist fraternity in public. Vietnam's real motives were masked by the language of "special brotherly relations between the three countries" and the need for "mutual assistance" through all-sided and long-term economic, cultural, and technological cooperation. In its internally circulated comprehensive economic study of the Committee on Economic Relations with Foreign Countries, which was presented to the Politburo and the Standing Committee of the Council of Ministers in July 1982, the document shows Hanoi's long-term economic plan for a Vietnam-dominated Indochina. Documents in preparation for the high-level summit on February 22–23, 1983, further reveal the long-term strategic thinking of Vietnam's economic planners.

In a top-secret economic research report, dated July 17, 1982, prepared for the Council of Ministers to present to the Politburo, a research group of the Committee on Economic Relations with Foreign Countries drafted a master plan for Vietnam's economic cooperation with Cambodia and Laos from 1983 to 2000.[120] This report was completed on June 30, 1982. Then it was sent on July 2 to the Office of the Council of Ministers for further review and additional ideas. In a revised version of the "economic cooperation plan," the research group provided an in-depth analysis of the need and potential of economic cooperation and integration between the three countries. Finally, the Committee on Economic Relations with Foreign Countries presented the study to the Politburo on July 17 so it could decide on a policy orientation. The Politburo was to convene a high-level party-government summit of the three countries in February 1983 to forge a trilateral agreement to deepen economic integration between the three Indochinese countries.

The study began by stressing the shift from Vietnam's nonrefundable aid to Cambodia (1979–81) and Laos (1965–81) to building independent socialist regimes in the two countries and to economic cooperation after 1982 to oppose the Sino-American alignment and its attempt to weaken the solidarity of the three countries. In the Vietnamese analysis, four factors (politics, geography, economic resources, and history) were singled out as representative of the commonality the three countries shared, and these factors also laid a strong foundation for integrated economic regionalism in Indochina. Politically, the three nations were to be the vanguard of socialism in Southeast Asia, and they were under a growing economic threat from China and Thailand, which were aligned with the United States. At the same time, China and Thailand attempted in every way to drive a wedge among the three countries and between them and the Soviet Union by stoking Cambodian and Laotian fears of Vietnamese hegemonism.[121]

Geographically the three countries are closely linked on the same Indochinese peninsula, sharing the Mekong River and a few million hectares of land rich in natural resources along their land borders. In terms of economic resources, each country had different strengths and weaknesses and could benefit by forging collective efforts to step up economic productivity and exports to the Soviet Union and other COMECON countries in Eastern Europe. Historically, colonial France had crafted a long-term plan to exploit the natural resources of Indochina by building a transportation system that crisscrossed the peninsula. Later, the first half of the 1970s saw the failed attempt by the United States to connect Cambodia and Laos with western Thailand's economy. Yet, from the perspective of Hanoi's economic planners, the regional economic blueprint of the French colonialists remained useful for Indochinese economic integration and to advance socialist industrialization in the region.

The Vietnamese plan was that economic cooperation between Vietnam and Cambodia and Laos would begin in the 1980s in the form of Vietnamese loans to the other two nations. The three countries could collaborate to construct industrial projects but would seek support from the Soviet Union and other COMECON countries.[122] Vietnam's long-term plan of economic regionalism was to more effectively exploit the natural resources (land, labor, forests, fish, and mineral resources) of the three countries, especially the largely untapped natural resources of Cambodia and Laos, to meet domestic needs and increase surpluses for export to the Soviet Union and other COMECON countries. In return, the three countries were to import from the Soviet Union and Eastern European countries modern technology and the industrial equipment needed to industrialize their respective economies. This plan would secure economic growth and enhance national defense, which in turn would serve the twin strategies of defending and building socialism in each country.[123]

Notably, the Council of Ministers' study, which was more detailed and official after it was reviewed by the Politburo, revealed Hanoi's deep strategic motive behind Vietnam-led Indochinese regionalism, that is, the linkage between economic and security cooperation in Indochina. On August 24, 1982, the Office of the Council of Ministers sent back suggestions about the content of economic, cultural, technical, and scientific cooperation between the three Indochinese countries to the MOFA and the CECC–Laos and Cambodia. First, it shared the research group's rationale that the three Indochinese countries shared a common struggle and a common destiny and therefore Indochinese regionalism was a natural development. Vietnam, Cambodia, and Laos were geographically connected, suffered economic hardship because of the thirty-year war (against the French, the Americans, and then the Chinese), and were similar in terms of their current stage of economic development, that is, small-scale production and a natural-resource-based economy. The Vietnamese Council of Ministers stressed what economists call "comparative advantage" in that "Cambodia and Laos possess abundant and diverse natural sources that have been underexploited due to the severe lack of human resources, equipment, infrastructure, capital, and technological capacity. However, Vietnam possesses a much larger force of skilled labor and stronger technological and industrial foundations."[124] The Council of Ministers also emphasized the importance of convincing Cambodia and Laos that "this economic regionalism would create necessary material foundations for an Indochinese [security] alliance."[125]

In addition to Vietnam's military domination of Cambodia and Laos, Vietnam was superior regarding its technological capacity, skilled labor force, economic management and size, and population. Hanoi's top economic planners envisioned a transition from economic cooperation to integration,[126] resembling an economic bloc. Vietnam would begin by concentrating on the most important projects, including exploitation of the water resources of the Mekong River; mining natural resources, especially minerals in the highlands of the three countries (Tay Nguyen in Vietnam, northeastern of Cambodia, and lower Laos, with combined virgin land of four million hectares); and improving the transportation system (land, water, rail, air, and pipeline) that connected them all. Such projects were of strategic importance for long-term cooperation, which would increase each country's economic strength and the collective economic power of all three.[127]

Hanoi's strategy of developing Vietnam-led Indochinese regionalism was revealed in greater detail in a study by an economic advisory committee within Office 7 of the Council of Ministers. Six key economic and cultural sectors, in Hanoi's plan, that were targeted for short- and long-term cooperation (at least until the year 2000) included (1) agricultural production; (2) the exploitation and preservation of forest resources; (3) the development of industry and manufacturing of consumption goods; (4) transportation, telecommunications, and post; (5) foreign trade, air travel, and tourism; and (6) culture. The six areas of trilateral cooperation were ranked from high to low priority in that order. First and foremost, in agriculture Vietnamese economic planners desired to significantly widen and deepen trilateral cooperation to expand food production, to address shortages of food in each country, and to develop and process agricultural products for export to the Soviet bloc.[128] From the Vietnamese economic planners' perspective, annual rice production was 300 kilograms per person on average, in Laos 335 kilograms per person, and in Cambodia 230 kilograms per person. This level of productivity was too low to keep up with the rate of population growth in each country (Vietnam at 2.6 percent per year, Laos at 2.4 percent, and Cambodia at 2.8 percent).[129]

The food shortages in the three countries, in Hanoi's view, could be easily resolved in a short span of time, but Vietnam had to spearhead trilateral collaborative efforts to develop and exploit the combined agricultural land and resources of Cambodia and Laos by utilizing Vietnamese human resources and technology. To the Vietnamese planners, Laos and Cambodia possessed far greater potential for agricultural productivity than did Vietnam. By 1982 Laos was able to cultivate only one-fourth of its available agricultural land and grew rice only once a year; its enormous amount farmland had not been used due to the lack of irrigation systems, machinery, and labor in the early 1980s. Rice growing in Laos still used traditional primitive methods, that is, it depended on manual labor and plowed its rice fields using oxen and buffalo. The result was a low rice yield, only 1.2 tons per hectare per year. If modern farming techniques were applied, the rice yield could reach five tons per hectare in some regions.

In Cambodia, in Hanoi's view, agricultural production was the same as it was in Laos; only one-forth of the country's agricultural land, or 1.3 to 1.5 million hectares of rice paddies, were cultivated in the early 1980s. However, in the late 1960s, 2.5 million hectares were cultivated during the Sihanouk regime. Rice was farmed only once a year, and farmers did not use modern methods of high-yield farming. The annual rice yield was only one ton per hectare.[130]

On the other hand, Vietnam's agricultural sector was more developed than those of Cambodia and Laos. Vietnam applied high-yield farming techniques, increased rice-growing seasons, expanded fruit-tree growing, acquired experience building large-scale irrigation systems, and had plant- and animal-breeding research centers and animal disease control center. Vietnam harvested 2.1 tons per hectare each rice-growing season in the early 1980s. The Vietnamese economic planners wanted to share these experiences to help their Cambodian and Laotian comrades increase their agricultural production to address domestic shortages in each country and contribute Indochina's exports of agricultural products to the Soviet Union and other Eastern European countries.[131] The Vietnamese also desired to cooperate with Cambodia in exploiting and processing freshwater fish in the Tonle Sap, the great lake of Cambodia.[132]

In the short term, the Vietnamese were to provide expertise, technology, equipment, and machinery of various kinds to exploit the agricultural resources of Laos and Cambodia, process them, and get their share of agricultural production or purchase it at "socialist" prices, meaning below international market prices. The Vietnamese planners reasoned that "Thailand, with a population of 46 million people and 6 million hectares of rice paddies, annually exported agricultural products worth US$8 billion (an average of US$170 per person), whereas in 1983 the three Indochinese countries had a combined population of more than 62 million people and more than 20 million hectares of rice paddies and could only export agricultural products worth US$350 million per year (an annual average of US$5 to $6 per person)."[133] The Vietnamese planners continued to speak zealously of the potential of exploiting the rich national resources of Laos and Cambodia. In their assessment report, they wrote:

> The Indochinese agricultural export potential is enormous, especially the highlands that join the three countries, with nearly four million hectares of fertile soil suitable for growing rubber, coffee, cacao, tea, and fruit. The Cambodian highlands comprise approximately 900,000 hectares; the Bolaven Plateau of Laos comprises over 1 million hectares. And in 1983 most of the highlands in the two countries has not been farmed, the dense forest in these regions is underexploited, forest products have not been processed, and therefore their value for export remains low.[134]

For long-term cooperation, the Vietnamese planners were thinking of starting several big projects to exploit the land and water of the Mekong River to boost the economy of each country. Those projects included hydropower plants in Pa Mong (Laos) and Stung Treng (Cambodia), water transportation, freshwater fish farming, fresh drinking water facilities, and irrigation projects. The Vietnamese were also planning to establish "a rice-seeding research center for all of Indochina."[135]

Economically minded and reformist leaders within the Council of Ministers also proposed a "preferential trade system for Indochina," especially a trade system that could meet the food supply needs of Vietnamese experts, workers, and volunteer troops in Laos and Cambodia. They suggested that in those countries Vietnamese military units be allowed to cultivate and produce food to meet their needs and mitigate Vietnam's economic burden.[136]

Vietnam's national interests were front and center in forestry cooperation. The Vietnamese economic planners saw enormous economic potential for exploiting the diverse and rich forest resources of Laos and Cambodia. In each country, logging alone, according to the Vietnamese estimate, would produce approximately 1 billion cubic meters of fine timber. In Laos, the Phin Xavanna-khet forest covers more than 18 million hectares and has more than 18 million cubic meters of high-quality wood of various kinds. The forest in the Muang Phin (Xiang Khuang Province) and Nakai (Khammuon Province) covers between 400,000 and 500,000 hectares of land and has not been exploited. In addition, Cambodia's northeastern region has a rich and dense forest, and it has not been exploited either. Both Laos and Cambodia were not capable of processing forest products and faced many difficulties due to the lack of laborers, transportation, processing equipment, and adequate roads.[137]

For technical cooperation, the Vietnamese saw an opportunity to export their processing equipment and expertise to Cambodia and Laos. In addition, they wanted to partner with their Cambodian and Laotian comrades to exploit the latter's forest resources and increase exports to the Soviet Union and other Eastern European countries.[138] For long-term cooperation, the Vietnamese planners envisioned building a joint forest-industrial complex, including wood processing, the production of wood products for consumption, and school products such as paper, pencils, and blackboards. These products would provide easily accessible resources for each country's lucrative export industry.[139]

For heavy industry, the Vietnamese aimed to create a pan-Indochina industrial complex. Vietnam's industrial capacity, including energy generation, mining, metallurgy, chemical processing, and manufacturing of construction materials, was already much stronger than those of Laos and Cambodia. Certainly Vietnam would take the lead in this area. Specifically, Vietnam saw an enormous market in Laos and Cambodia for its manufactures, including machinery and equipment to develop their agricultural sectors, forestry, road construction, and irrigation systems. Tens of thousands of small manufacturers in the industrial hub of Ho Chi Minh City would grow quickly as the demand for machinery, equipment, construction materials, and consumption goods in Cambodia and Laos was enormous.[140] Vietnam's manufacturing sector was running well below capacity due to the endemic shortages of raw materials, and as a result unemployment remained high. For this reason, the Vietnamese planners targeted Cambodia and Laos as easily accessible sources of raw materials to increase Vietnam's production of consumption goods and provide more jobs to Vietnamese workers.[141] In return, Vietnam would trade its manufactured goods for important natural resources such as forest products and other raw materials. The Vietnamese planners reasoned:

> Every year Laos and Cambodia spend tens of millions of US dollars to import
> consumption goods from Thailand. If we use our full industrial capacity and
> labor force in Vietnam to produce consumption goods for Laos and Cambodia,
> we can bring enormous benefit to the three Indochinese countries and save
> each country foreign currency, increase the quantity of consumption goods,
> reduce unemployment, and limit the effects of economic pressure and sanctions
> imposed by China and Thailand. Vietnam will replace Thailand as the supplier
> of consumption goods to Cambodia and Laos, putting an end to the flow of gold
> from Indochina to Thailand [through unofficial cross-border trade]. In the long
> run, a pan-Indochina trade bloc and a unified system of industrial production
> will be created for Indochina.[142]

On transportation, the Vietnamese planners desired to use the existing French transportation system (roads, waterways, and airways) to connect the three countries and facilitate the movement of goods and people in Indochina.[143] Vietnam was thinking in terms of a comparative advantage for each Indochinese country and that each country could compliment the others. Vietnam's comparative advantage was its skilled labor, technical expertise, and a more developed industrial capacity (manufacturing ships, boats, ferries, repair stations, spare parts, and machinery).[144] Moreover, Vietnam could develop its air industry and markets for tourism throughout Indochina.[145]

Clearly the Vietnamese had short- and long-term strategic visions of Vietnam-led Indochinese economic regionalism, which would more closely integrate the three socialist countries' economies with the Soviet-led COMECON; help address Vietnam's domestic needs such as food supply, markets for its consumption goods, raw materials for its industries, and unemployment; boost Vietnam's leadership role in Indochina, and allow the three countries to circumvent China's and Thailand's economic pressure.

In Hanoi's strategic thinking about post-1979 nation building after overthrowing the Pol Pot genocidal regime, top Vietnamese economic planners counseled the leadership of the PRK regime to request massive material aid from the Soviet Union and other socialist countries to reduce Vietnam's burden of aiding Cambodia. In the early phase of nation building in Cambodia (1979–81) the Soviet Union provided most of the material foundation of the PRK regime, including technology, industrial equipment, transport vehicles, telecommunications equipment, military hardware, fuel, and food. During this period, Vietnam, which was heavily dependent on large amounts of aid from the Soviet Union and other socialist countries, could provide Cambodia with only limited material aid, which included mostly supplementary food supplies and consumption goods to prevent starvation, restore agricultural production, and health. However, Hanoi's planners concentrated most of Vietnam's human resources and energy on building a client state in Cambodia modeled after its own party and government structure by dispatching large numbers of Vietnamese advisers in all fields, from the military, police, economic and cultural affairs, and top party and government leaders to district administrators. In short, Hanoi sought to exercise rather exclusive political and military influence in Cambodia, but it did so by shifting the burden of material and technological aid to the Soviet Union and other socialist members of the Soviet-led COMECON and tapping Cambodia's natural resources.

In 1983 the reformist leaders proposed to reduce Vietnam's provision of massive assistance to Cambodia and Laos and implement gradual shift toward Vietnam-dominated economic regionalism in Indochina in 1985–90. Under such regionalism, Laos and Cambodia would also benefit, though to a much lesser extent, due to their close cooperation with Vietnam in exploiting their natural resources, especially agricultural land, extensive forests, fisheries, and rich mineral deposits.

In domestic politics, after a four-year military mobilization and confrontation in Cambodia and against China, the economic reformist faction managed to convince the old guard within the CPV leadership to consider the costs of the two-front war and change the course of Vietnam's foreign policy. The nature of the threat also changed, as in 1983 the economic threat loomed even larger than the military one. As China's military threat declined, the economic and political threat from China and Thailand rose, causing the Vietnamese leadership to fear Chinese economic pressure and the drain of gold and foreign currency from Indochina to Thailand.

Internationally, Vietnam-led Indochinese economic regionalism would not only enable Vietnam to take advantage of the international division of labor with the Soviet-led COMECON but would also allow Vietnam to ward off the economic threat from the West. The economic crisis in Poland in 1980–81 alarmed the Vietnamese leadership, demonstrating that dependence on loans from the West ran the risk of political instability. The shift from military confrontation to economic integration of the three countries was also justified by structural change in great power politics from military escalation after the Soviet Union's invasion of Afghanistan in 1979 to détente and peaceful coexistence in

1982 as the political and economic power of the Soviet Union significantly declined in the last two years of Brezhnev's rule (1980–82). Regionally, China's troubled relationship with the United States and ASEAN's fragile unity regarding the resolution of the Cambodian problem led Vietnam's top diplomats to believe that China and ASEAN would prefer dialogue over military confrontation. This turned out to be true for ASEAN, but China was not giving up its military confrontation with Vietnam along the Sino-Vietnamese border while Vietnamese troops were present in Cambodia. In summary, the shift in Hanoi's strategic thinking from military confrontation to economic integration of the three Indochinese countries in 1982–83 was driven by both domestic economic imperatives and structural changes following Vietnam's invasion of Cambodia in and the Soviet Union's invasion of Afghanistan.

The impetus for course correction was additionally driven by impersonal material factors in 1983–85. The growing costs of the two-front war in Cambodia and with China, combined with the burden of nation building in postgenocide Cambodia and assistance to Laos, rapidly increased along with the prospect that Vietnam was at great risk of being bogged down in a protracted military conflict in Cambodia and China with no end in sight. Large-scale battles in summer of 1984 in Cambodia and battles the mountains against Chinese troops at Vi Xuyen (a district in Ha Giang Province), in which Vietnam suffered unprecedented casualties in a span of a few weeks, further illuminated the stalemate in this protracted war. Clearly Vietnam was fighting an unwinnable two-front war by 1985.

6

The Road to *Doi Moi*

1 9 8 6

This chapter delves into the historic period of the mid-1980s when the *Doi Moi* (renovation) policy, adopted by the Sixth Party Congress of the CPV in December 1986, marked the most transformative transition in Vietnam's modern political history from the Marxist central-planning model to a market-oriented economy. In the realm of international relations, Vietnam's perspective shifted from the Cold War "two-camp" worldview, that is, the zero-sum competition between socialism and capitalism, to a broad-based multidirectional foreign policy. The existing scholarship on this subject offers a dichotomous explanation of the emergence of *Doi Moi* in 1986, either internal economic and political causes or external pressure:[1] the erosion of Soviet economic and political power and the cost of Vietnam's occupation of Cambodia and economic sanctions imposed by the West.[2] Is *Doi Moi* an internal process of change or the effect of external pressure for change? Then there is a debate between the ideational shift toward and material causes of *Doi Moi*.

The two important debates about the *Doi Moi* policy have been unresolved. First, it was between the proponents of ideology and those of the material consequences as the cause of *Doi Moi*.[3] Most recently, an ardent proponent of this theory is the political scientist Tuong Vu. He writes, "Studies of economic reform in Vietnam since the late 1980s have downplayed the influence of foreign ideas or models on the event. Although it is true that the Vietnamese reform had many distinctive features, Vietnam's reformist ideas and policies followed closely those of the Soviet Union."[4] The most prominent reformist leaders who translated these reform ideas into policies are, according to conventional wisdom, Truong Chinh, Nguyen Van Linh, and Vo Van Kiet. Second, as Elliott put it, *Doi*

Moi is "either part of a self-generated process, driven by impersonal forces rather than considered policy, or a societal transformation taking place at the grassroots level, independent of any formal governmental design—or both."[5]

I argue that impersonal domestic and external forces (the protracted economic crisis and rising cost of two-front war in Cambodia and against China) in 1979–85 made it possible for reformist ideas to prevail over continued war and a state-planned economy while growing popular discontent with the party, beginning 1978 as a result of the economic crisis (as discussed in chapter 2), facilitated it. Competing ideas within Vietnam's political class matter, but it took the impersonal domestic and external forces to lead one set of ideas to prevail over all others. I also argue that Nguyen Co Thach was the earliest, most consistent, and strongest advocate for economic reform and opening to members of the old guard, namely, Le Duan, Truong Chinh, Pham Van Dong, Le Thanh Nghi, and Le Duc Tho, after the PPA was concluded in January 1973. Then vice-minister Nguyen Co Thach, whom the Politburo entrusted to do research on the Soviet Union's and Eastern European countries' economic relations with the West during the US-Soviet détente (1972–73), took a great interest in how to modernize Vietnam's economy after the Vietnam War. And it was Thach, who had the tenacity to speak frankly to the Politburo about the need for Vietnam to adapt to an increasingly interdependent world economy in which advanced technology, economic efficiency, and competitiveness were intertwined and decisive to avoid economic backwardness and overdependence on China and the Soviet Union. He was able to do so in part because he had the backing of the economically minded leaders Pham Van Dong and Le Thanh Nghi and had earned the trust of Le Duc Tho, for whom he worked as a senior adviser and assistant during the US-Vietnam negotiations to end the Vietnam War in the early 1970s.

Evidence from internal discussions within the inner circle of the Vietnamese leadership presented in this chapter corroborates Tuong Vu's argument that Vietnamese reformists keenly observed and learned reform practices and ideas from the Soviet Union and Eastern Europe from the 1970s to the mid-1980s. However, this explanation is incomplete. The Vietnamese knowledge of Soviet reformist ideas could only be pulled together into a concrete policy by the gravity of the material forces, that is, domestic economic imperatives and external systemic pressures that had built up since the Fourth Party Congress in December 1976 and explosively converged in the mid-1980s. Drawing on new documentary evidence from the Vietnamese archives, I argue that the either/or arguments failed to capture the complexity of what happened because their respective explanations were too simplistic. My account expands Elliott's multi-causal, multilevel framework, which recognizes the complexity, the nature of

incremental changes, and the convergence of changes at the individual, domestic, and international levels. Those interrelated factors were the changes in
political leadership with the rise of reformist leaders in Vietnam, the domestic
economic distress and political fallout in Vietnam, and the changes in the Soviet
Union under the reformist leader Mikhail Gorbachev.[6] Unlike Elliott's, however, my argument stresses material forces as the most important cause of the
collective ideational changes on the eve of the Sixth Party Congress in December 1986 while ideational factors, particularly the Vietnamese knowledge of reformist ideas acquired from the Soviet Union, as Tuong Vu argues, allowed the
reformists to push their ideas to the front and center of Vietnam's foreign policy
decision making. The change in collective ideas, which culminated in the *Doi
Moi* policy of 1986, was a self-generated process driven by domestic and external forces, which in turn propelled reformists and their ideas into the center of
foreign policy making. It is the convergence of domestic and external imperatives in the first half of 1980s that caused the reformist ideas to prevail over the
status quo of continued military confrontation with China and nation building
in Cambodia.

The result was, as Benedict J. Tria Kerkvliet argued, "worsening economic
conditions and widespread rural yet unorganized discontent [with the party]
in the form of resistance to the state-imposed collective farming strengthened
arguments in national offices that concessions to household farming were the
sensible course to take."[7] As pointed out in chapter 2, popular discontent with
and resistance to the party, which manifested in thousands of complaints
against the widespread corruption of local party officials in 1978, alarmed the
top party leadership. As Hanoi's top economic planner, deputy prime minister
and chairman of the State Planning Committee Le Thanh Nghi acknowledged
the problem of local party officials' widespread practices of ballooning the
amount of resources needed to meet the central government's quotas in late
1977. In 1978 Nghi called for economic decentralization, which would allow
city and district party leaders to plan their own economies with the central government's guidance and supervision. The convergence of these factors forced
the top Vietnamese leadership to tolerate local "fence breaking" in the south, of
which the most prominent leader was Ho Chi Minh City's party secretary Vo
Van Kiet in the early 1980s.[8]

By mid-1980s, external forces led to greater support for reformist ideas
than for the conservative and military-firsters' status quo policy of a centrally
planned economy and military confrontation with China. *Doi Moi* occurred
in 1985–86 because the prolonged economic crisis and poverty inside Vietnam were dire and the time was "ripe" for Vietnam to change course toward
economic reforms and opening to adapt to the prevailing global forces of the

technological and scientific revolutions. The Soviet bloc's demand for reciprocity in economic relations with Vietnam, meaning that Vietnam's imports of raw materials from the bloc would depend on its export capability, coupled with China's entrance into the market of the Soviet bloc, threatening Vietnam's exports, compelled Vietnam to quickly improve its economic efficiency and competitiveness even in the socialist bloc's market. By mid-1980s, the Vietnamese collective leadership came to the sobering conclusion that economically lagging behind other countries, especially China, threatened Vietnam's economy and national sovereignty and, by extension, the political survival of the CPV. Without the convergence of these material imperatives at the domestic and international levels at one critical juncture (in 1985), the ideas of Vietnamese reformists like Chairman of the State Planning Committee Vo Van Kiet and Foreign Minister Nguyen Co Thach could not have prevailed over the status quo. By no means do I claim that the reformist ideas did not matter. But if the focus here is about causation, then these ideational concepts were not independent of domestic and external material imperatives.

As I discuss in more detail below, the origins of these reformist ideas can be traced back to the PPA between Vietnam and the United States between 1968 and 1973, during which an outgoing and open-minded vice-minister of foreign affairs, Nguyen Co Thach, directly injected his ideas about economic reform and opening to the West in order to obtain advanced technology and modern industrial equipment into the inner circle of the Vietnamese leadership, the Politburo. However, such ideas were muted or brushed aside by the conservative Marxist-Leninist ideologues for more than a decade, during which the old wartime mentality of Stalinist-style state central planning and heavy reliance on foreign aid (mainly from China and the Soviet Union during the Vietnam War, 1965–73, and then mostly the Soviet Union after 1975) was too slow to change. It is hardly surprising that collective ideas in any country change slowly and only shift dramatically after a series of systemic shocks or crises. Not only that, but the military-first faction dragged Vietnam into a costly two-front war in Cambodia and with China for seven years (1979–85). During this period, despite massive aid from the Soviet bloc, Vietnam's economy continued to be inefficient, suffered a growing import-export deficit, and drove the country into excessive debt.

The Rise of the Reformists, 1985–86

Beyond Indochina were Vietnam's great power allies, the Soviet Union and Eastern Europe, the most important sources of Vietnam's economic development and modernization for its next FYP, 1986–90. The year 1986 was a pivotal one, for it ushered in the *Doi Moi* policy, which set Vietnam on the course of transformative economic reform, although the ground already had been shifting toward this trend a year earlier. In March 1985, the Foreign Economic Relations Research Group (To kinh te doi ngoai) of the Council of Ministers, under the leadership of the council vice-chairman Vo Van Kiet,[9] published an important and comprehensive study of Vietnam's foreign economic relations with the socialist bloc, nonsocialist developing countries, and the developed capitalist bloc. This report reveals the top Vietnamese planners' view of Vietnam's position within the changing international economic situation in the second half of the 1980s. The Research Group concluded, "For the 1986–90 five-year plan, Vietnam could no longer rely on the Soviet Union and Eastern Europe for vital nonrefundable aid, and economic reciprocity (mutually beneficial economic transactions) would become the new principle of Vietnam's economic relations with the Soviet Union and other members of the Council of Mutual Economic Assistance."[10]

The Research Group argued that Vietnam's export expansion during the next five years would require economic efficiency and modern industrial equipment—a greater output with less use of labor and energy, the restructuring of its economic system, and the application of technological innovation to the manufacturing of goods to reduce the cost of energy.[11] Increasing economic efficiency and export volume required economic reform at home and a broad-based foreign economic policy beyond the socialist bloc. That meant that Vietnam needed to develop economic relations with developed capitalist countries.

From 1975 to 1985, after its national unification, Vietnam's economic and security reliance on the Soviet Union increased steadily as Sino-Vietnamese relations plunged into war and military confrontation after the Chinese invasion of Vietnam in February 1979. Looking back at this turbulent decade, the Vietnamese viewed themselves as the victims of Chinese aggression and concluded that an alliance with the Soviet Union was necessary to counter the China threat. However, by 1985 Hanoi's economic planners were increasingly alarmed by the steady decline of Soviet economic power and economic deterioration in the COMECON countries, which were accumulating mounting debt to Western European countries.

Hanoi's economic planners divided the decade 1975–85 into three periods of Vietnam's economic relations with the Soviet bloc. During the first period, from 1975 to 1978, when China openly opposed Vietnam, the Soviet Union canceled Vietnam's wartime debt and additionally provided a large loan of 2.4 billion rubles at low interest rates.[12] However, in Hanoi's view, the relations between the Soviet Union and Vietnam during this period were not as closely connected as Soviet relations with other Eastern European countries. Vietnam's foreign policy did not always align with that of the Soviet Union.[13] As the Research Group summarized in March 1983, "Although the Soviet Union and other socialist countries increased their economic assistance to us during the period 1975–78, compared to a decade earlier, their total aid package was inadequate to compensate us for the loss of Chinese aid during this period."[14]

During this period, Hanoi's leaders believed that because the capitalist and nonsocialist countries wanted to limit the influence of the Soviet Union and China in Vietnam, Indochina, and Southeast Asia as a whole, Vietnam was granted loans totaling US$950 million from these countries and various international financial organizations.[15] Hanoi's economic planners viewed the period of 1975–78 as a regrettable missed opportunity to further develop economic relations with advanced western countries beyond the "exploration" (*tham do*) of business opportunities by Sweden, France, Australia, and Japan and postwar "humanitarian aid" (*vien tro nhan dao*) from international organizations, including the Food and Agriculture Organization of the United Nations and the United Nations Children's Fund (UNICEF).[16] Nonetheless, the loans from these nonsocialist countries made a significant contribution to Vietnam's agriculture, fisheries, and basic development, including the improvement of irrigation systems, reforestation, the seafood industry, and cement production.[17]

To meet the goals of production, construction, and living standards set in the 1986–90 FYP, the need to import raw materials, fuel, construction materials, and equipment and parts would increase significantly. Compared to 7.5 billion rubles in 1981–85, total import costs for 1986–90 were projected to be approximately 10 billion rubles, of which 6 billion would be used to pay for imports of four main items: fuel, steel, fertilizer, and cotton.[18] The Soviet Union and other members of the COMECON agreed to allow Vietnam to import goods worth 5.5 to 6 billion rubles on the condition that Vietnam would be able to export goods to them worth 3.5 billion rubles. Vietnam had to secure additional capital of US$4 to 4.5 billion from nonsocialist financial markets.[19] Yet, from 1986 to 1990, Vietnam had to pay a debt of 2.8 billion rubles (2.4 billion in principle loans plus 400 million in accrued interest) to the socialist bloc,[20] as well as an additional debt of US$1.9 billion (US$1.35 billion principle plus US$550 million in accrued interest) to the nonsocialist bloc.[21] This staggering amount of accumulated debt was indicative of Vietnam's growing trade deficit with other countries, which stemmed from its economic inefficiency, low-quality products, and, more important, the ever-growing detrimental effects of its "all for the frontline" mobilization for the two-front war in Cambodia and with China in 1979–85.

Without pointing the finger directly at the conservative and military-first leaders Le Duan, Le Duc Tho, General Van Tien Dung, and General Chu Huy Man, this group of reformists under Vo Van Kiet's leadership clearly and strongly advocated a course correction for the country. This group drew its conclusion from a comprehensive analysis of Vietnam's economy during the decade 1975–85.

During the second period (1979–81), China aligned itself with the United States, imposed economic sanctions on Vietnam, and initiated its military attacks. At this point, it was necessary for Vietnam to begin a new phase of strategic alliance with the Soviet Union and other socialist countries and greater reliance on Soviet aid. However, to Hanoi's top economic planners, the Soviet aid during this period arrived at the end of Vietnam's first FYP, 1976–80, and therefore took the form of "supplementary aid" to address the immediate economic impact of China's invasion of and military confrontation with Vietnam.[22] Soviet aid during this period covered the construction of several major projects for which China had eliminated aid after 1976. The Soviet aid additionally rebuilt a number of factories destroyed by the Chinese invading troops in the northern provinces of Vietnam and paid for imports of raw materials, equipment, and consumption goods necessary to maintain economic production and support people's livelihoods.[23] During this period, the Soviet Union and other socialist countries were sympathetic to Vietnam's economic hardship and enthusiastic about assisting the country. On the contrary, Vietnam faced stiff economic sanctions by capitalist and nonsocialist countries alike during this period. Its inability to repay the loans from to these countries and other international creditors further limited Vietnam's capacity to expand its economic relations with them.[24]

During the third period (1981–85), Vietnam received a generous aid package worth 4.5 billion rubles, twice the amount given to Vietnam during the preceding five-year period, from the Soviet Union and other COMECON countries.[25] The Soviet aid was meant to cover not just the major items, including raw materials, fuel, parts, and industrial equipment, that the Soviets had provided to Vietnam in the late 1970s, but it also paid for items that Vietnam had previously imported from the capitalist and nonsocialist countries, including steel, fuel, fertilizer, cotton, vehicles, tractors, and construction equipment.[26]

Notably, however, during the period 1981–85 the Soviet Union and other COMECON countries pressured Vietnam harder to develop mutually beneficial economic relations and significantly increased its exports to restore the export-import balance. Furthermore, although the Soviet Union and other COMECON countries allowed Vietnam to import significantly more goods than it exported, they imposed regular interest rates on Vietnam's loans and shorter deadlines for repayment of those loans. In addition, they imposed higher prices for the goods Vietnam imported from them and a higher standard of quality for goods Vietnam exported to them.[27] In 1984–85, China began economic cooperation with Eastern European countries, exporting labor-intensive products similar to what Vietnam did.[28] Vietnam's top economic planners saw this growing trend as an economic threat China posed to its markets in Eastern Europe.[29]

After 1983 Vietnam saw positive signs of resuming economic exploration with the nonsocialist and capitalist countries, starting with small-scale economic cooperation in a number of fields. In a March 1985 report, the reformists informed the party leaders that "capitalist nations and international economic organizations refused to enter into large-scale economic cooperation with us because of political issues [US economic sanctions against Vietnam] and regional conflict [Vietnam's military presence in Cambodia].[30]

The Fifth Party Congress in March 1982 elevated Vietnam's export sector to a strategic objective as increased agricultural production had stabilized people's livelihoods.[31] In April the reformist Vo Van Kiet was promoted to the chairmanship of the State Planning Committee and appointed deputy prime minister, replacing Nguyen Lam. Even in 1985, Vietnamese reformists like Vo Van Kiet were frustrated that the Party's collective ideas were too slow to permeate the party and government apparatus and be translated into actions and policies at various levels below the top echelon of the party and government.[32] The Research Group, under Vo Van Kiet's leadership, wrote in 1985:

> From the beginning (after Vietnam's national unification in 1975), we did not recognize the reality that our economic relations with other countries were based on the principle of mutual interests, reciprocity, and loans with interest. We did not clearly understand the important strategic role of our export sector in developing the economy from small-scale to large-scale socialist production, in increasing imports, and in building the material and technological foundations of socialism. Our psychology of reliance on outsiders was deep, widespread, and resistant to change. Because of that, we were not able to exploit our strength and potential in our country to widen our economic relations with other countries, particularly to increase our exports. We did not see as important investments in building infrastructure and material foundations in service of large-scale exports. We were too slow to determine the necessary policies and measures to strengthen our export sector.[33]

This statement was evidently a thinly veiled criticism Vo Van Kiet and his economic team leveled against his predecessor Le Thanh Nghi, who was by no mean a conservative but an economically minded leader. And the criticism did not stop there. Kiet's Research Group also criticized the conduct of Vietnam's foreign economic policy under Le Thanh Nghi's leadership. The ill-conceived import-export plans and the disconnect between foreign economic relations and the objectives of Vietnam's national economy prevented Vietnam from exploiting the economic potential of its abundant labor, land, and natural resources to boost its exports to friendly markets in the Soviet Union and other Eastern European countries.

In the agricultural sector, which was the most important sector for the first FYP (1976–80), outside assistance failed to bring it from small-scale to large-scale production because there was a mismatch between imported goods and the actual domestic needs of Vietnam. For instance, for 1976–80, Vietnam imported tractors in excess of its real need while falling far short of fertilizer and pesticides, which were important to boost production. For 1975–80, imports of machinery and equipment were too large (almost 15,000 tractors, 13,000 transport vehicles, and 2,000 excavators). The massive imports of machinery and equipment were in enormous excess of the domestic need and the country's ability to use such equipment at that time, leading to a significant waste of resources. However, in reaction to that, from 1981 to 1984, imports of machinery and equipment such as tractors, excavators, and bulldozers were reduced by more than 90 percent. Additionally, the imported machinery and equipment were not complete, and shortages of spare parts further reduced their use, worsening waste over time.[34]

In the industrial sector, Vietnam used up an enormous amount of foreign aid to build too many big and expensive projects and imported too much heavy machinery, construction materials, and manufacturing equipment. For example, Vietnam imported too many transport vehicles and big excavators and built six cement factories, each with a capacity of producing one million tons of cement, and dozens of concrete factories. These did not suit Vietnam's economic development stage, which was heavily dependent on agriculture and light industry.[35] The Research Group reported, "The dire consequences of these mistakes in economic planning, that is, too many big and expensive projects incompatible with Vietnam's real economic development needs, led to the widespread waste of capital, time-consuming construction, slow mobilization of resources, and costly economic inefficiency. Factories meant to produce major products such as fertilizer, coal, and construction equipment and materials begun in the years 1975–76 remain under construction in early 1985 and are unlikely to move into production by the end of the year.[36]

Concerning exports, for the first FYP after unification (1976–80), Vietnam's total export value was 1.5 billion rubles and US dollars, and it doubled, amounting to 3 billion rubles and US dollars during the second FYP (1981–85). As Vo Van Kiet's Research Group summed it up, "Although Vietnam was able to gradually bridge the gap between exports and imports, the discrepancy remained very large," referring to import value far in excess of export value.[37] The group pointed out that the system of exports was never renovated or improved; Vietnam exported everything it could, and the improvement of product quality was too slow. As a result, Vietnam did not have exportable products in large quantities that could compete in the world market; a number of Vietnam's products were actually at risk of losing market value.[38] Vietnam's exports and imports were not in sync with each other, and as a result the exports did not serve as the foundation for the import sector while imports failed to ensure that certain raw materials and equipment necessary to produce goods for export were not depleted.[39]

During the decade after unification (1975–85), Vietnam's imports relied on loans and nonrefundable aid from both socialist and nonsocialist countries. The import sector was very important and significantly affected the stability of economic production and construction in the postwar decade. During this decade, Vietnam's imports did not increase much; it was actually forced to decrease its imports of very important items like spare parts and industrial equipment after the invasion of Cambodia in late 1978 when the capitalist and nonsocialist countries eliminated aid and imposed economic sanctions on Vietnam. As a result, shortages of spare parts and equipment had a significant negative impact on production, construction, and livelihoods in Vietnam, especially in 1983–84.[40]

As Vietnam's top economic planners crafted their third FYP (1986–90) after unification, one of the major considerations was the changing configuration of international economic power, with the Soviet-led COMECON facing an alarming number of major economic problems. There were three areas of great concern to the Vietnamese. First, the COMECON countries faced growing shortages of energy and raw materials and therefore had difficulty meeting the needs of their national economies. Second, they suffered an enormous balance of payments deficit. Third, they were confronted with shortages of food.[41] In the Vietnamese view, except for the Soviet Union, members of the COMECON had never been able to secure sufficient energy sources and raw materials—these are two of the major decisive factors in a country's economy—to meet their needs. In the Soviet Union, oil reserves in the heart of Europe gradually were depleted, and oil production had to be moved to remote regions on the country's northern and eastern frontiers, increasing the cost of oil extraction due to difficult geography and transportation. To complicate matters, the price of fuel and raw materials on the world market increased significantly, and imports of such scarce resources from developing countries were expected to drop as well. As a result, COMECON countries were forced to mobilize strategic resources inside each country and deepen their participation in the international division of labor (*phan cong quoc te*) to meet their national needs and increase their efficiency in using fuel and raw materials. The entire production system had to be renovated to consume less energy but increase output by importing advanced energy-efficient technology from the West. In foreign economic relations, the socialist bloc, from the perspective of Hanoi's economic planners, had difficulty producing such modern technologically powered equipment, food supplies, and some kinds of mineral resources. Moreover, in the past the Soviet Union had exported raw materials to other members of the COMECON at prices lower than the market price, but from 1985 on the Vietnamese anticipated a decline in the Soviet ability to do this. In addition, by 1985 all COMECON countries faced difficulties in securing sufficient food supplies.[42] The Vietnamese economic planners informed their top leadership that all these external economic pressures mandated that Vietnam, like the other COMECON countries, must increase the efficiency of its national economy while increasing savings to address shortages of labor, energy, and raw materials; a lack of capital investment, and demands for infrastructure improvement and environmental protection.[43]

Vietnamese economic planners counseled their leaders that Vietnam should implement the economic reforms being adopted by Eastern European countries. These reforms (1) applying advanced science and technology to increase the quality and quantity of products to save energy and raw materials, (2) changing the economic system to one that used less energy and fewer raw materials, (3) integrating the international division of labor and stronger alignment with socialist economies, (4) using labor to create professions and skills appropriate for the society's needs, (5) enacting policies to conserve energy and raw materials, and (6) reforming labor organization and economic management to conform to the country's development level and production capabilities.[44]

However, Vietnam had no alternative but to continue to rely on the Soviet Union as long as the West refused to lift economic sanctions. The lifting of economic sanctions was conditional upon Hanoi's complete withdrawal of the Vietnamese occupying forces in Cambodia. Faced with economic sanctions by the West, the Soviet Union remained the main source of capital, fuel, raw materials, equipment, and technology and the largest market for Vietnam's exports.[45] On June 27, 1985, General Secretary Le Duan visited the Soviet Union, and Moscow pledged to increase economic assistance to Vietnam by doubling the amount offered during 1981–85, totaling 8.7 billion rubles in loans. In return the Vietnamese leadership completely supported Moscow's foreign policy line.[46] Although the Vietnamese leaders were well aware of the economic decline of the Soviet bloc, they were stuck with it for the long haul. In 1986–90, the Soviet Union, on the one hand, continued to offer Vietnam, Cuba, and Mongolia preferential trade status.[47] On the other, the Soviets and other Eastern European countries insisted that Vietnam broaden mutually beneficial economic cooperation with them based on the principle of reciprocity.[48] To boost its exports to the Soviet bloc, Vietnam was to concentrate on a number of sectors, including agriculture, the food industry, forest products, logging and wood processing, seafood, the garment industry, light industry products, mining, and oil production.[49]

Vietnam's projected imports of raw materials, especially fuel, for 1986–90 was nearly 10 billion rubles and US dollars, equal to the previous decade (4.6 billion rubles and dollars in 1976–80 and 5 billion in 1981–85).[50] Imports of fuel were to increase from 8.5 million tons (1981–85) to 15 million (1986–90).[51] Vo Van Kiet's Research Group projected that to meet Vietnam's import needs and enable the country to pay any of its creditors in 1986–90 (2.8 billion rubles to the socialist bloc and 1.9 billion US dollars to nonsocialist countries), the Vietnamese government would have to increase its export capacity up to tenfold or to a gross value of 6.5 to 7 billion rubles for 1986–90.[52] For 1985–90, the group proposed an export plan as follows: (1) agricultural products worth 3 to 3.5 billion rubles, (2) seafood worth 800 million rubles, (3) forest products worth 250 to 300 million rubles, (4) handicraft and light industry products worth more than 2 billion rubles, and (5) mineral resources worth 300 to 350 million rubles. If this export target were achieved, Vietnam's export value would be roughly 7 billion rubles. Besides exports, the Research Group counseled the Vietnamese government to strengthen its service sector, including financial services, tourism, and the commercial air industry, to accumulate between 400 and 500 million rubles.[53]

In summary, 1985 marked significant domestic and international changes that provided additional impetus for reform and opening in Vietnam. Domestically, the detrimental effects of the two-front war on Vietnam's economy was enormous in spite of massive aid from the Soviet bloc, not to mention the human cost; the war clearly had reached a stalemate, and war weariness was widespread in Vietnamese society. Within the party and government, the prevailing strategic thinking shifted toward economic reform and opening, meaning broad-based foreign economic relations beyond the Soviet bloc. The Soviet Union's economic reforms under Mikhail Gorbachev's "new thinking" in 1985 lent support to reformists within the CPV. Globally, in 1985, the pendulum of technological revolution had also swung in the direction of the West, and as the Soviet bloc was struggling economically, the new principle of economic reciprocity had replaced the nonrefundable aid. China's export-led growth under Deng Xiaoping's reform policy threatened Vietnam's export market in Eastern Europe, adding another layer of the China threat to Vietnam's national security.

The Origins of *Doi Moi* Ideas

In his seminal book *Changing Worlds: Vietnam's Transition from Cold War to Globalization*, international relations scholar David W. P. Elliott referred to Foreign Minister Nguyen Co Thach as "one of the leading reform voices of the 1980s."[54] I agree with Elliott and further argue that Nguyen Co Thach played a more crucial role in shaping the decision-making process leading to the adoption of the *Doi Moi* policy in 1986 than did Nguyen Van Linh and Vo Van Kiet, who are conventionally known as the heroes of *Doi Moi*.

In July 1986, in his lengthy report to the National Assembly, vetted by the Politburo of the Party Central Committee, Foreign Minister Nguyen Co Thach made a strong case for the need to adopt economic reform in order to adapt to the changing configuration of the global political economy.[55] Six months later, in December 1986, during the Sixth Party Congress, Thach presented another report on world politics and Vietnam's foreign policy to the National Assembly, making a more forceful case for a rapid shift toward economic reform at home and a broad-based foreign economic policy in "the age of technological revolution," to use Thach's own terms.[56] With the two detailed reports, Foreign Minister Nguyen Co Thach was entrusted by the Politburo to explain Vietnam's foreign policy to the National Assembly within the framework of the Politburo's political report presented at the Sixth Party Congress. What is striking in the December 1986 report is a direct reference to "a major shift in socioeconomic strategies in the socialist bloc, which developed out of basic changes in thinking, particularly economic thinking."[57] Thach began by highlighting "the revolutionary reorientation of the socioeconomic strategy" of the Soviet Union and other Eastern European countries at the Twenty-Seventh Congress of the Communist Party of Soviet Union concluded on March 6, 1986.[58]

> Notably this new thinking emerged from the socialist bloc's deeper recognition of the political influence of the basic changes in global economic foundations. The new phase of technological and scientific revolution that began in the 1970s and continued up to the present has brought about a new and powerful

transformation in global production forces, completely changed the global economic system, increasingly widened and deepened the process of internationalizing economic life and the division of labor, and heightened the level of trade and economic cooperation in the world. The global economic foundation is actually one whole body (*mot tong the*) in which every country's economy and every economic system is an inseparable part. Two opposing economic systems [capitalist and socialist] can simultaneously compete as well as closely cooperate with each other. This technological and scientific revolution and the trend of internationalization of economic life are so forceful that they will compel all nations, big or small, capitalist or socialist, to change their respective economic structures and management systems and rethink their socioeconomic strategies in order to reap the benefits of this global economic transformation to advance the development of their national economies and avoid the danger of lagging behind (*bi tut lai*) and falling deep into a situation of underdevelopment (*lun sau trong tinh trang lac hau*).[59]

Foreign Minister Nguyen Co Thach, in early 1986, forcefully convinced Vietnam's top foreign policy decision makers to shift from the two-camp worldview—the theoretical and philosophical question of who prevails over whom in the zero-sum competition between capitalist and socialist systems—to a broad-based foreign policy, especially in foreign economic relations. In the journalist Huy Duc's account, it was Foreign Minister Nguyen Co Thach, not those who were in charge of economic planning, who was the first member of the Politburo to have a thorough understanding of the market economy and to have compiled Politburo Resolution 13, which set in motion a historic shift to a multidirectional foreign policy. As foreign minister, Thach was a leader who was keen on bringing back to Vietnam intellectuals who understood the market economy. According to Duc, in a Politburo meeting on February 19–20, 1986, Thach bluntly told the entire Politburo, "The economic strength of socialism and the dictatorship of the proletariat cannot go in opposition to economic laws (*quy luat kinh te*). If we follow the economic law and know how to take advantage of that law in favor of socialism, then we can develop based on the strength of the economic law."[60] Here he was recasting the applied social Darwinism of the late nineteenth century to push for reforms in Vietnam if the CPV and its socialist revolution were to survive in an economically interdependent world.

Although Nguyen Co Thach has been credited in history as one of the leaders who reoriented a multidirectional foreign policy, his exact role was not known until now. Thach himself never publicly claimed to have been a key mover and shaper of the *Doi Moi* policy in 1986. Now there is revealing evidence that Thach was a strong and consistent advocate for economic reform within the inner circle of the Vietnamese leadership since the PPA of January 1973, and his central role in policy making led to the adoption of the *Doi Moi* policy in 1986.

During a historic negotiation between the DRV and the United States between 1968 and 1973 to end the Vietnam War, then Vice-Minister Nguyen Co Thach was a close aide to the chief negotiator, Le Duc Tho, and served as head of the Vietnamese experts group. In addition, he had another secret mission: directly assisting the Politburo in following the negotiation process and researching the inconspicuous economic relations between Western and Eastern Europe.[61] In short, he was the eyes and ears of the Politburo.

In a top secret report entitled "A Number of Situations about Economic Cooperation between the Soviet Union and Eastern Europe and Western Countries," dated September 1973, Nguyen Co Thach informed—actually educated if one were to peel back the Communist jargon—Politburo members about economic relations between the Soviet-led economic bloc, COMECON, and some Western European nations. Thach told Politburo members that in spite of the ideological and political conflicts between the two blocs during the Cold War, economically the two sides were trading with each other.[62] Very early on, on the eve of the PPA in January 1973, this young diplomat took a particular research interest in market economies and the transformative role of scientific and technological advancement in the global economy. Thach's research interests could have been perceived as revisionist, if not reactionary, by the conservative ideologues, who firmly viewed Cold War international relations through their two-camp lenses at that time. Yet, with direct access to the Politburo, Thach cautiously crafted his reform ideas into a report about the Soviet Union's and other Eastern European countries' economic relations with the capitalist West, suggesting that if the Soviets did that in order to find a shortcut to communism faster, then Vietnam should follow suit. In his September 1973 report to the Politburo, he wrote that the Soviet Union and Eastern European countries

> desire to develop fast, strengthen their economic foundations, and accelerate the process of development especially the quality of products. The Soviet Union and Eastern Europe are five to ten years behind the West in terms of technological development. The Soviets and Eastern European countries set the goal of catching up with the West and taking the lead in technological development in about ten to fifteen years. To meet that goal, they need to strengthen investment, renovate equipment and expand scientific research, and apply [scientific findings]

effectively. At the same time, they are taking the opportunity to attract capital investment and modern technology from western countries.[63]

Thach further reported to his leaders that in 1972–73 the United States and other capitalist countries widened their economic relations with the Soviet Union and other Eastern European countries, ending the twenty-year economic sanctions against the eastern bloc from 1951 to 1971. This new trend resulted from the market crisis, oil crisis, and shortages of raw materials and cheap labor, accompanied by stiff economic competition in the West especially among Western Europe, Japan, and the United States. In addition, the economic cooperation between East and West was mutually beneficial.[64] Thach had the tenacity to explain to the Politburo how the global political economy works. He wrote, "The US shift from economic sanctions to economic cooperation with the Soviet Union and Eastern Europe was first and foremost an imperative of economic interests. But at the same time it served the US political objective of transitioning from the policy of confrontation to peaceful coexistence between the East and West. And the Soviet Union and Eastern Europe knew the imperialist clique's political motive behind such their economic transactions with the West. They put political and ideological differences aside and prioritized importing modern technology from the West to modernize their economies, increase production efficiency, and raise the quality of their products."[65]

In his September 1973 report, Thach counseled the Politburo that Vietnam must reorient its foreign economic policy from heavy reliance on the Soviet and Chinese nonrefundable aid to loans, purchases on credit, and manufacturing joint ventures with both advanced socialist and capitalist countries to import modern machinery and industrial equipment.[66] Simply put, he suggested diversification of Vietnam's foreign economic relations beyond the socialist bloc. His economic vision after the PPA was for Vietnam to have a more economically independent and efficient foundation that could accelerate its economy from small- to large-scale production. He reasoned:

> Importing modern technology and equipment is extremely important for economic development. If we want to speed up economic development, we must increase exports, which requires importing modern equipment. For instance, for Hungary to increase its gross domestic product to 6 percent annually, it had to increase its exports by 12 percent annually. . . . We need to use the products we manufacture to pay for imports of modern equipment. Besides a number of projects, including seaports, irrigation systems, and power plants, [we] need to tightly connect our imports of modern equipment to our exports, using the products from those factories to pay down our import debt.[67]

To achieve this vision, Thach further counseled the Politburo, "We continue to rely on the advanced socialist countries as our main base of support, but at the same time we must take the opportunity to import modern technology from the capitalist countries. We need to take advantage of the opportunity to demand that the Americans pay compensation for their war of destruction in Vietnam, of the market crisis and fierce economic competition in the capitalist world, and of the rivalry between major powers in Indochina and Southeast Asia."[68] His strategic thinking reflects a realist worldview par excellence and well ahead of his time. As it turned out, it took more than a decade for his ideas to take root and be accepted as the prevailing collective ideas of the Politburo in 1985, on the eve of the Sixth Party Congress in December 1986.

The convergence of domestic and external forces that culminated in 1985 set Vietnam on a pathbreaking course toward economic reform and a broad-based foreign economic policy. In 1985–86, the rise of the reformists within the CPV was made possible, in part, by the deteriorating health and natural death of the most powerful leader of the conservative and military-first camp. Le Duan, the party secretary, died on July 10, 1986. Before he died, he put Truong Chinh, a conservative turned reformist, at the helm of the party Politburo. The transition was not without opposition. In December 1985, Le Duc Tho, Le Duan's longtime ally, persistently encouraged the dying Le Duan to name him as his replacement.[69] Le Duan made clear his distaste for Le Duc Tho's audacious ambitions by instructing him to stop chairing Politburo meetings. In April 1986, just before the Sixth Party Congress commenced, Le Duc Tho and his wife went to Le Duan's bedside to ask for his support Duan scolded Tho, saying, "You are strange. I already rejected [your request]. . . . I said Truong Chinh."[70] The most plausible explanation as to why Le Duan came to favor a conservative turned reformist like Truong Chinh over his long-term ally Le Duc Tho as the next party secretary has to be found in Truong Chinh's dealings with Vietnam's economic crisis since the Fifth Party Congress in 1982. Le Duc Tho's military allies, General Van Tien Dung and Chu Huy Man, who were the war hawks in the military-first faction, lost party support and their Politburo seats at the Sixth Party Congress in December 1986. Two other leading members of the military-first faction died in 1986. General Hoang Van Thai suddenly died on July 2, just months before the congress, and General Le Trong Tan died on December 1.[71] General Le Duc Anh, however, emerged from his command of the Vietnamese troops in Cambodia as a rising star in the military. One of his signature military strategies was to drive Cambodian resistance forces into Thai territory in the summer offensives of 1984–85, and he also carried out the K5 project in 1985, in which tens of thousands of Cambodian youths were forced by the PRK regime to clear eight hundred kilometers along Cambodia's border with Thailand so it could be planted with land mines and other barriers to prevent the Khmer Rouge forces from returning. According to former Vietnamese ambassador Ngo Dien's estimate, nearly 7 million workdays were dedicated to the completion of the K5 project. General Le Duc Anh hoped to enable the Cambodian armed forces to gain strength and allow the Vietnamese troops to withdraw from Cambodia by the end of the 1980s.[72]

According to the reformist Phan Van Khai, a member of the Party Central Committee in 1986, Truong Chinh reformist ideas and his determination to change the party's thinking between 1982 and 1986 had received growing support from the majority of party members.[73] Six months later, in December 1986, a reformist leader, Nguyen Van Linh, replaced the elderly Truong Chinh as party secretary. Nguyen Van Linh appeared to be a compromise candidate between reformist leader Truong Chinh and conservative leaders Le Duc Tho and Pham Hung, with the support for Linh by Prime Minister Pham Van Dong.[74] In 1985, it was Truong Chinh, who reintroduced Nguyen Van Linh into the Politburo and restored the rest of his other portfolio as a permanent member of the General Secretariat, a position a conservative, To Huu, wanted.[75]

At the Tenth Plenum of the Fifth Party Central Committee in May 1986, the internal struggle between the conservatives and reformists in the economic sphere ended in a further victory for the latter. Deputy Prime Minister To Huu and other conservatives lost their seats in the Council of Ministers.[76] The Eighth Plenum of the Fifth Central Committee voted to reinstate Nguyen Van Linh as a member of the Politburo and restore his previous party portfolio. New policies dealt head-on with basic inefficiencies in the economy, and the logical starting point was to reexamine the mistakes for the past ten years from 1975 to 1985.

At the policy level, the March 1985 report of the Foreign Economic Relations Research Group, under Vo Van Kiet's leadership at the Council of Ministers, called for a radical change in economic thinking, washing away the old wartime thinking that led to an overreliance on foreign aid, wasteful practices, economic inefficiency, bureaucratic bottlenecks, and a disconnect between import and export plans.[77] Three major past mistakes cited in that report were "knowledge" (*nhan thuc*), "orientation" (*chu truong*), and "import and export." First, after a two-decade-long war, the Vietnamese leaders were too slow to recognize that economic relations with other countries, including the socialist ones, were based on the principle of "mutual interests, reciprocity, and loans that must be paid back."[78]

> We failed to recognize the strategic relationship between exports and imports, which in turn affected our ability to transition from small-scale to large-scale

production; we did not understand the relationship between exports and building the material and technological foundation of a socialist economy. We were steeped in the wartime mentality of passively relying on outsiders and slow to recover. Because of these problems, we have not fully exploited the economic potential of our domestic resources and strengths to expand economic relations with other countries. Especially, we failed to increase exports, did not see the importance of building a material foundation in service of large-scale exports, and were slow in issuing policies and measures to boost exports.[79]

Second, for the reformists in 1985, there was a disconnect between Vietnam's foreign economic policy and the country's economic development objective of the previous ten years, causing a failure to adequately exploit the country's economic strengths, including a large labor force, land, natural resources, skills, and existing production capacity to concentrate on building the most important pillars of the economy. For instance, in 1976–80 Vietnam imported too many tractors and other agricultural machinery, but the most important goods, especially fertilizers and pesticides to guarantee the success of production plans were in short supply.[80] During this period, Vietnam imported nearly 150,000 tractors, more than 130,000 heavy-duty trucks, and 2,000 rice mills; these massive imports of agricultural machinery far surpassed country's need for and capacity to use them, while consumption goods and food were in short supply.[81]

Third, Vietnam's exports were not sufficient to guarantee basic imports of raw materials, and the trade deficit, though gradually reduced, remained very large during the 1975–85 period.[82] Vietnam owed the socialist bloc 2.6 billion rubles (2.4 billion in original loans and 200 million in accrued interest) by 1985, and payment was due in the next five years, 1986–90. In addition, Vietnam failed to repay 200 million rubles in 1981–85. It also owed the nonsocialist countries a total of US$1.9 billion (an original loan of 1.35 billion and accrued interest of US$550 million). Thus the total amount of Vietnam's national debt to be paid in 1986–90 was 2.8 billion rubles to the socialist bloc and US$1.9 billion to the capitalist and nonsocialist countries.[83] In addition, Vietnam's import need for 1986–90 was estimated to have increased from 7.5 billion rubles in 1981–85 to 10 billion rubles, of which 6 billion were used to import four important items, namely, oil (increasing from 8.5 million tons in 1981–85 to more or less 15 million tons in 1986–90), steel (1.8 million tons in 1981–85 slightly dropping to 1.3 million tons in 1986–90), fertilizer (from 13 million tons in 1981–85 to 6 million tons in 1986–90), and cotton (320,000 tons in 1981–85 to 237,000 tons in 1986–90). Vietnam expected to get loans of 5.5 to 6 billion rubles from the Soviet bloc and had to find an additional loan of US$4 to 4.5 billion if it was to import goods from the nonsocialist market.[84] This group of economists from the Council of Ministers recommended increased efforts to expand trade with the Soviet bloc while creating conditions favorable for mutually beneficial economic relations with nonsocialist countries.[85]

With respect to foreign economic policy, Nguyen Co Thach's 1986 foreign policy report more forcefully stressed the inherent transformative changes in the global economic configuration that compelled Vietnam to adopt economic reforms or else risk lagging behind. The Vietnamese learned a crucial lesson by closely observing international politics in the mid-1980s during which great power relations among the Soviet Union, China, and the United States were characterized by both conflict and cooperation. In other words, ideological conflicts between nations did not necessarily prevent them from engaging in mutually beneficial economic relations in an increasingly internationalized global economy. As Thach explained to his comrades at the National Assembly in 1986, the global economy was "one whole body" of which Vietnam's economy was a part, and Vietnam had to reform quickly and adopt broad-based economic relations to avoid being left behind.

Due to increased economic internationalization, all Party Congresses of the COMECON countries agreed on the following basic socioeconomic strategies: (1) obey the objective law of technological and scientific evolution. (2) completely change the production structure. (3) reform the management system by putting an end to bureaucratic centralism and subsidies (*tap trung quan lieu bao cap*) and replacing them with self-supporting enterprises and a socialist market economy, (4) promote business initiatives and human capital, and (5) mobilize and broaden economic levers in the country.[86] During the summit of the COMECON countries in November 1986, the general secretaries of the Party Central Committees issued a joint resolution to change the entire structure of economic cooperation within the COMECON bloc to one of strengthening joint corporate ventures and specialization in sectors that required the application of advanced technology.[87] Thach told his comrades, "In international economic relations, other socialist countries have now given up the old thinking and opened economic relations with Western Europe and participated in the GATT [General Agreement on Tariffs and Trade] and IMF [International Monetary Fund] to allow their domestic enterprises to directly participate in the global market."[88] Thus, the ideas of reform and opening behind Vietnam's *Doi Moi* policy, as this internal report shows, were accepted by the top leadership in 1985–86. This occurred because Vietnam had arrived at a critical historical juncture where the domestic shift from a foreign-aid-dependent mentality to economic reform thinking converged with external shocks; that was the prevailing new thinking about economic strategies in the Soviet Union and other COMECON countries and the advent of the technological revolution. The new thinking that emerged in the Soviet Union in 1985 lent support to the indigenous ideas of the reformists in Vietnam who sought ways to make Vietnam's economy more efficient and competitive.

Thanks to reform initiatives in 1986, the initial economic payoffs in the Soviet Union and other Eastern European countries further incentivized Vietnam's collective ideas about economic reforms. Foreign Minister Nguyen Co Thach told his comrades at the National Assembly, "The total production output in the socialist bloc in 1986 is predicted to increase to 4 percent from 3.2 percent in 1985. The gross national product of the Soviet Union for the past ten months of 1986 increased to 4.3 percent, exceeding the projected growth of 3.9 percent. Soviet industrial production rose to 5.1 percent, exceeding the projected growth of 4.3 percent. Labor productivity in the Soviet Union increased to 4.8 percent from the projected target of 4.1 percent for the whole year. This economic growth was the highest in nine years. Likewise, economic growth in East Germany, Bulgaria, and Czechoslovakia also met or exceeded their targets."[89]

In 1985–86, reformists pushed the idea that the risk of economically lagging behind China and other ASEAN countries posed a greater threat to Vietnam's national security in the future than the Chinese military threat. In Nguyen Co Thach's view, by the mid-1980s, the Cold War ideological fault line not only had given way to growing economic interdependence in which science, technology, and free markets were driving trade across national and ideological boundaries but also had succumbed to realpolitik in international relations where strategic interests prevailed over ideological affinity. In the political report of the Sixth Party Congress, one of the four lessons learned from forty years of national struggle for independence was "combining the strengths of the nation and of the era," which was enshrined as part of Ho Chi Minh's diplomatic thought.[90]

This principle, Thach argued, required that Vietnam correct its course of action according to the global trend. The underlying philosophical premise, as Thach reasoned with his colleagues, is that mankind has evolved according to the prevailing law of nature, which in turn determines the trends of existence and development of mankind in the world. Any nation that follows the prevailing trend and evolutionary law in history tends to grow strong. On the contrary, Thach argued, even a country as powerful as the imperialist United States of America, when it went against the prevailing trend and evolutionary law at the time, became weak and eventually met its defeat in Vietnam.

Adapting this philosophical belief to the stage of Vietnam's socialist economic development, Thach maintained:

To reach socialism fast from small-scale to large-scale production, we must go through the capitalist development phase of socialism, and we need to tightly combine our national strengths and those of the era. The technological and scientific revolution in the global economy in the 1980s has opened up a path for us to industrialize our economy quickly, faster than the global industrialization process that occurred two hundred years ago. On the contrary, the penetrating transformation in technology and science and global economic structure is putting our country, and other less-developed countries, in great danger because if we fail to economically develop fast enough, the gap between our less-developed country and the developed ones will further widen, and consequentially the hazard of our economic underdevelopment will become a threat to our political stability, security, and national defense.[91]

Thach proposed that Vietnam should invest aggressively in science and technology to turn the technological revolution into a locomotive of economic modernization. He believed that Vietnam should start by carving out an economic niche for itself in the COMECON bloc, and the most favorable position for Vietnam in the international division of labor was the production of "cheap and high-quality goods. Furthermore, although we prioritize its relations with the Soviet Union and other socialist countries, we have to open up economic relations with other countries as the trend of internationalization of global economy dictates."[92]

However, from 1986 to 1990, the Soviet Union and other Eastern European countries remained the most reliable and strongest supporters of Vietnam's economic reforms. During this period, the Soviet Union doubled its financial support with a total loan of approximately 8.7 billion rubles while Eastern Europe pledged approximately the same level of financial aid as it did during 1981–85. In addition, sympathetic to Vietnam's economic difficulties, Moscow decided to provide Hanoi with supplementary aid, including food, fertilizer, fuel, and consumption goods, which covered 90 percent of the total amount in the agreement.[93]

However, for many years Vietnam failed to increase its exports to the Soviet Union and other Eastern European countries to compensate for its large numbers of imports from them. Thach warned his comrades, "Besides the negative impact of our inability to increase exports in our economic relations with the Soviet Union, we must calculate and be mindful of a new factor—China is flooding the Soviet and Eastern European market with many products identical to ours but in much larger quantities with better quality, cheaper prices, and more timely delivery."[94] From Hanoi's vantage point, the threat emanating from China before the Sixth Party Congress in December 1986 had more of an economic nature than China's outright military attacks on Vietnam. As Thach explained, "China wants Vietnam's economic difficulties to worsen, which in turn would create internal divisions in our society, and our country would plunge into a serious political crisis. Our enemy [China] at the same time has increased military pressure along the border and heightened its propaganda to further divide and weaken us internally."[95]

Since 1983, Vietnam had faced a China that was aggressively making inroads into markets in the Soviet bloc and undercutting Vietnam's exports to those markets. As relations between China and the Soviet bloc improved, China gained access to its markets. Under Deng Xiaoping's leadership, China continued to amass capital strategically and advance technology to speed up the modernization of its economy. At the same time, China desired Soviet technological equipment and the markets of the Soviet Union and Eastern Europe. China's relations with the Soviet Union and Eastern Europe improved in 1985 as the Soviets exploited the conflict between China and the United States in their favor. To entice China, the Soviets agreed to help restore Soviet industrial projects of the 1950s, and the State Planning Committees of the two countries signed a long-term economic cooperation agreement in 1986.[96] Thach further maintained, "In 1986, China's main strategy was to take advantage of the conflict between the Soviet Union and the United States, between the West and East, and between revolutionary and antirevolutionary forces. In general, China avoided siding with one side against the other side."[97] Given China's economic statecraft in service of its economic modernization, top Vietnamese diplomats such as Nguyen Co Thach were confident that the Chinese leadership would have to negotiate with Vietnam when the military confrontation between Vietnam and China reached a stalemate. In the ninth round of negotiations between China and the Soviet Union and at the Sixth Party Congress in December 1986, Vietnam made clear its intention to negotiate with China to solve the Cambodian problem and create peaceful coexistence with China.[98]

It was the fear of being slowed down in their economic development, combined with the reformist leaders' articulation of economic backwardness as a threat to national security that compelled the military-first faction within the CPV to retreat from continued military confrontation. The ideas of leaders of the reformists or economy-firsters,[99] like Foreign Minister Nguyen Co Thach and chairman of the State Planning Committee Vo Van Kiet, did not prevail by defeating the conservative and military-first faction. Specifically, their ideas about economic reform and political and diplomatic solutions to the Cambodia problem did not replace but rather built on military strategies and victories, which the reformists themselves attributed to Vietnamese military leaders like General Le Duc Anh, who commanded the Vietnamese army in Cambodia.

It is not historically accurate to describe Vietnam's *Doi Moi* policy in 1986 as a single successful reform that completely replaced the formerly failing Marxist central-planning model or the reformists' economic engagement totally defeating the conservatives and military-first faction. Members of the military wing of the party and government were recognized for their major military victories during the summers of 1984–85 on the Cambodian battlefield in the southwest and for preventing China from launching another military invasion of Vietnam from the north, also referred to as the "second lesson" China threatened to teach Vietnam.

Vietnam's major military offensives against the Cambodian resistance forces inside Cambodia and Chinese military positions along its northern border in 1984–85 were designed to project an image of military strength into Vietnam's diplomacy. In its first six-month report on foreign affairs in 1986, the Vietnamese Ministry of Foreign Affairs wrote:

> After the severe military defeat of the Khmer reactionary forces in the two summers of 1984–85 and China's failure to teach us "a second lesson" during the past six years, the Chinese expansionists now pushed the Khmer reactionary forces to launch a campaign of destruction inside Cambodia, including using the pretext of "national reconciliation" to strengthen their psychological warfare and conceal their hidden agents within the masses. . . . However, the Cambodian armed forces together with the Vietnamese volunteer troops have bravely defended the PRK and built border defenses [known as K5 project] along the Thai-Cambodian border.[100]

The Vietnamese leadership was confident that by 1986 the PRK, with the help of the Vietnamese troops, would decisively thwart China's attempt to topple the Phnom Penh regime.

On the basis of this military victory and within the context of international politics shifting from confrontation to dialogue and peaceful coexistence in 1985–86, reformists like Nguyen Co Thach launched a diplomatic offensive to compel China to approach the negotiating table to find a solution to the Cambodian problem. Hanoi's public diplomacy throughout 1985 was designed to crystalize Vietnam's intention to completely withdraw all its troops from Cambodia in 1990, hoping to undermine China's strategy of using the presence of Vietnamese troops in Cambodia to maintain a united front against Vietnam in Southeast Asia and to bog Vietnam down in costly and protracted guerrilla warfare in Cambodia.

Despite of costly military intervention and national building in Cambodia and assistance to Laos, Vietnam was not prepared to relinquish its influence in those countries. To the reformists, the status quo policy of nation building in Cambodia while fighting the China-supported Cambodian resistance forces there and China along the northern border became clearly untenable and very harmful to Vietnam's economy by 1984–85. Along came the idea of establishing a Vietnam-led Indochinese economic bloc of to strengthen mutual assistance and maintain socialist solidarity among Vietnam, Cambodia, and Laos.

The Abandonment of Vietnam-Led Indochinese Regionalism

Three years after the summit of the three Indochinese countries in Vientiane in February 1982, Hanoi's top economic planners were much less enthusiastic about the idea of Vietnam-led economic integration in Indochina, preferring the more economically beneficial bilateral relations between Vietnam and its two smaller neighbors Cambodia and Laos. On January 12, 1985, in a top-secret memo to the secretariat of the Party Central Committee and other executive branches of the government, the Council of Ministers revealed its frustration with the slow progress in economic integration of the three countries. It was at this point that the Politburo instructed the State Planning Committee and the CECC–Laos and Cambodia to focus on strengthening Vietnam's economic co-operation with Laos and Cambodia based on the principle of "equality, fraternity, mutually beneficial (transactions), [and] preferential trade agreements with each other" and to optimize the effectiveness of Vietnamese assistance to the two countries so that they would be more self-reliant.[101] After 1986 Vietnam focused on bilateral trade with Cambodia and Laos. It had already cut off all nonrefundable aid to Cambodia and later to Laos by 1985.

What explained such a shift in Vietnam's foreign economic policy toward Cambodia and Laos? The answer lies in the systemic underdevelopment and deep poverty in the three countries. In other words, a poor Vietnam simply did not have enough economic power to shoulder the growing burden of lifting up its two poorer neighbors to create a strong and economically integrated bloc as anticipated by Hanoi's top economic planners in early 1982. In 1983–84, Vietnam was able to organize interagency coordination, namely, the economic and cultural committees for the three countries, and synchronize economic planning. Overall trade among the three countries remained very low, falling far short of Hanoi's expectations, and Vietnam's burden of aid to Laos and Cambodia continued unabated.

Dang Thi, Chairman of CECC–Laos and Cambodia, reported to the Council of Ministers on November 11, 1984, that after the summit of the three Indochinese countries in Vientiane in February 1983 the three economic and cultural cooperation committees of Laos, Cambodia, and Vietnam speedily established organizational mechanisms to deepen economic integration of the three countries. Most notable among those mechanisms were organizing the structure of economic relations among the three committees, drafting a joint economic cooperation plan for 1984–85, planning research efforts for the 1986–90 economic plan, creating a subcommittee for transportation, and deciding on principles governing trade, labor, imports and exports, currency exchange, and payments.[102] Besides these accomplishments, there emerged a myriad of issues ranging from Vietnam's aid burden in Laos and Cambodia to the rising cost of transshipping material aid from Vietnam to Laos and Cambodia, the growing cost of training Cambodian and Laotian officials and Vietnamese experts working in Laos and Cambodia, and Vietnam's debt to Cambodia.

Vietnam's debt to Cambodia became a sensitive issue in early 1985 and came to the attention of Hanoi's top leadership. Since 1979, due to the shortages of consumption goods and food in Vietnam, the Vietnamese government, with the Cambodian government's approval, used some of material aid given by the Soviet Union and other socialist countries and recorded it as a Cambodian loan to Vietnam. Vietnam's prolonged delay in paying Cambodia back negatively affected Vietnam's image of assisting Cambodia as Hanoi's leaders desired Cambodian gratitude and recognition of Vietnam's vital assistance to the its revolution.[103] Dang Thi, in a report to the Council of Ministers, dedicated a lengthy section to detailing the sensitivity of Vietnam's debt to Cambodia. He wrote, "Besides providing [food] for us [Vietnamese troops and experts] to consume in Cambodia, our Cambodian comrades allowed us to consume some rice, flour, and beans that other socialist countries gave Cambodia and transshipped via Vietnam. We have paid back some, but up to early 1984 we still owe Cambodia 7.089 million rubles and 13 million riels. In 1984, we can only pay back roughly 10 percent of the total amount. Our Cambodian comrades have expressed their hope that we will soon pay them back in goods. For the past several years, we have not done that."[104] In 1985, Dang Thi also proposed that the Vietnamese government allocate 400 million VND, in addition to repaying the financial loan (mentioned above), in order to pay for the balance of goods Vietnam owed Cambodia.[105]

At the meeting with the CECC–Laos and Cambodia, the State Planning Committee, and other concerned authorities on January 3, 1985, the Standing Committee of the Council of Ministers instructed that Vietnam's debt to Cambodia be divided into two categories: (1) material goods from other socialist countries that Cambodia had given to Vietnam and (2) food supplies the Cambodian government had allocated to feed the Vietnamese occupying troops.[106] The State Planning Committee, together with other concerned ministries such as Finance, Food and Material Supply, Internal Trade, and Transport, were scheduled to arrange payment of the first category of debt to Cambodia. Yet the second category of debt—food supplies, including rice and meat consumed by the Vietnamese troops and security forces in Cambodia—was to be left to the CECC–Laos and Cambodia and the leadership of the Vietnamese experts in Cambodia to be negotiated with the Cambodia government.[107] The term *negotiation* here implies that Vietnam's debt to Cambodia was to be nullified because it was used to feed the Vietnamese troops and experts that were helping the Cambodian government strengthen its national defense and economy.

During 1983–84, the Vietnamese government allocated more than one billion VND for the CECC–Laos and Cambodia to provide economic aid to and deepen cooperation with Laos and Cambodia. And during these years, Vietnam's bilateral economic assistance to Laos and Cambodia was used to ensure that their foreign policies would stay in line with Vietnam's.[108] During this period, the three countries helped each other address urgent economic problems. Vietnam provided experts, training of cadres, and basic evaluation to increase production and exploitation of agriculture, forests, and fisheries; to develop small industries; and to address the shortages of consumption goods.[109] In 1983–84, Laos and Cambodia requested—and Hanoi agreed—that Vietnam annually dispatch 3,500 professional and technical experts (this figure excluded Vietnamese cadres who helped Cambodia and Laos at the party level). One thousand Vietnamese experts were dispatched to Laos and 2,500 to Cambodia. The majority of these experts were in the fields of agriculture, fishing, health, education, economic management, public security, and national defense.[110] In addition, Vietnam annually provided scholarships to a large number of Cambodian and Laotian students and officials, between 6,500 and 7,000 (4,000 from Laos and 2,500 to 3,000 from Cambodia per year), to receive training in Vietnam. Vietnam also sent a large number of trainers and professors to the two countries.[111] Although the Cambodian and Laotian governments praised and never ceased to show their gratitude to the Vietnamese leaders for their significant contribution to the developing countries, the soaring cost and burden of Vietnam's aid to its two brotherly neighbors emerged as a contentious issue within the inner circle of the Vietnamese leadership.

Moreover, Vietnam shouldered the huge burden of transshipment of material aid from the Soviet Union and other socialist countries to Laos and Cambodia, registering between 150,000 and 170,000 tons passing through Vietnam's ports every year. That quantity included 40,000 to 50,000 tons of fuel transferred to Laos annually via a pipeline. Vietnam took responsibility for helping transporting goods it bought from Laos to Vietnam. For instance, in 1984, out of 70,000 tons of plaster (construction material) purchased from Laos, the Laotian government could only transport 15,000 tons to Vietnam, so the Vietnamese Ministry of Transport had to bring the rest to Vietnam at its own expense.[112] Similar burdens existed in the Vietnamese-Cambodian dyad with respect to the transshipment of foreign aid and transportation of commercial goods in that the Vietnamese had to assume much greater responsibility and bear more of the expense.

Dang Thi told the Council of Ministers that many problems emerged with the transshipment of foreign aid to Cambodia and Laos and the transportation of commercial goods. These problems ranged from goods being scattered about, misplaced, or damaged to other negative phenomena, including theft and looting. This problem caused growing friction between the Vietnamese and the Cambodian and Laotian authorities. Vietnamese transport units also faced increased difficulty with shortages of spare parts and fuel, bad roads, and security threats in remote areas, especially in Cambodia. All these obstacles further increased the cost of transport for Vietnam.[113] Moreover, Vietnam's assistance in the areas of road construction, irrigation, and storage and house construction also fell short of its plan and suffered delays due to Vietnam's own shortages of raw materials, fuel, spare parts, and modern equipment for these construction projects.[114] One can only infer from Dang Thi's frustrating report that the Vietnamese leaders were not pleased with their increased burden of transshipment and transport of Laotian and Cambodian goods.

Yet Vietnam also gained a trade benefit, though modest, from exchanges of its industrial products for agricultural products, forest products, and other specialties. Laos and Cambodia benefited from trade with Vietnam. Vietnam helped Laos and Cambodia by importing the majority of goods that were not of high quality and failed to meet the standards of export to the Soviet Union and Eastern European countries.[115] And bilateral trade turnover remained very low, recording 5.5 million rubles per year (Vietnamese-Laotian trade amounted to 3 million rubles and Vietnamese-Cambodian trade 2.5 million rubles). The main reason for this is simply that the three countries produced similar goods, leaving only a small number of tradable items. As Dang Thi lamented, "Cambodia and Laos had great potential to export agricultural products, forest products, and specialty products like rubber, coffee, and fruit, but their governments did not receive sufficient goods from their people to exchange for those products, and their economic organization was poor. As a result, they faced difficulty in mobilizing and collecting such products for export. For our part, we run short of goods to exchange for those products from Cambodia and Laos."[116] In Dang Thi's evaluation, "Cambodia and Laos desired to enlarge official economic cooperation with Vietnam and placed great hope and confidence in Vietnam, but our economic difficulty limited our ability to do so."[117] He further stressed that unofficial cross-border trade at the local level had increased much faster than the official trade among the three countries since 1979. He asked the Council of Ministers to look into the policy of encouraging mutually beneficial cross-border trade between local authorities of the three countries as Cambodia and Laos desired local trade between border provinces. He further suggested that the central government provide raw materials and equipment to local enterprises to increase the production of consumption goods to trade for other goods from Cambodia and Laos deemed important for the local economy of provinces along the border.[118]

Up to 1985, the CECC–Laos and Cambodia was Vietnam's top agency for dealing with economic cooperation between the two countries. This committee received capital for investment and a budget for expenses from the central government and made its own decisions quite independently; it was required only to consult the State Planning Committee. However, Deputy Prime Minister Vo Van Kiet, who was also chairman of the State Planning Committee, proposed in a letter dated August 9, 1985, to Prime Minister Pham Van Dong that from 1986 onward, the CECC–Laos and Cambodia would serve under the State Planning Committee, which would oversee the central economic planning for cooperation with Laos and Cambodia. In his reply on August 13, 1985, Prime Minister Pham Van Dong, who was also chairman of the Council of Ministers, agreed with Kiet's proposal.[119] The diminishing role of the CECC–Laos and Cambodia after 1986 demonstrated the waning importance of the idea of Vietnam-led economic regionalism in Indochina. At the same time, it was indicative of the rise of a leading reformist, Vo Van Kiet, within the Council of Ministers and his power as chairman of the State Planning Committee and vice-chairman of the council.

In 1985 Vietnam's nonrefundable aid to Laos and Cambodia was further reduced to an insignificant level while Hanoi continued to provide substantial technical support and training to its two socialist neighbors as part of its efforts to prop up client regimes in Cambodia and Laos. Vietnam's Council of Ministers decided to allocate 1.260 billion VND for aid to Laos and Cambodia; 950 million VND, of which 650 million was loan, was for Laos, 150 million VND was for nonrefundable aid to Cambodia, and 160 million VDN was allocated to service economic cooperation between Vietnam and Cambodia.[120] In addition, 400 million VND was allocated to pay the old debt to Cambodia.[121]

Most of the Vietnamese aid to Laos and Cambodia in 1985 was concentrated in three areas: (1) basic assessment, research, and design for various projects in the fields of agriculture, forestry, fisheries, irrigation, hydropower, transportation, and so on; (2) basic construction (irrigation systems, hydropower, bridges, hospitals, schools, and so on; (3) training in Vietnam of 4,500 Laotian students and cadres from various fields in 1984–85 (Vietnam accepted 1,100 more in 1985–86).

By November 1984, there were a total of 2,610 Cambodian cadres receiving training in Vietnam, of which 600 were in economic and cultural fields, 1,710 from the PRK's Ministry of Defense, and 300 from the Ministry of the Interior. For 1985–86, Vietnam agreed to train 1,992 Cambodian government and party officials, including 1,411 trainees from Cambodia's two key sectors (311 from the economic field and 1,100 in military affairs), 169 cadres from the Party Center, and 312 midlevel officials and technicians. Moreover, as requested by Laos and Cambodia, Vietnam in 1985 dispatched 120 Vietnamese experts for long-term stays and 1,000 experts in the field of agriculture in Laos. Vietnam also dispatched 846 short-term experts to Cambodia, and 150 rounds of experts were to be sent to Cambodia to train Cambodian officials on the spot. In addition, 700 Vietnamese experts from the party and armed forces were to be sent to Cambodia that year.[122]

In the field of economic cooperation in 1985, Hanoi directed its support for Laos and Cambodia toward exploitation of natural sources for import to Vietnam. For instance, Vietnam provided Laos with technical support to produce 200,000 tons of plaster (construction material) per year. In 1984 it bought 60,000 tons of plaster from Laos and planned to purchase 100,000 more in 1985. Vietnam planned to help Laos increase its extraction of minerals up to 200,000 tons per year in 1987–90.[123] The second area of economic cooperation with Laos in which Hanoi was interested was logging and wood processing. Laos and Vietnam agreed to produce between 15,000 and 20,000 cubic meters of high-quality logs in 1985. In Cambodia the Vietnamese authorities in the southern provinces of Long An, Dong Nai, Cuu Long, Quang Nam, and Da Nang were put in charge of cooperating with their Cambodian counterparts in the area of forestry. For 1985 Vietnam planned to import from Cambodia nearly 10,000 cubic meters of high-quality logs (from Kampong Thom 10 cubic meters of logs per day, from Kampong Speu 10 cubic meters of logs per day, and from Kratie 6 cubic meters of logs per day).[124]

For 1986–90, Vietnam expected to continue the course of bilateral economic cooperation that had brought about mutual benefit. Vietnam would provide expertise and sophisticated equipment to improve agricultural production and irrigation systems, grow rubber, exploit forests and process wood products, increase fish extraction, and upgrade transportation in Cambodia and Laos.[125] In return, Vietnam would take a share of those products or enjoy access to such products at a price below market rate. In 1985 the best Hanoi's top economic planner could hope for was to continue to "do research" on the economic strategy and the potential of economic integration of the three countries for the next FYP, 1986–90.[126] Thus, the vision of Vietnam-led economic regionalism remained far-fetched, if not completely scrapped, by 1985, a year before Vietnam was about to enter its transformative era of *Doi Moi*. Vietnam's economic assistance to Cambodia and Laos dropped significantly in the 1986–90 period.

On foreign policy, the Politburo of the CPV convinced the Politburo of the Kampuchea People's Revolutionary Party during a summit in Hanoi on August 9–10, 1985, to agree to Hanoi's plan to withdraw all Vietnamese troops from Cambodia in 1990.[127] It was a decisive shift to the strategy of a diplomatic offensive after the major victory of joint military offensives against the Cambodian resistance armed forces in the summers of 1984 and 1985. On August 13, the secretariat of the Party Central Committee dispatched Foreign Minister Nguyen Co Thach to Vientiane to inform Kaysone Phomihane, general secretary of the Laos People's Revolutionary Party, of the content of the meeting, and Phomihane completely agreed with Hanoi's strategy. After receiving instructions from Le Duan, Truong Chinh, Pham Van Dong, and Le Duc Tho, the Eleventh Conference of Foreign Ministers from the three Indochinese countries took place in Phnom Penh on August 15–16 to assess the development of the three countries' struggle during the previous six years (1978–84) with special attention to the years 1984–85. In addition, the conference assessed the three countries' diplomatic offensive in 1984–85 and agreed on the direction and strategy of diplomatic offensives in 1985–86. The three countries were pleased with the political and military victories in the summers of 1984 and 1985 in Cambodia and the Laotian people's victory against Thailand's territorial aggression in three provinces of Laos. Hanoi took note of the two countries' gratitude toward the Vietnamese and their recognition of the big role Vietnam played in the victories in Cambodia and Laos.[128] In a secret report that emerged from the

Eleventh Conference of Foreign Ministers, the Vietnamese believed—and their Cambodian and Laotian comrades agreed—that they had defeated China's attempt to "teach Vietnam a second lesson" in both Cambodia and the battlefield along the Sino-Vietnamese border during the previous six years. They were also optimistic because since 1985 dialogue had been increasing as Sino-Soviet relations improved and American-Soviet relations had shifted from confrontation to negotiation.

The leadership of the Vietnamese MOFA believed that Vietnam's diplomatic offensive after 1985 was important, timely, and suitable after the six-year military confrontation had ended in a stalemate and a political solution to the Cambodian problem was inevitable. The two-pronged strategy of complete withdrawal of Vietnamese troops from Cambodia in 1990 and the PRK leaders' explicit expression of their desire to negotiate with the Cambodian resistance forces was timed to go into effect before Vietnam's planned dialogue with Indonesia and the United States in August 1985, a United Nations General Assembly meeting in September, and an American-Soviet summit in November.[129] This strategy was designed to undermine Thailand's and China's most lethal diplomatic weapon—the presence of the Vietnamese occupying force in Cambodia—and drive a wedge between China and ASEAN and between a more cooperative Indonesia and anti-Vietnam hawks, including Thailand, Singapore, and Malaysia, in this regional organization.[130] The grand objective of Vietnam's diplomacy offensive was to bring all the major powers involved to the negotiation table to find a political solution to the Cambodian conflict and restore peace and stability in Southeast Asia. The Vietnamese believed that negotiations would bring the regional peace necessary for Vietnam, Laos, and Cambodia to focus on building their respective economies and ward off economic threats from China and the American-Japanese alliance.[131]

In 1986 the reformist leaders won the argument that China posed a long-term economic and political threat to Vietnam's national security, a major shift from the conservatives' and military-firsters' status quo of military confrontation with China and military intervention in Cambodia. In mid-1986, Nguyen Co Thach delivered a fifty-seven-page foreign affairs report to the National Assembly. In this report, he fired the first shot, warning his colleagues of China's future economic threat to Vietnam and the end of the Soviet Union's generosity. He stated,

> For the past five years (1981–85), the Soviet Union provided Vietnam with a total of about 8.7 billion rubles in capital, doubling the amount of the previous five years (1976–80). In addition, Eastern Europe provided more or less the

same amount of aid as they did during 1976–80. In addition, the Soviets provided additional food supplies, fertilizer, fuel, consumption goods, and so on. The combined aid from the Soviet bloc covered 90 percent of the total amount pledged. That is valuable assistance. However, we have not fulfilled our duty properly [as a worthy economic partner] as we did for many years. Besides the adverse effects of their trust in us as a reliable economic partner, we need to awaken ourselves to, and remind ourselves of, a new factor—that is, China is making great efforts to enter the market of our socialist brother countries. The Chinese entered those markets with a diverse array of goods, most of which were similar to our products, but they can supply those goods in larger quantities; with better quality, better packaging, and cheaper prices; and in a timely manner.[132]

Thach concluded his report to the National Assembly by stressing this.

The Sixth Party Congress restored Vietnamese people's confidence and unity with the party, won the respect of foreigners, and shocked the world. That is the bravery of facing the truth and daring to criticize and self-criticize. That is the determination to renovate (*Doi Moi*): new thinking (*doi moi tu duy*), open democracy, and the determination to overcome every obstacle. That is the political genius, resolve, and unity of our people in determining our country's direction. . . . The fact that our revolutionary leaders voluntarily withdrew from leadership positions in the party and designated the younger generation as their successors is a shining example and noble gesture that deserves the respect of the entire party, Vietnamese people, and friends alike.[133]

In an attempt to salvage Vietnam's influence in Cambodia and Laos, Foreign Minister Nguyen Co Thach, as Vietnam began to implement the *Doi Moi* policy in 1986, spoke of "the urgent need to complete the economic link between the three Indochinese countries, Vietnam, Cambodia, and Laos, to prevent the enemy, meaning China, from undermining their unity and the need to give up the old way of cooperating with Cambodia and Laos [Vietnam-led economic regionalism] because it is no longer suitable for the new situation."[134] In January 1986, Vietnam's Council of Ministers proposed that the Council of State to bestow its highest awards on the six most powerful members of the PRK Politburo for "strengthening the spirit of solidarity, special friendship, and all-around cooperation between Vietnam and Cambodia."[135] After 1987 the chairman of the Council of Ministers Hun Sen became the leader of economic reforms in Cambodia. Cambodia's economic reforms were largely influenced by a combination of external pressures and learning from the reforms taking place in Vietnam and the Soviet Union. With the death of Party Secretary Le Duan in July 1986 and the rise of southerners Nguyen Van Linh and Vo Van Kiet and a younger reformist, Nguyen Co Thach, in the CPV, Hanoi counseled the PRK Politburo to pursue economic reform. In 1987 Moscow significantly curtailed its aid commitment to the PRK, pushing the regime to think about economic self-sufficiency and a political solution to the Cambodian conflict.[136] Hun Sen's close relationship with his counterparts Vietnamese foreign minister Nguyen Co Thach and Soviet foreign minister Eduard Shevardnadze certainly influenced his thinking about economic reforms in Cambodia.

In 1987, in a concerted effort to end the military conflict with China, Hanoi pressured the PRK Politburo to accept what Le Duc Tho called the "Red Solution," to the dislike of its most powerful member, Hun Sen. On March 7, 1987, the Vietnamese Politburo discussed diplomatic strategies and came up with three options to deal with China: (1) continued fighting, (2) peaceful coexistence, and (3), friendly cooperation. On the diplomatic front, Vietnam proposed secret Sino-Vietnamese negotiations to find a solution to the Cambodian conflict, as well as counseling the PRK to declare a policy of national reconciliation.[137] On April 9, 1987, the MOFA established an internal research group, with the code name CP 87,[138] led by Vice-Minister Tran Quang Co and Dang Nghiem Hoanh (director of General Department of Foreign Relations) to conduct research on the policy of normalization with China and a solution to the Cambodian problem. At the end of April 1987, Le Duc Tho and General Le Duc Anh flew to Phnom Penh, bringing the leaders of CP 87 with them. Le Duc Tho suggested the Red Solution—that is, ending the Cambodian conflict, by means a reconciliation and compromise between the PRK and the Pol Pot clique, and creating a new socialist regime in Cambodia that would be acceptable to both Vietnam and China. According to Tran Quang Co's account, Le Duc Tho's idea met a cold reception from the PRK leadership, especially Hun Sen.[139] Two years later, in 1989, Hun Sen called it "wrong and dangerous" to the Cambodian people.[140] On October 12, 1989, Hun Sen told Vietnamese ambassador Ngo Dien, after complaining about Moscow's political concessions to Beijing and pressure on Cambodia to compromise with China and the Khmer Rouge, "Some Vietnamese comrades said we need to make some concessions to save China's face. . . . After meeting Khieu Samphan, I clearly realized in [1987] that I cannot get along with this [Pol Pot] clique."[141] To Hun Sen and his colleagues in the PRK Politburo, the Red Solution demonstrated Hanoi's and Moscow's changing politics without considering the desires of the PRK, a small ally, in this asymmetrical relationship. Perhaps for the first time Hun Sen had to confront and accept realpolitik.

Vietnam's *Doi Moi* policy formulated at the Sixth National Party Congress in 1986 was the result of two factors that converged on the eve of the party congress in 1985: (1) the prevailing collective ideas of economic reforms after years of failed economic development and (2) external economic pressures. First, the new thinking about economic reforms emerged to orient Vietnam's economy and foreign economic relations when Deputy Prime Minister Vo Van Kiet (1982–88) replaced Deputy Prime Minister Le Thanh Nghi (1974–80) and Nguyen Lam (1980–82). As chairman of the State Planning Committee, Nguyen Lam had steered Vietnam's economic planning based primarily on large amounts of aid from the Soviet Union and other Eastern European countries. Yet I contend that the external objective and subjective pressures provided ammunition reformist leaders, including Chairman Vo Van Kiet and Foreign Minister Nguyen Co Thach, used to convince the old guard, especially General Secretary Le Duan, president and chairman of the Council of State Truong Chinh, Prime Minister Pham Van Dong, and senior Politburo member Le Duc Tho, in the final year of their power. Without the crumbling economic power of the Soviet Union and its negative impact on Vietnam's import-export industries, the cornerstone of the Vietnamese economy, the reformists' economic ideas would not have prevailed in 1985. The death of Le Duan in July 1986 provided the pretext if not the catalyst for the rise of the second-generation reformists and many of the changes that ensued.[142]

The decline in the economic power of Vietnam's communist superpower ally, the Soviet Union, had a ripple effect on all other members of the COMECON, including Vietnam. First, foreign aid from the Soviet Union and other, more developed Eastern European countries shifted from nonrefundable aid, accounting for the majority of aid in 1975–80, to long-term loans in 1981–85 and then to short-term loans and the principle of reciprocity in economic relations from 1986 to 1990. This shift forced Vietnam to substantially increase its exports to bridge the export-import gap and reduce its balance of payments deficit. Second, as the main supplier of raw materials, fuel, and technology at a rate well below market prices to other COMECON countries, the Soviet Union could no longer shoulder that burden alone as the costs of extraction and transportation had increased substantially. As the cheap supply of energy and raw materials from the Soviet Union dwindled and the market price of strategic goods was much higher than that offered by the Soviets, the COMECON countries, including Vietnam, sought to purchase energy-efficient technology from the West and improve the efficiency of their economic production systems. Worse than Eastern European countries, Vietnam had faced economic sanctions by the West and ASEAN countries since its invasion of Cambodia in December 1978.

In 1985 it was forced to reduce waste and significantly increase the efficiency of its economic production, producing more with less energy, and to improve the quality of its export products as demanded by the Soviet Union and other Eastern European countries.

Vietnam learned from the Eastern Europeans that to survive in the new international division of labor, less-developed countries had to reform economically and adapt quickly to take advantage of prevailing trends in the global economy. In this new line of thinking, the grave threat to Vietnam's security after the mid-1980s was no longer China's military attacks but economic competition. China's success in implementing economic reforms and its access to Eastern Europe threatened Vietnam's most important and reliable markets. China's dumping of cheap goods similar the those Vietnam exported to Eastern Europe seriously threatened Vietnam's economic development and political stability in the long run.

To hasten its economic reforms, Vietnam had to reduce the costs of its occupation of Cambodia and significantly curtail aid to Cambodia and Laos, abandoning the idea of Vietnam-led economic regionalism in Indochina, which it could not longer finance by 1985. Two years after they conceived the idea of Vietnam-led economic integration, after the summit of the three countries in Vientiane in February 1983, Vietnam's top economic planners came to the sobering conclusion that Cambodia's and Laos's economies were too weak and without massive aid from the Soviet Union Vietnam's own weak economy could no longer shoulder the burden of aiding its two poorer neighbors. There was the prospect of long-term economic benefits, including taking advantage of Cambodia's and Laos's national resources (rich forests, fisheries, vast rice paddies, and raw materials) that economic regionalism was promising, but short- and medium-term investment in the two poorer countries would add a significant burden to Vietnam's struggling economy. Well before the Sixth Party Congress in December 1986, Hanoi had already hatched a strategic plan with Phnom Penh to announce the complete withdrawal of the Vietnamese occupying troops from Cambodia by 1990 and shifted its strategy from military confrontation to negotiation with China to find a political solution to the Cambodian problem.

Conclusion

Vietnam's decision to invade Cambodia was driven not by hegemonic ambition, nor by Marxist-Leninist ideology and the resultant socialist affinity with the Soviet Union against China, nor by an altruistic humanitarian impulse to save the Cambodian people from the genocide perpetrated by the Pol Pot regime. Rather, Hanoi's leaders were strategists attuned to a realpolitik interpretation of international relations and their rational consideration of strategic and material interests at the heart of Vietnam's national security. Their decision was rationalized by the full backing of the Soviet Union to address a dual national security crisis of homegrown economic hardship and two-front threats that the Chinese–Khmer Rouge alliance posed to Vietnam's national security. Domestic imperatives, specifically the socioeconomic crisis and widespread corruption within the party-state apparatus in the late 1970s, undermined the legitimacy of CPV rule by 1978 and threatened Vietnam's national defense in the midst of the Khmer Rouge attacks on Vietnam from the southwest and increased armed clashes with the Chinese along the Sino-Vietnamese border in the north.

Abundant documentary evidence in this book opens up the "black box" regarding the dynamics affecting the strategic thinking of different factions within the CPV and organs of the government about how to maximize Vietnam's national interests and security. Facing the duality of economic crisis and military threat from the Sino–Khmer Rouge alliance, Hanoi's leadership abandoned Ho Chi Minh's longtime stance of a balanced position between great power rivals and opted for a formal alliance with the Soviet Union in 1978. Hanoi's military leaders, led by General Secretary Le Duan and his close ally Le Duc Tho, took a calculated risk in invading Cambodia to topple the China-backed

Khmer Rouge regime and thus strengthen Vietnam's alliance with China's rival, the Soviet Union. The CMC, the top military decision-making body, drew up a decisive military plan, approved by the Politburo, to invade Cambodia and topple the Khmer Rouge as early as January 1978, well before Vietnam decided, in June 1978, to join the COMECON and form a military alliance with the Soviet Union in November of that year. Moderate and economically minded leaders led by Prime Minister Pham Van Dong and Deputy Prime Minister Le Thanh Nghi jumped on the bandwagon with the militant faction because they expected to secure greater economic aid, including modern technology, from the Soviet Union and other Eastern European countries in the CMECON to alleviate Vietnam's economic crisis.

China's massive invasion of Vietnam in February 1979 following Vietnam's invasion of Cambodia in December 1978 dragged Vietnam into a protracted two-front war in Cambodia and against China. The military-firsters' endless demands for massive mobilization on the frontlines in the early 1980s caused a wider rift between them and the economy-firsters, who were increasingly alarmed by the human and material costs the war was inflicting on Vietnam's economy. In addition to factional politics within the Vietnamese Politburo, important roles were played by specialized agencies within the prime minister's cabinet and party committees at the policy-input level. Competing coalitions, including ad hoc party-directed research committees and specialized government agencies, under the leadership of the Council of Ministers, were formed and allowed to present their ideas to the Politburo of the party and the Council of State for internal deliberation. Within the Council of Ministers, the Prime Minister's Office played a crucial role in policy input. Rather than a stovepipe decision-making process, there was a strong feedback loop characterized by the relationship between the Politburo (the top decision-making body) and the Council of Ministers, headed by the prime minister (the executive). Subsequently, the Politburo presented a draft resolution first to the Party Central Committee for approval and then to the National Assembly for promulgation. Beneath the public display of collective leadership and unity, Vietnam's national security decision making was shaped and influenced by competing personalities, factions, and ideas in internal party politics. There were heated contestations over ideas and policies, especially at times of crisis decision making, such as the decision to invade Cambodia in 1978 or national militarization in 1980–81 following the Chinese invasion of Vietnam in February 1979.

The most important decisions about national security were made collectively by the Politburo, which was dominated by four members of the old guard—Le Duan, Truong Chinh, Pham Van Dong, and Le Duc Tho—who were long-standing leaders of the party and government. However, policy research and input by groups of political elites, including vice-ministers, general directors of departments, and heads of party or government committees, significantly shaped and influenced the top decision makers' thinking. At times these power groups, including the military faction led by Defense Minister General Van Tien Dung and economic planners led by Deputy Prime Minister Le Thanh Nghi, differed in terms of their influence on policy. For instance, in 1975–77, Politburo member and deputy prime minister Le Thanh Nghi, who also chaired the State Planning Committee, were very influential in planning the economy and shaping economic foreign policy. Nghi's power derived from the party-state's ultimate objective of economic recovery and modernization. As Vietnam was confronted with a growing national security threat and economic crisis at home in 1978, top economic planner Le Thanh Nghi, decorated for revolutionary and wartime accomplishments, was largely discredited and forced to admit major mistakes in the internal self-criticism style of the CPV. Other moderate and economically minded leaders, especially Prime Minister Pham Van Dong, supported Vietnam's invasion of Cambodia and direct involvement in regime change there because they hoped to acquire more economic aid, including advanced industrial equipment, from the Soviet Union and other Eastern European countries. Nghi's influence rapidly declined; he was demoted in 1982 and drifted to a peripheral role in the party thereafter.

From the perspective of the military-firsters led by Le Duan and Le Duc Tho, the economic crisis was extremely detrimental to national defense and the legitimacy of the party, and they used it to justify their preference for an all-out war with the China-backed Khmer Rouge. From 1978 to 1984, the conservatives and their military-first allies were the dominant voices within the party and government. As early as January 1978, the CMC was all powerful again as national security became the top priority. Notably, General Van Tieng Dung, General Le Duc Anh, and Chu Huy Man played crucial roles in strengthening the military and planning the invasion of Cambodia. Members of the economics-first faction could only protest in private, although they were alarmed by the rapid depletion of vital material and human resources due to Vietnam's military-first policy during this period.

Five years into the war, the rising cost of the two-front conflict in Cambodia and against China had squandered foreign aid from the Soviet Union and other socialist countries and undercut economic reforms, thus giving reformist leaders more influence in foreign policy decision making by 1983–84. The economics-firsters successfully persuaded the old guard to embrace economic reform and a shift from total reliance on the Soviet bloc to a broad-based economic foreign policy. After the PPA was signed in January 1973, then vice-minister Nguyen Co Thach was among the few high-ranking officials entrusted by the Politburo with conducting research on the potential for expanding economic relations with the West. Thach believed that the Soviet Union and Eastern Europe were lagging behind the West in the technological revolution of the 1970s. During the Cold War period of peaceful coexistence in the early 1970s, the Soviet Union and some Eastern European countries led the way in showing the Vietnamese that economic cooperation with the West to obtain modern technology did not necessarily undermine socialist ideology. Nguyen Co Thach directly counseled the conservative-dominated Politburo in September 1973 that Vietnam could engage in economic cooperation with the West while ideologically and politically siding with the Soviet Union. Indeed, Nguyen Co Thach's role in collective idea change was far more significant than conventional wisdom acknowledges.

At this early stage, young reformists like Thach recognized the transformative role of technology in increasing Vietnam's economic efficiency and exports, but such reform thinking was far ahead of its time given the Politburo's focus on the war effort to reunite the country. It took the increasing human and material costs of Vietnam's two-front war for the second-generation reformists and their new thinking (*tu duy moi*) to dominate Vietnam's collective decision making by 1985–86. Nguyen Co Thach was promoted to minister of foreign affairs in 1982 and played a central role in formulating the *Doi Moi* policy in 1986.

Today, forty years after the onset of the Third Indochina War (1978–88), there are two conflicting historical narratives of Vietnam's invasion of Cambodia in December 1978 and China's invasion of Vietnam in February 1979. First, the historical memory of the Sino-Vietnamese border war in February 1979 is deeply contested in both Vietnam and China today. China's historical representation of the war as a punitive action against an ungrateful Vietnam is a thorn in Sino-Vietnamese relations. Until recently the war with China was a strictly forbidden topic in Vietnam because Hanoi has attempted to avoid provoking anti-Vietnam hostility from a rising China. The official publication of a history of China's war of aggression against Vietnam in August 2017 in a new fifteen-volume *History of Vietnam* provides a narrative of the Vietnamese people's heroic fight against Chinese invaders to defend their nation.[1] As in the case of Vietnam's intervention in Cambodia, the official version of this highly sensitive episode in the 1979 Sino-Vietnamese border war is not only a counternarrative to Chinese nationalist history, but it also serves the national purpose of memorializing the Vietnamese people's sacrifice and heroism in defending their country from China's aggression, as their ancestors did for two millennia.

Regrettably, such a nationalist history requires a truncated narrative bleached of its complexity and unflattering past, including the heavy toll the military confrontation in Cambodia and against China in the 1980s took on Vietnam's economy and the suffering that ordinary Vietnamese people endured.

Second, in Cambodia opinions are highly divided. Many Cambodians attribute Vietnam's intervention to "Vietnam's imperial ambitions over Cambodia." The ruling CPP and its supporters, on the contrary, view this as "Vietnam's liberation of Cambodia." The Vietnamese government today reminds Cambodia of Vietnam's sacrifice for and liberation of the Cambodian people from the Pol Pot genocidal regime. The official history of Vietnam's intervention in Cambodia constructs a metanarrative of Vietnam's sacrifice in fulfilling its international duty to assist the Cambodian revolution (1978–89).[2] Both narratives are inaccurate in light of this book's findings. Ample evidence shows that the Vietnamese leaders did not invade Cambodia with imperial ambitions in mind, though neither did Vietnam's top economic planners shy away from promoting Vietnam-dominated economic regionalism in the first half of the 1980s.

Pham Van Dong's fear that the prolonged presence of Vietnamese troops in Cambodia would stir up anti-Vietnamese sentiment was justified. The Vietnamese army's heavy-handed purges and torture of Cambodian officials in its campaign against the "two-faced" enemy burrowing within the PRK in 1983 undermined Vietnam's efforts to win the hearts and minds of the Cambodian people. The influx of Vietnamese people into Cambodia and Vietnamese mistreatment of Cambodian villagers easily fueled anti-Vietnamese sentiment throughout the 1980s. All these factors played into the hands of Cambodian resistance leaders, who wanted Cambodians to view the Vietnamese as occupiers and turned the Vietnamese intervention into a protracted, unwinnable, and costly war. To reduce their respective burdens of assisting the PRK, reformist leaders in Vietnam and the Soviet Union in 1986 encouraged economic reforms in Cambodia and Laos. In Cambodia, Prime Minister Hun Sen had no other choice as nonrefundable aid from the Soviet Union and Vietnam had dried up by 1986. That marks the beginning of a gradual lessening of Vietnamese influence over Cambodia.

Vietnam's *Doi Moi* policy in 1986 would never have occurred had Vietnam not endured the most turbulent period of socioeconomic crises threatening the CPV after national unification in 1975, followed by the costly two-front military confrontation from 1979 to 1985. Similarly, Vietnam's integration into the world economy today owes its success to the *Doi Moi* policy of 1986. In other words, post-1986 economic integration does not erase the periods before it. Instead, it builds on the foundation and orientation of the *Doi Moi* policy. The trajectory of Vietnam's drive toward economic modernization and national sovereignty remains the ultimate twin objective of the CPV. Vietnam's multi-directional foreign policy is designed to allow its leaders the flexibility to maneuver strategies and tactics to quickly achieve economic modernization and strengthen national defense. Toward such a strategic objective, Vietnam will need a peaceful and stable regional environment, making any military confrontation with China over the South China Sea detrimental to that goal.

Nonetheless, the Sino-American rivalry in Asia, particularly in the South China Sea, has offered Vietnam ample opportunity to maneuver around great power rivalries to further its national interests, defined in terms of economic and military modernization and stalwart defense of maritime claims in the South China Sea in the age of China's new assertiveness. The US commitment to Vietnam is based purely on Vietnam's usefulness in Washington's grand strategy of containing China. For Vietnam the US market, investment, and advanced military technology are crucial to its economic integration and efforts to beef up its national defense against potential threats by China down the road. However, Vietnam has no appetite for another episode of military confrontation with a China far more powerful militarily and economically than the one the Vietnamese fought against in the 1979–88.

Brantly Womack argues—and I agree—that stability in China-Vietnam relations or the absence of Vietnam's balance of power against China should not be attributed to Chinese domination, as is implicit in David Kang's China-centered hierarchical system, but rather to a mechanism of asymmetric interactions between the two neighbors. China learned the "habits of self-restraint in its relationship with smaller neighbors like Vietnam" while the Vietnamese learned to "fashion their interactions with China into their own cultural learning curve."[3] One of the important lessons China may have learned from its conflict with Vietnam in the second half of the 1970s is that if Vietnam perceives China to be a threat to its national security and sovereignty, it would not hesitate to side with China's great power rival and engage in military confrontation with China. A sobering lesson the Vietnamese political elites have learned is that Vietnam ought to avoid tacit military alliances with extraregional great powers like the Soviet Union against China. As the consequences of this war clearly show, even China in 1979, which was much weaker in terms of economic and military power than it is today, could inflict massive destruction on Vietnam's society and economy. The Soviet Union had global interests and was willing to change its own politics without honoring its alliance commitments. It did not send ground troops to Vietnam after the Chinese invasion in 1979 but only sent economic and military assistance to Vietnam. By the same token, Hanoi's leaders have even more reason to distrust any military alliance commitment by an extraregional great power like the United States. Given this history, Hanoi's leaders will be even more reluctant to enter into an official military alliance with the United States to counterbalance a much more powerful China in the foreseeable future. Nonetheless, Vietnam is not simply acquiescent to China.

I have written elsewhere that a pattern of resistance and deference to China is a recurring feature of Vietnam's dealings with its more powerful northern neighbor but rather displays astute entrepreneurial thinking about foreign policy strategies and diplomatic tactics to adjust to China's changing power, as it has done for the past two millennia.[4] In modern Vietnam, Ho Chi Minh's strategic thinking, applied to the situation Vietnam now faces, is instructive of Vietnam's foreign policy belief system: (1) avoid direct confrontation with great powers, (2) find ways to compromise with them, (3) exploit inherent contradictions and conflicts between them, (4) exercise skillful and flexible diplomacy, and (5) refrain from getting involved in conflicts between them.[5] These are instructive of Vietnam's strategic thinking about its foreign policy and its strategy for coping with China's rise.

Notes

Introduction

1. For this study, the conservative camp consists of proponents of military strength, adherents of the orthodox Marxist-Leninist ideology, and firm believers in the idea that "the Socialist bloc will prevail over the capitalist-imperialist camp."

2. The great divide between the conservative and reformist camps boils down to their different emphasis on defining Vietnam's national security. While conservatives and their military-first allies gave priority to military victory and strength and Marxist-Leninist ideological commitment to the Soviet Union, the economically minded and reformist faction prioritized the task of economic development and modernization in the context of an economically interdependent world and therefore pragmatic economic engagement with the West. The reformist camp views the "two-camp" ideology as not only outdated but also threatening to Vietnam's long-term national security. I hope my narrative will elucidate these deceptively dichotomous terms.

3. For a general theory of asymmetric conflicts, see T. V. Paul, *Asymmetric Conflicts: War Initiation by Weaker Powers* (New York: Cambridge University Press, 1994). For a "resource-extraction" model of the state in neoclassical realism, see Norrin M. Ripsman, Jeffrey W. Taliaferro, and Steven E. Lobell, *Neoclassical Realist Theory of International Politics* (New York: Oxford University Press, 2016), 24.

4. Although I contend that the documentary evidence presented here is of high quality and is much less tainted by current nationalist histories published in Vietnam, I cannot be certain that these documentary sources are entirely immune to ideological forces.

5. For the role of ideology, see Tuong Vu, *Vietnam's Communist Revolution: The Power and Limits of Ideology* (New York: Cambridge University Press, 2016), 22–23.

6. Ibid., 23.

7. For the role of Vietnamese elites' hegemonic political culture, see Stephen J. Morris, *Why Vietnam Invaded Cambodia: Political Culture and the Cause of War* (Stanford, CA: Stanford University Press, 1999).

8. David W. P. Elliott, *Changing Worlds: Vietnam's Transition from Cold War to Globalization* (New York: Oxford University Press, 2012), 6.

9. Paul, *Asymmetric Conflicts*, 16.

10. Ibid.

11. While systemic variables have causal primacy in shaping states' strategic ideas and behaviors, domestic-level variables intervene to determine the types of strategies they are likely to pursue. However, rather than privileging systemic effects on Vietnam's foreign policy, as conventional neorealist theory posits, this book shows how factionalism within Vietnam's decision-making processes intervenes to shape its foreign policy outcomes. I draw on Jeffrey W. Taliaferro's concept of the "resource-extractive state" for my analysis. For more details, see his "State Building for Future Wars: Neoclassical Realism and the Resource-Extractive State," *Security Studies* 15, no. 3 (July–September 2006): 464–95.

12. Paul, *Asymmetric Conflicts*, 16.

13. Joe D. Hagan, "Domestic Political Explanations in the Analysis of Foreign Policy," in *Foreign Policy Analysis: Continuity and Change in Its Second Generation*, edited by Laura Neack, Jeanne A. K. Hey, and Patrick J. Haney (Englewood Cliffs, NJ: Prentice Hall, 1995), 121–23; Robert D. Putnam, "Diplomacy and Domestic Politics: The Logic of Two-Level Games," *International Organization* 42, no. 3 (Summer 1998): 427–69.

14. Elliott, *Changing Worlds*, 32–34, 49–51; Lien-Hang T. Nguyen, *Hanoi's War* (Chapel Hill: University of North Carolina Press, 2012), 42–45; Pierre Asselin, *Hanoi's Road to the Vietnam War, 1954–1965* (Berkeley: University of California Press, 2013), 15–16.

15. Domestically, the economic threat consisted of economic inefficiency, the wasteful use of material and human resources, a growing debt to the Soviet Union and other socialist countries, and the loss of access to the Soviet bloc's market due to China's more competitive goods. Externally, in 1979–81, Vietnam's economic relations with capitalist countries after 1975 came to an abrupt end with the exception of small loans from Sweden, Denmark, and Finland. While economic relations with the Soviet bloc significantly expanded in scope and scale, economic reciprocity quickly replaced nonrefundable aid from 1981 onward. As a result, imports of important raw materials largely depended on Vietnam's capacity to export better-quality goods to the Soviet bloc. See To Kinh te Doi ngoai, Hoi Dong Bo Truong, 3/1985, Gui Uy Ban Ke Hoach Nha Nuoc (Foreign Economic Relations Research Group of the Council of Ministers to the State Planning Commmittee, March 1985), "Bao cao cua To kinh te doi ngoai Hoi Dong Bo Truong" (Report of the Foreign Economic Policy Group of the Council of Ministers), Phu Thu Tuong (Office of the Prime Minister, hereafter PTT), *ho so* (archival file, hereafter h.s.) 13234, 5–6, 13–14.

16. Thu Truong Vo Dong Giang, K/T Bo Truong Bo Ngoai Giao (Foreign Affairs Vice-Minister Vo Dong Giang on behalf of the foreign affairs minister),

4/19/1983, gui van phong Quoc hoi va Hoi dong Nha nuoc (sent to the office of National Assembly and the State Council), "Bao cao ket qua hoi nghi bat thuong Bo Truong ngoai giao Lao, Campuchia, Viet-Nam tai Phnom Penh, 4/12/1983" (Report on the results of the extraordinary summit of foreign ministers of Laos, Cambodia, and Vietnam in Phnom Penh on April 12, 1983), PTT, h.s. 5575, 1–4.

17. PTT, h.s. 13234, 4.

18. For details on the Politburo of the Fifth Party Congress held in March 1982, see Van Canh Nguyen, *Vietnam under Communism, 1975–1982* (Stanford, CA: Hoover Institution Press, 1985), 63–74.

19. General Secretary Le Duan took over General Vo Nguyen Giap's post as secretary of the Central Military Commission after the Fifth Party Congress in March 1982. Real power was in the hands of Le Duan and his ally Le Duc Tho. Both controlled the key appointments to important ministries, including foreign affairs, the state security apparatus, and the army.

20. Le Duc Tho was one of the most influential leaders of the CPV after the January 1973 agreement on ending the Vietnam War and restoring peace in Vietnam. Tho was head of the Central Organization Committee of the party and therefore was in charge of placing high-ranking party cadres in the party apparatus and state agencies. He oversaw Vietnam's invasion and occupation of Cambodia. He desired to become the general secretary of the party by taking over the post from Le Duan after the latter died on July 10, 1986, but he lost the trust of the Politburo. For more details, see Huy Duc, *Ben Thang Cuoc I: Giai Phong* (The winning side, part 1: Liberation) (Los Angeles: OsinBook, 2012), 352–53.

21. A longtime ally of Le Duan and Le Duc Tho, Pham Hung (a southerner) became deputy prime minister in 1976 and replaced Tran Quoc Hoan as minister of the interior in February 1980. At the December 1986 Party Congress, he moved up to the number two slot in the party Politburo, behind the new general secretary, Nguyen Van Linh. Hung was a military hardliner and a conservative opposed to economic reform initiatives in the early 1980s. See Elliott, *Changing Worlds*, 34; Nguyen, *Hanoi's War*, 303.

22. This faction, as historian Pierre Asselin characterized it, is the party's hardline, risk-taking "militant" wing (Asselin, *Hanoi's Road to the Vietnam War*, 15–16). See also Nguyen, *Hanoi's War*, 42–45). Their hawkish position did not change, favoring a full-blown invasion of Cambodia and taking the risk of military confrontation with China, when Vietnam faced the China-backed Khmer Rouge military attacks on Vietnam in 1977–78.

23. Nguyen, *Hanoi's War*, 43.

24. In February 1980, Phan Trong Tue, minister of transportation and communications, was replaced by Dinh Duc Thien, who is Le Duc Tho's brother (Nguyen, *Vietnam under Communism*, 71–72).

25. Ibid., 71.

26. General Van Tien Dung, already a full member of the Politburo by the Fourth Party Congress in December 1976, was promoted to sixth place in the Politburo and took over from General Vo Nguyen Giap as minister of defense after the March 1982 Fifth Party Congress. Van Tien Dung, along with To Huu, was dropped from the Politburo at the Sixth Party Congress in December 1986 for his conservative stance regarding Cambodia (Nguyen, *Hanoi's War*, 302).

27. Between 1977 and 1986, General Chu Huy Man headed the General Political Department of the PAVN, which commanded all political officers. In July 1982 he was promoted to vice-chairman of the Council of State and member of the Politburo at the March 1982 Fifth Party Congress.

28. Lieutenant General Le Duc Anh played a central role in Vietnam's invasion of Cambodia in late December 1978 and went on to play an even more significant role in building up the armed forces of the People's Republic of Kampuchea after toppling the Khmer Rouge regime. On January 5, 1979, Le Duc Tho, General Le Trong Tan, and Lieutenant General Le Duc Anh on behalf of the Central Military Commission, the highest organ of the CPV in charge of military affairs, delivered an additional order to Military Region 9 to attack and take over Pochentong Airport, the Military Command of the DK regime, the Prime Minister's headquarters, radio stations, and the Monivong Bridge. After the liberation of Phnom Penh on August 21, 1979, the Central Committee of the CPV made a decision to establish Committee K (Kampuchea), a unified organ that represented the Vietnamese government, the Party Centre, and the Central Military Commission, to oversee Vietnam's assistance to the PRK. Committee K was also in charge of all Vietnamese specialists dispatched to assist the new revolutionary government in Cambodia. Le Duc Tho was the chairman of Committee K, and Le Duc Anh was the first deputy chairman of this committee. The other two deputies were Nguyen Con and Hoang The Thien. In addition to this role, Le Duc Anh was also vice-minister of defense and the commander of the Vietnamese Volunteer Army in Cambodia. In February 1980 the Politburo of the CPV made a decision to create the General Unit of Specialists and place it under General Le Duc Anh's direct command. That made him Vietnam's most powerful man in Cambodia, and he earned the reputation as the "Tiger of Cambodia." General Le Duc Anh was promoted to full membership of the Politburo under the March 1982 Fifth Party Congress.

29. Le Thanh Nghi, who was a member of the Politburo of the CPV and deputy prime minister and chairman of the State Planning Committee, was put in charge of the country's economy after the Fourth Party Congress in December 1976. Nguyen Lam took over his post as chairman of the State Planning Committee in February 1980. At the Fifth Party Congress in March 1982, Le Thanh Nghi (along with Vo Nguyen Giap, Nguyen Duy Trinh, Tran Quoc Hoan, Le Van Luong, and Nguyen Van Linh) was dropped from the Politburo

primarily because he was blamed for failing to curb the economic crisis in 1978–80.

30. Deputy Prime Minister Do Muoi was promoted to full membership in the Politburo and put in charge of the country's economy by the 1982 Fifth Party Congress. He succeeded Nguyen Van Linh as general secretary of the party in June 1991 and held that post until December 1997.

31. "Bai noi chuyen cua Pho Thu tuong Le Thanh Nghi tai hoi nghi can bo lanh dao cac co quan Trung uong, cac tinh, thanh pho ngay 5/12/1978 ve thuc hien ke hoach nam 1978 va ke hoach nam 1979" (Deputy Prime Minister Le Thanh Nghi's speech at the Party Central, Province, and City Leadership Conference on May 12, 1978), PTT, h.s. 787, 1–11.

32. I use the term "economy-firsters" to refer to economically minded reformists, broadly speaking. I adapted it from actual groups or committees, including To Kinh Te and Ban Kinh Te, found in documentary evidence. For instance, Deputy Prime Minister Le Thanh Nghi and Tran Phuong (vice-chairman of the State Planning Committee), not just Vo Van Kiet, belonged to this group. However, there is no original term *Quan vu tren het* (military-firster) per se; I use it to refer to hawkish military leaders who favored military strength as the main pillar of national security. General Van Tien Dung and General Chu Huy Man, members of the Central Military Commission, belonged to this faction.

33. Truong Chinh was the hero of Vietnam's *Doi Moi* in Vietnamese journalist Huy Duc's account and was extolled by Elliott as an "unlikely reformer" who brought together a group of North Vietnamese economists with new thinking to solve Vietnam's economic crisis. See Huy Duc, *Ben Thang Cuoc I*, 323–28; Elliott, *Changing Worlds*, 38–39.

34. Truong Chinh, the ideological mentor of the old guard and longtime member of the Politburo, changed his position from the hardline conservative camp to the reform-minded camp in the early 1980s, lending support to reformist leader Vo Van Kiet (Huy Duc, *Ben Thang Cuoc I*, 324–59). He was briefly general secretary of the party from July to December 1986 and chairman of the Council of State from 1981 to 1987.

35. Nguyen Van Linh became general secretary of the party, taking over the post from Truong Chinh, and served from December 1986 to June 1991. Linh was a political compromise born out of a bitter contest between Le Duc Tho and Truong Chinh for the top post. Linh, a revolutionary who looked to preserve the status quo, was never a true reformist but continued the course of the reform already set in motion when he took the mantle in 1986.

36. Vo Van Kiet, who served as Ho Chi Minh City party secretary until November 1981, was promoted to full membership in the Politburo under the March 1982 Fifth Party Congress. In April 1982 Kiet was appointed vice-chairman of the Council of Ministers, as well as chairman of the State Planning Committee, replacing Nguyen Lam.

37. Tran Phuong, who was vice-chairman of the State Planning Committee and Vo Van Kiet's deputy in the early 1980s, expressed his concerns to the party leadership about the drain of resources into the war effort in 1980. See Tran Phuong, Pho Chu Nhiem Uy Ban Ke Hoach Nha Nuoc, kinh gui Thu Tuong Chinh Phu, va kinh gui Bo Quoc Phong (Vice-Chairman of the State Planning Committee Tran Phuong to the prime minister of the government and a copy sent to the Ministry of National Defense), "Bao cao tinh hinh thuc hien Quyet dinh 58-CP cho Hoi dong Chinh phu ve viec san sang dong vien khi co chien tranh" (Report on the implementation of Decision 58-CP to the Council of Ministers about our readiness to mobilize for war), 3/5/1980, PTT, h.s. 16381, 113–18. According to an insider within the reformist faction, Tran Phuong was "the most progressive in the conservative camp." For more on Tran Phuong, see Huy Duc, *Ben Thang Cuoc I*, 341.

38. Nguyen Co Thach became consul general in India in 1956 and was a senior adviser and aide to Chief Negotiator Le Duc Tho during the Paris peace talks with the United States from 1968 to 1973. On May 24, 1979, he was appointed minister in charge of assisting the prime minister in foreign affairs before officially replacing Nguyen Duy Trinh as the minister of foreign affairs in 1980 at the age of fifty-two. He was promoted to an alternate member of the Politburo by the March 1982 Fifth Party Congress. In 1986, he was promoted to a Politburo member and a year later he gained another position of vice-chairman of the Council of Ministers, equivalent to the position of deputy prime minister.

39. Pho Thu Tuong To Huu, T/M Hoi Dong Chinh Phu (Deputy Prime Minister Tu Huu on behalf of the Council of Government), 2/11/1980, "Quyet dinh cua Hoi Dong Chinh Phu ve cong tac dong vien tuyen quan nam 1980" (Directive of the Council of Government about the tasks of mobilizing military conscripts in 1980), PTT, h.s. 16381, 1–3.

40. Thu Truong Vu Xuan Chiem, T/M Bo Truong Bo Quoc Phong (Vice-Minister of Defense Vu Xuan Chiem on behalf of the minister of national defense), "Bao cao tinh hinh thuc hien quyet dinh 58-CP ngay 2/25/1980 cua Hoi dong Chinh phu" (Report on the implementation of Directive 58 of the Council of Government on February 25, 1980), PTT, h.s. 16381, 42.

41. PTT, h.s. 16381, Tran Phuong, 117–18.

42. Nguyen Duy Trinh, Bo Truong Bo Ngoai Giao, kinh gui Thu Tuong Chinh Phu (Minister of Foreign Affairs Nguyen Duy Trinh to the Prime Minister [Pham Van Dong]), "Tiep theo bao cao cua Quan Uy Trung uong, toi xin bao cao de xin chu truong ve tien cong ngoai giao va tranh thu du luan quoc te ve van de bien gioi Viet-Nam-Campuchia" (Following the Central Military Commission's report, I would like to report and ask for directions about diplomatic offensives and efforts to win world public opinion about the border problem between Vietnam and Cambodia), PTT, h.s. 16137, 15–22.

43. Chu Huy Man, Pho Bi Thu T/M Thuong Vu Quan Uy Trung Uong, van phong Dang Cong San Viet-Nam Ban Chap Hanh Trung Uong, No. 42-SL/TW, kinh gui cac dong chi trong Bo Chinh Tri, Ban Bi thu (Deputy Secretary of the Standing Committee of the Military Central Commission, the Secretariat of the Central Committee of the Communist Party of Vietnam, to comrade leaders of the Politburo and the party), 8/28/1977, "Bao cao tinh hinh quan doi va cong tac quan su trong 6 thang qua" (Report on the military situation and military affairs in the past six months), PTT, h.s. 15860, 1–7.

44. PTT, h.s. 787, 5–9.

45. Ibid., 1–2.

46. "Bao cao cua Thu Tuong Pham Van Dong truoc ky hop thu tu—Quoc hoi Khoa VI, ngay 23–12–78 tai Hoi truong Ba-Dinh, Hanoi [Chep tu bang ghi am]" (Prime Minister Pham Van Dong's report to the Fourth Plenary Session of the Sixth National Assembly Plenum on December 23, 1978 at the National Assembly Hall Ba Dinh, Hanoi [note taking from his speech]), QH, h.s. 2354, 1–25. Dong delivered a foreign affairs speech to the National Assembly on December 23, 1978, to reassure National Assembly members about Vietnam's pending invasion of Cambodia. He stressed the importance of Soviet economic and military aid under the Soviet-Vietnamese friendship treaty of November 1978 and the necessary military-political solutions to the Cambodian problem.

47. "Tap hop tai lieu ve hoi nghi cap chuyen vien kinh te 3 nuoc Dong Duong nam 1982–83" (Compilation of documents on Conferences of Economic Experts of the Three Indochinese Countries in 1982–83), PTT, h.s. 12589, 23–39, 40–56.

48. To nghien cuu, Uy ban Lien lac Kinh te voi Nuoc ngoai (Research Group of the Committee on Economic Relations with Foreign Countries) gui lanh dao UBLKT voi Nuoc ngoai (sent to the leadership of the Committee on Economic Relations with Foreign Countries), 7/17/1982, "De an ve hop tac kinh te van hoa va khoa hoc ky thuat giua Viet Nam-Laos-Campuchia (de trinh BCT)" (Plan for economic, cultural, and scientific cooperation between Vietnam, Laos, and Cambodia [to be presented to the Politburo]), PTT, h.s. 12589, 23–38. This report was part of a cluster of files produced by the Research Group, which was spearheaded by economists under the supervision of the party-level Committee of Economic Relations with Foreign Countries, on Vietnam's plan for economic cooperation with Cambodia and Laos. See PTT, h.s. 12589, "Tap hop tai lieu ve hoi nghi cap chuyen vien kinh te 3 nuoc Dong Duong nam 1982–83."

49. Nguyen Dinh Bin, *Ngoai Giao Viet Nam, 1945–2000* (Vietnam's Diplomacy, 1945–2000) (Hanoi: Nha Xuat Ban Chinh Tri Quoc Gia, 2015), 297.

50. PTT, h.s. 5575, 1–2.

51. Ibid., 2.

52. Hoang Bich Son, Thu Truong T/M Bo Truong Bo Ngoai Giao [Nguyen Co Thach] gui Hoi Dong Nha Nuoc va Van Phong Quoc Hoi (Vice-Minister of Foreign Affairs Hoang Bich Son on behalf of Foreign Affairs Minister [Nguyen Co Thach] to the Council of State and the National Assembly on 8/19/1985), "Bao cao cua Bo Ngoai Giao ve ket qua Hoi Nghi Bo Truong Ngoai giao Lao, Campuchia and Viet-Nam lan thu 11 ngay 5/16/1985 tai Phnom Penh" (The Foreign Affairs Ministry's report on the results of the Eleventh Conference of Foreign Affairs Ministers of Laos, Cambodia, and Vietnam held on May 16, 1985, in Phnom Penh), PTT, h.s. 5595, 1–4.

53. Ibid., 1–2.

54. Ibid., 3.

55. Nguyen Co Thach, Bo Truong Bo Ngoai Giao (Minister of Foreign Affairs Nguyen Co Thach), "Mot so tinh hinh ve hop tac kinh te giua Lien Xo va Dong Au voi cac nuoc phuong tay" (A number of situations concerning the Soviet Union's and Eastern Europe's economic cooperation with other western countries), September 1973, PTT, h.s. 9061, 1–7.

56. Phan Doan Nam, "Aligning the Strength of the Nation with the Power of the Age (1987)," in *Sources of Vietnam's Tradition*, edited by George Dutton, Jayne Werner, and John Whitmore, 579 (New York: Columbia University Press, 2012) (original Vietnamese text was published in *Tao Chi Cong San* [Communist review], no. 1]1987]); Nguyen Dinh Bin, *Ngoai Giao Viet Nam*, 451; Nguyen Dy Nien, *Tu Tuong Ngoai Giao Ho Chi Minh* (Ho Chi Minh's thought on diplomacy) (Hanoi: Nha Xuat Ban Chinh Tri Quoc Gia, 2009), 95.

57. Nguyen Co Thach gui Van Phong Quoc Hoi (Ministry of Foreign Affairs to the National Assembly), ([undated] 1986), "Bao cao ve tinh hinh the gioi va cong tac doi ngoai cua Viet-Nam nam 1986" (Report on world affairs and our foreign policy in 1986 [Read at the National Assembly session in December 1986]), QH, h.s. 5607, 27–57.

58. George Dutton, Jayne Werner, and John Whitmore, eds., *Sources of Vietnamese Tradition* (New York: Columbia University Press, 2012), 584.

Chapter 1. Impact of the Economic Crisis, 1975–1978

1. Adam Fforde and Stefan de Vylder, *From Plan to Market: The Economic Transition in Vietnam* (Boulder, CO: Westview Press, 1996), 12.

2. See, for example, Beresford Malenie and Dang Phong, *Economic Transition in Vietnam: Trade and Aid in the Demise of a Centrally Planned Economy* (Cheltenham: Edward Elgar, 2000); Fforde and de Vylder, *From Plan to Market*; Gareth Porter, *Vietnam: The Politics of Bureaucratic Socialism* (Ithaca, NY: Cornell University Press, 1993); Canh, *Vietnam under Communism*.

3. Elliott, *Changing Worlds*, 35.

4. Ibid., 26.

5. Ibid., 47–48.

6. Ibid., 30, 47–48. Elliott cites a recollection by Vo Van Kiet.

7. Ibid., 25–57.

8. Between party congresses, the Central Committee is the supreme leading organ of the CPV, and it determines major foreign and domestic policies at its twice-yearly meetings. The Political Bureau, or Politburo, is the inner core of the party leadership. It has full authority to provide strategic direction to the party between plenums of the Central Committee by translating Central Committee resolutions into concrete policy guidelines for the party. The most influential post of the Central Committee is that of general secretary, held by Le Duan from 1960 to 1986. See Porter, *Vietnam*, 66.

9. Elliott, *Changing Worlds*, 47.

10. Elliott writes, "In terms of 'ideological hegemony,' the transition in new thinking was from socialist orthodoxy to the quest of the early nationalist modernizers for 'wealth and power'" (*Changing Worlds*, 15).

11. Vu, *Vietnam's Communist Revolution*, 1–2.

12. Ibid., 230–31.

13. Ibid., 212, 222–23.

14. Ibid., 234–35.

15. Nguyen, *Tu Tuong Ngoai Giao Ho Chi Minh*, 95.

16. Le Duan, *Bao cao chinh tri cua ban chap hanh trung uong Dang tai dai hoi dai bieu toan quoc lan thu IV* (Political report of the Party Central Committee at the Fourth Party Congress) (Hanoi: Nha Xuat Ban Su That, 1977), 48.

17. Nguyen, *Tu Tuong Ngoai Giao Ho Chi Minh*, 164, 247.

18. Bo Ngoai giao (Ministry of Foreign Affairs), "Bao cao cong tac 6 thang dau nam 1975 cua Bo Ngoai giao" (Ministry of Foreign Affairs report on its work during the first six months of 1975), PTT, h.s. 9599, 4.

19. Ibid.

20. Van Loi Luu, *50 Years of Vietnamese Diplomacy, 1945–1995,* vol. 1: *1945–1975* (Hanoi: The Gioi Publisher, 2000), 26.

21. PTT, h.s. 9599, 4. See also Stephen Morris, "The Soviet-Chinese-Vietnamese Triangle in the 1970s: The View from Moscow," in *Behind the Bamboo Curtain: China, Vietnam, and the World beyond Asia*, edited by Priscilla Roberts (Stanford, CA: Stanford University Press, 2006), 414.

22. Shu Guang Zhang, *Beijing's Economic Statecraft during the Cold War, 1949–1991* (Washington, DC: Woodrow Wilson Center Press, 2014), 258–59.

23. Ibid., 258.

24. Ly Ban, "Bao cao tinh hinh lam viec voi Trung Quoc tu cuoi thang 8 den nay" (Report on the negotiations with China from the end of August to the present [November 1975]), PTT, h.s. 10088, 1–5. Ly Ban was Vietnam's chief negotiator in Beijing.

25. Ibid.

26. Morris, "Soviet-Chinese-Vietnamese Triangle," 41.

27. "Bao cao ket qua dam phan kinh te voi 8 nuoc xa hoi chu nghia cho 5 nam 1976–1980" (Report on the results of economic negotiations with eight socialist countries for the five-year [plan], 1976–1980), November 28, 1975, PTT, h.s. 9833. 3.

28. Ibid., 3, 41.

29. Ibid., 11.

30. Robert S. Ross, *The Indochina Triangle: China's Vietnam Policy, 1975–79* (New York: Columbia University Press, 1988); Nicholas Khoo, *Collateral Damage: Sino-Soviet Rivalry and the Termination of the Sino-Vietnamese Alliance* (New York: Columbia University Press, 2011).

31. PTT, h.s. 9833, "Bao cao ket qua dam phan kinh te voi 8 nuoc," 3.

32. Ibid.

33. Ibid., 13; Le Duan, *Bao cao chinh tri*, 47–48. See also Luu, *50 Years of Vietnamese Diplomacy*, 26.

34. All-round, first-order relations were established with socialist countries, second-order relations were limited to the political and economic spheres for nationalist countries, and only economic ties were sought with capitalist countries. See Vu, *Vietnam's Communist Revolution*, 233. Based on the same 1976 MOFA report in the context of debating how to achieve the economic objectives of the Fourth Party Congress in December of that year, my interpretation of Hanoi's thinking about Vietnam's foreign relations as "strategic" differs from Vu's contention that such a broad-based foreign policy reorientation was not significant and could be subsumed under Hanoi's socialist orthodoxy of vanguard internationalism.

35. See Le Duan's speech in *Bao cao chinh tri*, 45–46, 57–58. In his speech, Prime Minister Pham Van Dong further stressed that the economic objective of the FYP was to "strengthen socialist industrialization, build the technical and material basis of socialism, and bring our economy from small-scale to large-scale socialist production." Pham Van Dong, *Phuong huong, Nhiem vu va Muc Tieu Chu yeu cua Ke hoach 5 nam, 1976–1980* (Orientation, tasks, and main objectives of the five-year plan, 1976–80) (Hanoi: Nha Xuat Ban Su That, 1977), 9.

36. Le Duan, *Bao cao chinh tri*, 49–50. The three revolutions were inscribed in the new constitution of the Socialist Republic of Vietnam (SRV). For details, see Nguyen, *Vietnam under Communism*, 79–84.

37. PTT, h.s. 9599, 8.

38. Ibid., 6.

39. Ibid., 8.

40. Luu, *50 Years of Vietnamese Diplomacy*, 24. The documents of the Fourth Party Congress have similar content.

41. PTT, h.s. 9599, 13.

42. "Bao cao tinh hinh cong tac sau thang dau nam 1976 cua Bo Ngoai Giao" (Ministry of Foreign Affairs' first six months report of 1976), PTT, h.s. 9833, 8–10.

43. For more details on the legislative process of North-South governmental unification, see Luu, *50 Years of Vietnamese Diplomacy*, 13–19.

44. Ibid., 21.

45. "Bao cao tinh hinh cong tac doi voi chuyen gia trong thoi gian qua va nhung van de can giai quyet de cai tien cong tac doi voi chuyen gia nuoc ngoai" (Report on our work with foreign specialists over the years and problems to be resolved in order to improve our work with them), CCG, h.s. 2228,1–7; "Bao cao ve tinh hinh quan ly va su dung chuyen gia nuoc ngoai nam 1977" (Report on the management and use of foreign specialists for 1977), CCG, h.s. 2399, 2.

46. CCG, h.s. 2399, 2; CCG, "Bao cao tinh hinh cong tac doi voi chuyen gia trong thoi," h.s. 2228, 2.

47. CCG, h.s. 2399, 9. In 1977, although the central government instructed the local authority to educate the Vietnamese people to stop speaking ill of Chinese specialists or behaving in an unfriendly manner toward them, the damage had already been done, and Beijing intended to recall all its foreign specialists in 1978. For details on China's complaint on this issue, see CCG, h.s. 2228, 31.

48. CCG, h.s. 2399, 3–4.

49. Ibid., 10.

50. For details on this subject, see Nguyen, *Vietnam under Communism*, 29, 195–96.

51. Triple-digit inflation reduced the value of the Vietnamese VND from 2.75 to a US dollar in 1976 to 9 to a US dollar in 1978 (see ibid., 45).

52. CCG, h.s. 2228, "Bao cao tinh hinh cong tac doi voi chuyen gia trong thoi," 7.

53. Ibid., 1.

54. CCG, h.s. 2399, 16.

55. Bo Ngoai giao (Ministry of Foreign Affairs), "Bao cao Cong tac 6 Thang dau nam 1977 cua Bo Ngoai giao" (Ministry of Foreign Affairs report on its work for the first six months of 1977), PTT, h.s. 10160, 7–8.

56. Ibid., 7.

57. Ibid., 9.

58. Vu, *Vietnam's Communist Revolution*, 221.

59. Desaix Anderson, *American in Hanoi: America's Reconciliation with Vietnam* (Norwalk, CT: EastBridge, 2002), 132. In the late 1970s, Anderson served under Richard Holbrooke in the Bureau of East Asian and Pacific Affairs and was involved in efforts to normalize US relations with Vietnam.

60. "Ban trinh bay cua dong chi Le Thanh Nghi ve ke hoach nam 1978 va muc phan dau den nam 1980 o Hoi Nghi lan thu ba cua Ban Chap Hanh Trung

Uong Dang" (Comrade Le Thanh Nghi's presentation on the 1978 [economic] plan and the level of collective endeavors through 1980 at the Third Conference of the Party Central Committee), 1–36, 12/6/1977, PTT, h.s. 786, 2.

61. Ezra R. Vogel, *Deng Xiaoping and the Transformation of China* (Cambridge, MA: Belknap Press of Harvard University Press, 2011), 311–12.

62. For details on the sequence of positions adopted by American and Vietnamese negotiators, see Anderson, *American in Hanoi*, 132–34.

63. On May 19, Deng Xiaoping declared, "China is NATO in the East" and "Vietnam is Cuba in the East." On May 20 National Security Advisor Zbigniew Brzezinski visited Beijing. According to Tran Quang Co, Washington scrapped normalization with Vietnam in May 1978.

64. For details on the evolution of Vietnamese-American normalization talks, see Tran Quang Co, *Hoi uc va Suy nghi* (Memoir and thought) (Hanoi: unpublished memoir, 2003), 13–23.

65. Vu, *Vietnam's Communist Revolution*, 221. Vu cited Tran Quang Co, who opined that in his view some aspects of Hanoi's foreign policy thinking (*tu duy doi ngoai*) at the time of its negotiations with the United States were so rigid that Vietnamese policy makers were slow to react to the rapid transformation of global politics and great power strategies after 1975, and as a result they did not dare respond with flexible policies or do so soon enough to serve Vietnam's national interests (see Tran Quang Co, *Hoi uc va Suy nghi*, 28).

66. Anderson, *American in Hanoi*, 28.

67. Ibid., 132.

68. Ibid., 133–34.

69. Phan Hien, Bo Ngoai Giao ([Vice-Minister] Phan Hien, Ministry of Foreign Affairs), March 31, 1978, "Bao cao dam phan 6 thang 10/1977 den 3/1978" (Report on negotiations for six months from October 1977 to March 1978), PTT, h.s. 10776, 1–7.

70. For details on the impact of China's economic sanctions on Vietnam's economy, see Kosal Path, "China's Economic Sanction against Vietnam, 1975–78," *China Quarterly* 212 (December 2012): 1040–58.

71. "Phuong huong, nhiem vu, muc tieu chu yeu cua ke hoach 5 nam 1976–1980 do Thu Tuong Pham Van Dong and Pho Thu Tuong Le Thanh Nghi trinh bay tai Dai hoi Dang lan thu IV nam 1976" (The orientations, tasks, and main objectives of the five-year plan 1976–1980 presented by Prime Minister Pham Van Dong and Deputy Prime Minister Le Thanh Nghi at the Fourth Party Congress in 1976), PTT, h.s. 611, 22.

72. Ibid., 8.

73. Ibid., 16.

74. Ibid., 27.

75. Ibid., 29–30.

76. Ibid.

77. Ibid.

78. Ibid., 6.

79. Ibid.

80. Ibid., 7. In 1977 Vietnam planned to graduate 3,000 cadres with post-graduate degrees, 160,000 with university degrees, and 350,000 with diplomas. There would also be one million skilled laborers and tens of thousands of experienced cadres in charge of cooperative farming.

81. Ibid.

82. "De cuong phat bieu cua Pho Thu Tuong Le Thanh Nghi tai ky hop thu nhat cua Uy Ban Phan Vung Kinh Te T. W. ngay 10/1/1977" (Draft of the fundamentals of Deputy Prime Minister Le Thanh Nghi's speech at the first meeting of the Central Economic Zoning Commission on October 1, 1977), PTT, h.s. 724, 1–2. On September 30, 1977, the Council of Ministers, headed by Prime Minister Pham Van Dong, swiftly issued Decision 269-CP to establish the Central Economic Zoning Commission, led by a small group of economically minded deputy prime ministers, including Le Thanh Nghi (chairman), Do Muoi (executive vice-chairman), and Vo Chi Cong (vice-chairman).

83. PTT, h.s. 786, 5–6.

84. Ibid., 6.

85. Ibid., 2.

86. Ibid., 2. In 1975–78, half a million army officers and civil servants of the former regime were sent to so-called reeducation camps in the jungle and mountainous areas to clear land for cultivation. See Nguyen, *Vietnam under Communism*, 29.

87. For more on Vietnam's thought reform and reeducation in the late 1970s, see Nguyen, *Vietnam under Communism*, 188–89, 208–25.

88. PTT, h.s. 786, 3.

89. Ibid., 10–11.

90. Ibid., 12.

91. Beresford and Phong, *Economic Transition in Vietnam*, 11.

92. Ibid.

93. PTT, h.s. 786, 13.

94. Ibid., 14.

95. Ibid., 15.

96. Ibid., 16.

97. Beresford and Phong, *Economic Transition in Vietnam*, 31.

98. The Council of Ministers was the central policy-making body within the state structure under the chairmanship of Prime Minister Pham Van Dong (see Porter, *Vietnam, the Politics of Bureaucratic Socialism*, 78).

99. PTT, h.s. 787, 3.

100. The top economic planners who led the conference included Deputy Prime Minister Le Thanh Nghi, Chief of the Prime Minister's Office Vu Tuan, Deputy Prime Minister Tran Phuong, and Minister of Labor Dao Thien Thi.

101. PTT, h.s. 787, 2.

102. Ibid., 4.

103. Ibid.

104. Ibid., 5.

105. Ibid., 9.

106. Beresford and Phong, *Economic Transition in Vietnam*, 24.

107. PTT, h.s. 787, 3.

108. Porter, *Vietnam*, 50; Nguyen, *Vietnam under Communism*, 29.

109. Bo Quoc Phong (Ministry of National Defense), *Nganh tai chinh quan doi nhan dan Viet Nam: 50 nam xay dung, phuc vu va truong thanh* (Finance branch of the Vietnamese People's Army: Fifty years of construction, services, and growth) (Hanoi: Nha Xuat Ban Quan Doi Nhan Dan, 1996), 56, luu hanh noi bo (internally circulated only).

110. Since the Politburo's March 1976 decision to deploy the armed forces to bolster the economy, many army units (some under the direct supervision of the MoD and others under various divisions of the military regions or army corps) were sent to economically poor corners of the country. PTT, h.s. 786, 5; Bo Quoc Phong, *Nganh tai chinh quan doi nhan dan Viet Nam*, 54.

111. Bo Quoc Phong, *Nganh tai chinh quan doi nhan dan Viet Nam*, 57.

112. PTT, h.s. 786, 27.

113. Cuc Van Tai, Tong Cuc Hau Can (Department of Transportation of the General Department of Logistics), *Bien nien su kien van tai quan su, 1975–1995* (Factual records of military transport, 1975–1995) (Hanoi: Nha Xuat Ban Quan Doi Nhan, 1999), 105–21.

114. PTT, h.s. 787, 13.

115. Ibid., 13.

116. Ibid., 1. Le Thanh Nghi's December 6 presentation was an attempt to additionally clarify some of the important points in the Politburo's report on the 1978 plan to the members of the Party Central Committee for further discussion.

117. Ibid., 34.

118. PTT, h.s. 786, 18.

119. Ibid.

120. Ibid., 1–21.

121. Ibid., 13–15.

122. Ibid., 14–15.

123. Ibid., 16.

124. Ibid., 16–17.

125. Beresford and Phong, *Economic Transition in Vietnam*, 32.

126. PTT, h.s. 786, 17.

127. Ibid., 18.

128. Ibid., 19–20.

129. Ibid.

130. Beresford and Phong, *Economic Transition in Vietnam*, 13.

131. Le Trong Tan, "Hai khau then chot cua cong tac quan su dia phuong" (Two key elements in local military work), *Tap Chi Cong San* (Communist review), September 1978, 14. General Le Trong Tan was chief of the General Staff of the PAVN in 1978.

132. PTT, h.s. 787, 16.

133. "The right of collective mastery" in the field of economy, as Le Duan outlined in the December1976 political report, entailed that the means of economic production (labor, production organization and management, and distribution) in Vietnamese society belonged to the peasants and workers. It therefore required the eradication of private property and the creation two forms of socialist ownership: all people's property (*so huu toan dan*) and collective property (*so huu tap the*). See Le Duan, *Cach Mang Xa Hoi Chu Nghia o Viet Nam* (Socialist revolution in Vietnam) (Hanoi: Nha Xuat Ban Su That, 1980), 53–54.

134. Huy Duc, *Ben Thang Cuoc I*, 100. Le Duan's intention to ban Chinese residents from commercial activities was corroborated by the deputy party secretary of Ho Chi Minh City, Tran Quoc Huong, who was summoned by Le Duan to report on the commercial activities of Chinese residents in the city.

135. Ibid.

136. Ibid., 101. According to Ho Chi Minh City's own records, before April 30, 1975, 200 Chinese business families left Cho Lon (the Chinese residents' commercial hub) in Saigon city. The remaining 98 Chinese business owners out of 161 private compradors were persecuted from September 1975 to 1977. In 1978, under the campaign of combating private ownership spearheaded by Do Muoi, at least four thousand Chinese business families were "reformed," meaning that they were stripped of their private possessions and sent to reeducation camps. An additional 3,494 families were deported to various provinces under the guise of "registering for transfer to New Economic Zones."

137. Ibid., 101.

138. Marjorie Niehaus, "Vietnam 1978: The Elusive Peace," *Asian Survey* 19, no. 1 (January 1979): 86–87.

139. Nguyen Hai Hong, "Resilience of the Communist Party of Vietnam's Authoritarian Regime since Doi Moi," *Journal of Current Southeast Asian Affairs* 35, no. 2 (2016): 31–55.

140. Niehaus, "Vietnam 1978," 86–87.

141. PTT, h.s. 786, 18–19.

142. Nguyen, *Vietnam under Communism*, 44–45. The official value of the dong in 1976 was 2.75 per US dollar, but it was drastically devalued to 9 per dollar in 1978.

143. Ibid., 45.

144. The Supreme People's Procuracy is the state agency tasked with carrying out public prosecutions, including regulating and limiting the power of the

government. It is administratively distinct from the Ministry of Justice and reports to the National Assembly on a semiannual basis. But it served the party, and in 1978 the it was given very broad powers of investigation sanctioned by Politburo Resolution 228.

145. Tran Huu Duc, Vien Truong Vien Kiem Sat Nhan Dan Toi Cao (Prosecutor general of the Supreme People's Procuracy of Vietnam), December 18, 1978, "Bao cao cua Vien Truong Vien Kiem Sat Nhan Dan Toi Cao truoc Quoc Hoi Khoa VI, ky hop thu 4" (Report of Supreme People's Investigation Bureau during the Fourth Session of the Sixth Plenum of National Assembly), PTT, h.s. 2354, 25–31.

146. Ibid., 26.

147. Ibid., 27–28. The 1,706 units investigated during this nine-month period included 332 agricultural units, 78 forestry units, 8 fishing units, 166 hydraulic units, 258 rice-purchasing units, 233 trade units, 48 manufacturing units, 20 transportation units, and 13 construction units, among others.

148. Ngo Vinh Long, "Reform and Rural Development: Impact on Class, Sectoral, and Regional Inequalities," in *Reinventing Vietnamese Socialism: Doi Moi in Comparative Perspective*, edited by William S. Turley and Mark Selden (Boulder, CO: Westview Press, 1993), 173.

149. This referred to the majority of rank-and-file soldiers because families of most military officers above the army rank of captain reportedly received sufficient food during this period. According to Huy Duc, however, Nguyen Thanh Tho, deputy party secretary of Ho Chi Minh City and member of the Party Central Committee (1975–79), recalled that the wife of an army general who was once his doctor came knocking at his door one evening to ask for some rice to eat; out of pity for her desperate hunger, Tho gave her his last bag of rice (Huy Duc, *Ben Thang Cuoc I*, 287).

150. "Bai noi cua Pho Thu Tuong Le Thanh Nghi ve mot so viec can lam sau khi gia nhap HDTTKT [Hoi dong Tuong tro Kinh Te] ngay 20/7/1978" (Deputy Prime Minister Le Thanh Nghi's speech on a number of tasks that need to be carried out after Vietnam's entry into the Council for Mutual Economic Assistance), PTT, h.s. 10568, 3.

151. Ibid., 4–5.

152. Ibid., 8–9.

Chapter 2. The Decision to Invade Cambodia, December 1978

1. See Morris, *Why Vietnam Invaded Cambodia*; David W. P. Elliott, ed., *The Third Indochina Conflict* (Boulder, CO: Westview Press, 1981); Nayan Chanda, *Brother Enemy: The War after the War, a History of Indochina since the Fall of Saigon* (Orlando, FL: Harcourt Brace Jovanovich, 1986); Odd Arne Westad and Sophie Quinn-Judge, eds., *The Third Indochina War: Conflict between*

China, Vietnam, and Cambodia, 1972–79 (London: Routledge, 2006); Xiaoming Zhang, *Deng Xiaoping's Long War: The Military Conflict between China and Vietnam, 1979–1991* (Chapel Hill: University of North Carolina Press, 2015); Andrew Mertha, *Brothers in Arms: Chinese Aid to the Khmer Rouge, 1975–1979* (Ithaca, NY: Cornell University Press, 2014); Brantly Womack, *China and Vietnam: The Politics of Asymmetry* (New York: Cambridge University Press, 2006).

2. Gareth Porter, "Vietnamese Policy and the Indochina Crisis," in *The Third Indochina Conflict*, edited by David W. P. Elliott, 69–138 (Boulder, CO: Westview Press, 1981), 69–138; Chanda, *Brother Enemy*; Morris, *Why Vietnam Invaded Cambodia*; Vu, *Vietnam's Communist Revolution*.

3. For details on this subject, see Morris, *Why Vietnam Invaded Cambodia*, 215–18; Dmitry Mosyakov, "The Khmer Rouge and the Vietnamese Communists: A History of Their Relations as Told in the Soviet Archives," in *Genocide in Cambodia and Rwanda*, edited by Susan E. Cook (New Haven, CT: Yale Genocide Studies Program, 2004), 54–94.

4. Morris, *Why Vietnam Invaded Cambodia*, 16–18.

5. Ibid., 229.

6. In Cambodia today, the theory that Vietnam's long-standing hegemonism over Indochina was at play still strongly resonates with the anti-Vietnam nationalist discourse of the Cambodian National Rescue Party (CNRP), the main opposition to the ruling Cambodian People's Party (CPP), whose predecessor, the Kampuchean People's Revolutionary Party, was pro-Vietnam.

7. Porter, "Vietnamese Policy," 69.

8. Odd Arne Westad, "Introduction," in *The Third Indochina War: Conflict between China, Vietnam, and Cambodia, 1972–79*, edited by Odd Arne Westad and Sophie Quinn-Judge (London: Routledge, 2006), 7.

9. Hoang Minh Vu, "Facing the Inevitable? Vietnam's Decision to Invade Cambodia, 1977–78" (B.Sc. thesis, International Relations and History, London School of Economics and Political Science, 2014), 10.

10. Womack, *China and Vietnam*, 188.

11. Ibid.

12. Vu, *Vietnam's Communist Revolution*, 18, 223. Note that Vu's book focuses on the Sino-Vietnamese conflict, not the conflict between Vietnam and DK, between 1975 and 1979.

13. Ibid., 226–27.

14. Ibid., 235.

15. For more details on factional politics within the Vietnamese leadership as revealed by Soviet sources, see Morris, "Soviet-Chinese-Vietnamese Triangle," 415–18.

16. Paul, *Asymmetric Conflicts*, 16.

17. Ibid.

18. Porter, "Vietnamese Policy," 71.

19. Ibid., 72.

20. Chanda, *Brother Enemy*.

21. Vu, "Facing the Inevitable?"

22. Ibid., 17.

23. Among the existing works that emphasize the structural determinant, see Khoo, *Collateral Damage*.

24. Ben Kiernan, "Myth, Nationalism, and Genocide," *Journal of Genocide Research* 3, no. 2 (2001): 187–206, 192.

25. For details, see Elizabeth Becker, *When the War Was Over: Cambodia and the Khmer Rouge Revolution* (New York: Public Affairs, 1986), 113.

26. Bo Quoc Phong, Vien Lich Su Quan Su Viet Nam (Military History Institute of Vietnam, Ministry of Defense), *Lich su khang chien chong My cuu nuoc, 1954–1975* (History of anti-American resistance and national liberation, 1954–1975), vol. 9 (Hanoi: Nha Xuat Ban Chinh Tri Quoc Gia, 2013), 524.

27. Becker, *When the War Was Over*, 139.

28. Bo Quoc Phong, *Lich su khang chien chong My cuu nuoc*, 524–25.

29. The underground PRG opposed to the Republic of Vietnam (RVN) government of President Nguyen Van Thieu and its military arm, the National Liberation Front (NLF), referring to the communist Viet Cong in the southern part of Vietnam, was established on June 8, 1969. It was the temporary political administration of southern Vietnam under the leadership of the NLF. They sought to undermine the legitimacy of the Republic of Vietnam.

30. Nguyen Thi Binh, *Family, Friends, and Country* (Hanoi: Tri Thuc Publishing House, 2015), 241–45.

31. Ibid., 244.

32. Becker, *When the War Was Over*, 147–48.

33. Ibid., 149.

34. Here I use Khmer Rouge and DK interchangeably.

35. Chanda, *Brother Enemy*, 13.

36. "Bao cao so ket cong tac bien gioi nam 1976–77 cua Uy Ban Bien Gioi" (Border Commission summary report on border tasks in 1976–77), PTT, h.s. 15969, 9.

37. Ibid.

38. Ibid., 10.

39. Bo Ngoai Giao (Ministry of Foreign Affairs), "Ve tien cong ngoai giao va tranh thu du luan quoc te ve van de bien gioi Viet Nam-Campuchia" (On launching a diplomatic offensive and drawing the support of world opinion regarding the border issue between Vietnam and Cambodia), PTT, h.s. 16137, 15–22.

40. PTT, h.s. 15969, 1.

41. For details on the KR view of Kampuchea Krom, see Ben Kiernan, *The Pol Pot Regime: Race, Power, and Genocide in Cambodia under the Khmer*

Rouge, 1975–1979, 3rd ed. (New Haven, CT: Yale University Press, 2008), 360–64.

42. Vu, "Facing the Inevitable?," 14.

43. Sophie Richardson, *China, Cambodia, and the Five Principles of Peaceful Coexistence* (New York: Columbia University Press, 2010), 91.

44. For details on China's aid to DK in 1975, see Mertha, *Brothers in Arms,* 121.

45. In 1976 China sent DK antiaircraft guns and airport equipment for its air force, tanks for a tank regiment, and escort ships and torpedo boats for its navy. For details, see "Excerpts of Speech by Wang Shang Rhung [Wang Shangrong], Deputy Chief of the General Staff of the Chinese Army at the Talks with Son Sen (6/2/1976)," Phnom Penh, National Archives, file 31, 38. Wang Youping shared this document with me.

46. Bo ngoai giao (Ministry of Foreign Affairs), "Bao cao tinh hinh va cong tac doi ngoai sau thang dau nam 1976" (Report on the foreign affairs situation and work for the first six months of 1976), PTT, h.s. 9833, 1–2.

47. Ibid.

48. Bo Quoc Phong, Vien Lich Su Quan Su Viet Nam (Military History Institute of Vietnam, Ministry of Defense), *Lich su quan tinh nguyen va chuyen gia quan su Viet Nam giup cach mang Campuchia (1978–1989)* (A history of Vietnam's volunteer army and military specialists' assistance to the Cambodian revolution, 1978–1989) (Hanoi: Nha Xuat Ban Quan Doi Nhan Dan, 2010), 26, luu hanh noi bo (internally circulated only).

49. For details, see Kosal Path, "The Sino-Vietnamese Dispute over Territorial Claims, 1974–1978: Vietnamese Nationalism and Its Consequences," *International Journal of Asian Studies* 8, no. 2 (2011): 213.

50. Mosyakov, "Khmer Rouge," 65.

51. Ibid.

52. Bac si Nguyen Tien Buu (Dr. Nguyen Tien Buu), Vien Sot Ret (Antimalaria Institute), 11/18/1976, "Bao cao dot di cong tac tai Campuchia Dan chu tu ngay 1 thang 11 den ngay 16 thang 11, 1976" (Report on a trip to Democratic Kampuchea from 11/1 to 11/16/1976), PTT, h.s. 9961, 3.

53. Chanda, *Brother Enemy,* 186.

54. Mosyakov, "Khmer Rouge," 68.

55. Huy Duc, *Ben Thang Cuoc I,* 157.

56. PTT, h.s. 9833, "Bao Cao Tinh Hinh va Cong Tac Doi Ngoai Dau Nam 1976," 8.

57. Huy Duc, *Ben Thang Cuoc I,* 154.

58. Ibid.

59. PTT, h.s. 15860, 6. Only eighteen copies of this report were made, suggesting circulation within a small circle of the top leaders of the CMC and the Politburo of the Central Committee of the CPV.

60. Ibid., 1.

61. Ibid., 5.

62. Huy Duc, *Ben Thang Cuoc I*, 157.

63. PTT, h.s. 611, 64.

64. Ibid., 63.

65. Ibid., 72.

66. PTT, h.s. 10160, 1–2.

67. PTT, h.s. 15860, 3.

68. Ibid., 4.

69. Ibid.

70. Ibid., 5.

71. Vu Tuan, Bo Truong Phu Thu Tuong (Prime Minister's Office), "Chi Thi ve viec to chuc chon cat cong nhan, vien chuc Nha nuoc va quan nhan cach mang chet o cac tinh phia Nam" (Directive on the task of preparing burials for government employees and revolutionary soldiers who died in southern provinces), PTT, h.s. 15945, 1.

72. PTT, h.s. 15860, 7.

73. Ibid., 6.

74. Ibid., 5.

75. Ibid., 6.

76. Ibid., 4.

77. Ibid., 7.

78. See Path, "China's Economic Sanctions," 1040–45.

79. Tran Quang Co, *Hoi uc va Suy nghi*, 18.

80. Ibid., 19–20.

81. Anderson, *American in Hanoi*, 110.

82. PTT, h.s. 10568, 4.

83. Ibid., 5.

84. Ibid., 8, 14.

85. PTT, h.s. 611, 6.

86. Ibid.

87. Ibid., 7.

88. PTT, h.s. 786, 2.

89. Ibid.

90. Ibid.

91. QH, h.s. 2354, Tran Huu Duc, 27–28.

92. PTT, h.s. 786, 2–3.

93. Huy Duc, *Ben Thang Cuoc I*, 157. On Le Duan's view, Duc relied on an interview he conducted with Tran Phuong, who served as Le Duan's assistant at that time.

94. Wilfred Burchett, *The China-Cambodia-Vietnam Triangle* (Chicago: Vanguard Books, 1981), 159–60.

95. Huy Duc, *Ben Thang Cuoc I*, 157.

96. PTT, h.s. 10160, 1–2.

97. Pho Thu Tuong Le Thanh Nghi gui Pho Thu Tuong Ly Tien Niem 11/77 (Deputy Prime Minister Le Thanh Nghi to Vice-Premier Li Xiannian, 11/77), "Bao cao ket qua dam phan kinh te voi Trung Quoc nam 1976" (Report on economic negotiations with China in 1976), PTT, h.s. 8600, 1–2.

98. For details see Dang Uy-Chi Huy Trung Doan Bo Binh 1 (Party Committee and Command of Infantry Battalion 1), *Lich su Trung Doan Bo Binh 1 Su Doan 330, Quan Khu 9, 1963–2003* (History of Infantry Battalion 1, Division 330, of Military Region 9, 1963–2003) (Hanoi: Nha Xuat Ban Quan Doi Nhan Dan, 2005), 148–50, luu hanh noi bo (internally circulated only).

99. Huy Duc, *Ben Thang Cuoc I*, 156–57.

100. Ibid., 161.

101. PTT, h.s. 10088, "Bao cao ket qua dam phan kinh te voi Trung Quoc nam 1976" (Report on the results of economic negotiations with China for 1976), August 31, 1975, 2.

102. PTT, h.s. 10088, Ly Ban, 3–4.

103. Ibid., 5.

104. PTT, h.s. 10461, Do Muoi to the Politburo and General Secretary Le Duan, December 7, 1976, "Bao cao ket qua lam viec voi d/c lanh dao Trung Quoc 5–6 thang 12 nam 1976" (Report on the results of working with Comrade Chinese leaders, December 5–6, 1976), 24.

105. Huy Duc, *Ben Thang Cuoc I*, 163.

106. "Bien ban cuoc gap go giua Thu Tuong Pham Van Dong va Pho Thu Tuong Ly Tien Niem tai Bac kinh 10/6/1977" (Minutes of the meeting between Prime Minister Pham Van Dong and Vice-Premier Li Xiannian in Beijing on June 10, 1977), PTT, h.s. 10460, 15. Present at the meeting on the Vietnamese side were Dinh Duc Thien, minister and chief of the Prime Minister's Office; Nguyen Co Thach, vice-minister of foreign affairs; and Ambassador Nguyen Trong Vinh. Present on the Chinese side were Hoang Hoa, minister of foreign affairs, and Han Hien Long, vice-minister of foreign affairs.

107. For more details, see Vogel, *Deng Xiaoping*, 198–99. In July 1977, having survived the purges of the Mao Zedong–inspired Cultural Revolution, Deng Xiaoping officially returned to all the positions he had held before 1976: member of the Central Committee, member of the Standing Committee of the Politburo, vice-chairman of the party, vice-chairman of the Central Military Commission, vice-premier, and chief of General Staff of the People's Liberation Army (PLA).

108. PTT, h.s. 10461, "Chuong trinh chuyen di huu nghi o Trung Quoc cua dai dien Dang and Chinh phu, ngay 20 thang 11 nam 1977" (Program of the party and government delegation's visit to China, November 20, 1977), 4. This observation was on the program by an unidentified close aid to Le Duan.

109. Ban Doi Ngoai, Ban Chap Hanh Trung Uong Dang Cong San Viet Nam (Foreign Affairs Committee of the Central Committee of the Communist Party of Vietnam), October 28, 1977, "Bao cao ve viec dong chi Saplin, Dai Su Lien Xo tai Viet Nam thong bao y kien Chinh Phu Lien Xo tra loi thu cua dong chi Pham Van Dong ve vien tro quan su cho Viet Nam nam 1976–1980" (Report of Soviet ambassador Chaplin's conveyance of the Soviet government's reply to Comrade Pham Van Dong regarding military aid to Vietnam, 1976–1980), 1–8, PTT, h.s. 10007, 1. This report was sent to Anh Ba (Le Duan) and Anh Nghi (Le Thanh Nghi).

110. Ibid., 5.

111. Chanda, *Brother Enemy*, 216.

112. Morris, *Why Vietnam Invaded Cambodia*, 108.

113. Bo Quoc Phong, *Lich su quan tinh nguyen*, 38–39.

114. Ibid., 10.

115. "Du luan the gioi ve Tuyen bo cua Chinh phu ta ve van de bien gioi Viet Nam-CPC" (World opinion concerning our government's declaration about the border issue between Vietnam and Cambodia, January 1, 1978), PTT, h.s. 16137, 24–25.

116. PTT, h.s. 15969, 9.

117. PTT, h.s. 10776, Phan Hien, 2–3.

118. Bo Tu Lenh CANDVT, Bo Noi Vu (Police Commission of the Ministry of the Interior), February 1978, "Bao cao tin nhan duoc ngay 5–6/2/1978" (Report on information received on February 5–6, 1978), PTT, h.s. 16137, 30–34.

119. Nguyen Duy Trinh, Bo Truong Bo Ngoai Giao, kinh gui Thu Tuong Chinh Phu (Minister of Foreign Affairs Nguyen Duy Trinh to Prime Minister [Pham Van Dong]), "Tiep theo bao cao cua Quan uy Trung uong, toi xin bao cao de xin chu truong ve tien cong ngoai giao va tranh thu du luan quoc te ve van de bien gioi Viet-Nam-Campuchia" (Following the Central Military Commission's report, I would like to report and ask for directions about diplomatic offensives and efforts to win world opinion regarding the border problem between Vietnam and Cambodia), PTT, h.s. 16137, 15–16.

120. Ibid.

121. Ibid., 16.

122. Ibid.

123. For more on the role of ideology in Vietnam's foreign policy, see Vu, *Vietnam's Communist Revolution*.

124. "Trich thu cua phong vien TTXVN tai Bac Kinh ngay 1/19/1978" (Note on the Vietnam News Agency report of January 19, 1978), PTT, h.s. 16137, 6–9. The report was sent to the Prime Minister's Office, 6, 9.

125. Nguyen Van Bang, Ban Lien Lac Doi Ngoai Tinh Kien Giang (Foreign Relations Committee of Kien Giang Province) gui den Ban Doi Ngoai TW va Bo

Ngoai Giao (to the Foreign Affairs Committee of the Party Central Committee and the Ministry of Foreign Affairs). "Bao cao tong ket Quy II 1978" (Summary report for the second quarter of 1978), PTT, h.s. 16049, 15.

126. PTT, h.s. 16137, Bo Ngoai Giao, 16.
127. Ibid., 18, 20.
128. Ibid., 22.
129. PTT, h.s. 787, 4.
130. Huy Duc, *Ben Thang Cuoc I*, 165.
131. Chanda, *Brother Enemy*, 257.
132. Ibid., 257–58.
133. Ibid., 258.
134. PTT, h.s. 2354, "Bao cao cua Thu Tuong Pham Van Dong," 1–3.
135. Ibid.
136. Huy Duc, *Ben Thang Cuoc I*, 165.

Chapter 3. Mobilization for a Two-Front War, 1979–1981

1. These resistance forces consisted of a loose alliance among the Khmer People's National Liberation Front, led by Son Sann; the royalist resistance movement, Movement for the National Liberation of Kampuchea (MOULINAKA); and the Khmer Rouge forces. In October 1980 the General Assembly of the United Nations had voted, by an even greater majority than in the previous year, to continue to seat the exiled DK regime. In February 1981 Sihanouk called for "a United Front against Vietnamese Colonization of Cambodia." Evan Gottesman, *Cambodia after the Khmer Rouge: Inside the Politics of Nation Building* (Chiang Mai, Thailand: Silkworm Books, 2003), 115.

2. For instance, Tuong Vu writes, "Vietnam's high international prestige would be sufficient to deter China. Their pride in their belief that Vietnam had selflessly been at the forefront of world revolution made Vietnamese leaders complacent and blind to the blowback that was coming from [China]." Vu, *Vietnam's Communist Revolution*, 228.

3. Zhang, *Deng Xiaoping's Long War*, 4.
4. Ibid., 109.

5. Le Kien Thanh recalled that on the morning of January 17, 1979, when the Chinese troops stormed across the border into Vietnam, his air force commander phoned, ordering him to return to the base. Still in his sleeping pajamas, he asked his father, Le Duan, whether or not he should postpone his wedding. Le Duan told his son not to postpone the wedding. Truong Chinh, Pham Van Dong, and Le Duc Tho were among the attendees at that one-hour wedding. For details, see Lan Huong To, "Thai do cua TBT Le Duan voi lanh dao Trung Quoc" (General Secretary Le Duan's attitude toward Chinese leaders),

SOHA.vn, February 16, 1979, http://soha.vn/thai-do-cua-tbt-le-duan-voi-lanh
-dao-trung-quoc-truoc-trong-va-sau-chien-tranh-bien-gioi-20190216095400
546.htm.

6. "Bon bai hoc tu cuoc chien chong Trung Quoc xam luoc nam 1979"
(Four lessons from the war against China's invasion in 1979), *VNExpress*,
February 18, 2019, https://vnexpress.net/40-nam-cuoc-chien-bao-ve-bien-gioi
-phia-bac/bon-bai-hoc-tu-cuoc-chien-chong-trung-quoc-xam-luoc-nam
-1979-3882107.html.

7. Tran Quang Co, *Hoi Uc va Suy Nghi*, 19–27.

8. Ibid., 28.

9. Dat Phat Nguyen, "Chien Tranh 1979: Gay suc ep voi TQ, Lien Xo dat 6
quan khu trong tinh trang san sang chien dau" (The 1979 war: Pressure on
China—the Soviet Union dispatched six military regions ready for war [with
China]), *SOHA.vn*, February 18, 2019, http://soha.vn/chien-tranh-1979-gay
-suc-ep-voi-tq-lien-xo-dat-6-quan-khu-trong-tinh-trang-san-sang-chien
-dau-20190217163738078.htm.

10. Ibid.

11. Phan Hong Ha, "Chien tranh bien goi 1979: 30 tau chien Lien Xo da san
sang o Bien Dong" (The 1979 war: Thirty Soviet warships ready [for war] in the
East Sea), *SOHA.vn,* February 18, 2019, http://soha.vn/chien-tranh-bien-gioi
-1979-30-tau-chien-lien-xo-da-san-sang-o-bien-dong-20190218003717671
.htm. Hong Ha cited Alexander Okorokov, *Nhung cuoc chien tranh bi mat cua
Lien Xo* (The Soviet Union's secret wars) (Moscow: Nxb. Yauza Eksmo, 2008)
(in Russian).

12. Nguyen, "Chien Tranh 1979."

13. Bo Quoc Phong, *Lich su quan tinh nguyen*, 77.

14. Pham Gia Duc and Pham Quang Dinh, eds., *Lich Su Quan Doan 2,
1974–1994* (History of the Second Corps, 1974–1994) (Hanoi: Nha Xuat Ban
Quan Doi Nhan Dan, 2004), 303 (book internally circulated within the army,
not for sale). See also Zhang, *Deng Xiaoping's Long War*, 110.

15. Pham and Pham, *Lich Su Quan Doan 2*, 391.

16. Ibid., 392.

17. Phu Thu Tuong (The Prime Minister's Office), gui Van phong Quoc hoi
(sent to the National Assembly), March 1979, "Bao cao cua van phong Phu Thu
Tuong ve dot di cong tac len cac tinh bien gioi phia Bac va nhung viec can lam
ngay de giai quyet hau qua chien tranh sau khi Trung Quoc rut nam 1979" (Report of the Prime Minister's Office about the trip to border provinces in the
north and the immediate tasks to overcome the negative effects of the war after
the Chinese troops withdrew in [March] 1979), PTT, h.s. 16327, 76–78.

18. Van Phong 8 (Office 8), February 15, 1980, "Chuong Trinh Qui I nam
1979" (Program for the first quarter of 1979), PTT, h.s. 16028, 1–2.

19. Phuong Minh Nam, Pho Chu Nhiem Van Phong PTT (Phuong Minh Nam, vice-chief of the Prime Minister's Office), January 15, 1980, "Bao cao tong ket cong tac nam 1979" (Summary report of 1979 work), PTT, h.s. 16028, 7.

20. Pham and Pham, *Lich Su Quan Doan 2*, 392.

21. Luu, *50 Years of Vietnamese Diplomacy*, 370.

22. Ibid., 373.

23. Ibid., 375.

24. QH, h.s. 2354, "Bao cao cua Thu Tuong Pham Van Dong," 3–4.

25. Ibid., 4.

26. Ibid., 20.

27. Nguyen Co Thach, "Bao cao ve tinh hinh the gioi va cong tac doi ngoai cua ta trong nam 1986" (Report on world affairs and our foreign policy in 1986 [read at the National Assembly session in December 1986]), 53, PTT, h.s. 5607.

28. QH, h.s. 2354, "Bao cao cua Thu Tuong Pham Van Dong," 17–18.

29. Ibid., 19.

30. Ibid., 17.

31. Ibid., 16.

32. Ibid., 20–21.

33. Ibid., 22–33.

34. Ngo Thi Thanh Tuyen, "Lich su chien tranh chong Khome Do xam luoc Viet Nam tren huong Tay Nam" (History of the war against the Khmer Rouge invasion in southwestern Vietnam) (MA thesis, Truong Dai Hoc Khoa Hoc Xa Hoi va Nhan Van, Dai hoc Quoc gia Thanh Pho Ho Chi Minh [University of Social Sciences and Humanities, Vietnam National University, Ho Chi Minh City], 2008), 1–216, 158–59.

35. QH, h.s. 2354, "Bao cao cua Thu Tuong Pham Van Dong," 8.

36. Ibid.

37. Christopher Goscha, *Vietnam: A New History* (New York: Basic Books, 2016), 379.

38. Ibid.

39. Rewi Alley, *Refugees from Viet Nam in China* (Beijing: New World Press, 1980), 4–6, 19. At the July 1979 Geneva Conference, deputy foreign minister of the PRC Zhang Wenjin claimed that China had allocated more than US$450 million to meet the needs of a quarter million Chinese refugees from Vietnam.

40. For personal accounts of Chinese refugees feeling persecuted in Vietnam at that time, see ibid.

41. Ibid., 22–23.

42. PTT, h.s. 16208, Van Phong 8, 4–9.

43. Ibid., 6.

44. Ibid., 5. Duong Van Phu, vice-chief of the Prime Minister's Office, was put in charge of advising the Council of Government on national defense policy.

45. PTT, h.s. 16208, Phuong Minh Nam, 4–7.

46. Ibid., 8.

47. With the exception of the Japanese mistreatment of Chinese residents in Indochina after overthrowing the French administration in March 1945, according to historian David G. Marr, "Most Vietnamese considered resident Chinese (*Hoa Kieu*) overall to have enjoyed favorable treatment under French colonialism, enabling them to get rich at the expense of the *kinh* (or Vietnamese) majority. With the arrival of the Chinese Army [of the Nationalist Party of China or *Guagmindang*] in September, Vietnamese immediately suspected local Chinese would link up with the occupation authorities for mutual gain." However, after the French returned to recolonize Indochina after September 1945, Vietnamese and Chinese residents joined forces in anticolonial resistance in Indochina. Overseas Chinese associations in North Vietnam contributed to the early stages of nation building in communist North Vietnam. In response, DRV president Ho Chi Minh encouraged the formation of Sino-Vietnamese friendship associations. For more on this subject, see David G. Marr, "Vietnamese, Chinese, and Overseas Chinese during the Chinese Occupation of Northern Indochina (1945–1946)," *Chinese Southern Diaspora Studies* 4 (2010): 134–35. From the late 1940s to the early 1970s, the North Vietnamese government treated the Chinese in North Vietnam with special respect and offered them special rights in order to solidify Sino-Vietnamese friendship. Many joined the Vietnamese Workers' Party and the Communist Youth League, and some became officials of the Vietnamese government and army. For details, see Xiaorong Han, "From Resettlement to Rights Protection: The Collective Actions of the Refugees from Vietnam in China since the late 1970s," *Journal of Chinese Overseas* 10 (2014): 197–219.

48. Luu, *50 Years of Vietnamese Diplomacy*, 380–81.

49. PTT, h.s. 16137, Bo Tu Lenh CANDVT, 30–34.

50. Dai tuong Vo Nguyen Giap, Uy vien Bo Chinh Tri Trung uong Dang, Pho Thu tuong Chinh phu kiem bo truong Bo Quoc phong (General Vo Nguyen Giap, member of the Politburo of the Party Central Committee and deputy prime minister with a portfolio of minister of defense), Quoc Hoi Khoa VI, ky hop thu 5 (Sixth session of the Fifth Plenum of the National Assembly), May 28, 1979, "Bao cao cua Hoi dong chinh phu ve thang loi vi dai cua hai cuoc chien tranh bao ve To quoc va nhiem vu cua toan dan va toan quan ta truoc tinh hinh moi" (Report of the Council of Government about the great victory of the two wars of defending our motherland and the duty of our people and army in the new situation), 14, QH, h.s. 2374.

51. Nguyen Huy Toan, Vu Tang Bong, Nguyen Huy Thuc, Nguyen Viet Binh, and Nguyen Minh Duc, *Su that ve nhung lan xuat quan cua Trung Quoc*

va quan he Viet-Trung (The truth about the Chinese military deployments and China-Vietnam relations) (Da Nang: Nha Xuat Ban Da Nang, 1996), 88–89.

52. PTT, h.s. 16327, Phu Thu Tuong, 1–2.

53. PTT, h.s. 16327, Bo Noi Thuong gui Phu Thu Tuong, 63.

54. Ibid.

55. Ibid., 64. By March 5, these provinces had received the following percentages of the plan: Lang Son received 54 out of 275 tons in the plan; Cao Bang 17 out of 275 tons; Bac Thai 541 tons, 141 tons over the plan of 400 tons; Ha Tuyen 191 out of 400 tons; Lai Chau 61 out of 200 tons; and Son La 136 out of 300 tons, 99 out of 400 tons, and 224 out of 450 tons.

56. Ibid., 61.

57. Ibid.

58. Ibid., 64.

59. PTT, h.s. 16028, Phuong Minh Nam, 4–9.

60. Zhang, *Deng Xiaoping's Long War*, 118.

61. Ibid.

62. In the north, there were three Military Regions, 1, 2 and 3.

63. QH, h.s. 2374, Dai tuong Vo Nguyen Giap, 9–10.

64. The forty-three-page report, marked "unofficial," was distributed to all National Assembly representatives for debate and comments in small groups and on the National Assembly floor for two days before an official report was released to the entire nation. None of the criticisms appeared in the official report.

65. "Phien hop sang 30/5/1979 Tham luan cua cac DBQH ve viec day manh san xuat, san sang chien dau, tang cuong dao tao can bo KHKT" (Session on the morning of May 30, 1979, speeches of National Assembly members about boosting [economic] production, preparing for battle, and enhancing and training of economic science cadres), PTT, h.s. 2378, 97–99.

66. Ban tap hop y kien cua dai bieu Quoc Hoi trong ky hop Thu 5 Quoc hoi Khoa VI (tu 28 den 30/5/1979) ve Bao cao cua Hoi dong Chinh phu, "Thang loi vi dai cua hai chien tranh bao ve To quoc va nhiem vu cua toan dan va toan quan doi ta truoc tinh hinh moi" (Collection of opinions of National Assembly members during the fifth session of the Sixth Plenum of the National Assembly from 28 to 30 May 1979 concerning the Council of Government's report entitled "The Great Victory of the Two Wars to Defend Our Motherland and the Duties of Our People and Military in the New Situation"), PTT, h.s. 2374, 116–29. The minutes are handwritten, with the notation "Secret" underlined and "6 copies" written in the left margin of the first page. The six copies were most likely sent the six ranking Politburo members, including Le Duan, Le Duc Tho, Truong Chinh, Pham Van Dong, General Vo Nguyen Giap, and Pham Hung.

67. Ibid., 100.

68. Ibid.

69. From 1976 to 1980, Nguyen Ky Uc served as deputy general secretary of the province of Cuu Long. On April 8, 1984, the Politburo appointed him party secretary of the province.

70. QH, h.s. 2374, Ban tap hop y kien cua Dai Bieu Quoc Hoi, 101.

71. Ibid., 102–3.

72. In the Battle of Bach Dang River near Ha Long Bay (Vietnam) in 938, the Vietnamese dealt a decisive blow to an invading Chinese army, and in January 1789 Quang Trung (Nguyen Hue) led the Vietnamese people to defeat an invading Chinese army and drove it from Vietnam. On February 9, 2019, the Vietnamese government commemorated the 230th anniversary of this great military victory over the Chinese (1789–2019), and tens of thousands of Vietnamese people flocked to pay homage to King Quang Trung at "Go Dong Da or Dong Da Hill." See "PM Phuc Joins Thousands at Dong Da Festival," *Voice of Vietnam*, February 9, 2019, https://english.vov.vn/society/pm-phuc-joins-thousands-in-attendance-at-dong-da-festival-391842.vov#p5).

73. QH, h.s. 2374, Ban tap hop y kien cua dai bieu Quoc Hoi, 103.

74. Ibid., 117–18.

75. Ibid., 114.

76. Ibid., 113.

77. Ibid.

78. Ibid., 128.

79. QH, h.s. 2374, Dai tuong Vo Nguyen Giap, 15.

80. QH, h.s. 2374, Ban tap hop y kien cua dai bieu Quoc Hoi, 101.

81. Ibid., 10.

82. Tran Duc Cuong, Vien Su Hoc, Vien Han Lam Khoa Hoc Xa Hoi Vietnam (Institute of History, Vietnam Academy of Social Science), *Lich Su Vietnam*, tap 14: *Tu nam 1975 den nam 1986* (Vietnam's history, vol. 14: 1975 to 1986) (Hanoi: Nha Xuat Ban Khoa Hoc Xa Hoi, 2017), 335. In an official history, Vietnam claimed to have taken 62,500 Chinese soldiers out of the battle. See also Luu, *50 Years of Vietnamese Diplomacy*, 381.

83. King C. Chen, *China's Wars with Vietnam, 1979* (Stanford, CA: Hoover Institution Press, 1987), 113–14.

84. Zhang, *Deng Xiaoping's Long War*, 119.

85. Ibid., 118, 238. On page 238, Zhang cited Chinese government sources: Party History and Political Work Department, "Issues on Political Work at Company Level during the Counterattack in Self-Defense on the Sino-Vietnamese Border (draft for discussion)," in *Zhong Yue bianjing ziwei fanji zuozhan zhengzhi gongzuo ziliao* (Materials on political work during the counterattack in self-defense on the Sino-Vietnamese Border), no. 14 (Guilin: Guangzhou junqu bubing xuexiao, 1979), 1; and Min Li, *Zhong Yue zhanzheng shinian* (Ten years of the Sino-Vietnamese War) (Chengdu: Sichuan daxue, 1993), 65.

86. Zhang, *Deng Xiaoping's Long War*, 238, n16.

87. QH, h.s. 2374, Dai tuong Vo Nguyen Giap.

88. General Li Zoucheng, a decorated hero of the Sino-Vietnamese War in 1979, was promoted in August 2017 as the new chief of the Joint Chiefs Department of the PLA. See Liu Caiyu, "Appointment of the New Chief to Raise the Military's Combat Ability: Expert," *Global Times*, August 27, 2017.

89. See QH, h.s. 2374, Dai tuong Vo Nguyen Giap.

90. Pham and Pham, *Lich Su Quan Doan 2*, 396.

91. QH, h.s. 2374, 508, 579.

92. For more details on the socially constructed tradition of resistance to foreign aggression in the national history of Vietnam in the 1950s and 1960s, see Patricia Pelley, "The History of Resistance and the Resistance to History in Post-colonial Constructions of the Past," in *Essays into Vietnamese Past*, edited by K. W. Taylor and John K. Whitmore, 234–35 (Ithaca, NY: Southeast Asia Program, Cornell University, 1995). As Pelley noted, Ngo Si Lien, the fifteenth-century compiler of *Dai Viet Su ky Toan Thu* and a revered scholar in Vietnam, located the origins of the Hung king in 2879 B.C.E. so that the mythical origins of Vietnam would predate the mythical origins of China.

93. QH, h.s. 2354, Tran Huu Duc, 26.

94. Ibid., 30.

95. Ibid.

96. Ibid., 32.

97. Ibid., 33.

98. Ibid., 45–46.

99. Ibid., 48–49.

100. QH, h.s. 2374, Dai tuong Vo Nguyen Giap, 10–12.

101. Ibid., 9.

102. Party Secretary Le Duan told his assistants in 1986, "I only know 20 of the 150 members of the Party Secretariat. The rest were appointed by Tho" (Huy Duc, *Ben Thang Cuoc I*, 362).

103. QH, h.s. 2374, Dai tuong Vo Nguyen Giap, 38.

104. Ibid., 29–30, 38.

105. Tran Dang Khoa, "Bao cao cua Uy ban thuong vu Quoc Hoi" (Report of the Standing Committee of the National Assembly at the fifth session of the Sixth Plenum of the National Assembly), May 24, 1979, QH, h.s. 2374, 5.

106. QH, h.s. 2374, "Ban tap hop y kien cua dai bieu Quoc Hoi," 114.

107. Ibid., 115.

108. QH, h.s. 2374, Tran Dang Khoa, 8.

109. "Dien Van Khai Mac, 5/24/1979" (Opening remarks [by Truong Chinh] on May 24, 1979), QH, h.s. 2374, 1.

110. Ibid., 4.

111. Truong Chinh, *On Kampuchea* (Hanoi: Foreign Languages Publishing House, 1980), 13.

112. QH, h.s. 2374, Tran Dang Khoa, 5; Cuong, *Lich Su Vietnam*, 356.

113. QH, h.s. 2374, Tran Dang Khoa, 5.

114. Ibid., 2.

115. Ibid., 6.

116. QH, h.s. 2374, "Dien Van Khai Mac (by Truong Chinh)," 7–8. Truong Chinh reiterated the victory speech by General Hoang Van Thai in his opening remark.

117. Ibid., 6.

118. Ibid., 8.

119. QH, h.s. 2374, Bao cao cua Uy ban thuong vu Quoc hoi, 10–11.

120. Ibid., 6–7.

121. PTT, h.s. 16381, Pho Thu Tuong To Huu, 1–3.

122. Ibid., 2.

123. Ibid., 1.

124. Ibid., 1–3.

125. Pho Thu Tuong To Huu, T/M Hoi Dong Chinh Phu (Deputy Prime Minister To Huu on behalf of the Council of Government), 58-CP, February 11, 1980, "Quyet Dinh cua Hoi Dong Chinh Phu ve viec giao ke hoach san sang dong vien phuc vu nhu cau quoc phong khi co chien tranh" (Directive of the Council of Government about planning and readiness to meet the needs of national defense when war breaks out), PTT, h.s. 16381, 4.

126. Pho Thu Tuong To Huu (Deputy Prime Minister To Huu), "V/v tam hoan viec thuc hien ke hoach tuyen quan" (About postponing military conscription), PTT, h.s. 16381, 4–5. This directive was also copied to General Secretary Le Duan and the General Political Department of the PAVN.

127. Ibid., 19.

128. Pham Nien, Tong Cuc Truong Tong Cuc Buu Dien (Pham Nien, general director of the General Directorate of Telecommunications and Post), Thu So 657/KH (Letter 657/KH), "V/v bao cao ket qua thuc hien QD 58-CP to Thu Tuong Chinh Phu" (Report of the result of implementing Directive 58-CP), PTT, h.s. 16381, 20.

129. Ibid., 31–34.

130. Binh Tam, Thu Truong Bo Giao Thong Van Tai (Binh Tam, vice-minister of Transport), Thu So 1118 BC/KH, 8/5/1980, gui Thu Tuong Chinh Phu, Uy Ban Ke Hoach Nha Nuoc, Bo Quoc Phong (to the prime Minister, the State Planning Committee, and the Ministry of Defense, May 8, 1980), "Bao cao thuc hien QD 58-CP" (Report on the implementation of Directive 58-CP), 55–57, PTT, h.s. 16381.

131. Ibid., 57.

132. Ibid., 58.

133. Bo Quoc Phong /Y Te, No. 49/QD-LNQPTY (Ministry of Defense/ Ministry of Health), "Quy Dinh cua Lien Bo Quoc Phong-Y T ve viec thuc hien quyet dinh cua Hoi Dong Chinh Phu giao ke hoach san sang viec phuc vu quoc phong khi co chien tranh" (Directive of the Ministry of Defense/Health inter-ministerial agreement on the implementation of the decision of the Council of Government regarding mobilization for national defense), PTT, h.s. 16381, 18–20.

134. Ibid., 21.

135. PTT, h.s. 16381, Thu Truong Vu Xuan Chiem, 39–40.

136. Ibid., 39.

137. Ibid., 60.

138. Thu Truong Le Hoa (Vice-Minister Le Hoa), Bo Vat Tu (Ministry of Materials Supply), So 116 VT/HK, May 16, 1980, "V/v chuan bi kim khi phuc vu nhu cau quoc phong khi co chien tranh" (About preparing hardware to serve the needs of national defense), PTT, h.s. 16381, 62–64.

139. Ibid., 64.

140. Ibid., 65–66.

141. PTT, h.s. 16381, Thu Truong Vu Xuan Chiem, 42.

142. Bo Vat Tu (Ministry of Materials Supply), PTT, h.s. 16381, 65–67.

143. PTT, h.s. 16381, Tran Phuong, 117.

144. Phuong Minh Nam, Thu Truong Phu Thu Tuong (Phuong Minh Nam, Vice-minister of the Prime Minister's Office), So 4235-V8, October 7, 1980, "Thong bao tinh hinh thuc hien Quyet Dinh 58-CP ngay 25/2/1980 cua Hoi Dong Chinh Phu ve viec giao ke hoach san sang dong vien phuc vu nhu cau khi co chien tranh" (Report on implementing Directive 58-CP on February 25, 1980 of the Council of Government regarding the mobilization plan to meet the needs [for national defense] when war breaks out), PTT, h.s. 16381, 18–19.

145. Ibid., 19.

146. QH, h.s. 2374, "Dien Van Khai Mac (by Truong Chinh)," 10.

147. Zhang, *Deng Xiaoping's Long War*, 143.

148. Ngo Tuyen, "Lich Su Chien Tranh Chong Khome Do," 178–79. According to Ngo Tuyen, who had access to internal records of the MoD, from September 1977 to December 1978 the Vietnamese military claimed to have taken 32,727 Khmer Rouge soldiers out of battle (meaning it had injured 32,727), killed 18,407, captured 7,035, and taken in 10,835 defectors, but the Vietnamese had far from destroyed all the main Khmer Rouge forces.

149. Ho Son Dai, ed., *Lich Su Quan Doan 4, 1974–2004* (History of the Fourth Army Corps) (Hanoi: Nha Xuat Ban Quan Doi Nhan Dan, 2004), 355–92, luu hanh noi bo (internally circulated only).

150. Zhang, *Deng Xiaoping's Long War*, 146.

151. General Van Tien Dung was minister of defense from February 1980 to February 1987.

152. Pho Thu Tuong To Huu (Deputy Prime Minister To Huu), So. 333-CP (Directive 333-CP), "Quyet Dinh Cua Hoi Dong Chinh Phu ve cong tac tuyen quan dot II nam 1980" (Directive of the Council of Government concerning the tasks of military conscription in Round II in 1980), PTT, h.s. 16381, 5–9.

153. Ibid., 6.

154. Ibid.

155. Luu, *50 Years of Vietnamese Diplomacy*, 383. To support his claim, top Vietnamese diplomat Luu Van Loi cited a Vietnamese translation of Sa Luc–Man Luc (Sa Li and Min Li), *9 lan xuat quan lon cua Trung Quoc* (Nine great military expeditions of China) (Sichuan, China: Nxb. Van Nghe Tu Xuyen, 1992), 45. The Vietnamese viewed the publication of this book by Chinese scholars as a "revisionist history" justifying China's aggression in Vietnam. In February 1996 cadre historians on the Vietnamese side were permitted by the Vietnamese government to publish 3,700 copies of this book entitled *Su that ve nhung lan xuat quan cua Trung Quoc va quan he Viet-Trung* (The truth about the Chinese military deployments and China-Vietnam relations).

156. David Wurfel, "*Doi Moi* in Comparative Perspective," in *Reinventing Vietnamese Socialism*, edited by William S. Turley and Mark Selden (Boulder, CO: Westview Press, 1993), 23.

157. Ibid.

158. Ibid.

159. Ibid.

160. Ibid., 24.

161. Ibid., 24–25.

162. Ibid., 25.

Chapter 4. The Two-Faced Enemy in Cambodia, 1979–1985

1. Elliott, *Changing Worlds*. Elliott cites a remark to this effect by Major General Tran Cong Man, editor of the *Army People's Daily*, quoted from Steven Erlanger, "Vietnam's Vietnam: Scars from Cambodia," *New York Times*, April 9, 1989.

2. Elliott, *Changing Worlds*, 69.

3. Ibid.

4. Ibid., 68–69.

5. Gottesman, *Cambodia after the Khmer Rouge*, 44, 139.

6. I use the term "nation building" as that is the way the Vietnamese often referred to their mission in Cambodia, but I am mindful of the fact that this term is controversial in Cambodia today and widely contested in its political discourses.

7. Astrid Norén-Nilsson, *Cambodia's Second Kingdom: Nation, Imagination, and Democracy* (Ithaca, NY: Southeast Asia Program, Cornell University, 2016), 117, 131.

8. "A Tribute to Vietnam's 'Buddha Army' Who Fought and Died in Cambodia," editorial, *Tuoi Tre News*, January 7, 2017, http://tuoitrenews.vn/poli tics/38919/a-tribute-to-vietnams-buddhas-army-that-fought-and-died-for -cambodians. When Prime Minister Hun Sen visited the southern Vietnamese province of Dong Nai on January 2, 2012, to dedicate a historical monument commemorating Division 125, the predecessor of the Kampuchean United Front for National Salvation (KUFNS), which fought to topple the Khmer Rouge regime, he dubbed the Vietnamese soldiers who helped Cambodia "Buddha's army."

9. Nguyen Van Hong, *Cuoc chien tranh bat buoc* (A necessary war) (Hanoi: Nha Xuat Ban Quan Doi Nhan Dan, 2013), 117.

10. Anna C. Merrit, Daniel A. Affron, and Benoi Monin, "Moral Self-Licensing: When Being Good Frees Us to Be Bad," *Social and Personality Psychology* 4, no. 5 (2010): 355.

11. Ibid.

12. Bo Quoc Phong, *Lich su quan tinh nguyen*, 108–9.

13. Ibid., 110.

14. Ibid. Infantry Regiment 775 was stationed at Sandan Commune, Regiment 747 at Baray Commune, Regiment 115 at Staung Commune, and Artillery Regiment 770b at Santuk Commune in Kampong Thom Province.

15. Nguyen, *Cuoc chien tranh bat buoc*, 116.

16. Ibid.

17. Ibid., 111–12. These included Tank and Armored Vehicle Regiment 145, Artillery Regiment 488, Antiaircraft Regiment 594, Information Regiment 611, and two units of military specialists (7704 and 7705). The remaining forces of Military Region 7 became Front 779, which was put in charge of the battlefront east of Phnom Penh, covering the provinces of Kampong Cham, Kampong Thom, Kratie, Svay Rieng, and Prey Veng.

18. Ibid.

19. Bo Nong Nghiep (Ministry of Agriculture), "Ke hoach chi vien cho K de on dinh doi song cap bach cua nhan dan va khoi phuc san xuat 1979" (Plan to help Cambodia stabilize people's basic livelihood and restore productivity in 1979), PTT, h.s. 11120, 1–29, 20.

20. Ibid.

21. Ibid., 21.

22. Le Tuan, Truong Van Phong 6 (Le Tuan, head of Office 6 [of the Prime Minister's Office]), "Bao cao mot so van de trong cong tac K" (Report on a number of issues pertaining to our work in Cambodia), March 13, 1980, PTT, h.s. 11353, 2.

23. Nguyen, *Cuoc chien tranh bat buoc*, 136–37.

24. Ibid., 138.

25. Benedict J. Tria Kerkvliet, *The Power of Everyday Politics: How Viet-namese Peasants Transformed National Policy* (Ithaca, NY: Cornell University Press, 2005), 9–10.

26. Pham Chung, deputy chief of Specialists Group B68, recalled Le Duc Tho's instructions. See Pham Chung, "Anh Le Duc Tho voi nghia vu quoc te giup ban Campuchia (hoi ky)" (Comrade Le Duc Tho and his international duty to assist Cambodia [memoir]), in *Le Duc Tho, nguoi cong san kien cuong nha lanh dao tai nang* (Le Duc Tho, an ardent socialist and talented leader), edited by Van Duc Thanh (Hanoi: Nha Xuat Ban Chinh Tri Quoc Gia, 2011), 672.

27. Ibid.

28. Le Duc Tho, *Thuc hien mot su chuyen bien sau sac ve to chuc nham tang cuong lanh dao va quan ly ve moi mat nhat la kinh te* (Achieve organizational transformation to strengthen leadership and management of all fields, especially the economy) (Hanoi: Nha Xuat Ban Su That, 1983), 9.

29. Huy Duc, *Ben Thang Cuoc I*, 378.

30. Ibid., 380–81.

31. Le Duc Anh, *Cuoc doi va su nghiep cach Mang (hoi ky)* (Life and the revolutionary profession [memoir]) (Hanoi: Nha Xuat Ban Chinh Tri Quoc Gia, 2015), 282.

32. Chung, "Anh Le Duc Tho voi nghia vu quoc te giup ban Campuchia," 671–72.

33. Bo Quoc Phong, *Lich su quan tinh nguyen*, 150.

34. Ibid.

35. Ibid., 147.

36. Ibid., 151. Military Region 5 was in charge of 5501 (Rattanakiri), 5502 (Mundolkiri), 5503 (Stung Treng), and 5504 (Preah Vihear). Military Region 7 was in charge of 7701 (Kampong Thom), 7702 (Kampong Cham), 7703 (Svay Rieng), 7704 (Battambang), 7705 (Siem Reap), 7706 (Prey Veng), 7707 (Kratie), and 7708 (Phnom Penh City). Military Region 9 was in charge of 9901 (Kampong Speu), 9002 (Kampong Chhnang), 9903 (Pursat), 9905 (Takeo), 9906 (Kandal), and 9907 (Koh Khong).

37. Ibid., 153.

38. Nguyen, *Cuoc chien tranh bat buoc*, 132.

39. Ibid. Also see Bo Quoc Phong, *Lich su quan tinh nguyen*, 175, which quotes a report dated January 2, 1982, on the enemy situation in the fourth quarter of 1981 by the Research Department of the Chief of Staff.

40. Le Duc Anh, *Quan Doi Nhan Dan Viet Nam va Nhiem Vu Quoc Te Cao Ca Tren Dat Ban Campuchia* (People's Army of Vietnam and its lofty international duty in Cambodian territory) (Hanoi: Nxb. QDND, 1986), 71.

41. Bo Quoc Phong, *Lich su quan tinh nguyen*, 160.

42. Nguyen, *Cuoc chien tranh bat buoc*, 171.

43. Ibid., 189.

44. Adapted from Nguyen Thanh Nhan, *Away from Home Season: The Story of a Vietnamese Volunteer Veteran in Cambodia* (Midtown, DE: By the author, 2010), 184. Thanh Nhan is a former Vietnamese volunteer veteran who lived and fought in Cambodia from December 1984 to July 1987. He arrived in Cambodia in the midst of Vietnam's major military offensives to drive Cambodia resistance forces across the Cambodian-Thai border, followed by the massive construction of a defense belt, called K5, to prevent the resistance forces from crossing into the interior of Cambodia.

45. Author's interview with the former chief of Chi Kreng district (Siem Reap Province), Kham Sokhom, January 19, 2016.

46. Ibid.

47. Ibid.

48. QH, h.s. 2374, Ban Tap Hop, 115.

49. Gottesman, *Cambodia after the Khmer Rouge*, 143.

50. Author's interview with Kham Sokhom.

51. Nguyen, *Cuoc chien tranh bat buoc*, 124–25. Cambodian villagers in this region warmly welcomed the Vietnamese soldiers with water, bananas, and coconuts when they arrived in their villages.

52. Author's interview with Kham Sokhom.

53. Gottesman, *Cambodia after the Khmer Rouge*, 143.

54. Both served in Regiment 4, Division 5, Front 479. Huy was sent to Cambodia in 1983, but Quan is a veteran of Front 479.

55. Adapted from Nguyen Thanh Nhan, *Away from Home Season*, 87.

56. Author's interview with Kham Sokhom.

57. Gottesman, *Cambodia after the Khmer Rouge*, 139.

58. Huy Duc, *Ben Thang Cuoc I*, 382.

59. Ibid., 190.

60. Ibid.

61. Huy Duc's books, composed after many years of in-depth research and with access to a vast array of interviews with key players in communist politics in Vietnam, provide new insight into the murky period of Vietnam's social and political transformation after 1975. Huy Duc's pathbreaking books break from Vietnam's official history, written by cadre historians with close ties to the party and government in Vietnam, because they speak truth to power and penetrate sensitive subjects that are still taboo in Vietnam today. When asked about his personal motivation for writing the two-volume *Ben Thang Cuoc* (The winning side), self-published in 2012, this Vietnamese journalist and former military expert of the PAVN in Cambodia told his audience (at an Association for Asian Studies seminar in March 2018 in Washington, DC), "Vietnam's history is mostly written by the Vietnamese elites about their roles or officials in the royal

palace about kings and queens; there were few stories of common Vietnamese people. That is why I wanted to write my books *The Winning Side* about common citizens who became victims of the Communist Party of Vietnam's policy of Northernification of the South after 1975."

62. Huy Duc, *Ben Thang Cuoc I*, 379.

63. Gottesman, *Cambodia after the Khmer Rouge*, 141.

64. Huy Duc, *Ben Thang Cuoc I*, 383.

65. Author's interview with Kham Sokhom.

66. Gottesman, *Cambodia after the Khmer Rouge*, 141.

67. Author's interview with Kham Sokhom.

68. Le Duc Anh, *Cuoc doi va su nghiep cach Mang*, 288.

69. Author's interview with Kham Sokhom.

70. When Hun Sen resumed the chairmanship of the Council of Ministers in 1985, he referred to Ambassador Ngo Dien as "my greatest teacher," the man who taught him everything he knew about foreign affairs. Huy Duc, *Ben Thang Cuoc I*, 381.

71. Ibid., 383.

72. Ibid., 379–83.

73. Le Duc Anh, *Cuoc doi va su nghiep cach Mang*, 288.

74. Huy Duc, *Ben Thang Cuoc I*, 383.

75. Ibid.

76. Ibid., 186–87. Also see Le Duc Anh, *Cuoc doi va su nghiep cach Mang*, 289.

77. Le Duc Anh, *Cuoc doi va su nghiep cach Mang*, 288–89.

78. Huy Duc, *Ben Thang Cuoc I*, 383.

79. Le Duc Anh, *Cuoc doi va su nghiep cach Mang*, 289.

80. Ibid., 287–88.

81. Ibid., 289.

82. Ibid. See also Huy Duc, *Ben Thang Cuoc I*, 382–83. Huy Duc cited Ngo Dien, *Campuchia nhin lai va suy nghi* (Cambodia: Revisit and reflect) (Hanoi: Unpublished memoir, 1992).

83. Huy Duc, *Ben Thang Cuoc I*, 377. In June 1978, Le Duc Tho flew to Saigon to create B68, a leadership committee for "solving problems related to the war in the southwest [against the Khmer Rouge regime] and fulfilling the international duty to help the new Cambodian revolution." Le Duc Tho, according to General Le Duc Anh, made all the big decisions, including the building of the armed forces and military planning.

84. Huy Duc, *Ben Thang Cuoc I*, 383.

85. Ibid.

86. Nguyen Thanh Nhan, *Away from Home Season*, 171–72.

87. Ibid., 174.

88. Ibid.

89. PTT, h.s. 5575, 1–4.

90. Nguyen Thanh Nhan, *Away from Home Season*, 170.

91. Author's interview with Kham Sokhom.

92. Huy Duc, *Ben Thang Cuoc I*, 383.

93. Ibid., 382.

Chapter 5. Economic Regionalism in Indochina, 1982–1985

1. For proponents of this view, see Vu, *Vietnam's Communist Revolution*, 242–43.

2. Gottesman, *Cambodia after the Khmer Rouge*, 168.

3. Ibid., 169.

4. The French privileged association—a strong type of cooperation between colonial and native in which economic cooperation and development could take place under peaceful, even harmonious conditions—over assimilation. The French and indigenous peoples would therefore cooperate, with the French fulfilling their charge as protectors by facilitating the entrance of local peoples into the world economy and their advancement into modernity. See David W. Del Testa, "'Imperial Corridor': Association, Transportation, and Power in French Colonial Indochina," *Science, Technology, and Society* 4, no. 2 (1999): 320–21.

5. Phu Thu Tuong (Prime Minister's Office), April 30, 1979, "Bao cao ve tinh hinh kinh te Campuchia sau ngay giai phong va nhung nhiem vu kinh te cap bach cua Campuchia" (Report on the economic situation in Cambodia after liberation and Cambodia's urgent economic tasks), PTT, h.s. 11104, 43.

6. QH, h.s. 2354, "Bao cao cua Thu Tuong Pham Van Dong," 18.

7. Ibid., 18–19.

8. Le Tuan, Phu Thu Tuong (Prime Minister's Office) to [General Secretary] Le Duan, ban so 066 (Report no. 066), "Giup do ban on dinh nhan dan, khoi phuc san xuat, tung buoc xay dung kinh te van hoa trong thoi gian truoc mat" (Help our [Cambodian] friends to stabilize people's [livelihoods], restore production, and gradually build economy and culture in the immediate future), 1979, PTT, h.s. 11104, 1.

9. Ibid.

10. Ibid., 2.

11. Note that Hanoi used the economy during the last year of Sihanouk's reign in 1969 as the baseline for economic recovery in postgenocide Cambodia. Back then Cambodia had more than 3 million hectares of cultivated land, of which rice paddies covered 2.5 million hectares and rubber plantations 600,000. Cambodia annually produced 200,000 tons of sesame; 50,000 tons of industrial crops such as cotton; 60,000 tons of tea (Kirirum), coffee (Pailin), and pepper (Kampot and Koh Kong); 50,000 tons of sugar; and a large quantity of fruit. In

addition, Cambodia had more than 1 million buffaloes, 2.8 million cows, 1.5 million pigs, and more than 6 million chickens and other birds. Cambodia's forests covered 13 million hectares and produced high-quality wood. Its Tonle Sap Lake produced about 130,000 tons of freshwater fish annually. Ibid., 2–4.

12. Margaret Slocomb, *The People's Republic of Kampuchea, 1979–1989: The Revolution after Pol Pot* (Chiang Mai, Thailand: Silkworm Books, 2003), 112.

13. PTT, h.s. 11104, Le Tuan, 4.

14. For a more detailed discussion of *krom samaki*, see Slocomb, *People's Republic of Kampuchea*, 96–98.

15. Ibid., 99.

16. PTT, h.s. 11104, Le Tuan, 10.

17. Bo Quoc Phong, *Lich su quan tinh nguyen*, 83.

18. Committee B68 was a military advisory committee under the oversight of the CMC. After Le Duc Tho established B68 in Ho Chi Minh City in June 1978, Tran Xuan Bach, a member of the CMC, was put in charge of it until March 1982. After that General Le Duc Anh took over B68 as part of his overall command in Cambodia. Huy Duc, *Ben Thang Cuoc I*, 378. Below Le Duc Anh, Nguyen Xuan Hoang, deputy director of the Military Science Academy of Vietnam, was appointed committee chairman. The four deputy chairmen included Tran Van Phac, vice-chairman of the General Department of Political Affairs; Doan The, vice-chief of staff; Dan Thanh, vice-chairman of the General Department of Logistics (the MoD); and Nguyen Huu Tai, chairman of the Foreign Affairs Committee of the CMC. Bo Quoc Phong, *Lich su quan tinh nguyen*, 42–43.

19. PTT, h.s. 11104, Le Tuan, 2. Nguyen Thuan was appointed head of Group 478 and Le Chieu political commissar. On January 24, 1979, Group 478 was transferred from B68 to the Vietnamese MoD. Bo Quoc Phong, *Lich su quan tinh nguyen*, 53–54, 76.

20. The A40 committee was led by a group of top economic planners of the Vietnamese party and government. The chairman of A40 was Nguyen Con, who was also chairman of the Economic and Planning Committee of the CMC and a member of the Central Committee of the CPV. The two vice-chairmen of A40 were Ho Viet Thang, vice-chairman of the State Planning Committee, and Nguyen Tuan, vice-minister of energy and coal. The six members of A40 included vice-ministers from various ministries of the government, including Tran Khai (Ministry of Agriculture), Nguyen Huu Bao (Ministry of Internal Trade), Dang Van Thong (Ministry of Transport), Pham Van Son (Ministry of Forestry), Le Thanh Cong (Ministry of Culture and Information), and Nguyen Duy Cuong (Ministry of Health). Bo Quoc Phong, *Lich su quan tinh nguyen*, 81–82.

21. PTT, h.s. 11104, Le Tuan, 11.

22. Bo Quoc Phong, *Lich su quan tinh nguyen*, 127–28.

23. Ibid.

24. For more about Le Duc Tho's role in Cambodia in 1979–81, see Huy Duc, *Ben Thang Cuoc I*, 377–83; Le Duc Anh, *Cuoc doi va su nghiep cach Mang*, 170–71.

25. "Ket luan cua Anh Do Muoi tai Hoi nghi khoi phuc thu do Phnom Penh ngay 25–26/2/1979" (Conclusion of [Deputy Prime Minister] Do Muoi at the conference on reconstruction of the Phnom Penh capital on February 25–26, 1979), PTT, h.s. 11104, 65, 69.

26. Bo Quoc Phong, *Lich su quan tinh nguyen*, 149; PTT, h.s. 11353, Le Tuan, 5. The idea of merging B68 and A40 was proposed by Le Tuan, chief of Office 6 of the Prime Minister's Office.

27. Le Duc Anh, *Cuoc doi va su nghiep cach Mang*, 170.

28. Ibid.

29. In the sister provinces and cities model, the pairing was as follows: Kien Giang (Vietnamese Province) and Kampot (Cambodian Province), An Giang-Takeo, Dong Thap-Prey Veng, Long An-Svay Rieng, Tay Ninh-Kampong Cham, Song Be-Kratie, Dak Lak-Mondulkiri, Gai lai and Kon tum-Rattanakiri, Dong Nai-Kampong Thom, Cuu Long-Kampong Speu, Hau Giang-Battambang, and Ben Tre-Siem Reap.

30. Bo Quoc Phong, *Lich su quan tinh nguyen*, 84–85.

31. PTT, h.s. 11353, Le Tuan, 2.

32. Ibid., 12.

33. Ibid., 2.

34. Ibid., 4.

35. Nguyen Mai, Chanh van phong Ban to chuc Ban chap hanh trung uong (Head of the Organization Committee Office of the Party Central Committee), Ban To Chuc No. 384 (Organization Committee No. 384), March 13, 1980, Kinh gui Dong chi Chu nhiem Van phong Phu thu tuong (to Comrade Chief of the Prime Minister's Office), "Ve viec dat khoan phu cap biet tieng Lao va Campuchia cho can bo nhan vien cua ta sang giup Ban" (About allocating allowances to learn Laotian and Cambodian languages for our cadres and officials who are assisting our friends [Cambodia and Laos]), PTT, h.s. 11353, 1.

36. PTT, h.s. 11104, Le Tuan, 5–6.

37. Chinh Phu C.H.X.H.C.N. Vietnam (Government of the Socialist Republic of Vietnam) gui Hoi dong Cach mang Campuchia (to the Revolutionary Council of Kampuchea), March 7, 1979, PTT, h.s. 11634, 54.

38. Several reports referred to Do Muoi as the top government planner at the Office of the Prime Minister in charge of coordinating foreign aid, including aid from the Soviet Union and other socialist countries, to Cambodia. See, for example, "Bao cao Anh Muoi" (Report to Brother Muoi), 6/23/1980, PTT, h.s. 11634, 9. In this handwritten letter from Office 7 (in charge of the economic affairs) of the Prime Minsiter's Office, Nguyen Con, A40 chief in Cambodia,

asked the deputy prime minister and vice-chairman of the Council of Ministers Do Muoi for ideas regarding the content of the meeting with a group of Soviet officials from the Soviet Committee on Economic Relations with Foreign Countries and two Soviet foreign affairs officials who would arrive in Vietnam on February 2, 1980.

39. Phu Thu Tuong (Prime Minister's Office), So 88/TTg., March 14, 1979, "Quyet dinh cua Thu Tuong Chinh Phu ve nhiem vu van chuyen va dam bao giao thong trong thoi gian truoc mat" (The Prime Minister's decision regarding the task of transporting and guaranteeing transportation in the weeks and months ahead), PTT, h.s. 11104, 15–16.

40. Hanoi immediately restored National Road 1, which connected Go Dau, Tay Ninh Province (Vietnam), crossing the Bavet border pass in Svay Rieng Province (Cambodia), Neak Luong, and then Phnom Penh. The Vietnamese also restored Cambodia's National Road 5 from Phnom Penh to Udong and National Road 6 from Udong to Skun (Kampong Thom Province). They rebuilt National Road from Skun to Chup, Soung, and Kraek (Kampong Cham Province) and National Road 22 from Kreak to Tay Ninh Province (Vietnam). In addition, the Vietnamese rebuilt Cambodia's National Road 3, connecting Song Be Province of Vietnam to Kratie Province of Cambodia, and National Road 9 running from Pleiku (Vietnam) to Ban Lung (Cambodia). Vietnam built three ferry stations, at Neak Luong (in Prey Veng Province) to cross the Mekong River, at Prek Kdam to cross Tonle Sap Lake at Udong, and at Kampong Cham Province to cross the Mekong River.

41. PTT, h.s. 11634, Chinh Phu C.H.X.H.C.N. Vietnam, 34–35.

42. PTT, h.s. 11104, Phu Thu Tuong, "Bao cao ve tinh hinh kinh te Campuchia," 45.

43. Ibid., 36–37, 39–40.

44. Ibid., 41.

45. Ibid., 43.

46. Ibid., 44.

47. Ibid.

48. QH, h.s. 2374, Tran Dang Khoa, 6.

49. A40 Doan Chuyen Gia Giao Duc (A40 Education Specialist Group), January 26, 1981, "Bao cao so ket cong tac chuyen gia giao duc tinh, thanh pho tai Kampuchea" (Report on the work of education specialists in provinces and cities in Cambodia), BGD, h.s. 161, 88–109.

50. "Bao cao so bo ve tinh hinh giao duc Phnom Penh sau 7/1/79 cua doan khao sat giao duc thanh pho Ho Chi Minh" (A preliminary report about the situation of education in Phnom Penh after January 7, 1979, by the Education Inspection Group of Ho Chi Minh City), BGD, h.s. 153, 157–58.

51. BGD, h.s. 161, 90.

52. Ibid.

53. Ibid., 100.

54. A40 Doan Chuyen Gia Giao Duc (A40, Education Specialist Group), June 7, 1979, "Bao cao mot so net ve tinh hinh va cong tac giao duc truoc mat hien nay can giup Ban" (Report on a number of observations and the situation of our immediate educational tasks to help our friends), BGD, h.s. 153, 1–3.

55. Cong Hoa Nhan Dan Campuchia, Hoi Dong Nhan Dan Cach Mang (People's Republic of Kampuchea, People's Revolutionary Council of Kampuchea), "Chi thi ve cong tac giao duc trong thoi gian truoc mat" (Directive regarding the immediate educational task), BGD, h.s. 146, 1–12. This document was submitted to B68 for comments (1).

56. Bo Giao Duc (Ministry of Education), "Bao cao tong ket 10 nam hop tac va giup nganh giao duc Campuchia" (Summary report on the ten-year cooperation with and assistance to Cambodia in the field of education), BGD, h.s. 477, 1.

57. Nguyen Con, Truong doan Chuyen gia Kinh te va Van hoa (Chief of Economic and Cultural Experts), Phnom Penh, April 12, 1980, "Bao cao ke hoach vien tro kinh te nam 1980 Viet Nam KPC" (Report on Vietnam's economic assistance to Cambodia in 1980), PTT, h.s. 11633, 66–69. This report was sent to the Standing Committee of the government, Do Muoi, Nguyen Lam, and the Ministry of Finance (66–67). The amount included 30 million VND for the recovery of agriculture and fisheries, 22.5 million for food production, 18.5 million for transportation and communications, 29 million for other sectors, and 30 million for building the Cambodian revolutionary army.

58. Ibid., 67.

59. Ibid., 68.

60. PTT, h.s. 11353, Le Tuan, 3–4. For 1980, Hanoi created a separate budget of 24.3 million VND to purchase food supplies for the Vietnamese experts in Cambodia.

61. Tran Xuan Bach, Truong Ban B68 (head of the B68 committee), So 359/B68, February 26, 1980, kinh gui dong chi Pho Thu Tuong Do Muoi (to Deputy Prime Minister Do Muoi), "Ve viec bao dam cung cap vat chat cho cac Doan chuyen gia Viet Nam cong tac tai Campuchia" (About guaranteeing material supply for groups of Vietnamese experts working in Cambodia), PTT, h.s. 11353, 7–8, 10.

62. Gottesman, *Cambodia after the Khmer Rouge*, 84–85.

63. These heavy-duty trucks included 100 UAZ-452Ds, 100 Gaz-53As, and 160 Zil-131s.

64. These consisted of 35 Gas-24 vehicles, 70 Moskvich 412, 50 Uaz-469, 100 Vaz35 Gas-24, 70 Moskvich 412, 50 Uaz-469, and 100 Vaz.

65. This included 15,000 tons of automobile gasoline, 10,000 tons of diesel, 10,000 tons of crude oil, and 15,000 tons of low-quality oil.

66. "Danh muc hang hoa duoc cung cap khong hoan lai tu Lien Bang Cong hoa Xa hoi Chu nghia Xo Viet sang nuoc Cong Hoa Nhan Dan Campuchia

trong nam 1979" (List of goods in nonrefundable aid from the Soviet Union to the People's Republic of Kampuchea), PTT, h.s. 11634, 65–67.

67. "Danh muc hang hoa yeu cau Lien Xo vien tro bo sung cho Cong Hoa Nhan Dan Campuchia trong nam 1979" (List of goods [Vietnam] requested the Soviet Union to provide to the People's Republic of Kampuchea as supplementary nonrefundable aid in 1979), PTT, h.s. 11634, 44.

68. Nguyen Van Dao, Thu Truong Bo Ngoai thuong (Vice-Minister of the Ministry of Foreign Trade), August 10, 1979, "Bao cao tom tat tinh hinh dam phan giua doan chuyen vien kinh te Lien Xo va Campuchia" (Brief report on the negotiations between the Soviet economic experts and their Cambodian counterparts), PTT, h.s. 11634, 59–61. This report was sent to VP6 (K), referring to Office 6 (about Kampuchea), and was also copied VP7 (Office 7) of the Prime Minister's Office (59).

69. Ibid.

70. Ibid., 60.

71. Ibid.

72. Duong Van Dat, Thu truong Bo Tai Chinh gui Bo Truong Phu Thu Tuong Vu Tuan (Finance Vice-Minister Duong Van Dat to Chief of the Prime Minister's Office Vu Tuan), November 10, 1979, "Ve giao nhan, thanh toan, van chuyen hang vien tro K qua canh Viet Nam" (About delivery, payment, and shipment of aid to Cambodia via Vietnam), November 10, 1979, PTT, h.s. 11634, 62–66. The report was also sent to Nguyen Con, chairman of A40 committee, 63.

73. Ibid., 65.

74. PTT, h.s. 11634, "Danh muc hang vien tro cua Lien Xo cho Campuchia nam 1980," 22–23.

75. Ibid., 23–24.

76. Ibid., 24–29.

77. In 1979, Pen Sovann was vice-chairman of the People's Revolutionary Council of Kampuchea in charge of economic affairs, commander-in-chief of the army, and was also defense minister. After the Fourth Party Congress held May 26–29, 1981, Pen Sovann became the General Secretary of the Party Central Committee of the Kampuchean People's Revolutionary Party, which consisted of twenty members. Sovann played a central role in establishing a seven-member political bureau of the Party Central Committee, which consisted of Pen Sovann, Chea Sim, Hun Sen, Chea Sot, Chan Si, Say Phouthang, and Mat Ly. Out of the Fourth Party Congress, Chea Sim became president of the newly established National Assembly on June 6, 1981; Heng Samrin became the president of the State Council. Sovann was the first prime minister of the PRK. He was accused of being anti-party and anti-Vietnam by his main opponents, Say Phouthang and Hun Sen, and four other Politburo members on November 30, 1981, and purged on the same day. On December 3, he was flown to Hanoi

where he was imprisoned until December 5, 1991. See Pen Sovann, *Brief Biography and National Cause* (Khmer language) (Seattle, WA: Khmer Vision Publishing Company, 2002), 181–83, 234.

78. I. A-ro-khi-pop (Ivan Arkhipov), Pho Chu Tich Hoi dong Bo truong Lien Xo (Vice-Chairman of the Council of Ministers of the Soviet Union) to Dong chi Pen-Xo-Van (Comrade Pen Sovann) on 6/16/1980, PTT, h.s. 11634, 12–13.

79. Ibid., 13.

80. Ibid.

81. Ibid.

82. "Hiep dinh thuong mai giua Chinh phu nuoc Cong hoa Xa hoi Chu nghia Viet Nam va Hoi dong Nhan dan Cach mang nuoc Cong hoa Nhan dan Kampuchea" (Agreement on trade between the government of the Socialist Republic of Vietnam and the People's Revolutionary Council of the People's Republic of Kampuchea), Hanoi, May 2, 1981, PTT, h.s. 12028, 28–29.

83. Ibid., 30.

84. "Hiep dinh vien tro khong hoan lai giua Chinh phu nuoc Cong hoa Xa hoi Chu nghia Viet Nam va Hoi dong Nhan dan Cach mang Nuoc Cong hoa Nhan dan Kampuchea" (Agreement on nonrefundable aid between the government of the Socialist Republic of Vietnam and the People's Revolutionary Council of Kampuchea), Hanoi, May 2, 1981, PTT, h.s. 12028, 31.

85. "Hiep dinh giua chinh phu Cong hoa Xa hoi Chu nghia Viet Nam, Hoi dong Nhan dan Cach mang Kampuchea va chinh phu Lien bang Cong hoa Xa hoi Chu nghia Xo Viet ve phoi hop su giup do trong viec khoi phuc va xay dung o Cong hoa Nhan dan Kampuchea cac cong trinh ghi trong cac hiep dinh Kampuchea—Lien Xo" (Agreement between the government of the Socialist Republic of Vietnam, the People's Revolutionary Council of People's Republic of Kampuchea, and the government of the Union of Soviet Socialist Republics about the coordination of assistance to the PRK's recovery and construction of projects signed in the agreement between the PRK and the Soviet Union), Phnom Penh, March 2, 1981, PTT, h.s. 12028, 26–27. For implementation, the agreement was sent on April 18, 1981, to the Office of the Prime Minister, the State Planning Committee, the Committee on Economic Relations with Foreign Countries, the Ministry of Finance, the Soviet Union Department, and the Vietnamese ambassador to Cambodia.

86. Ibid. Vietnam's Committee on Economic Relations with Foreign Countries, Cambodia's Office of Economic Affairs of the People's Revolutionary Council of the PRK, and the Soviet State Committee on Economic Relations with Foreign Countries were directly responsible for implementing this agreement.

87. PTT, h.s. 11104, Phu Thu Tuong, "Bao cao ve tinh hinh kinh te Campuchia sau ngay giai phong," 39.

88. Vo Dong Giang, Uy vien Ban tru bi hoi nghi cap cao cua Vietnam ([Vice-Minister of Foreign Affairs] Vo Dong Giang, member of Vietnam's Preparatory Committee on the high-level summit), kinh gui Thuong vu Hoi Dong Bo Truong (to the Standing Committee of the Council of Ministers), December 27, 1982, "To trinh ve to chuc hoi nghi chuyen vien kinh te, van hoa, khoa hoc ky thuat de tru bi them cho hoi nghi cap cao 3 nuoc Lao-Campuchia-Viet Nam" (Proposal regarding the organization of a conference of economic, cultural and technological experts in additional preparation for the high-level summit of the three countries Laos, Cambodia and Vietnam), PTT, h.s. 12589, 69. The Office of the Council of Ministers in Hanoi covered the cost the conference; the Cambodian and Laotian delegations only needed to pay their airfare.

89. PTT, h.s. 12589, "Tap hop tai lieu ve hoi nghi cap chuyen vien kinh te 3 nuoc Dong Duong nam 1982–83," 1.

90. Vo Dong Giang, Thu Truong Bo Ngoai giao (Vice-Minister of Foreign Affairs Vo Dong Giang), March 14, 1983, "Bao cao ve Hoi Nghi cap cao khong lien ket lan thu 7 o New Delhi" (Report on the Seventh Summit of the Nonaligned Movement in New Delhi), PTT, h.s. 12594, 81–97, 91.

91. Vladislav M. Zubok, *A Failed Empire: The Soviet Union in the Cold War from Stalin to Gorbachev* (Chapel Hill: University of North Carolina Press, 2007), 263, 268.

92. Ibid., 269.

93. Ibid., 268.

94. Beresford and Phong, *Economic Transition in Vietnam*, 44.

95. Ibid., 124.

96. Ibid., 129.

97. Ibid., 128.

98. Ibid., 118.

99. Zhang, *Beijing's Economic Statecraft*, 362.

100. Ibid., 288.

101. The Office of the Council of Ministers approved the MOFA request, dated February 4, 1983, to send sixteen high-ranking officials of the MOFA, four from the Ministry of Culture, nine from the Radio and Television Broadcasting Committee, four from the People's Committee of Hau Giang Province, two from the Vietnam News Agency, one from the Nhan Dan editorial board, and one from the Foreign Affairs Committee of the PCC. Nguyen Van Ich, Pho Chu Chiem Van Phong Hoi Dong Bo Truong (Nguyen Van Ich, vice-chief of the Office of the Council of Ministers), 2/9/1983, "Ve cu can bo sang giup Lao chuan bi hoi nghi cap cao 3 nuoc Dong Duong" (About sending officials to assist Laos to prepare for the summit for the three Indochinese countries), PTT, h.s. 12589, 70.

102. PTT, h.s. 12594, "Bao cao ve hoi nghi cap cao lan thu 7," 75.

103. Ibid., 86.

104. Ibid., 85.

105. Vo Nguyen Viet Dung, Chu Nhiem Van Phong Quoc Hoi va Hoi dong Nha Nuoc (chief of the Office of the National Assembly and the Council of State), "Bien ban phien hop 19 cua Hoi dong Nha nuoc ngay 29 va ngay 30 thang 3, 1983" (Minutes of the nineteenth meeting of the Council of State on March 29–30, 1983), PTT, h.s. 12594, 5–30. Nguyen Co Thach reported to the nineteenth Council of State meeting chaired by Truong Chinh and attended by other council members, including Nguyen Huu Tho, Le Thanh Nghi, [General] Chu Huy Man, Vu Quang, Dam Quang Trung, Ngo Duy Dong, and Le Thanh Dao (Nguyen Thi Dinh and Nguyen Duc Thuan were absent). Also in attend_ance were Tran Phuong, vice-chairman of the Council of Ministers; Nguyen Huu Thu, chief of the Office of the Council of Ministers; Phan Hien, Minister of Justice; and others (24).

106. PTT, h.s. 12594, "Bao cao ve hoi nghi cap cao lan thu 7," 76.

107. Ibid.

108. Ibid., 77.

109. Ibid.

110. Ibid., 77–78.

111. Ibid., 78.

112. Ibid.

113. Ibid., 80.

114. Ibid., 79.

115. PTT, h.s. 12589, "Tap hop tai lieu ve hoi nghi cap chuyen vien kinh te 3 nuoc Dong Duong nam 1982–83," 68; PTT, h.s. 12589, Vo Dong Giang, 69.

116. PTT, h.s. 12589, Nguyen Ngoc Thai, 57.

117. Ibid., 58–61.

118. Ibid., 59.

119. Ibid., 60–61.

120. PTT, h.s. 12589, To nghien cuu, 23–39; "De cuong ve hop tac kinh te va khoa hoc ky thuat giua Viet Nam-Lao-Campuchia" (Proposal for economic, technical and scientific cooperation between Vietnam, Lao and Cambodia), 6/30/1982, PTT, h.s. 12589, 40–56.

121. PTT, h.s. 12589, To nghien cuu, 24.

122. Ibid., 26.

123. Ibid., 27.

124. Van phong Hoi dong Bo truong gui Bo Ngoai giao va Uy ban Hop tac Kinh te Van hoa voi Lao va Campuchia (The Office of the Council of Ministers sent to the Ministry of Foreign Affairs and the Committee on Economic and Cultural Cooperation with Lao and Cambodia), July 17, 1982, "Ban goi y ve chuong trinh va noi dung hop tac kinh te, van hoa, khoa hoc ky thuat giua ba nuoc Dong Duong" (Suggestions concerning the program and content of economic, cultural, technical and scientific cooperation between the three Indo-chinese countries), PTT, h.s. 12589, 3–4.

125. Ibid., 1–2.
126. Ibid., 3.
127. Ibid.
128. Ibid., 3–4.
129. Ibid., 4.
130. Ibid.
131. Ibid.
132. Ibid., 5.
133. Ibid., 7.
134. Ibid., 6.
135. Ibid., 7.
136. Ibid.
137. Ibid., 8.
138. Ibid., 9.
139. Ibid.
140. Ibid., 10.
141. Ibid.
142. Ibid., 11–12.
143. Ibid., 12.
144. Ibid., 13–14.
145. Ibid., 15–16.

Chapter 6. The Road to *Doi Moi*, 1986

1. Fforde and De Vylder contend, "The Vietnamese transition, although certainly strongly influenced by such external factors as the aid cuts of 1978–79, and 1989–90, as well as the high levels of COMECON aid in the mid-1980s, was mainly determined by internal factors" (*From Plan to Market*, 15). Although evidence discussed in this chapter corroborates their characterization of the *Doi Moi* policy as "responsive" rather than "proactive," I disagree with them, believing that the Vietnamese leadership was simply responsive to domestic economic and political imperatives. As the new evidence in this chapter reveals, the Vietnamese leadership was, by 1985, under enormous external influences in terms of both ideational factors (learning from the Soviet Union and other Eastern European countries in their economic dealings with the West) and material systemic change in global market forces (the dire need to boost exports and its relations with necessary imports of modern technology to improve economic efficiency and product quality).

2. See Womack, *China and Vietnam*, 204–5.

3. See Porter, *Vietnam*, 188. New evidence reveals that ideas about the interdependence of states and market forces and the role of modern technology permeated and aroused the interest of the Vietnamese top decision-making body as early as the PPA in 1973, that is, the Politburo, long before the Sixth Party

Congress in December 1986, the date Porter claimed to be the starting point of the transition in Hanoi's worldview from an orthodox Marxist-Leninist ideology to a recognition of the interdependence of states and economic constraints on conflict.

4. Vu, *Vietnam's Communist Revolution*, 245–47. Mostly relying on publicly available party records, especially *Van Kien Dang Toan Tap* (Collected Party Documents), 54 vols. (Hanoi: Chinh Tri Quoc Gia, 1999–2007), published by the CPV, Vu almost exclusively attributed the reformist ideas to Truong Chinh. In his pathbreaking book *Ben Thang Cuoc*, Vietnamese journalist Huy Duc also cast Truong Chinh as the *Doi Moi* hero.

5. Elliott, *Changing Worlds*, 34. Elliott is among few scholars who downplay the role of personality in the *Doi Moi* process.

6. For details, see ibid., 48–51.

7. Kerkvliet, *Power of Everyday Politics*, 189.

8. Elliott, *Changing Worlds*, 34.

9. Vo Van Kiet was in charge of economic planning. For details, see Huy Duc, *Ben Thang Cuoc II: Quyen Binh* (The winning side, part 2: Power) (Saigon: OsinBook, 2012) 101.

10. PTT, h.s. 13234, 25.

11. Ibid., 25–26.

12. Ibid. See also Nguyen Dinh Bin, *Ngoai Giao Viet Nam*, 297.

13. PTT, h.s. 13234, 3.

14. Ibid.

15. Ibid., 4–26.

16. Ibid., 4. Most of the aid was for postwar economic recovery and included fuel, fertilizer, tractors, and basic consumption goods such as food, public health, and school supplies.

17. Ibid., 4.

18. Ibid., 25.

19. Ibid.

20. Ibid., 25–26. The original amount borrowed from the socialist bloc during the second half of the 1970s was 2.4 billion rubles. Vietnam was not able to repay this loan during the period 1981–85. Therefore, it was rolled over to the period 1986–90, and the total interest of 400 million rubles was added to the original amount.

21. Ibid., 26. According to Vietnam's commercial bank, the original debt as of December 31, 1984, was US$1.6 billion, including US$924 million owed to other countries, US$208 million owed to international organizations, US$317 million owed to international banks, and US$215 million owed to private creditors. US$630 million was scheduled to be paid back during the 1986–90 period, and US$950 million was rolled over from the 1981–85 period during which Vietnam was unable to pay.

22. Ibid., 5.

23. Ibid.
24. Ibid., 6–7.
25. Nguyen Dinh Bin, *Ngoai Giao Viet Nam*, 297.
26. PTT, h.s. 13234, 7.
27. Ibid., 8.
28. Ibid., 21.
29. Ibid.
30. Ibid.
31. Ibid., 9.
32. Ibid., 10.
33. Ibid.
34. Ibid., 14.
35. Ibid.
36. Ibid., 11–12.
37. Ibid., 12.
38. Ibid., 12–13.
39. Ibid., 13.
40. Ibid.
41. Ibid., 16.
42. Ibid., 17.
43. Ibid.
44. Ibid.,18.
45. Ibid., 20.
46. Nguyen Dinh Bin, *Ngoai Giao Viet Nam*, 298.
47. PTT, h.s. 13234, 19.
48. Ibid., 20, 28.
49. Ibid.
50. Ibid.
51. Ibid., 25.
52. Ibid., 34.
53. Ibid., 35.
54. Elliott, *Changing Worlds*, 16.
55. Nguyen Co Thach, "Bao cao ve tinh hinh the gioi va cong tac doi ngoai cua ta trong nam 1986" (Report on world affairs and our foreign policy in 1986 [Read at the National Assembly session in December 1986])," QH, h.s. 5607, 1–26.
56. Ibid., 27–57.
57. Ibid., 28.
58. Ibid., 1.
59. Ibid., 2.
60. Huy Duc, *Ben Thang Cuoc II*, 216.
61. Nguyen Co Thach, "Hiep Dinh Paris Voi Su Nghiep Giai phong mien nam," in *Mat Tran Ngoai Giao Voi Cuoc Dam Phan Paris ve Viet Nam* (The

diplomatic front at the Paris negotiations about Vietnam), edited by Bo Ngoai giao, 2nd ed. (Hanoi: Nha Xuat Ban Chinh Tri Quoc Gia-Su That, 2015), 399.

62. Nguyen Co Thach, Bo Truong Bo ngoai giao (Nguyen Co Thach, Minister of Foreign Affairs), "Mot so tinh hinh ve hop tac kinh te giua Lien Xo va Dong Au voi cac nuoc phuong tay" (A number of situations about economic cooperation between the Soviet Union and Eastern Europe and other western countries), September 1973, PTT, h.s. 9061, 1.

63. Ibid., 1.

64. Ibid., 2.

65. Ibid., 2–3.

66. Ibid., 6.

67. Ibid.

68. Ibid.

69. Huy Duc, *Ben Thang Cuoc I*, 352. Huy Duc cited Doan Duy and Hoang Tung (chief of party propaganda).

70. Ibid.

71. Ibid., 361.

72. Ibid., 272.

73. Ibid., 351, 365. In an internal preliminary survey leading up to the Sixth Party Congress, 900 out of 1,129 party members present voted to retain Truong Chinh as the general secretary of the party.

74. For the final power struggle on December 12, 1986, just three days before the Sixth Party Congress on December 15, between Truong Chinh and Le Duc Tho, backed by Pham Hung, see ibid., 365–67.

75. Ibid., 353.

76. Wurfel, "*Doi Moi* in Comparative Perspective," 27.

77. PTT, h.s. 13234, 9–15.

78. Ibid., 10.

79. Ibid.

80. Ibid., 11.

81. Ibid., 14.

82. Ibid., 13.

83. Ibid., 25–27.

84. Ibid., 25.

85. Ibid., 28.

86. Ibid., 29.

87. Ibid.

88. Ibid., 30.

89. Ibid., 30.

90. Ibid., 50–51.

91. QH, h.s. 5607, 51.

92. Ibid., 52.

93. Ibid., 53.

94. Ibid.

95. Ibid., 55.

96. Ibid., 39–40.

97. Ibid., 40.

98. Ibid., 48.

99. Note that here I use the terms "economy-firsters" and "reformists" interchangeably.

100. QH, h.s. 5607, 13.

101. Doan Trong Truyen, Bo Truong Tong Thu ky Hoi dong Bo Truong (Chief of the General Secretariat of the Council of Ministers), So 01-TB, 01/12/1985, "Thong bao ve Hoi nghi Thuong truc Hoi dong Bo truong ban ve mot so van de hop tac kinh te, van hoa, khoa hoc ky thuat giua Viet Nam voi Lao va Campuchia" (Declaration of the Standing Committee of the Council of Ministers at the conference on issues related to economic and cultural cooperation with Laos and Cambodia), PTT, h.s. 13410, 5–6.

102. Dang Thi, Chu nhiem Uy ban Hop tac Kinh te Van hoa voi Lao va Campuchia (Chairman of the Committee on Economic and Cultural Cooperation with Laos and Cambodia), 11/29/1984, gui Thuong vu Hoi dong Bo Truong (to the Standing Committee of the Council of Ministers), "Bao cao tinh hinh thuc hien hop tac kinh te, van hoa, khoa hoc-ky thuat giua nuoc ta voi hai nuoc ban va nhiem vu ke hoach nam 1985" (Report on the situation of implementing economic, cultural, technical, and scientific cooperation between our country and Laos and Cambodia and the tasks of planning for 1985), PTT, h.s. 1340, 7–8.

103. Doan Trong Truyen, Bo Truong Tong Thu ky Hoi dong Bo Truong (Chief of the General Secretariat of the Council of Ministers), So 999, 28/8/1985, Gui Anh To, Anh Lanh, Anh Tran Quynh (to Brother To [Prime Minister Pham Van Dong], Brother Lanh [unidentified], and Tran Quynh [Deputy Prime Minister and Vice-Chairman of the Council of Ministers]), PTT, h.s. 1340, 1–2.

104. PTT, h.s. 1340, Dang Thi, 14.

105. Ibid.

106. PTT, h.s. 1340, Doan Trong Truyen, 5. The Council of Ministers' decision was sent to the secretariat of the Party Central Committee, the Foreign Affairs Committee of the PCC, the State Planning Committee, and other offices of the Council of Ministers.

107. Ibid.

108. PTT, h.s. 1340, Dang Thi, 11.

109. Ibid., 12.

110. Ibid.

111. Ibid.

112. Ibid., 13.

113. Ibid.

114. Ibid.

115. Ibid.

116. Ibid.

117. Ibid., 15.

118. Ibid.

119. PTT, h.s. 13410, Doan Trong Truyen, 1–2.

120. Hoi Dong Bo Truong (Council of Ministers), "Quyet Dinh cua Hoi Dong Bo Truong ve viec xet duyet nhiem vu vien tro va hop tac kinh te van hoa va khoa hoc ky thuat voi CHDCND Lao va CHNH Campuchia trong nam 1985" (The Decision of the Council of Ministers regarding the aid and economic, cultural, and technical cooperation with the governments of Laos and Cambodia in 1985), PTT, h.s. 13414, 3–4.

121. Ibid., 4.

122. Ibid.

123. Ibid., 19.

124. Ibid., 20.

125. PTT, h.s. 1340, Dang Thi, 16.

126. Ibid.

127. PTT, h.s. 5595, 1. In actuality, Vietnam withdrew all its troops a year before scheduled.

128. Ibid.

129. Ibid., 2.

130. Ibid.

131. Ibid., 2–3.

132. PTT, h.s. 5607, 53.

133. Ibid., 55–56.

134. Ibid., 54.

135. Hoi dong Bo truong (Council of Ministers), "Cong van cua HDBT ve viec khen thuong 6 can bo lanh dao Campuchia nam 1986" (Letter of the Council of Ministers about awarding six leaders of Cambodia in 1986), 1/30/1986, QH, h.s. 5618, 1–3. The general secretary of the party, Heng Samrin, received a Gold Star medal. Five Ho Chi Minh medals went to the president of the National Assembly Chea Sim, chairman of the Council of Ministers and Minister of Foreign Affairs Hun Sen, chairman of the Party Organization Committee Say Phouthang, vice-chairman of the Council of Ministers and minister of defense Bou Thang, and vice-chairman of the Council of Ministers and minister of planning Chea Sot.

136. Gottesman, *Cambodia after the Khmer Rouge*, 276–77.

137. Co, "Hoi uc va Suy nghi," 54.

138. Ibid., 55–56. Members of the CP 87 team included Nguyen Phuong Vu (director of the China Department) and Tran Xuan Man (director of the Asia

Department). Trinh Xuan Lang was put in charge of the Cambodian issue, and Trang Quang Co was to provide direct guidance on Cambodian affairs.

139. Ibid., 75.

140. Ibid. Tran Quang Co cited Hun Sen's book in Vietnamese: Hun Xen, *10 nam qua trinh Campuchia (1979–1989)* (Hanoi: Vien Lich Su Quan Su Viet Nam, 2002).

141. Co, "Hoi uc va Suy nghi," 78.

142. Le Duan died in Hanoi on July 10, 1986, at the age of seventy-eight. The other three leaders were forced to leave the party and government due to old age and poor health after the Sixth Party Congress in December 1986.

Conclusion

1. See Cuong, *Lich su Vietnam*, 342–59.

2. See, for example, Bo Quoc Phong, *Lich su quan tinh nguyen*.

3. Brantly Womack, *Asymmetry and International Relationships* (New York: Cambridge University Press, 2016), 30–31.

4. For a detailed critique of David Kang's model of a China-centered hier-archical order, see Kosal Path, "The Duality of Vietnam's Resistance and Defer-ence to China," *Diplomacy and Statecraft* 29, no. 93 (2018): 499–521.

5. An inference I drew from an in-depth reading of a number of national security writings by contemporary Vietnamese diplomatic veterans and strat-egists: Nguyen Dy Nien, *Ho Chi Minh Thought on Diplomacy* (Hanoi: Gioi Pub-lishers, 2004); Tran Quang Co, *Hoi uc va Suy Nghi* (Memory and thought) (Hanoi: Unpublished memoir, 2003); Nguyen Tran Bat, *Tinh The va Giai Phap: Doi Thoai* (Circumstance and solution: A dialogue) (Hanoi: Nhan Xuat Ban Hoi Nhan Van, 2015); Duong Danh Dy, "Some Thoughts about China."

BIBLIOGRAPHY

Archival Sources

The number preceding each entry corresponds to the archival file (*ho so* [h.s.]) containing the documents cited. File codes PTT (Office of the Prime Minister) and QH (Office of the National Assembly) are used in the catalog of Luu Tru Quoc Gia 3 (Vietnamese National Archive No. 3).

After the initial full citation for a document in the notes, ensuing short citations include an abbreviation for the name of the collection (i.e., PTT, QH, BGD, or CCG), file numbers (and the title of a particular document if an archival file contains more than one document), and page numbers.

Office of the Prime Minister
(Phu Thu Tuong, PTT)

611—"Phuong huong, nhiem vu, muc tieu chu yeu cua ke hoach 5 nam 1976–1980 do Thu Tuong Pham Van Dong and Pho Thu tuong Le Thanh Nghi trinh bay tai Dai hoi Dang lan thu IV nam 1976" (The orientations, tasks, and main objectives of the five-year plan, 1976–1980, presented by Prime Minister Pham Van Dong and Deputy Prime Minister Le Thanh Nghi at the Fourth Party Congress in 1976), 1–99.

724—"De cuong phat bieu cua Pho Thu Tuong Le Thanh Nghi tai ky home thu nhat cua Uy Ban Phan Vung Kinh Te T. W. ngay 10/1/1977" (Draft of the fundamentals of Deputy Prime Minister Le Thanh Nghi's speech at the first meeting of the Central Economic Zoning Commission on October 1, 1977), 1–7.

786—"Ban trinh bay cua dong chi Le Thanh Nghi ve ke hoach nam 1978 va muc phan dau den nam 1980 o Hoi Nghi lan thu ba cua Ban Chap Hanh Trung Uong Dang" (Comrade Le Thanh Nghi's presentation on the 1978 [economic] plan and the level of collective endeavors through 1980 at the Third Conference of the Party Central Committee), 12/6/1977, 1–36.

787—"Bai noi chuyen cua Pho thu tuong Le Thanh Nghi tai hoi nghi can bo lanh dao cac co quan Trung uong, cac tinh, thanh pho ngay 5/12/1978 ve thuc hien ke hoach nam 1978 va ke hoach nam 1979" (Deputy Prime Minister Le Thanh Nghi's speech at the Party Central, Province, and City Leadership Conference on May 12, 1978), 1–11.

1340—Dang Thi, Chu nhiem Uy ban Hop tac Kinh te Van hoa voi Lao va Cam-puchia (Chairman of the Committee on Economic and Cultural Coopera-tion with Laos and Cambodia), 29/11/1984, gui Thuong vu Hoi dong Bo Truong (to the Standing Committee of the Council of Ministers). "Bao cao tinh hinh thuc hien hop tac kinh te, van hoa, khoa hoc-ky thuat giua nuoc ta voi hai nuoc ban va nhiem vu ke hoach nam 1985" (Report on the situa-tion of implementing economic, cultural, technical, and scientific coopera-tion between our country and Laos and Cambodia and the tasks of planning for 1985), 7–19.

1340—Doan Trong Truyen, Bo Truong Tong thu ky Hoi dong Bo Truong (Minister of the General Secretary of the Council of Ministers), So 999, 28/8/1985. "Gui Anh To, Anh Lanh, Anh Tran Quynh" (to Brother To [Prime Minister Pham Van Dong], Brother Lanh [unidentified], and Tran Quynh [Deputy Prime Minister and Vice-Chairman of the Council of Min-isters]), 1–2.

5575—Thu Truong Vo Dong Giang, K/T Bo Truong Bo Ngoai Giao (Foreign Affairs Vice-Minister Vo Dong Giang on behalf of the foreign affairs minis-ter), 19/4/1983, gui van phong Quoc hoi va Hoi dong Nha nuoc (sent to the office of National Assembly and the State Council). "Bao cao ket qua hoi nghi bat thuong Bo Truong ngoai giao Lao, Campuchia, Viet-Nam tai Phnom Penh, 12/4/1983" (Report on the results of the extraordinary sum-mit of foreign ministers of Laos, Cambodia, and Vietnam in Phnom Penh on April 12, 1983), No. 39/VP, 1–4.

5595—Hoang Bich Son, Thu Truong T/M Bo Truong Bo Ngoai Giao [Nguyen Co Thach] gui Hoi Dong Nha Nuoc va van phong Quoc Hoi (Vice-Minister of Foreign Affairs Hoang Bich Son on behalf of Foreign Affairs Minister [Nguyen Co Thach]), to the Council of State and National Assembly on 8/19/1985. "Bao cao cua Bo Ngoai Giao ve ket qua Hoi Nghi Bo Truong Ngoai giao Laos, Campuchia, and Viet-Nam lan thu 11 ngay 16/5/1985 tai Phnom Penh" (The Foreign Affairs Ministry's report on the results of the Eleventh Conference of Foreign Affairs Ministers of Laos, Cambodia, and Vietnam held on May 16, 1985, in Phnom Penh), 1–4.

8600—Pho Thu tuong Le Thanh Nghi gui Pho Thu tuong Ly Tien Niem 11/77 (Deputy Prime Minister Le Thanh Nghi to Vice-Premier Li Xiannian, 11/77). "Bao cao ket qua dam phan kinh te voi Trung Quoc nam 1976" (Re-port on economic negotiations with China in 1976), 1–3.

9061—Nguyen Co Thach, Bo truong Bo ngoai giao (Nguyen Co Thach, Minis-ter of Foreign Affairs). "Mot so tinh hinh ve hop tac kinh te giua Lien Xo va Dong Au voi cac nuoc phuong tay" (A number of situations about economic cooperation between the Soviet Union and Eastern Europe and other west-ern countries), September 1973, 1–12.

9599—Bo ngoai giao (Ministry of Foreign Affairs). "Bao cao cong tac 6 thang dau nam 1975 cua Bo ngoai giao" (Ministry of Foreign Affairs report on its work for the first six months of 1975), 1–10.

9689—Bao cao Dai Tieng Noi Viet Nam (Report on the Voice of Vietnam). "Giup do cach mang Campuchia" (Assistance to the Cambodian revolution), May 1975, 1–3.

9833—"Bao cao ket qua dam phan kinh te voi 8 nuoc xa hoi chu nghia cho 5 nam 1976–1980" (Report on the results of economic negotiations with eight socialist countries for the five-year [plan], 1976–1980), November 28, 1975, 1–25.

9833—"Bao cao tinh hinh cong tac sau thang dau nam 1976 cua Bo Ngoai Giao" (Ministry of Foreign Affairs first six months report of 1976), 1–18.

9833—Bo ngoai giao (Ministry of Foreign Affairs). "Bao cao tinh hinh va cong tac doi ngoai sau thang dau nam 1976" (Report on the foreign affairs situation and work for the first six months of 1976), 1–20.

9961—Bac Si Nguyen Tien Buu (Dr. Nguyen Tien Buu), Vien Sot Ret (Anti-malaria Institute), 11/18/1976. "Bao cao dot di cong tac tai Campuchia Dan chu tu ngay 1 thang 11 den ngay 16 thang 11, 1976" (Report on the trip to Democratic Kampuchea from 11/1 to 11/16/1976), 1–2.

10007—Ban Doi Ngoai, Ban Chap Hanh Trung Uong Dang Cong San Viet Nam (Foreign Affairs Committee of the Central Committee of the Communist Party of Vietnam), October 28, 1977. "Bao cao ve viec dong chi Saplin, Dai Su Lien Xo tai Viet Nam thong bao y kien chinh phu Lien Xo tra loi thu cua dong chi Pham Van Dong ve vien tro quan su cho Vietnam nam 1976–1980" (Report on Soviet ambassador Chaplin's conveyance of the Soviet government's reply to Comrade Pham Van Dong regarding military aid to Vietnam, 1976–80), 1–8.

10088—"Bao cao ket qua dam phan kinh te voi Trung Quoc nam 1976" (Report on the results of economic negotiations with China for 1976), August 31, 1975, 10–15.

10088—Ly Ban. "Bao cao tinh hinh lam viec voi Trung Quoc tu cuoi thang 8 den nay" (Report on the negotiations with China from the end of August to the present [November 1975]), 1–5.

10160—Bo Ngoai giao (Ministry of Foreign Affairs). "Bao cao Cong tac 6 Thang dau nam 1977 cua Bo Ngoai giao" (Ministry of Foreign Affairs report on its work for the first six months of 1977), 1–18.

10460—"Bien ban cuoc gap go giua Thu Tuong Pham Van Dong va Pho Thu Tuong Ly Tien Niem tai Bac kinh 10/6/1977" (Minutes of the meeting between Prime Minister Pham Van Dong and Vice-Premier Li Xiannian in Beijing on June 10, 1977), 1–20.

10461—"Chuong trinh chuyen di huu nghi o Trung Quoc cua dai dien Dang and Chinh phu, ngay 20 thang 11 nam 1977" (Program of the party and government delegation's visit to China, November 20, 1977), 4–24.

10461—Do Muoi to the Politburo and General Secretary Le Duan, December 7, 1976. "Bao cao ket qua lam viec voi d/c lanh dao Trung Quoc 5–6 thang 12 nam 1976" (Report on the results of working with Comrade Chinese leaders, December 5–6, 1976), 24–6.

10568—"Bai noi cua Pho Thu Tuong Le Thanh Nghi ve mot so viec can lam sau khi gia nhap HDTTKT [Hoi dong Tuong tro Kinh Te] ngay 20/7/1978" (Deputy Prime Minister Le Thanh Nghi's speech about a number of tasks after [Vietnam's] integration into the Council of Mutual Economic Assistance on July 20, 1978), 1–18.

10776—"Bao cao tinh hinh 6 thang dam phan ve bien gioi Viet Nam va Trung Quoc, 10/1977–3/1978" (Report on the situation of border negotiation for the past six months from October 1977 to March 1978), 1–6.

10776—Phan Hien, Bo Ngoai Giao ([Vice-Minister] Phan Hien, Ministry of Foreign Affairs), March 31, 1978. "Bao cao dam phan 6 thang 10/1977 to 3/1978" (Report on negotiations for six months from October 1977 to March 1978), 1–7.

11120—Bo Nong Nghiep (Ministry of Agriculture). "Ke hoach chi vien cho K de on dinh doi song cap bach cua nhan dan va hoi phuc san xuat 1979" (Plan to help Cambodia stabilize people's basic livelihoods and restore productivity in 1979), 1–29.

11353—Le Tuan, Truong Van Phong 6 (Le Tuan, head of Office 6 [of the Prime Minister's Office]). "Bao cao mot so van de trong cong tac K" (Report on a number of issues pertaining to our work in Cambodia), March 13, 1980, 1–12.

11353—Nguyen Mai, Chanh van phong Ban to chuc Ban chap hanh trung uong (Head of the Organization Committee Office of the Party Central Committee), Ban To Chuc No. 384 (Organization Committee No. 384), March 13, 1980, Kinh gui Dong chi Chu nhiem Van phong Phu thu tuong (to Comrade Chief of the Prime Minister's Office). "Ve viec dat khoan phu cap biet tieng Lao va Campuchia cho can bo nhan vien cua ta sang giup Ban" (About allocating allowances to learn Laotian and Cambodian languages for our cadres and officials who are assisting our friends [Cambodia and Laos]), 1.

11353—Tran Xuan Bach, Truong Ban B68 (head of the B68 committee), So 359/B68, February 26, 1980, kinh gui dong chi Pho Thu Tuong Do Muoi (to Deputy Prime Minister Do Muoi). "Ve viec bao dam cung cap vat chat cho cac Doan chuyen gia Viet Nam cong tac tai Campuchia" (About guaranteeing material supply for groups of Vietnamese experts working in Cambodia), 7–10.

11633—Nguyen Con, Truong doan Chuyen gia Kinh te va Van hoa (Chief of Economic and Cultural Experts), Phnom Penh, April 12, 1980. "Bao cao ke hoach vien tro kinh te nam 1980 Viet Nam KPC" (Report on Vietnam's economic assistance to Cambodia in 1980), 66–69.

11634—"Bao cao Anh Muoi (Report to Brother Muoi)," 6/23/1980, 9.

11634—"Chinh Phu C.H.X.H.C.N. Vietnam gui Hoi dong Cach mang Campuchia" (Government of the Socialist Republic of Vietnam to the Revolutionary Council of Kampuchea), March, 7, 1979, 34–35.

11634—"Danh muc hang hoa duoc cung cap khong hoan lai tu Lien Bang Cong hoa Xa hoi Chu nghia Xo Viet sang nuoc Cong Hoa Nhan Dan Campuchia trong nam 1980" (List of goods in nonrefundable aid from the Soviet Union to the People's Republic of Kampuchea in 1980), 65–67.

11634—"Danh muc hang hoa yeu cau Lien Xo vien tro bo sung cho Cong Hoa Nhan Dan Campuchia trong nam 1979" (List of goods [Vietnam] requested the Soviet Union to provide to the People's Republic of Kampuchea as supplementary nonrefundable aid in 1979), 44.

11634—"Danh muc hang vien tro cua Lien Xo cho Campuchia nam 1980 (Hiep dinh ky ket 5/2/1980)" (List of Soviet material aid to Cambodia for 1980 [Agreement concluded on February 5, 1980]), 22–25.

11634—Duong Van Dat, Thu truong Bo Tai Chinh gui Bo Truong Phu Thu Tuong Vu Tuan (Finance Vice-Minister Duong Van Dat to Chief of the Prime Minister's Office Vu Tuan). "Ve giao nhan, thanh toan, van chuyen hang vien tro K qua canh Viet Nam" (About delivery, payment, and shipment of aid to Cambodia via Vietnam), November 10, 1979, 62–66.

11634—I. A-ro-khi-pop (Ivan Arkhipov), Pho Chu Tich Hoi dong Bo truong Lien Xo (Vice-Chairman of the Council of Ministers of the Soviet Union) to Dong chi Pen-Xo-Van (Comrade Pen Sovann) on 6/16/1980, 11–14.

11634—Nguyen Van Dao, Thu Truong Bo Ngoai thuong (Vice-Minister of the Ministry of Foreign Trade). "Bao cao tom tat tinh hinh dam phan giua doan chuyen vien kinh te Lien Xo va Campuchia" (Brief report on the negotiations between the Soviet economic experts and their Cambodian counterparts), August 10, 1979, 59–61.

11634—"Quyet dinh Chinh phu Viet Nam ngay 23/12/1978 ve dot chi vien dau tien ve kinh te va hang hoa giup nhan dan giai phong khoi phuc lai doi song binh thuong" (The Vietnamese government's decision on December 23, 1978 to provide its first round of aid to the [Cambodian] people to restore and normalize their livelihood after liberation), 54.

12028—"Hiep dinh giua chinh phu cong hoa xa hoi chu nghia Viet Nam, Hoi dong Nhan dan Cach mang Kampuchea va chinh phu Lien bang Cong hoa xa hoi chu nghia Xo Viet ve phoi hop su giup do trong viec khoi phuc va xay dung o cong hoa nhan dan Kampuchea cac cong trinh ghi trong cac hiep dinh Kampuchea—Lien Xo" (Agreement between the government of the Socialist Republic of Vietnam, the People's Revolutionary Council of

Kampuchea, and the government of the Union of Soviet Socialist Republics about the coordination of assistance to the PRK's recovery and construction of projects signed in the agreement between the PRK and the Soviet Union), Phnom Penh, March 2, 1981, 26–27.

12028—"Hiep dinh thuong mai giua Chinh phu nuoc Cong hoa Xa hoi Chu nghia Viet Nam va Hoi dong Nhan dan Cach mang nuoc Cong hoa Nhan dan Kampuchea" (Agreement on trade between the government of the Socialist Republic of Vietnam and the People's Revolutionary Council of Kampuchea), Hanoi, May 2, 1981, 28–29.

12028—"Hiep dinh vien tro khong hoan lai giua Chinh phu nuoc Cong hoa Xa hoi Chu nghia Viet Nam va Hoi dong Nhan dan Cach mang nuoc Cong hoa Nhan dan Kampuchea" (Agreement on nonrefundable aid between the government of the Socialist Republic of Vietnam and the People's Revolutionary Council of Kampuchea), Hanoi, May 2, 1981, 31–32.

12589—"De cuong ve hop tac kinh te va khoa hoc ky thuat giua Viet Nam-Lao-Campuchia" (Proposal for economic, technical and scientific cooperation between Vietnam, Lao and Cambodia), 6/30/1982, 40–56.

12589—Nguyen Van Ich, Pho Chu Chiem Van Phong Hoi Dong Bo Truong (Nguyen Van Ich, vice-chief of the Office of the Council of Ministers), 2/9/1983. "Ve cu can bo sang giup Lao chuan bi hoi nghi cap cao 3 nuoc Dong Duong" (About sending offcials to assist Laos to prepare for the summit for the three Indochinese countries), 70.

12589—"Tap hop tai lieu ve hoi nghi cap chuyen vien kinh te 3 nuoc Dong Duong nam 1982–83" (Compilation of documents on conferences of economic experts of the three Indochinese Countries in 1982–83), 1–86.

12589—To nghien cuu, Uy ban Lien lac Kinh te voi Nuoc ngoai (Research Group of the Committee on Economic Relations with Foreign Countries) gui lanh dao UBLLKT voi Nuoc ngoai (sent to the leadership of the Committee on Economic Relations with Foreign Countries), 7/17/1982. "De an ve hop tac kinh te van hoa va khoa hoc ky thuat giua Viet Nam-Laos-Campuchia (de trinh BCT)" (Plan for economic, cultural, and scientific cooperation between Vietnam, Laos, and Cambodia [to be presented to the Politburo), 23–39.

12589—Van phong Hoi dong Bo truong gui Bo Ngoai giao va Uy ban Hop tac Kinh te Van hoa voi Lao va Campuchia (The Office of the Council of Ministers sent to the Ministry of Foreign Affairs and the Committee on Economic and Cultural Cooperation with Lao and Cambodia), July 17, 1982. "Ban goi y ve chuong trinh va noi dung hop tac kinh te, van hoa, khoa hoc ky thuat giua ba nuoc Dong Duong" (Suggestions concerning the program and content of economic, cultural, technical and scientific cooperation between the three Indochinese countries), 3–4.

12589—Vo Dong Giang, Uy vien Ban tru bi hoi nghi cap cao cua Vietnam ([Vice-Minister of Foreign Affairs] Vo Dong Giang, member of Vietnam's Preparatory Committee on the high-level summit), kinh gui Thuong vu Hoi Dong Bo Truong (to the Standing Committee of the Council of Ministers), December 27, 1982. "To trinh ve to chuc hoi nghi chuyen vien kinh te, van hoa, khoa hoc ky thuat de tru bi them cho hoi nghi cap cao 3 nuoc Lao-Campuchia-Viet Nam" (Proposal regarding the organization of a conference of economic, cultural and technological experts in additional preparation for the high-level summit of the three countries Laos, Cambodia and Vietnam), 69.

12594—Vo Dong Giang, Thu Truong Bo Ngoai giao (Vice-Minister of Foreign Affairs Vo Dong Giang), March 14, 1983. "Bao cao ve Hoi Nghi cap cao khong lien ket lan thu 7 o New Delhi" (Report on the Seventh Summit of the Non-aligned Movement in New Delhi), 70–91.

12594—Vo Nguyen Viet Dung, Chu Nhiem Van Phong Quoc Hoi va Hoi dong Nha Nuoc (chief of the Office of the National Assembly and the Council of State). "Bien ban phien hop 19 cua Hoi dong Nha nuoc ngay 29 va ngay 30 thang 3, 1983" (Minutes of the nineteenth meeting of the Council of State on March 29–30, 1983), 5–30.

13234—To Kinh te Doi ngoai, Hoi Dong Bo Truong, 3/1985, Gui Uy Ban Ke Hoach Nha Nuoc (Foreign Economic Relations Research Group of the Council of Ministers to the State Planning Commmittee, March 1985). "Bao cao cua To kinh te doi ngoai Hoi dong Bo truong ve tinh hinh va phuong huong phat trien quan he kinh te giua Viet Nam voi cac nuoc nam 1985" (Report of the Foreign Economic Relations Research Group of the Council of Ministers about the situation and direction of developing economic relations between Vietnam and other countries in 1985), no. 6b, 3/1985, 1–36.

13410—Doan Trong Truyen, Bo Truong Tong Thu ky Hoi dong Bo Truong (Minister of the General Secretary of the Council of Ministers), So 01-TB, 1/12/1985. "Thong bao ve Hoi nghi Thuong truc Hoi dong Bo truong ban ve mot so van de hop tac kinh te, van hoa, khoa hoc ky thuat giua Viet Nam voi Lao va Campuchia" (Declaration of the Standing Committee of the Council of Ministers at the conference on issues related to economic and cultural cooperation with Laos and Cambodia), 5–6.

13414—Hoi Dong Bo Truong (Council of Ministers), "Quyet Dinh cua Hoi Dong Bo Truong ve viec xet duyet nhiem vu vien tro va hop tac kinh te van hoa va khoa hoc ky thuat voi CHDCND Lao va CHNH Campuchia trong nam 1985" (The Decision of the Council of Ministers regarding the aid and economic, cultural, and technical cooperation with the governments of Laos and Cambodia in 1985), 2–4.

15796—Nguyen Van Ngoc, Pho Truong Ban Bien Gioi HDCP, Chi thi Ban Bien Gioi cua Hoi Dong Chinh Phu (Vice-Chairman of the Border Committee of the Council of Government), So 91 (Letter No. 91), 10/8/1976. "BG/tm kinh gui Uy Ban Nhan Dan cac tinh Gia Lai, Kun Tum, Dac Lac, Song Be, Tay Ninh, Long An, Dong Thap, An Giang, and Kien Giang" (To People's Committees at Gia Lai, Kun Tum, Dac Lac, Song Be, Tay Ninh, Long An, Dong Thap, An Giang, and Kien Giang provinces), 1–2.

15860—Chu Huy Man, Pho Bi Thu T/M Thuong Vu Quan Uy Trung Uong, van phong Dang Cong San Viet-Nam Ban Chap Hanh Trung Uong, No. 42-SL/TW, kinh gui cac dong chi trong Bo Chinh Tri, Ban Bi thu (Deputy secretary of the Standing Committee of the Military Central Commission, the Secretariat of the Central Committee of the Communist Party of Vietnam, to comrade leaders of the Politburo and the party), 8/28/1977. "Bao cao tinh hinh quan doi va cong tac quan su trong 6 thang qua" (Report on the military situation and military affairs in the past six months), 1–7.

15945—Vu Tuan, Bo Truong Phu Thu Tuong (Prime Minister's Office). "Chi Thi ve viec to chuc chon cat cong nhan, vien chuc Nha nuoc va quan nhan cach mang chet o cac tinh phia Nam" (Directive on the task of preparing burials for government employees and revolutionary soldiers who died in southern provinces), 12–13.

15969—"Bao cao so ket cong tac bien gioi nam 1976–77 cua Uy Ban Bien Gioi" (Border Commission summary report on border tasks in 1976–77), 1–20.

16028—Phuong Minh Nam, Pho Chu Nhiem Van Phong PTT (Phuong Minh Nam, vice-chief of the Prime Minister's Office), January 15, 1980. "Bao cao tong ket cong tac nam 1979" (Summary report of 1979 work), 4–9.

16028—Van Phong 8 (Office 8), February 15, 1980. "Chuong trinh qui I nam 1979" (Program for the first quarter of 1979), 1–3.

16049—Nguyen Van Bang, Ban Lien Lac Doi Ngoai tinh Kien Giang (Foreign Relations Committee of Kien Giang Province) gui den Ban Doi Ngoai TW va Bo Ngoai Giao (to the Foreign Affairs Committee of the Party Central Committee and the Ministry of Foreign Affairs). "Bao cao tong ket Quy II 1978" (Summary report for the second quarter of 1978), 12–20.

16137—Bo Ngoai Giao (Ministry of Foreign Affairs). "Ve tien cong ngoai giao va tranh thu du luan quoc te ve van de bien gioi Viet Nam-Campuchia" (On launching a diplomatic offensive and drawing the support of world opinion regarding the border issue between Vietnam and Cambodia), 15–22.

16137—Bo Tu Lenh CANDVT, Bo Noi Vu (Police Commission of the Ministry of the Interior), February 1978. "Bao cao tin nhan duoc ngay 5–6/2/1978" (Report on information received on February 5–6, 1978), 30–34.

16137—"Du luan the gioi ve Tuyen bo cua Chinh phu ta ve van de bien gioi Viet Nam-CPC" (World opinion concerning our government's declaration about the border issue between Vietnam and Cambodia, January 1, 1978), 23–29.

16137—Nguyen Duy Trinh, Bo Truong Bo Ngoai Giao, kinh gui Thu Tuong Chinh Phu (Minister of Foreign Affairs Nguyen Duy Trinh to Prime Minister [Pham Van Dong]). "Tiep theo bao cao cua Quan uy Trung uong, toi xin bao cao de xin chu truong ve tien cong ngoai giao va tranh thu du luan quoc te ve van de bien gioi Viet-Nam-Campuchia" (Following the Central Military Commission's report, I would like to report and ask for directions about diplomatic offensives and efforts to win world opinion about the border problem between Vietnam and Cambodia), 15–22.

16137—"Trich thu cua phong vien TTXVN tai Bac Kinh ngay 19/1/1978" (Note on the Vietnam News Agency report of January 19, 1978), 6–9.

16327—Bo Noi Thuong gui Phu Thu Tuong (Ministry of Internal Trade to the Prime Minister's Office). "Bao cao tinh hinh cong tac noi thuong phuc vu chien dau tu 03 den 10 thang 03, 1979" (Report on the situation of the Ministry of Internal Trade's work in support of the battle from 3 to 10 March, 1979), 63–65.

16327—Phu Thu Tuong (The Prime Minister's Office), gui Van phong Quoc hoi (sent to the National Assembly), March 18, 1979. "Bao cao cua van phong Phu Thu Tuong ve dot di cong tac tinh bien gioi phia bac va nhung viec can lam ngay de giai quyet hau qua chien tranh sau khi Trung Quoc rut nam 1979" (Report of the Prime Minister's Office about the trip to border provinces in the north and the immediate tasks to overcome the negative effects of the war after the Chinese troops withdrew in [March] 1979), 1–76.

16381—Binh Tam, Thu Truong Bo Giao Thong Van Tai (Binh Tam, Vice-Minister of Transport), Thu So 1118 BC/KH, 8/5/1980, gui Thu Tuong Chinh Phu, Uy Ban Ke Hoach Nha Nuoc, Bo Quoc Phong (to the Prime Minister, the State Planning Committee, and the Ministry of Defense, May 8, 1980). "Bao cao thuc hien QD 58-CP" (Report on the implementation of Directive 58-CP), 55–57.

16381—Bo Quoc Phong /Y Te, No. 49/QD-LNQPTY (Ministry of Defense/ Ministry of Health). "Quy dinh cua lien Bo Quoc Phong-Y Te ve viec thuc hien quyet dinh cua Hoi dong Chinh phu giao ke hoach san sang viec phuc vu quoc phong khi co chien tranh" (Directive of the Ministry of Defense/Health interministerial agreement on the implementation of the decision of the Council of Government regarding mobilization for national defense), 18–20.

16381—Pham Nien, Tong Cuc Truong Tong Cuc Buu Dien (Pham Nien, general director of the General Directorate of Telecommunications and Post), Thu So 657/KH (Letter 657/KH). "V/v bao cao ket qua thuc hien QD 58-CP to Thu Tuong Chinh Phu" (Report of the result of implementing Directive 58-CP), 20–21.

16381—Pho Thu Tuong To Huu, T/M Hoi Dong Chinh Phu (Deputy Prime Minister Tu Huu on behalf of the Council of Government), No. 44-CP,

2/11/1980. "Quyet dinh cua Hoi Dong Chinh Phu ve cong tac dong vien tuyen quan nam 1980" (Directive of the Council of Government about the tasks of mobilizing military conscripts in 1980), 1–5.

16381—Pho Thu Tuong To Huu, T/M Hoi dong Chinh Phu (Deputy Prime Minister To Huu on behalf of the Council of Government), 58-CP, February 11, 1980. "Quyet dinh cua Hoi Dong Chinh Phu ve viec giao ke hoach san sang dong vien phuc vu nhu cau quoc phong khi co chien tranh" (Directive of the Council of Government about planning and readiness to meet the needs of national defense when war breaks out), 5–6.

16381—Pho Thu Tuong To Huu (Deputy Prime Minister To Huu), So. 333-CP (Directive 333-CP). "Quyet dinh Cua Hoi Dong Chinh Phu ve cong tac tuyen quan dot II nam 1980" (Directive of the Council of Government concerning the tasks of military conscription in Round II in 1980), 7–9.

16381—Pho Thu Tuong To Huu (Deputy Prime Minister To Huu). "V/v tam hoan viec thuc hien ke hoach tuyen quan" (About postponing military conscription), 4–5.

16381—Phuong Minh Nam, Thu Truong Phu Thu Tuong (Vice-Minister of the Prime Minister's Office), So 4235-V8, October 7, 1980. "Thong bao tinh hinh thuc hien quyet dinh So 58-CP ngay 25/2/1980 cua Hoi Dong Chinh Phu ve viec giao ke hoach san sang dong vien phuc vu nhu cau khi co chien tranh" (Report on implementing Directive 58-CP on February 25, 1980, of the Council of Government regarding the mobilization plan to meet the needs [for national defense] when war breaks out), 18–19.

16381—Thu Truong Le Hoa (Vice-Minister Le Hoa), Bo Vat Tu (Ministry of Materials Supply), So 116 VT/HK, May 16, 1980. "V/v chuan bi kim khi phuc vu nhu cau quoc phong khi co chien tranh" (About preparing equipment to serve the needs of national defense), 65–67.

16381—Thu Truong Le Hoa (Vice-Minister Le Hoa), Thu So 716/VT-KR, April 2, 1980. "Bao cao thuc hien quyet dinh 58/CP cua Thu Tuong Chinh Phu" (Report on the implementation of Directive 58-CP of the prime minister), 62–64.

16381—Thu Truong Vu Xuan Chiem, T/M Bo Truong Bo Quoc Phong (Vice-Minister of Defense Vu Xuan Chiem on behalf of the minister of national defense), No. 1287/QP. "Bao cao tinh hinh thuc hien quyet dinh 58-CP ngay 2/25/1980 cua Hoi dong Chinh phu" (Report on the implementation of Directive 58 of the Council of Government on February 25, 1980), 39–44.

16381—Tran Phuong, Pho Chu Nhiem Uy Ban Ke Hoach Nha Nuoc, kinh gui Thu Tuong Chinh Phu, va kinh gui Bo Quoc Phong (Vice-Chairman of the State Planning Committee Tran Phuong to the prime minister of the government and a copy sent to the Ministry of National Defense). "Bao cao tinh hinh thuc hien Quyet dinh 58-CP cho Hoi dong Chinh phu ve viec san sang dong vien khi co chien tranh" (Report on the implementation of Directive

58-CP to the Council of Ministers about our readiness to mobilize for war),
No. 534 UB/VI, 3/5/1980, 113–18.

Office of the National Assembly
(Van Phong Quoc Hoi, QH)

2158—"Bai phat bieu cua Chu Tich Nguyen Huu Tho tai Hoi nghi Hiep thuong
Chanh tri Thong nhat To Quoc" (Speech of President Nguyen Huu Tho at
the National Reunification Political Conference) (undated), 1–30.

2354—"Bao cao cua Thu Tuong Pham Van Dong truoc ky hop thu tu—Quoc
Hoi Khoa VI, ngay 23/12/78 tai Hoi Truong Ba-Dinh Ha-Noi" (Prime Minister Pham Van Dong's report before the fourth session of the Sixth Plenum
of the National Assembly on December 23, 1978 at Ba-Dinh).

2354—Tran Huu Duc, Vien Truong Vien Kiem Sat Nhan Dan Toi Cao (Prosecutor general of the Supreme People's Procuracy of Vietnam), December
18, 1978. "Bao cao cua Vien Truong Vien Kiem Sat Nhan Dan Toi Cao
truoc Quoc Hoi Khoa VI, ky hop thu 4" (Report of the Supreme People's
Investigation Bureau during the Fourth Session of the Sixth Plenum of National Assembly), 25–52.

2374—Ban tap hop y kien cua dai bieu quoc Hoi trong Ky Hop Thu 5 Quoc hoi
Khoa VI (tu 28 den 30/5/1979) ve Bao cao Cua Hoi dong Chinh phu.
"Thang loi vi dai cua 2 chien tranh bao ve to quoc va nhiem vu cua toan dan
va toan quan doi ta truoc tinh hinh moi" (Collection of opinions of National Assembly members during the fifth session of the Sixth Plenum of
the National Assembly from 28 to 30 May 1979 concerning the Council of
Government's report entitled "The Great Victory of the Two Wars to Defend Our Motherland and the Duties of Our People and Military in the
New Situation"), 100–115.

2374—Dai tuong Vo Nguyen Giap, Uy vien Bo Chinh Tri Trung uong Dang,
Pho Thu tuong Chinh phu kiem bo truong Bo Quoc phong (General Vo
Nguyen Giap, member of the Politburo of the Party Central Committee and
deputy prime minister with the portfolio of minister of national defense).
Quoc Hoi Khoa VI, ky hop thu 5 (Sixth session of the Fifth Plenum of the
National Assembly), May 28, 1979. "Bao cao cua Hoi dong chinh phu ve
thang loi vi dai cua hai cuoc chien tranh bao ve To quoc va nhiem vu cua toan
dan va toan quan ta truoc tinh hinh moi" (Report of the Council of Government about the great victory of the two wars of defending our motherland and the duty of our people and army in the new situation), 1–59.

2374—"Dien Van Khai Mac, 5/24/1979" (Opening Remarks [by Truong Chinh]
on May 24, 1979), 1–23.

2374—Tran Dang Khoa. "Bao cao cua Uy ban thuong vu Quoc Hoi" (Report of
the Standing Committee of the National Assembly at the fifth session of the
Sixth Plenum of the National Assembly), May 24, 1979.

2378—"Phien hop sang 30/5/1979, Tham luan cua cac DBQH ve viec day manh san xuat, san sang chien dau, tang cuong dao tao can bo KHKT" (Session on the morning of March 5, 1979, speeches of National Assembly members about boosting [economic] production, preparing for battle, and enhancing and training technical cadres), 79–126.

5607—Nguyen Co Thach gui Van Phong Quoc Hoi (Ministry of Foreign Affairs to the National Assembly). "Bao cao ve tinh hinh the gioi va cong tac doi ngoai cua ta trong nam 1986" (Report on world affairs and our foreign policy in 1986 [Read at the National Assembly session in December 1986]), 1–57.

5618—Hoi dong Bo truong (Council of Ministers). "Cong van cua HDBT ve viec khen thuong 6 can bo lanh dao Campuchia nam 1986" (Letter of the Council of Ministers about awarding six leaders of Cambodia in 1986), 1/30/1986, 1–3.

11104—"Ket luan cua Anh Do Muoi tai Hoi nghi khoi phuc thu do Phnom Penh ngay 25–26/2/1979" (Conclusion of [Deputy Prime Minister] Do Muoi at the conference on reconstruction of the Phnom Penh capital on February 25–26, 1979), 65–69.

11104—Le Tuan, Phu Thu Tuong (Prime Minister's Office to [General Secretary] Le Duan), ban so 066 (report no. 066). "Giup do ban on dinh nhan dan, khoi phuc san xuat, tung buoc xay dung kinh te van hoa trong thoi gian truoc mat" (Help our [Cambodian] friends to stabilize people's [livelihoods], restore production, and gradually build the economy and culture in the immediate future), 1979, 1–12.

11104—Phu Thu Tuong (Prime Minister's Office), April 30, 1979. "Bao cao ve tinh hinh kinh te Campuchia sau ngay giai phong va nhung nhiem vu kinh te cap bach cua campuchia" (Report on the economic situation in Cambodia after liberation and Cambodia's urgent economic tasks), 36–52.

11104—Phu Thu Tuong (Prime Minister's Office), So 88/TTg., March 14, 1979. "Quyet dinh cua Thu Tuong Chinh Phu ve nhiem vu van chuyen va dam bao giao thong trong thoi gian truoc mat" (The prime minister's decision regarding the task of transporting and guaranteeing transportation in the weeks and months ahead), 13–20.

Ministry of Education
(Bo Giao Duc, BGD)

146—Cong Hoa nhan dan Campuchia, Hoi Dong Nhan Dan Cach Mang (People's Republic of Kampuchea, People's Revolutionary Council of Kampuchea). "Chi thi ve cong tac giao duc trong thoi gian truoc mat" (Directive regarding the immediate educational task), 1–12.

153—A40 Doan Chuyen Gia Giao Duc (A40, Education Specialist Group), June 7, 1979. "Bao cao mot so net ve tinh hinh va cong tac giao duc truoc mat hien nay can giup Ban" (Report on a number of observations and the situation of our immediate educational tasks to help our friends), 1–6.

153—"Bao cao so bo ve tinh hinh giao duc Phnom Penh sau 7/1/79 cua doan khao sat giao duc thanh pho Ho Chi Minh" (A preliminary report about the situation of education in Phnom Penh after January 7, 1979, by the Education Inspection Group of Ho Chi Minh City), 157–60.

161—A40 Doan Chuyen Gia Giao Duc (A40, Education Specialist Group), January 26, 1981. "Bao cao so ket cong tac chuyen gia giao duc tinh, thanh pho tai Kampuchea" (Report on the work of education specialists in provinces and cities in Cambodia), 88–109.

477—Bo Giao Duc (Ministry of Education). "Bao cao tong ket 10 nam hop tac va giup nganh giao duc Campuchia" (Summary report on the ten-year cooperation with and assistance to Cambodia in the field of education), 1–57.

Department of Foreign Specialists
(Cuc Chuyen Gia, CCG)

2228—"Bao cao tinh hinh cong tac doi voi chuyen gia trong thoi gian qua va nhung van de can giai quyet de cai tien cong tac doi voi chuyen gia nuoc ngoai" (Report on our work with foreign specialists over the years and problems to be resolved in order to improve our work with them), 1–25.

2228—"Bao cao ve tinh hinh quan ly va su dung chuyen gia nuoc ngoai nam 1976" (Report on the management and use of foreign specialists for 1976), 31–35.

2228—"De cuong kiem diem cong tac doi voi chuyen gia trong thoi gian qua va nhung van de cap bach can giai guyet de cai tien cong tac doi voi chuyen gia nuoc ngoai" (Draft of the fundamentals of our work with foreign specialists over the past years and urgent problems to be resolved to improve our work with foreign specialists), 26–30.

2399—"Bao cao ve tinh hinh quan ly va su dung chuyen gia nuoc ngoai nam 1977" (Report on the management and use of foreign specialists for 1977), 1–35.

National Archives, Phnom Penh, Cambodia

"Excerpts of Speech by Wang Shang Rhung [Wang Shangrong], Deputy-Chief of the General Staff of the Chinese Army at the Talks with Son Sen (6/2/1976)." Phnom Penh, National Archives, file 31, 38–40.

Cambodian Secondary Sources

Pen Sovann and Neang Savun. *Chi-veak Pravoat sang-kheb Noeng Bupahet Chiet Mieto-phum kampuchea* (Brief biography and national cause). Seattle: Khmer Vision Publishing, 2002.

Vietnamese Secondary Sources

Ban Nghien Cuu Lich Su Ngoai Giao (Diplomatic History Research Committee). *Van dung tu tuong doi ngoai Ho Chi Minh thoi ky hoi nhap quoc te* (The use of Ho Chi Minh's diplomatic thought in the era of international integration). Hanoi: Nha Xuat Ban Chinh Tri Quoc Gia, 2009.

Bo Quoc Phong (Ministry of National Defense). *Nganh tai chinh quan doi nhan dan Viet Nam: 50 nam xay dung, phuc vu va truong thanh* (Finance branch of the Vietnamese People's Army: Fifty years of construction, services, and growth). Hanoi: Nhan Xuat Ban Quan Doi Nhan Dan, 1996. Luu hanh noi bo (internally circulated only).

Bo Quoc Phong, Vien Lich Su Quan Su Viet Nam (Military History Institute of Vietnam, Ministry of National Defense). *Lich su quan tinh nguyen va chuyen gia quan su Viet Nam giup cach mang Campuchia (1978–1989)* (A history of Vietnam's volunteer army and military specialists' assistance to the Cambodian revolution, 1978–1989). Hanoi: Nha Xuat Ban Quan Doi Nhan Dan, 2010. Luu hanh noi bo (internally circulated only).

———. *Lich su khang chien chong My cuu nuoc, 1954–1975* (History of anti-American resistance and national liberation, 1954–1975). Vols. 6 and 9. Hanoi: Nha Xuat Ban Chinh Tri Quoc Gia, 2013.

Cuc Van Tai, Tong Cuc Hau Can (Department of Transportation of the General Logistics Department). *Bien nien su kien van tai quan su, 1975–1995* (Factual records of military transport, 1975–1995). Hanoi: Nha Xuat Ban Quan Doi Nhan Nhan, 1999.

Cuong, Tran Duc, Vien Su Hoc, Vien Han Lam Khoa Hoc Xa Hoi Vietnam (Institute of History, Vietnam Academy of Social Science). *Lich su Vietnam, Tap 14: Tu nam 1975 den nam 1986* (Vietnam's history, vol. 14: 1975 to 1986). Hanoi: Nhan Xuat Ban Khoa Hoc Xa Hoi, 2017.

Dang Uy-Chi Huy Trung Doan Bo Binh 1 (Party Committee and Command of Infantry Battalion 1). *Lich su Trung Doan Bo Binh 1 Su Doan 330, Quan Khu 9, 1963–2003* (History of Infantry Battalion 1, Division 330, of Military Region 9, 1963–2003). Hanoi: Nha Xuat Ban Quan Doi Nhan Dan, 2005. Luu hanh noi bo (internally circulated only).

Duong Danh Dy. "Vai suy ngam ve Trung Quoc" (Some thoughts about China). September 6, 2006. Available at http://www.thoidai.org/ThoiDai8/200608_DuongDanhDy.htm]

Ho Son Dai, ed. *Lich Su Quan Doan 4, 1974–2004* (History of the Fourth Army Corps). Hanoi: Nha Xuat Ban Quan Doi Nhan Dan, 2004. Luu hanh noi bo (internally circulated only).

Hun Xen. *10 nam qua trinh Campuchia (1979–1989)*. Hanoi: Vien Lich Su Quan Su Viet Nam, 2002.

Huy Duc. *Ben Thang Cuoc I: Giai Phong* (The winning side, part 1: Liberation). Los Angeles: OsinBook, 2012.

———. *Ben Thang Cuoc II: Quyen Binh* (The winning side, part 2: Power). Sai-gon: OsinBook, 2012.

Le Duan. *Bao cao chinh tri cua ban chap hanh trung uong Dang tai dai hoi dai bieu toan quoc lan thu IV* (Political report of the Party Central Committee at the Fourth Party Congress). Hanoi: Nha Xuat Ban Su That, 1977.

———. *Cach Mang Xa Hoi Chu Nghia o Viet Nam* (Socialist revolution in Viet-nam). Hanoi: Nha Xuat Ban Su That, 1980.

Le Duc Anh. *Cuoc doi va su nghiep cach Mang (hoi ky)* (Life and the revolu-tionary profession [memoir]). Hanoi: Nha Xuat ban Chinh tri Quoc gia, 2015.

———. *Quan Doi Nhan Dan Viet Nam va Nhiem Vu Quoc Te Cao Ca Tren Dat Ban Campuchia* (People's Army of Vietnam and its lofty international duty in Cambodian territory). Hanoi: Nxb QDND, 1986.

Le Duc Tho. *Thuc hien mot su chuyen bien sau sac ve to chuc nham tang cuong lanh dao va quan ly ve moi mat nhat la kinh te* (Achieve organizational transformation to strengthen leadership and management of all fields, es-pecially the economy). Hanoi: Nha Xuat Ban Su That, 1983.

Ngo Dien. *Campuchia nhin lai va suy nghi* (Cambodia: Revisit and reflect). Hanoi: Unpublished memoir, 1992.

Ngo Thi Thanh Tuyen. "Lich su chien tranh chong Khome Do xam luoc Viet Nam tren huong Tay Nam" (History of the war against the Khmer Rouge invasion in southwestern Vietnam). MA thesis, Truong Dai Hoc Khoa Hoc Xa Hoi va Nhan Van, Dai hoc Quoc gia Thanh Pho Ho Chi Minh (Univer-sity of Social Sciences and Humanities, Vietnam National University, Ho Chi Minh City), 2008.

Nguyen, Van Hong. *Cuoc chien tranh bat buoc* (A necessary war). Hanoi: Nha Xuat Ban Quan Doi Nhan Dan, 2013.

Nguyen Co Thach. "Hiep Dinh Paris Voi So Nghiep Giai phong mien nam." In *Mat Tran Ngoai Giao Voi Cuoc Dam Phan Paris ve Viet Nam* (The diplo-matic front at the Paris negotiations about Vietnam), edited by Bo Ngoai Giao. 2nd ed. Hanoi: Nha Xuat Ban Chinh Tri Quoc Gia-Su That, 2015.

Nguyen Dinh Bin. *Ngoai Giao Viet Nam, 1945–2000* (Vietnam's diplomacy, 1945–2000). Hanoi: Nhan Xuat Ban Chinh Tri Quoc Gia, 2015.

Nguyen Dy Nien. *Tu Tuong Ngoai Giao Ho Chi Minh* (Ho Chi Minh's thought on diplomacy). Hanoi: Nha Xuat Ban Chinh Tri Quoc Gia, 2009.

———. *Ho Chi Minh Thought on Diplomacy.* Hanoi: Gioi Publishers, 2004.

Nguyen Huy Toan, Vu Tang Bong, Nguyen Huy Thuc, Nguyen Viet Binh, and Nguyen Minh Duc. *Su that ve nhung lan xuat quan cua Trung Quoc va quan he Viet-Trung* (The truth about the Chinese military deployments and China-Vietnam relations). Da Nang: Nha Xuat Ban Da Nang, 1996.

Nguyen Tran Bat. *Tinh The va Giai Phap: Doi Thoai* (Circumstance and solu-tion: A dialogue). Hanoi: Nhan Xuat Ban Hoi Nhan Van, 2015.

Pham Chung. "Anh Le Duc Tho voi nghia vu quoc te giup ban Campuchia (hoi ky)" (Comrade Le Duc Tho and his international duty to assist Cambodia [memoir]). In *Le Duc Tho, nguoi cong san kien cuong nha lanh dao tai nang* (Le Duc Tho, an ardent socialist and talented leader), edited by Van Duc Thanh, 671–75. Hanoi: Nha Xuat Ban Chinh Tri Quoc Gia, 2011.

Pham Gia Duc and Pham Quang Dinh, eds. *Lich Su Quan Doan 2, 1974–1994* (History of the Second Corps, 1974–1994). Hanoi: Nha Xuat Ban Quan Doi Nhan Dan, 2004. Book internally circulated within the army, not for sale.

Pham Van Dong. *Phuong huong, Nhiem vu va Muc Tieu Chu Yeu cua Ke hoach 5 nam, 1976–1980* (Orientation, tasks, and main objectives of the five-year plan, 1976–80). Hanoi: Nhan Xuat Ban Su That, 1977.

Sa Luc and Man Luc (Sa Li and Min Li). *9 lan xuat quan lon cua Trung Quoc* (Nine great military expeditions of China). Sichuan, China: Nxb. Van Nghe Tu Xuyen, 1992.

Tran Quang Co. *Hoi uc va Suy nghi* (Memory and thought). Hanoi: Unpublished memoir, 2003.

Van Kien Dang Toan Tap (Collected party documents), 54 vols. Hanoi: Chinh Tri Quoc Gia, 1999–2007.

Vien Lich Su Quan Su Vietnam, Bo Quoc Phong (Institute of Military History, Ministry of Defense). *Lich su khang chien chong My cuu nuoc* (History of resistance against the United States and national salvation). Vol. 9. Hanoi: Nhan Xuat Ban Chinh Tri Quoc Gia, 2013.

Vo Nguyen Giap. *Chien tranh giai phong dan toc va chien tranh bao ve to quoc* (War of national liberation and war of defending the nation). Hanoi: Nha Xuat Ban Su That, 1979.

Vu Duong Ninh. *Lich su quan he doi ngoai Viet Nam, 1940–2010* (History of Vietnam's foreign relations, 1940–2010). Hanoi: Nha Xuat Ban Chinh Tri Quoc Gia, 2015.

Secondary Sources in English

Anderson, Desaix. *American in Hanoi: America's Reconciliation with Vietnam.* Norwalk, CT: EastBridge, 2002.

Asselin, Pierre. *Hanoi's Road to the Vietnam War, 1954–1965.* Berkeley: University of California Press, 2013.

Becker, Elizabeth. *When the War Was Over: Cambodia and the Khmer Rouge Revolution.* New York: Public Affairs, 1986.

Beresford, Malenie, and Dang Phong. *Economic Transition in Vietnam: Trade and Aid in the Demise of a Centrally Planned Economy.* Cheltenham: Edward Elgar, 2000.

Burchett, Wilfred. *The China-Cambodia-Vietnam Triangle.* Chicago: Vanguard Books, 1981.

Chanda, Nayan. *Brother Enemy: The War after the War, a History of Indochina since the Fall of Saigon.* Orlando, FL: Harcourt Brace Jovanovich, 1983.

Chen, King C. *China's Wars with Vietnam, 1979*. Stanford, CA: Hoover Institution Press, 1987.

Chinh, Truong. *On Kampuchea*. Hanoi: Foreign Languages Publishing House, 1980.

Ciorciari, John. "The Balance of Great-Power Influence in Contemporary Southeast Asia." *International Relations of the Asia-Pacific* 9 (2009): 157–96.

Del Testa, David W. "'Imperial Corridor': Association, Transportation, and Power in French Colonial Indochina." *Science, Technology, and Society* 4, no. 2 (1999): 319–54.

Dutton, George, Jayne Werner, and John Whitmore, eds. *Sources of Vietnamese Tradition*. New York: Columbia University Press, 2012.

Elliott, David W. P. *Changing Worlds: Vietnam's Transition from Cold War to Globalization*. New York: Oxford University Press, 2012.

———, ed. *The Third Indochina Conflict*. Boulder, CO: Westview Press, 1981.

Fforde, Adam, and Stefan de Vylder. *From Plan to Market: The Economic Transition in Vietnam*. Boulder, CO: Westview Press, 1996.

Goscha, Christopher. *Vietnam: A New History*. New York: Basic Books, 2016.

Gottesman, Evan. *Cambodia after the Khmer Rouge: Inside the Politics of Nation Building*. Chiang Mai, Thailand: Silkworm Books, 2003.

Hagan, Joe D. "Domestic Political Explanations in the Analysis of Foreign Policy." In *Foreign Policy Analysis: Continuity and Change in Its Second Generation*, edited by Laura Neack, Jeanne A. K. Hey, and Patrick J. Haney, 117–43. Englewood Cliffs, NJ: Prentice Hall, 1995.

Han, Xiaorong. "From Resettlement to Rights Protection: The Collective Actions of the Refugees from Vietnam in China since the late 1970s." *Journal of Chinese Overseas* 10 (2014): 197–219.

Kang, David. *East Asia before the West: Five Centuries of Trade and Tribute*. New York: Columbia University Press, 2010.

Kerkvliet, Benedict J. Tria. *The Power of Everyday Politics: How Vietnamese Peasants Transformed National Policy*. Ithaca, NY: Cornell University Press, 2005.

Khoo, Nicholas. *Collateral Damage: Sino-Soviet Rivalry and the Termination of the Sino-Vietnamese Alliance*. New York: Colombia University Press, 2011.

Kiernan, Ben. *How Pol Pot Came to Power: Colonialism, Nationalism, and Communism in Cambodia, 1930–1975*. 2nd ed. New Haven, CT: Yale University Press, 2004.

———. "Myth, Nationalism, and Genocide." *Journal of Genocide Research* 3, no. 2 (2001): 187–206.

———. *The Pol Pot Regime: Race, Power, and Genocide in Cambodia under the Khmer Rouge, 1975–1979*. 3rd ed. New Haven, CT: Yale University Press, 2008.

Le Hong Hiep. "Vietnam's Hedging Strategy against China since Normalization." *Contemporary Southeast Asia* 35, no. 3 (2013): 333–68.

Liu Caiyu. "Appointment of the New Chief to Raise the Military's Combat Ability: Expert." *Global Times*, August 27, 2017.

Luu, Van Loi. *50 Years of Vietnamese Diplomacy, 1945–1995*. Vol. 1: *1945–1975*.
Hanoi: The Gioi Publisher, 2000.

Marr, David G. "Vietnamese, Chinese, and Overseas Chinese during the Chinese Occupation of Northern Indochina (1945–1946)." *Chinese Southern
Diaspora Studies* 4 (2010): 129–39.

Merrit, Anna C., Daniel A. Affron, and Benoi Monin. "Moral Self-Licensing:
When Being Good Frees Us to Be Bad." *Social and Personality Psychology* 4,
no. 5 (2010): 344–57.

Mertha, Andrew. *Brothers in Arms: Chinese Aid to the Khmer Rouge, 1975–
1979*. Ithaca, NY: Cornell University Press, 2014.

Morris, Stephen J. "The Soviet-Chinese-Vietnamese Triangle in the 1970s: The
View from Moscow." In *Behind the Bamboo Curtain: China, Vietnam, and
the World beyond Asia*, edited by Priscilla Roberts, 405–49. Stanford, CA:
Stanford University Press, 2006.

———. *Why Vietnam Invaded Cambodia: Political Culture and the Causes of
War*. Stanford, CA: Stanford University Press, 1999.

Mosyakov, Dmitry. "The Khmer Rouge and the Vietnamese Communists: A
History of Their Relations as Told in the Soviet Archives." In *Genocide in
Cambodia and Rwanda*, edited by Susan E. Cook, 54–94. New Haven, CT:
Yale Genocide Studies Program, 2004.

Ngo Vinh Long. "Reform and Rural Development: Impact on Class, Sectoral,
and Regional Inequalities." In *Reinventing Vietnamese Socialism: Doi Moi in
Comparative Perspective*, edited by William S. Turley and Mark Selden,
165–208. Boulder, CO: Westview Press, 1993.

Nguyen Hai Hong. "Resilience of the Communist Party of Vietnam's Authoritarian Regime since Doi Moi." *Journal of Current Southeast Asian Affairs* 35,
no. 2 (2016): 31–55.

Nguyen, Thanh Nhan. *Away from Home Season: The Story of a Vietnamese Volunteer Veteran in Cambodia*. Midtown, DE: By the author, 2010.

Nguyen, Lien-Hang T. *Hanoi's War*. Chapel Hill: University of North Carolina
Press, 2012.

Nguyen, Thi Binh. *Family, Friends, and Country*. Hanoi: Tri Thuc Publishing
House, 2015.

Nguyen, Van Canh. *Vietnam under Communism, 1975–1982*. Stanford, CA:
Hoover Institution Press, 1985.

Niehaus, Marjorie. "Vietnam 1978: The Elusive Peace." *Asian Survey* 19, no. 1
(1979): 85–94.

Norén-Nilsson, Astrid. *Cambodia's Second Kingdom: Nation, Imagination, and Democracy*. Ithaca, NY: Southeast Asia Program, Cornell University, 2016.

Okorokov, Alexander. *Nhung cuoc chien tranh bi mat cua Lien Xo* (The Soviet Union's secret wars). Moscow: Nxb. Yauza Eksmo, 2008.

Path, Kosal. "China's Economic Sanction against Vietnam, 1975–78." *China Quarterly* 212 (December 2012): 1040–58.

————. "The Duality of Vietnam's Deference and Resistance to China." *Diplomacy and Statecraft* 29, no. 93 (2018): 499–521.

————. "The Sino-Vietnamese Dispute over Territorial Claims, 1974–78: Vietnamese Nationalism and Its Consequences." *International Journal of Asian Studies* 8, no. 2 (2011): 189–220.

Paul, T. V. *Asymmetric Conflicts: War Initiation by Weaker Powers*. New York: Cambridge University Press, 1994.

Pelley, Patricia. "The History of Resistance and the Resistance to History in Post-colonial Constructions of the Past." In *Essays into Vietnamese Past*, edited by K. W. Taylor and John K. Whitmore, 232–45. Ithaca, NY: Southeast Asia Program, Cornell University, 1995.

Porter, Gareth. *Vietnam: The Politics of Bureaucratic Socialism*. Ithaca, NY: Cornell University Press, 1993.

————. "Vietnamese Policy and the Indochina Crisis." In *The Third Indochina Conflict*, edited by David W. P. Elliott, 69–138. Boulder, CO: Westview Press, 1981.

Putnam, Robert D. "Diplomacy and Domestic Politics: The Logic of Two-Level Games." *International Organization* 42, no. 3 (Summer 1998): 427–69.

Quinn-Judge, Sophie. "Victory on the Battlefield, Isolation in Asia: Vietnam's Cambodia Decade, 1979–1989." In *The Third Indochina War: Conflict between China, Vietnam, and Cambodia, 1972–1979*, edited by Odd Arne Westad and Sophie Quinn-Judge, 207–30. Abingdon, NY: Routledge, 2006.

Richardson, Sophie. *China, Cambodia, and the Five Principles of Peaceful Coexistence*. New York: Columbia University Press, 2010.

Ripsman, Norrin M., Jeffrey W. Taliaferro, and Steven E. Lobell. *Neoclassical Realist Theory of International Politics*. New York: Oxford University Press, 2016.

Ross, Robert S. *The Indochina Triangle: China's Vietnam Policy, 1975–79*. New York: Columbia University Press, 1988.

Slocomb, Margaret. *The People's Republic of Kampuchea, 1979–1989: The Revolution after Pol Pot*. Chiang Mai, Thailand: Silkworm Books, 2003.

Strangio, Sebastian. *Hun Sen's Cambodia*. New Haven, CT: Yale University Press, 2014.

Taliaferro, Jeffrey W. "State Building for Future Wars: Neoclassical Realism and the Resource-Extractive State." *Security Studies* 15, no. 3 (July–September 2006): 464–95.

Vogel, Ezra R. *Deng Xiaoping and the Transformation of China*. Cambridge, MA: Belknap Press of Harvard University Press, 2011.

Vu, Hoang Minh. "Facing the Inevitable? Vietnam's Decision to Invade Cambodia, 1977–78." B.Sc. thesis, International Relations and History, London School of Economics and Political Science, 2014.

Vu, Tuong. *Vietnam's Communist Revolution: The Power and Limits of Ideology*. New York: Cambridge University Press, 2016.

Vuving, Alexander. "Strategy and Evolution of Vietnam's China's Policy: A Changing Mixture of Pathways." *Asian Survey* 46, no. 6 (November–December 2006): 805–24.

Wade, Geoff. "Engaging with the South: Ming China and Southeast Asia in the Fifteenth Century." *Journal of the Economic and Social History of the Orient* 51 (2008): 578–638.

Westad, Odd Arne. "Introduction." In *The Third Indochina War: Conflict between China, Vietnam, and Cambodia, 1972–79*, edited by Odd Arne Westad and Sophie Quinn-Judge, 1–11. London: Routledge, 2006.

Westad, Odd Arne, and Sophie Quinn-Judge, eds. *The Third Indochina War: Conflict between China, Vietnam, and Cambodia, 1972–79*. London: Routledge, 2006.

Womack, Brantly. *Asymmetry and International Relationships*. New York: Cambridge University Press, 2016.

———. *China and Vietnam: The Politics of Asymmetry*. New York: Cambridge University Press, 2006.

Wurfel, David. "*Doi Moi* in Comparative Perspective." In *Reinventing Vietnamese Socialism*, edited by William S. Turley and Mark Selden, 19–52. Boulder, CO: Westview Press, 1993.

Zhang, Shu Guang. *Beijing's Economic Statecraft during the Cold War, 1949–1991*. Washington, DC: Woodrow Wilson Center Press, 2014.

Zhang, Xiaoming. *Deng Xiaoping's Long War: The Military Conflict between China and Vietnam, 1979–1991*. Chapel Hill: University Press of North Carolina, 2015.

Zubok, Vladislav M. *A Failed Empire: The Soviet Union in the Cold War from Stalin to Gorbachev*. Chapel Hill: University of North Carolina Press, 2007.

Newspapers and Periodicals

Anh, Viet. "Tong bi thu: 'Dien bien chinh tri the gioi vuot xa du bao thong thuong.'" *VNExpress*, August 13, 2018.

"Bon bai hoc tu cuoc chien chong Trung Quoc xam luoc nam 1979" (Four lessons from the war against China's invasion in 1979). *VNExpress*, February

18, 2019. https://vnexpress.net/40-nam-cuoc-chien-bao-ve-bien-gioi-phia
-bac/bon-bai-hoc-tu-cuoc-chien-chong-trung-quoc-xam-luoc-nam-1979
-3882107.html.

"Cambodia-China Relationship a 'Role Model' in Modern International Relations: Cambodian Ruling Party Lawmaker." Editorial. *Xinhua Economic
News*, January 10, 2018.

Doan, Xuan Loc. "Breaking a Taboo: Hanoi Recalls War with China." *Asia
Times*, February 23, 2017.

Erlanger, Steven. "Vietnam's Vietnam: Scars from Cambodia." *New York Times*,
April 9, 1989.

Lay, Samean. "Vietnam 'Not My King': PM." *Phnom Penh Post*, August 2, 2016.

Le Trong Tan. "Hai khau then chot cua cong tac quan su dia Phuong" (Two key
elements in local military work). *Tap Chi Cong San* (Communist Review),
September 1978, 8–14.

Nguyen, Dat Phat. "Chien Tranh 1979: Gay suc ep voi TQ, Lien Xo dat 6 quan
khu trong tinh trang san sang chien dau" (The 1979 war: Pressure on
China—the Soviet Union dispatched six military regions ready for war
[with China]). *SOHA.vn*, February 18, 2019. http://soha.vn/chien-tranh-1979
-gay-suc-ep-voi-tq-lien-xo-dat-6-quan-khu-trong-tinh-trang-san-sang
-chien-dau-20190217163738078.htm.

Ono, Yukako. "Hun Sen's 'Flawed' Victory Puts Cambodian Businesses at Stake."
Nikkei Asian Review, July 31, 2018.

Pham, Lan Huong, Central Commission for Foreign Relations. "Local External
Relations' Contributions to Socioeconomic Development and International
Integration." *Tap Chi Cong San* (Communist Review), June 21, 2016. http://
english.tapchicongsan.org.vn/Home/Foreign-Relations-and-Interna
tional-Intergration/2016/600/Local-external-relations-contributions-to
-socioeconomic-development-and-international-integration.aspx.

Phan, Hong Ha. "Chien tranh bien goi 1979: 30 tau chien Lien Xo da san sang o
Bien Dong" (The 1979 war: Thirty Soviet warships ready [for war] in the
East Sea). *SOHA.vn*, February 18, 2019. http://soha.vn/chien-tranh-bien-gioi
-1979-30-tau-chien-lien-xo-da-san-sang-o-bien-dong-201902180037
17671.htm.

"PM Phuc Joins Thousands at Dong Da Festival." *Voice of Vietnam*, February 9,
2019. https://english.vov.vn/society/pm-phuc-joins-thousands-in-attend
ance-at-dong-da-festival-391842.vov#p5.

To, Lan Huong. "Thai do cua TBT Le Duan voi lanh dao Trung Quoc" (General Secretary Le Duan's attitude toward Chinese leaders). *SOHA.vn*,
February 16, 1979. http://soha.vn/thai-do-cua-tbt-le-duan-voi-lanh-dao
-trung-quoc-truoc-trong-va-sau-chien-tranh-bien-gioi-20190216095400
546.htm.

"A Tribute to Vietnam's 'Buddha Army' Who Fought and Died in Cambodia." Editorial. *Tuoi Tre News*, January 7, 2017. http://tuoitrenews.vn/politics/38919/a-tribute-to-vietnams-buddhas-army-that-fought-and-died-for-cambodians.

Willemyns, Alex. "Cambodia Blocks ASEAN Statement on South China Sea." *Cambodia Daily*, July 25, 2016.

Zhang, Tao. "Cambodian Prime Minister: Cambodia Is Not Vietnam's Puppet." *China Military Online*, August 31, 2016. http://english.chinamil.com.cn/view/2016-08/31/content_7234553.htm.

INDEX

A40 (Vietnamese economic, educational, and cultural advisors), 8, 11, 117, 133, 138–39
A50 (education advisors), 138
agricultural sector, 38–39
air force base (Cambodia), 61
alliance: Sino-American, 32–33; Sino-Cambodian, 4, 5, 19, 20, 55–56, 62, 77; Soviet-Vietnamese, 13, 16, 20, 48–49, 55, 77; Vietnamese–Khmer Rouge, 56
Anderson, Desaix, 32
Arkhipov, Ivan, 149
Asselin, Pierre, 8
Assembly, 98, 100–101, 107, 123
Association of Southeast Asian Nations (ASEAN), 9, 17, 27, 132, 150–51, 153–54, 166, 187, 198, 201

B68 (Vietnamese Party Centre advisors to Cambodia), 8, 9, 11, 117, 133, 138–41, 145–46
Battambang province, 121
Battle of Bach Dang, 93
Battle of Dong Da, 93
Battle of Vi Xuyen, 166
Beresford, Melanie, 38, 45, 153
Binh Tam, 103
Border Commission, 58, 73
Brezhnev, Leonid, 93, 166
broad-based foreign economic policy, 27, 50
Brzezinski, Zbigniew, 33
Bui Thanh Van, 116

Cambodia National Rescue Party (CNRP), 114

Cambodian genocide, 3, 137; aftermath, 15
Cambodian People's Party (CPP), 114, 207
Cambodian resistance forces, 18, 105
Cam Ranh Bay, 23–24, 81
Cao Bang, 28, 83
Cao Van Khanh, 100
Carter, Jimmy, 30–32, 67
Central Economic Zoning Commission, 35
Central Military Commission (CMC), 8, 14, 62–64, 77, 97, 139, 204–5; economic role of the army, 65–66; military actions against the Khmer Rouge, 73–74; military duty in Cambodia, 125
Chanda, Nayan, 54, 73
Chaplin, B., 60, 72
chauvinism (Vietnam), 21, 133
Chi Kreng district, 123
China as a paper tiger, 81
Chinese residents (Hoa Kieu), 46, 87–88
Chu Huy Man, 10, 62, 66, 106, 129, 183
Coalition of Government of Democratic Kampuchea (CGDK), 131
collective ideas, 4, 18, 21
Command 719, 129
Committee for Foreign Economic Relations, 147, 154, 158
Committee K, 139
Committee on Economic and Cultural Cooperation with Laos and Cambodia (CECC–Laos and Cambodia), 157, 192–95
Committee Z, 139
Communist Party of Kampuchea (CPK), 59

285